To Renew Books
PHONE: (925) 969-3100

Women on Their Own

Women on Their Own

INTERDISCIPLINARY PERSPECTIVES ON BEING SINGLE

EDITED BY

RUDOLPH M. BELL

VIRGINIA YANS

Rutgers University Press
New Brunswick, New Jersey, and London

Library of Congress Cataloging-in-Publication Data

Women on their own : interdisciplinary perspectives on being single / edited by Rudolph M.
Bell and Virginia Yans.
    p. cm.
Includes bibliographical references and index.
ISBN 978–0-8135–4210–2 (hardcover : alk. paper)
ISBN 978–0-8135–4211–9 (pbk. : alk. paper)
 1. Single women—Social conditions. 2. Single women—Conduct of life. 3. Single
women—Psychology. 4. Single women—Case studies. I. Bell, Rudolph M. II. Yans-
McLaughlin, Virginia, 1943–
HQ800.2W66 2008
306.81'53091821—dc22   2007008412

A British Cataloging-in-Publication record for this book is available from the British Library.

Visit our Web site: http://rutgerspress.rutgers.edu

Manufactured in the United States of America

CONTENTS

Women on Their Own

Introduction

RUDOLPH M. BELL AND VIRGINIA YANS

The essays in this volume sustain a recently developed counternarrative of "singleness." This narrative is intent on correcting negative images of unmarried women without male partners. Three themes draw the writers of these pages into conversation with each other: choice, power, and diversity. The authors demonstrate that some women, at least some of the time and in some circumstances, choose singleness. And they show that some single women, at least some of the time and in some circumstances, exercise great power and authority over themselves and their surroundings. The essays acknowledge as well a remarkable diversity of situations and identities among a population who by choice or by chance were unmarried: women who chose never to marry; widows and divorcees who, having had the experience of marriage, chose not to repeat it; women who took vows of celibacy; women who lived with men but elected not to marry them; women who preferred female partners they could not marry; and women who through force of circumstance—war, economic crisis, physical disability, a husband's desertion or death—found themselves, often without their choosing, widowed or on their own.

As an initial step toward rendering this diverse, otherwise unwieldy group into a manageable category for analysis, contemporary scholars and population studies focus on singleness as a civil status—that is, the condition of not being married.[1] It is worth emphasizing the *not* at the outset: singleness for women, in a wide variety of societies, past and present, has been a negative—something missing, incomplete, or damaged, something without, even something pitied. There have always been women on their own, and societies have conjured up various ways to deal with them and evaluate their supposed shortcomings. Today, ironically, even as both men and women more widely embrace singleness as a viable alternative to marriage, mainstream attitudes still regard the choice as second best. Specialists generally attribute the stigma of singleness to a "pervasive ideology of marriage and family" stubbornly residing in both popular consciousness and social science literature. In the words of one sociologist, the emerging field of "singleness studies" attempts to open a "dialog about assumptions, theories, and terminology that implicitly (though sometimes quite openly) disparages the men and women who live outside the traditional married state."[2]

The essays in this volume document nineteenth- and twentieth-century North American and European women and twentieth-century women living in France, Ireland, Cuba, the Dominican Republic, and Puerto Rico. But the historians and social scientists of the modern era represented in this collection give greatest attention to the white majority culture that has produced and sustained marriage and the nuclear family as ideals, the same culture that produces a negative assessment of singleness. Particularly because their field is young, it should come as no surprise that as an initiating strategy, singleness studies scholars give priority to the deconstruction of mainstream, hegemonic family values rather than attending to a variety of alternative ethnic cultural ideals and practices. There are other good reasons for this approach, not the least of which is, as Anne Byrne and Deborah Carr, two of this volume's contributors, point out elsewhere,[3] the necessity to correct the normative pro-marriage biases of scholars who, significantly, support popular negative stereotypes of all single persons, regardless of class and race. These pro-marriage biases, as readily apparent in studies of middle-class single women as they are in analyses of poor, unwed African American mothers, mask two realities: namely, that the "not-marrieds" assume many lifestyle forms and social roles, ranging from cohabitation to widowhood; and, that irrespective of race and class differences, they share the same civil status as incomplete, second-class citizens. Moreover, as one scholar notes, stereotypes and prejudices toward unmarried adults are increasing, even as other biases "based on race, ethnicity, disability and sexual orientation are less tolerated."[4] The emphasis on shared civil status and mainstream ideology, does not, of course, exclude consideration of racial, ethnic, and other minority groups. In our collection, anthropologist Helen Safa's comparative analysis of Caribbean women and historian Catherine Kudlick's provocative essay on opposite marital choices made by two blind women, Helen Keller and Thérèse-Adèle Husson, make this clear. We anticipate that future research on minority women will benefit from the foundational exercises offered in this volume and elsewhere.[5] Indeed, a next step would be an attempt to understand what singleness scholars have already acknowledged, that is, the unexplored connections between singleness and such "master identities" as race, gender, ethnicity, and disability. Singleness is a social identity that, precisely because it embraces so many different kinds of individuals in so many different life situations, may well assume second place as a subjective identity for a single person belonging to other groups, including other minority groups. As an example, although many persons designate themselves as female, or Jewish, or physically disabled, and even declare themselves unmarried, some of these same individuals would not describe themselves as single. Perhaps future scholars of singleness will, like recent revisionists in the field of ethnic group studies, question the "group-ness" of their group, that is, we cannot assume a priori that single persons are a group. Instead, the revisionists suggest that groups (and class, as well) are historically situated in continually changing formations, not "continuing, trans-historical entities with agency, homogenous membership, and consensual goals."[6] That our singles group gains its definition from something that it is *not* (married) rather than from something that it *is* means that we must pay particular attention to this revisionist call for caution. The essays collected in this volume demonstrate the usefulness of singleness as a category for analysis. Still, their historicity and their attention to diversity are a caveat against the assumption that single persons are, and have been, an internally homogenous group continuing across historical time.

Categories and Analytic Strategies

Civil status offers a convenient and manageable criterion for determining who is, and who is not, single. In the modern world, where state rules regulate much of social life, including the legal control and privileging of marriage, the categories of never married, divorced, separated, widowed, and cohabiting offer a logical beginning for the study of women on their own. As some of the essays in this book suggest, however, the matter is more complex than such categories pertaining to marital status seem to allow. Some groups of unmarried cohabiting persons, for example, lesbians, may be legally prohibited from marrying each other, whereas another cohabiting group, heterosexual couples unwilling to make long-term commitments, may not wish to marry. Persons in each of these two groups organize their relationships outside of and without the support of state policy. Surely, however, the choice not to marry and the prohibition from marrying mark the categories of heterosexual not-married and lesbian as significantly different from each other.

Singleness is also a social construction carrying different meanings within different cultures and within different historical eras. Hence, as Anne Byrne observes, over the course of history and among various cultures, the single woman has been "variously constructed as an old maid, a spinster, an androgyne, a rebel, a marriage resister, sad, mad or bad, embittered, sexless, surplus, celibate, virtuous, a menace, homosexual, a bachelor woman, or an independent woman." To date, scholars themselves have not reached a consensus. We include widows within our universe of women on their own, whereas a recent pioneering collection excluded both widows and nuns.[7] Our decision to include widows does not mean that we minimize the distinctions among widowed, never-married, divorced, institutional single, and cohabiting individuals. But we do wish to emphasize similarities in the choices and exercise of power made by women in these varied circumstances. We refer readers to Bettina Bradbury's and Susan Ingalls Lewis's essays in this volume for outstanding examples of the sort of detailed scholarly reconstruction necessary to assess both similarities and differences in the circumstances of widows versus the never married.

Historians and social scientists need to converse with each other about how the constructions and the realities of being "not married" operated in premodern small-scale societies versus their modern, transnational manifestations. Can we, for example, assume that the Western constructions of singleness familiar to us have their analogs in other times and places? Or, if singleness is a historically specific category, is there any discernible common bond or common function to be found for singles across time and civilizations? To what extent, for example, do each and all of the not-married populations function as "maintenance workers," shoring up and naturalizing the cohabiting, reproductive family unit, whatever its actual local form? This question brings to mind another property of singleness as an analytic category. As Anne Byrne reminds us in her essay, singleness is "a discourse regulating conduct . . . a set of narratives through which subject positions and identity can be managed."

Singleness may be fruitfully studied from any of these perspectives. At the Rutgers Center for Historical Analysis (RCHA), which hosted the conference and yearlong seminar in 2003–2004 out of which *Women on Their Own* arose, we were fortunate to have an interdisciplinary group of participating historians and social scientists. Although most of the essays in this book are the products of historians' efforts, the advantages of our cross-disciplinary collaborations are clear in all these essays. The social scientists Anne Byrne, Deborah Carr, Helen Safa, and Eileen Yeo each in some way acknowledge the importance of a historical grounding or context. The historians, implicitly or explicitly, rely heavily on theory and on categories ordinarily employed by social scientists, meaning that they give attention to singleness as a social construct, an identity, a social group, and an analytic concept.

At the RCHA, seminar participants soon realized that an absence of the most basic classification schemes needed to communicate the availability and relevance of their work to the larger community badly hampered the nascent field of singleness studies. Whether using a Google search, a Library of Congress classification system, WorldCat, Ovid, or any of dozens of search engines, all discovered that it was no simple task to find out who was writing what about singleness. We were not alone in recognizing this deficiency, and within the span of only a few months, three independent Web-based bibliographies appeared. All three may be addressed from the home page of the RCHA bibliography (http://www.scc.rutgers.edu/rcha).

The initial compilations for all three bibliographies arranged materials according to fixed subcategories of discipline, time, place, literary genre, and intellectual focus. Jenéa Tallentire compiled the bibliography under the auspices of the Scholars of Single Women Network, and Bella M. DePaulo takes pride of authorship for "The Scientific Study of People Who Are Single: An Annotated Bibliography." Ours at RCHA, researched and edited by Dominique Padurano, brought together the results of hundreds of searches using electronic indexes for books and journal articles, which amounted to over 1,700 nonduplicate items. The public version now available on the Internet was then greatly enhanced by the work of Aki Beam, who redesigned a classification, update, and retrieval system developed at the Scholarly Communications Center of the Alexander Library of Rutgers University to apply it to the subject of singleness.[8] There is enough nonredundancy among the bibliographies that all three should be consulted, unless and until someone takes on the project of integrating them. Given the field's ongoing rapid development, the critical need is for continued updating, and the RCHA version has features that allow individual scholars to contribute entries directly and share them with the scholarly community. We invite our readers to participate in contributing entries.

Negotiating Singleness

The first three chapters of this volume reflect broadly on the meaning of singleness to the singles themselves and to their contemporaries. In the opening essay, sociologist Anne Byrne's "Single Women in Ireland," readers will find personal, firsthand accounts of how unmarried women born in the 1950s and 1960s manage, cognitively and emotionally, the distressing contradictions inherent in their "choice," as some describe it, or, as the less accepting would have it, their failure, in not having married. True to her discipline's practice, Byrne situates these individual experiences of being Irish and single within a wider social context. Caught in the contradictions of change, this generation of women, living in a rapidly modernizing and urbanizing Ireland, enjoy unprecedented benefits— such as emphasis on individualization, equality, and choice; newly available job opportunities; and economic independence—even as the Irish state and social norms continue to support conventional pro-family policies and women's roles. Using interviews of thirty Irish women as her research base, Byrne finds poignant documentation of what we have referred to as the discourse of being single, in this instance, from the point of view of single women themselves, as they struggle to make sense of their lives. From their words and thoughts, Byrne discerns how these unmarried individuals experience and negotiate hegemonic prescriptions about family, marriage, and identity. In their narratives, she finds palpable evidence of the internalization and naturalization of an external category—the family—and of the roles that women are destined to perform within it. Byrne asks us to observe the psychological and emotional labor required of these women if they are to release themselves from Irish idealizations of the family and "femininity." As they perceive their choices, it will either be autonomy and aloneness or femininity and loss of self. These are innovating, often accomplished women who nonetheless find themselves unable to imagine or to find new options for themselves in lives that would conjoin autonomy with intimacy. "Above all else," Byrne argues, "singleness is an identity issue." Moving back and forth between individual narratives and hegemonic discourses, Byrne powerfully backs up her claim. She concludes that "arguably, the identity of single women, of who and what one can be, is constrained at the ideological level by opposing societal accounts of womanhood and singleness and constrained at the personal level in internal dialogues constructing singleness as either negative or positive." Byrne concludes positively, nonetheless, that these self-reflective and often painful struggles with contradictions between femininity and autonomy contain the potential for "transformatory action and change."

Eileen Janes Yeo's "Virgin Mothers: Single Women Negotiate the Doctrine of Motherhood in Victorian and Edwardian Britain" takes us back in time by more than a century and focuses our lens onto never-married women in a Victorian setting. Against their self-esteem stood a fortress of public opinion constructed from a synergy comprised of scientific assertion, ascending middle-class sensibilities, and the full spectrum of Protestant ideology. Spinsters with shriveled wombs, aging hags, and hysterical maidens were said to be swelling the ranks of a rapidly growing population of surplus women who might best be exported to the colonies. The worst of them, those who reproduced outside the confines of marriage, were accused of being perverts, guilty of race impurity and deterioration. Single women, Yeo reports convincingly, did not fall entirely silent before the forces arrayed against them. A significant revival of a Catholic-based cult of the Virgin Mary developed, along with a corresponding role for the good, though unwed, mother who presided over a residential institution or home for girls, whether wayward or abandoned. Yeo finds that for these women, the spiritual, metaphysical, and emotional ties of motherhood might flourish independent of biological birth somehow embedded in the female essence. The human sphere, as opposed to imagined separate spheres, would work in greater harmony if love completed justice, inner spirit complemented external law, and intuition supplemented abstract intelligence. The mother/nurse and father/physician working together in hospital to heal their shared patient was the proof beyond challenge that interdependence could be fruitful, indeed, indispensable. The unequal hierarchical nature of such success was never entirely obscured to Victorian and Edwardian feminist thinkers, however. Throughout the lives of prominent single women there lurked crippling dependency on strong fathers, unfulfilled desires for biological offspring, bitter consequences of ill-chosen marriage partners, and the failures of adoptive motherhood. Yeo's essay forces us to examine the exercise of choice and power so circumscribed by contradictory consequences (to use her phrase) that one concludes the reading with a sense more of irony than of triumph.

Sociologist Deborah Carr's "Social and Emotional Well-Being of Single Women in Contemporary America" is a classic example of one sociologist interrogating the statistical interpretations of others. Using an already constructed set of evidence for her explorations, the 1995 Midlife Development in the United States (MIDUS) survey, a random sample of men and women aged twenty-five to seventy-four, Carr argues that existing sociological studies overstate the "negative psychological consequences of singlehood."

Carr hopes to determine if "the psychological costs of singlehood attenuate when attitudes about the desirability of marriage are considered," as they recently have in American society. Concurrently, she examines whether different age cohorts and categories of single women, for example, never-married and formerly married women, experience the same levels of psychological distress. Over the past half-century, she points out, the advantages typically attributed to marriage have lost appeal, even as new occupational opportunities and reproductive technologies have diminished women's dependency on male partners. Corresponding with these realities, the proportion of unmarried women in the United States has increased over the past fifty years. Carr's emphasis on the diversity of single women, including their differing age cohorts, prior relationship histories, and sexual orientation raises serious questions concerning the efficacy of studies purporting to compare married and single persons. Can these studies appropriately assume that the highly diverse populations of singles are a unified analytic category? If not, then these studies actually may not be measuring, as they purport to do, the consequences of group membership. Carr demonstrates, for example, that the causes for single women's "discontent" and problems of "psychological health" can be attributed to factors extraneous to marriage status itself, for example, education level, race, and a history of poor health. At the very least, statistical models comparing married and single persons must take these characteristics into account. Some of Carr's confirmed findings are not surprising; others raise interesting questions about the benefits of marriage. As an example, for both the never married and formerly married, absence of a continuing, available, and exclusive sexual relationship appears to explain much of their dissatisfaction. This reality-based complaint, however, does not apply to another population defined as single by statistical studies: today's cohabiting single women, for example, report greater satisfaction with their sexual relationships than do legally married women.

Historians almost never have at their disposal the rich data offered by such targeted population surveys as the MIDUS survey. Carr's methodology is statistical. Still, her thinking about the use and interpretation of this data resonates with the work of the historians in this volume. Her research strategy begins with an interest in the diversity of experiences among single women. And, acknowledging the serious limitations of cross-sectional "snapshot" statistical studies like MIDUS, Carr attempts to understand singleness in both historical and personal time. These emphases on diversity and change, in part an outcome of fruitful interdisciplinary collaboration, distinguish Carr's contribution and promise to enrich existing findings concerning the advantages of marriage and the disadvantages of singleness.

Widows as Public Agents

In the RCHA spring 2004 conference devoted specifically to "The Widow's Might," three papers addressing dissimilar historical circumstances reached congruent conclusions about the exercise of power—at the ballot box, the cash register, and the wealthy foundation. Revised versions of these presentations constitute the next segment of this collection, wherein the fascinating particulars of just how votes were cast and dollars were earned or distributed shed light on the inner workings of heretofore largely invisible roles for widows.

Bettina Bradbury's "Widows at the Hustings: Gender, Citizenship, and the Montreal By-Election of 1832" takes us to the British colonial possession of Lower Canada, where women who met moderate, gender-neutral property qualifications were eligible to vote. No explicit law gave them this right, but none denied it, and for decades some women had exercised the franchise. Women who held their wealth in common with a husband, as well as single women, did not often vote. Propertied widows, however, had political interests to defend, and they exercised their rights in sufficient numbers to become seen as a swing vote that might determine electoral outcomes, a milestone in the history of citizenship not to be passed over lightly. Bradbury portrays the physical setting of the poll, where each voter had to swear her eligibility and then shout out her preference in public, as a place of violence and intimidation, where Catholics and Protestants, working people and gentlemen, Patriots and Loyalists contested every vote with verbal abuse and even by physical threats and blockades. Chaos reigned, foul-mouthed drunks abounded, and a woman's respectable reputation suffered merely from being there. Moreover, in the Montreal 1832 election, a zealous official surreptitiously used color-coded marks to record whether would-be participants had been challenged and then how they had cast their ballots. Eligible women who chose to enfranchise themselves in these hostile circumstances, where more than half of them were forced to prove their qualification to vote, not only expressed a political preference but also served as frontline combatants against the trend toward excluding women from the electoral process. Bradbury's essay suggests as well that more attention might usefully be given to the gendering of public space from the mid-nineteenth century onward as a change, for the worse, from practices in early modern Europe and North America.

The next essay takes us from Montreal's contentious polling place, with its virulent hostility toward gentlewomen, to the humdrum of street life in nineteenth-century Albany, New York. On the basis of painstaking reconstructions drawn from city directories, federal and state censuses, and credit company records, Susan Ingalls Lewis, in "Business Widows in Nineteenth-Century Albany, New York, 1813–1885," captures the world of women, mostly widows, competing vigorously and successfully in business not only as the expected confectionary shop owners and tavern keepers but also as proprietresses of a large-scale plumbing enterprise, a notably fashionable hotel, and a highly prosperous dry-goods company. Alongside these fabulous successes, the records also show enterprising women breaking supposed barriers by engaging in occupations such as undertaker, blacksmith, livery stable owner, and cigar seller. Lewis argues persuasively that most of these widows did not suddenly find themselves in possession of a profitable establishment at the demise of their husbands but rather that they had been active partners in the businesses for years. The very category of "widow" was fluid, as much a perception, a marketing strategy, or a convenient way to hide a dark past as it might have been a demographic reality. The environment was not always good. Albany's women generally were deemed to be worthy of character but less often worthy of credit. Moreover, the city itself, and its economy, declined steadily through the century, falling from among the top ten cities in the United States in population and enterprise to a rather middling position, despite being the capital of the nation's richest state. Nonetheless, as of 1880, Albany's widowed proprietresses, 65 percent of whom were foreign born, had managed somehow to stay in business for impressively long periods, on average over a decade, certainly longer than their sisters who worked in factories or as domestic servants, although many only eked out a living, at least according to their potential creditors. Such reports are silent, however, on whatever pride these unspectacular women may have felt about their abilities to succeed on their own.

For something of a wickedly comic interlude, as least to judge from author Ruth Crocker's twinkle while presenting her original paper, the essay "'His Absent Presence': The Widowhood of Mrs. Russell Sage" considers the public agenda of the widowed Mrs. Russell Sage. When Russell, partner with the even better known financier Jay Gould, died a few weeks short of his ninetieth birthday, he left a huge estate, all of it to Mrs. Sage, because neither his first marriage nor this one of thirty-seven years had produced any children. Upon her husband's death, the reticent and heretofore inconsequential Olivia suddenly achieved the right to make decisions. Among the first of these was the question of how and where to place the corpse. The new widow boldly decided to bury Russell beside his first wife, many miles away from her own chosen future resting place next to her parents. In life, Russell had been frugal to a fault, never putting much faith in the value of charity, and his estate amounted in today's money to over a billion dollars, enough for the seventy-eight-year-old widow to do whatever she pleased. What she liked most was to have people, thousands of them, ask her for money, and then she would decide who would be rewarded or denied. This task was a continuation of what she had been doing for years but only very sparingly, due as much to Russell's extreme cheapness as to her internalized sense of wifely docility. Her previously timid voice on behalf of women's rights, attenuated both by Russell's shadow and by her own modest social background, thundered in widowhood, earning her an honorary degree from one donation-seeking university (alas, not including the institution publishing this volume, although Rutgers did woo her) and invitations to all the most glittering philanthropic functions. She reserved only enough money to cover her personal needs, including a chauffer-driven automobile, many fur coats, and a fabulous penthouse, but still there was plenty to give, and give again, to all she deemed worthy. To the local zoological society, to which she had been able to send only a token $25 when her husband was still alive, she gave $100,000 a few years later and then $800,000 in her will, when no one could laugh in her face. Under her stewardship the original billion grew nicely, and in her eleven remaining years she gave away three times that much and still had more to bequeath in her will. She was America's richest woman and the nation's largest taxpayer, yet she could not vote. After a time she surrounded herself with protectors, becoming reclusive and declining most visitors and social invitations, for these invariably turned into appeals for money. The rapidly increasingly value of the Manhattan real estate she had wisely invested in after her husband's demise left her uncertain about just how much she was actually worth, and increasingly she delegated the details of charity to others. She came to find enjoyment instead in being chauffeured to wherever a whim directed, and in her last year her legs felt better and she could walk a bit. She had established the Russell Sage Foundation to carry on her philanthropy, insisting that it be called exactly that and not the Sage Foundation, bringing us full circle to the enigma of women's choices tightly circumscribed by infused societal expectations of proper gender roles, even for a woman who could buy her every desire.

Not Married or No Longer Married

The assumption that marriage is the ideal state for women often goes unexamined. It remains powerful in our own time, as shown in the essays by Byrne and

Carr. Our interest, in the next three essays, turns to historical settings in which the fact of being not married—whether as the result of widowhood or of being deemed unfit for marriage—mattered enormously. In each of these essays the authors pay close attention to the women themselves, seeing them as protagonists, albeit ones enmeshed in less than ideal circumstances. Indeed, the state of being unmarried or no longer married comes to have positive qualities, turning societal prejudice on itself to forge an image of special virtue, never without sacrificial elements but containing as well elements of self-worth, legitimacy, and accomplishment.

Lee V. Chambers, in her essay "'Great Was the Benefit of His Death': The Political Uses of Maria Weston Chapman's Widowhood," trains her lens on Maria Weston Chapman, antislavery leader and widow of Henry Grafton Chapman, also an abolitionist. Henry died in 1842, but the crusade to free America's slaves lived on with ever-increasing stridency and success, thanks in no small part to this woman's public imaging of her husband's death and to her attentive refashioning of her own persona, which had veered chaotically among those of unfit mother, fiery opponent of deferential politics, and perceived madwoman. Maria reserved the unpleasant details of Henry's slow and painful death from tuberculosis for private family letters and instead declared to the news media that his passing, over which she had presided with no help from nurses, clergy, or even an undertaker, had been tranquil, even serene, "a good man & just, [who] died in sweet peace." She went on to tell the world that "his last thoughts & directions were about the cause[,] leaving me to its service, with the charge to lose no opportunity of promoting its interests." Having appointed herself as Henry's successor, Maria spun a narrative of devoted widowhood aimed at restoring her public image, which had suffered badly from suspicions that she was an unfit mother who four years earlier had abandoned the care of her infant children to attend an antislavery convention in Philadelphia and consequently had suffered a hallucinatory illness that doctors diagnosed as phrenitis, a brain inflammation caused by excessive passions. The transition from public madwoman and powerless laughing stock to reclusive widow and esteemed intellectual leader of the movement rested initially on the deathbed narrative Maria constructed for Henry, but her makeover then required careful choices over many years about what she would or would not do before the world's eyes. She was, as Chambers summarizes Maria's grandson's view, a fanatic, but perhaps one with a fair amount of chutzpah and a cunning intellect.

No such absence of verbal evidence characterizes the self-assertions of Confederate widows, the subject of Jennifer L. Gross's intriguing essay "The United Daughters of the Confederacy, Confederate Widows, and the Lost Cause: 'We Must Not Forget or Neglect the Widows.'" What agency can we ascribe to a collective of women who seemed to be living for the past, sacrificing their existences to perpetuate the memory of their dead husbands' valorous deeds on behalf of a lost cause? Were these women merely dupes, poignant victims of fading southern gentility and nostalgia, or did they somehow actively choose their historical fate, at least once the war had ended? Contradictions abound. By their chaste devotion to dead men, the United Daughters of the Confederacy reassured the masculinity of the soldiers who had survived such a crushing and senseless defeat. Moreover, by accepting rhetorical contributions and memorial parading of the flag, the women forgave their men for failing to provide them with pensions or other means of survival. Some militants chastised the men for not giving more in charity for truly indigent widows, but few presumed to seek politically funded benefit packages for the surviving victims of the South's political suicide. Eventually the states contributed to the costs of running homes for needy war widows, but that came only after decades of more important work. In the war's immediate aftermath, Confederate widows first attended not to their own needs but to the hopeless task of gathering together and bringing home the bits of bone, torn flesh, buttons, and insignia left in mass graves on distant battlefields. In this pre-DNA era, they made the necessary compromises, thousands of times over, to produce impressive memorial sites, ideally with the statue of a mounted warrior atop the most prominent available corpse and usually surrounded by organized rows of graves marked by individually inscribed granite headstones. The widows then took another symbolic step, notable as well for its affordability, and pushed successfully to obtain recognition of a single Confederate Memorial Day throughout the South. Memorialization of the gravesites, in perpetuity, united white men and women not only against the Yankees but also against their own black people, foreclosing potential alliances that the realities of class distinction might have suggested, at least for some of the poorer widows. In the celebratory orations there was much invention about how patriotic and brave the women had been during the war itself, but at the cemetery once a year and in the bedroom every day, there could be little doubt but that Confederate women actively chose to be chaste and loyal, giving rise to what came to be called the Cult of Dead Generals. Better an obituary lauding your faithful devotion to a dead hero than a death notice referring to a former life when you had known a true soldier. In the end, it was the widows who nurtured the South's fatal path toward white race solidarity, and it is fitting that the South they created died with them, as the last survivor was laid to rest in the 1950s.

Catherine Kudlick's "Modernity's Miss-Fits: Blind Girls and Marriage in France and America, 1820–1920" poses a jarring set of additional issues concerning the unmarried woman. It is woman's helplessness and dependency, say men, that makes marriage the only viable way to protect and cover her from life's vicissitudes, but if she is too helpless or dependent, then she is not fit for marriage. Drawing testimony from the blind French writer Thérèse-Adèle Husson and from history's most famous disabled woman, Helen Keller, Kudlick brings together the probing theoretical insights offered in disability scholarship and several key questions raised in the emerging field of singleness studies. Both women declared that blind girls should never marry, although they thought it appropriate for a blind man to wed a sighted woman. Kudlick forces us to question whether it is indeed the case that single is the appropriate status for a disabled woman—in early nineteenth-century France, in early twentieth-century America, and today? Before readers jump to the politically correct answer of no, we might ask ourselves how we would look on the marriage of our fully enabled son to a blind girl, or we might delve deeply into our consciences, as the blind women Husson and Keller did before reaching their harsh conclusion. Kudlick places their thoughts as bookends on a century of discussion in scientific circles, both biological and social, about the critical role of healthy family structures in preserving and improving the human race, with disability increasingly cast not simply as an individual mark of shame to be contained at the village level but as a peril that threatened society at large. The disabled were barred from international migration, from the workplace, from health insurance coverage, and from reproductive marriage. Women, seen by male luminaries ranging from Aristotle to Larry Summers as naturally less able, suffered most whenever the disabled came under attack. Singlehood, the category for women who failed to comply with the societal norm of marriage, was perfect for the disabled, who were misfits by definition. Marriage between genetically disabled persons, argued Alexander Graham Bell and many others, was a recipe for disaster, and so these unfortunates should not be encouraged to seek each other out in institutional settings where occasions for falling in love might occur, such as schools for the blind or deaf. Marriage between the disabled and the able polluted the race, thought leading eugenicists, and should be prohibited by law or severely discouraged. In short, blind girls should remain single and live either with their parents or with others of their kind, since sighted girls, while not dangerous as companions, should be married. For these thinkers, the horrors of sexuality among blind single girls could best be attenuated by infantilizing them, or else by keeping their behavior behind closed doors. Ultimately, both Husson and Keller were ready to ignore the expert advisers, including themselves. Husson married a blind man and bore two children, only to die tragically in a fire at the age of twenty-nine. Helen Keller had packed her bags and was ready to run off with a sighted lover who apparently had obtained a marriage license, only to have the elopement fizzle when he never came to their appointed meeting place in her hostile parents' parlor.

Women Alone: Male Breadwinners and Economic Change

The two final essays in our volume dig into the harsh economic realities faced by some women on their own. In fact, we see these women in some sense as alone, abandoned, or willfully left to fend for themselves by governmental agencies that could have then and now recognize the necessity to revise regulations and adapt policy in accord with the realities of economic change.

When we look at women who were homeless, as Elaine S. Abelson does in "The Times That Tried Only Men's Souls: Women, Work, and Public Policy in the Great Depression," her essay concentrating on urban America during the Great Depression, it is probably time to set aside the word "choice," although readers will see a clear logical flow here that leads from choices to consequences, with homelessness as an unpredictable and certainly not inevitable consequence of arguably reasonable decisions these women had made in more optimistic times. Whereas we might think of the homeless as people with no roof over their heads, perhaps huddled under newspapers and rags on a park bench, Abelson reminds us that in the early twentieth century, anyone in a short-term or unstable living arrangement would have been considered homeless—weekly renters of a furnished room or persons who flopped onto a friend's couch for a few days. When nondomiciled persons, the sort to whom you could not mail a letter because they had no address, came to include large numbers of women, including many of middle-class origin, the state began to take notice. Some of them were women who, having recently emancipated themselves during the prosperous 1920s, now found themselves independently impoverished. Among the last to be hired, they were the first to be fired, and even a few weeks of unemployment wiped out any savings they had managed to accumulate. Returning from the city to their families, often in the countryside, likely meant defeat, and they could not be sure of a welcome under any circumstances. Until New Deal policies became fully functional, the crisis of displaced schoolteachers, librarians, secretaries, bookkeepers, and telephone operators living hand-to-mouth existences in shabby rooming houses failed to compete successfully against the needs of families with dependent children, at least in the calculations of men who controlled the public coffers. A glimmer of hope came from the private sector, organized by Eleanor Belmont in New York and specifically aimed at providing clean, safe rooms for single women who could show they had no one else to call on for aid. But it was not enough, and the "Disaster Winter" of 1930–31 ensued. Not until Franklin and Eleanor Roosevelt had moved from the governor's mansion to the White House, and the shortcomings of New York's Temporary Emergency Relief Act (TERA) had been recognized and partially corrected in parallel federal legislation (FERA), did single women's lot begin to improve by the mid-1930s. Even then, the independent woman who fit as neither a daughter nor a wife remained something of an outcast, the last in line and the least deserving on the social agency agenda.

Continuing the discussion of the twentieth century, anthropologist Helen I. Safa, in "Globalization, Inequality, and the Growth of Female-Headed Households in the Caribbean," skillfully connects the growth of female-headed households in three Caribbean nations to an international market demand for cheap labor. In an essay that compares Cuba, the Dominican Republic, and Puerto Rico, she blends the local with the global and the recent present with the past, providing a model for researchers seeking to understand how gender roles influence and are influenced by globalization and state policy. Safa's essay choreographs women's choices in a variety of national contexts, testing and challenging assumptions concerning the influence of state policy on the life choices of mothers without male partners. Cuba's recognition of the legality of consensual marriages, free health care, and educational and occupational opportunities for women, Safa hypothesizes, enabled an increase in female-headed households there. Paradoxically, the United States' pro-family policy in Puerto Rico, of which Social Security requirements are an instance, also enabled the decline of nuclear, male-headed households. Still, Safa concludes that welfare policy alone does not explain the rise of Caribbean female-headed households, because the highest percentages exist not in Puerto Rico but in Cuba and the Dominican Republic, where state support of this kind does not exist. Paradoxically, as well, Safa demonstrates that within global capitalism's relentless search for ever cheaper labor, a drive that reduces the value of both male and female labor, women are given opportunities, and take them, to gain greater control over their own lives. Safa's interviews with Caribbean women offer testimony to the personal discontent with husbands and fathers of their children that motivates these women to resist marriage and to live without men. Historical recognition of female-headed households as a legitimate family form, coupled with child-care assistance from willing female kin, both of which are common in Cuba and the Dominican Republic, enables their decisions. Safa's cross-cultural analysis is a powerful demonstration of how a blend of ethnographic inquiry, subjective information, and macro-analysis can be employed to explain what she describes as a trend in cheap labor markets throughout the world, namely, women's resistance to marriage and the development of "more diverse intergenerational and intrafamiliar alliances" put to the service of raising children.

Acknowledgments

Before turning to the essays themselves, we take the final introductory words to express our profound thanks to all the contributors to this volume for their unfailing collegiality. The selections include only a fraction of the splendid academic work presented during the course of an academic year and within an intense weekend conference on widowhood. It was simply not possible to include the full range of activity within a single, coherent volume, and we are pleased to see that the fruits of our guests' labors already are appearing in a variety of other venues. In particular, we call our readers' attention to Katherine Holden's essay in the *Journal of Family History* (October 2005), "Imaginary Widows: Spinsters, Marriage, and the 'Lost Generation' in Britain after the Great War," which in an earlier version was presented at the RCHA.

We also acknowledge the outstanding support given throughout the Singleness Studies year at the RCHA and in the preparation of this volume by Tim Alves and Lynn Shanko. Tim Alves cheerfully and effectively did the heavy lifting in coordinating changes in drafts from authors spread around the world and separated in their writing styles by disciplinary barriers, not to mention his huge assistance in making notational formats consistent. In a similar vein, Kathryn Gohl's highly professional copyediting added greatly to the quality of the volume. We are grateful to the Rutgers University Research Council for conference support and assistance with photo reproduction costs. We appreciate deeply the confidence placed in us by Kendra Boileau, Melanie Halkais, and Marlie Wasserman at Rutgers University Press, as well as by Carol Berkin and two anonymous readers for their generous and insightful readings of the collection. Finally, we salute each other on a collaboration that has been fruitful and enjoyable.

Notes

1. For an important discussion of the state of singleness and singleness studies by psychologists and sociologists, see Bella M. DePaulo and Wendy L. Morris, "Singles in Society and Science," *Psychological Inquiry* 16, nos. 2/3 (2005): 57–83. Bella M. De Paulo, *Singled Out: How Singles Are Stereotyped, Stigmatized, and Ignored, and Still Live Happily Ever After* (New York: St. Martin's Press, 2006), offers a full study of singleness and social scientific approaches to singleness.

    Readers seeking historical bibliography should visit the singleness studies Web site constructed in conjunction with the yearlong seminar on single women and a related conference on widows sponsored by the Rutgers Center for Historical Analysis in 2003–2004. This and other bibliographies on single women are discussed and cited later in this introduction.

2. Tanya Koropeckyj-Cox, "Singles, Society and Science: Sociological Perspectives," *Psychological Inquiry* 16, nos. 2/3 (2005): 91–97. Koropeckyj-Cox also summarizes the demographics of single persons in recent American history (92). Briefly stated, the number of single persons has fluctuated over the course of the twentieth century, with the lowest numbers occurring during the post–World War II baby boom. According to the 2000 United States Census, 41 percent of men and 45 percent of women over age fifteen were single at the time of the census, including those never married, divorced, and widowed. Deborah Carr's essay in this volume offers more detailed commentary on the single population.

3. Anne Byrne and Deborah Carr, "Caught in the Cultural Lag: The Stigma of Singlehood," *Psychological Inquiry* 16, nos. 2/3 (2005): 84–91.

4. Koropeckyj-Cox, "Singles," 91.

5. For discussion of race, ethnicity, and singleness, see ibid., 94.

6. For a critique of what Rogers Brubaker calls the group ontology, see Rogers Brubaker, "Ethnicity without Groups," *Archives Europeenes des Sociologie* 42, no. 2 (2002): 163–189. See also Virginia Yans, "On Groupness," *Journal of American Ethnic History* 25, no. 4 (Summer 2006): 119–126. For a discussion of singleness and "master statuses," see Koropeckyj-Cox, "Singles," 94. Kipling D. Williams and Steve A. Nida, "Obviously Ostracizing Singles," *Psychological Inquiry* 16, nos. 2/3 (2005): 127–131, proposes that individuals have multiple identities and that particular social situations may evoke any one of them.

7. Judith M. Bennett and Amy M. Froide, *Singlewomen in the European Past, 1250–1800* (Philadelphia: University of Pennsylvania Press, 1999), 1–37.

8. Ronald Jantz and Rudolph M. Bell, "Do It Yourself Courseware," *Syllabus* 16, no. 7 (February 2003): 24–27, describes the platform used for this bibliographic system.

CHAPTER 1

Single Women in Ireland

ANNE BYRNE

The mid-twentieth century in Ireland marked a paradigmatic shift from a traditional, family-based, rural, monocultural society with circumscribed roles for women, unequal gender relations, and authoritative male privilege to a rapidly urbanizing society embracing individualization, equality, diversity, and choice. The accounts of thirty single women, born in the 1950s and 1960s, reveal the identity effects of the ideology of marriage and family that continues to resonate in contemporary Irish society despite the economic and social forces of modernity. Familistic ideologies positively support constructions of womanhood as married and mother, a context in which singlehood and the opposition between woman identity and single identity are problematic. In the absence of positive and powerful counternarratives, singlehood is disparaged and stigmatized, constraining the identity possibilities for all women.

This essay examines accounts of how women made sense of their single identity within an Irish sociological study of single women's lives. Utilizing a framework from a similar British study (from a psychosocial perspective), I explore the concept of interpretative repertoires and their constraining effects.[1] Some women speak of their own singleness as their failure to realize womanhood as traditionally endorsed. Others focus on the freedom that singleness brings, extolling the advantages of being alone and the autonomy of single independence. Accounts from both studies show that a negative construction of singleness disarms the capacity for innovatory action. A positive construction likewise constrains, so that possibilities for expanding the meaning of singleness to include intimacy and independence are not realized. Arguably, the identity of single women, of who and what one can be, is constrained at the ideological level by opposing societal accounts of womanhood and singleness and constrained at the personal level in internal dialogues constructing singleness as either negative or positive.

Despite these constraints, evidence from the Irish study suggests that awareness of the contradictions, combined with self-reflection, enables women's capacity for transformatory action and change. Four possible responses to opposing constructions of womanhood and singlehood are noted: compliance, acceptance, resistance, and transformation. Although a few women are "less successful" as single persons, most women work the available constructions, refusing to be constrained by them, and talk with awareness about the experiences, difficulties and contradictions of being "on the outside." In recognizing the internal contradictions in their own narratives and working with the polarities of woman identity and single identity, many women devise alternative ways of being single, arguing that singleness will become an acceptable social identity for women in Ireland.

Effects of the Ideology of Marriage and Family

Although the ideology of marriage and family has a long history and special significance in traditional, rural, familistic societies, familism, the "propagation of politically pro-family ideas," has come under much pressure from the individualistic tendencies of modern industrial societies.[2] Historically there is diversity in family forms, and research supports the view that kin as well as nonkin relationships can promote well-being. Nonetheless, the family unit of the heterosexual couple with dependent children only, based on love, marriage, and reproduction, is the ideal and highly rewarded social form. The family has prime responsibility for maintaining emotional, nurturing relationships, for reproduction, socialization, and care of children, for promoting individual well-being, and for encouraging normative behaviors such as sexual exclusivity with marital partners. The regulatory aspect of family life posits singles as outside the control of the family system and as being less invested in family matters. Bella DePaulo and Wendy Morris note that the idea of a happy single person challenges the security of the "meaning and hope" offered by an American cultural worldview that is pro-family. The "happy single" is also a challenge to the intensive, exclusive coupling demanded by this system.[3]

Accounting for the privileged, and idealized, status of family in private and public life, Pierre Bourdieu observes that this ideal model of human relations provides the "principles for the construction and evaluation of every social relationship." Relationships forged beyond the family model are ignored, deprecated, or rendered invisible. The perception of family as a naturally occurring universal social category arises, according to Bourdieu, because the external, objective category "family" is the basis for an internal subjective category that "is the matrix of countless representations and actions (e.g. marriages) which help to reproduce the objective social category." In Bourdieu's account, single women are specifically mentioned as a group marked by "social suffering," a consequence of their nonconformity to the cultural hegemony of marriage and family. Interviewing single women in France, he observes that women suffer harassment, are not taken seriously, and are regarded as inadequate or incomplete persons because they fail to "fall into line, to settle down and start a family." Despite the perceived "naturalness" of family as a social institution, a social grouping, and a mental structure in an age of individualism, the unit requires extensive maintenance: "the forces of fusion (especially the affective one) must endlessly counteract the forces of fission."[4] Single women are a "threat" to family—perhaps because they are perceived to be forces of fission.

Neither is the state insignificant in supporting and perpetuating familism, given that it performs "countless constituting acts which constitute family identity as one of the most powerful principles of perception of the social world and one of the most real social units."[5] Eileen Connolly's work on state gender systems characterizes the gender regime in Ireland up to the late 1950s as marked by gender difference, hierarchical ranking of male and female, separation of public and private spheres, and subjugation of individual rights within the family.[6] The gender system endorsed male privilege and authority in political, social, economic, legal, and family life, deeply circumscribing women's roles and life options. Profound struggles to reform the gendered state took place up to the 1990s, but as Connolly notes, once a gender contract is established it proves difficult to alter. The Irish state continues to privilege the marital family, discriminating against nonmarital families and single people. As a woman remarked in the Irish study: "I think everybody would much prefer if everybody else got married and it all worked all the time. . . . there is this feeling that the whole society revolves around marriage. . . . the assumption is, that this is the norm and everybody else is abnormal because we [single people] are not married and we don't have children" (interview with Anna, age 42).[7]

Singlism, a term coined by Bella DePaulo and Wendy Morris to characterize the stereotyping, prejudice, and discrimination to which, they argue, single people are subject, is a consequence of the uncontested set of beliefs associated with the ideology of marriage and family. The ideology of marriage and family is uncontested, they argue, because it offers "a simple and satisfying worldview" for both citizen and scientist. Singlism is based on the assumption "that the sexual partnership is the one truly important peer relationship and that people who have such partnerships are happier and more fulfilled than those who do not."[8] Permeated by the ideology of marriage and family, scientific and popular discourse support the view that married people are happier than those who are not married, but, ask DePaulo and Morris, why then are singles not miserable? Disputing the significance of the relationship between civil status and happiness, DePaulo and Morris present a robust counterargument to show that single people do have significant, lasting interpersonal relationships and live happy, content, joyful, and fulfilled lives.

Puzzled about the persistence of single stigma, Anne Byrne and Deborah Carr propose that singles are caught in a normative and cultural lag, "although demographic patterns and other major social changes are creating an historical and social context where singles may lead lives that are as rich and fulfilling as married persons, cultural values and attitudes still blithely endorse and perpetuate the ideology of marriage and family."[9] Byrne and Carr argue that pro-marriage ideology will persist until the privileged social status and institution of marriage are recognized and interrogated, until the embedded inequalities and flaws in the institution of marriage are recognized as public issues rather than private troubles, and until the adaptive and creative ways that unmarried persons construct and maintain "family" and other significant relationships are investigated. They propose that singleness studies as a field of academic inquiry may sensitize science and society to even unintentional singlism.

In terms of social identities, single women have to negotiate between two strong conceptions of womanhood: (1) a patriarchal conception of womanhood as heterosexual, married, and reproductive, and (2) a conception of single womanhood as lack, as deviant, and as a threat to the patriarchal order. Sociological (and to a lesser extent historical and psychoanalytical) studies of single women provide us with a variety of categories and labels that either purport to explain women's choices to remain unmarried or reveal the effects of prejudice suffered by those who do not conform. A single woman is variously constructed as an old maid, a spinster, an androgyne, a rebel, a marriage resister, sad, mad, or bad, embittered, sexless, surplus, celibate, virtuous, a menace, homosexual, a bachelor woman, or an independent woman. The stigmatizing of single women's reluctance or failure to construct their womanhood on the basis of a recognized, enduring socially approved sexual connection with a man demonstrates the extent to which heterosexuality matters in dominant modes of constructing womanhood. On the flip side, the valuing of independence and equality as a basis for composing the self is fundamentally challenging to concepts of dependence and inequality, implicit to male–female heterosexual relations. Single women are faced with the challenge of composing coherent self-identities and acceptable social identities; they are confronted with negotiating the space between woman perceived as wife/mother/carer and connected to others versus woman perceived as independent, a chooser, and separate from others. Above all else, singleness is an identity issue.

Single Women in Irish Society

Research on single women's identities in Irish society is scant and focuses on the indigenous population.[10] Byrne and Breeda Duggan maintain that approved social identities for women continue to be based on marriage and motherhood, despite Ireland's membership in the European Community, the influence of the women's movement, and the economic and educational expansion of women's choices in contemporary Irish society.[11] Marriage is perceived as a more desirable option for women, with little cultural validation for singleness. Duggan signals the difficulties involved in devising alternative identities: "It is difficult to resist the cultural and ideological pressures and to maintain a positive sense of choice and independence in the face of negative attitudes. Despite the greater sense of independence in the single or lesbian identity, the effects of the social prejudices continue to place constraints on the capacity for greater self determination." Constrained by the conception of singleness as a failed identity, some find it impossible to conceive of singleness as a self-conscious choice. Duggan considers those who "choose" a different lifestyle as change agents engaged in transformatory action and advises further research to investigate how women resist cultural and ideological pressures and "maintain a positive sense of choice and independence in the face of negative attitudes."[12]

Mairead Flynn, in her comparison of single women and married women in Ireland, concludes that being married and older contributes to self-actualization. After measuring fulfillment of love/belonging needs and self-esteem, she reports that older married women score highest, followed by older single women, then younger single women, and younger married women.[13] More young single women (about two-thirds) perceive themselves as less self-fulfilled compared with those in the other categories, and none of the single women regard themselves as "very self-fulfilled."

Despite extensive changes in Irish culture wrought by rapid modernization, the ideology of marriage and family continues to spread "ideological effects" evident at the social, structural, and individual level.[14] Ideology is implicated in knowledge production; those in control can prioritize their own truth claims, "thus limiting the formulation, availability, credibility of alternative accounts which may more fully reflect the interests of subordinated groups."[15] Interested in the effects of ideology on individual identities, I spoke with thirty "always single" women about singleness and identity issues. Women's narrative accounts reveal not only extensive stigma but also the difficulties in making sense of being a single woman in contemporary Ireland.[16] Ambivalence, contradictions, and confusion surround single identity. I was interested in women's descriptions of themselves, their reflections on their own and others' perceptions of singleness, and the consequences of dominant conceptions of womanhood for single identity. Other themes explored in the Irish study are the benefits and challenges of independence; the perceptions and significance of marital, sexual, mother–child, family, and friend relationships; the prioritizing of caring work, career work, and partner-seeking work; and singleness as an acceptable social identity.

Interpretative Repertoires: British Study of Singles

Jill Reynolds and Margaret Wetherell show that singleness in Britain, as in Ireland, is a "troubled category (difficult to align oneself with)."[17] Part of the difficulty they observe is that singleness is a social category, delimiting the single from the married, for example, and a socially constructed social category that has varied meanings, culturally and historically. Singleness is also a discourse that regulates conduct and a set of narratives through which subject positions and identity can be managed. Reynolds and Wetherell call for a feminist politics of singleness to permit women to position themselves "in more enabling ways."[18] From social, psychological, and discourse perspectives, their study on the meaning of singleness and identity management provides a valuable comparative framework for the study of singles in Ireland. The thirty participants in the Reynolds and Wetherell study are mainly heterosexual, middle-class, white, single women aged between thirty and sixty, living in Britain; eight of them are mothers. Unlike the Irish study, which focuses on the "always single," the study by Reynolds and Wetherell includes "single again" women. They acknowledge that the sample is diverse in terms of marital and motherhood status but stress that they are looking for the main patterns in how women speak about singleness and identity issues.

Reynolds and Wetherell identify the concept of interpretative repertoires as "the recognizable routines of arguments, descriptions, and evaluations found in people's talk . . . the building blocks through which people develop accounts and versions of significant events and through which they perform social life."[19] Accounts are variable and inconsistent, allowing ideological dilemmas to develop as discrepancies in and between accounts are talked about or reflected upon. Reynolds and Wetherell identify four repertoires through which single women talk about singleness, with two polarized as negative and denigrating and two as positive and idealized conceptions of singleness. The repertoires, used in combination, are singleness as personal deficit, as social exclusion, as independence and choice, and as self-actualization and achievement, forming an "uncomfortable discursive climate" for single women. The opposing repertoires represent "a discursive package creating a powerful set of ideological dilemmas without easy resolution," and they have consequences for single women's identity work.[20] If singleness is represented as a positive and desirable state, how does one talk about stepping outside the category? Women who denigrate singleness reveal themselves as personally deficient and failures at leaving the category. How do women manage the discursive space marked by the four repertoires? One positive strategy identified by Reynolds and Wetherell is that women are aware of, and talk about, the dilemmas. They discerned that, in interviews, some women tended to "develop a reflexive account and talk about the dilemmas per se rather than alternating between each side of them as experiential truths."[21]

Using this framework, I ask how singleness is spoken about in Ireland, to what extent is an "uncomfortable discursive climate" evident in narrative accounts of single women, and how do women position themselves in relation to dominant constructions of womanhood and singlehood.

Interpretative Repertoires: Irish Study

Women are discouraged from talking about the experiences and meaning of singleness. Silenced by the taken-for-granted backdrop of familism, women do not speak about their singleness with friends, family, or in the public domain. It is acceptable for persons with partners and families to talk freely about the ups and downs of family life, sexual relationships, and childbearing and rearing in both private and public settings. In contrast, for single women, the discursive context is primarily evoked by others who call on women to account for their single status, who tease, insult, or make hurtful remarks about or to single women, or who completely ignore any reference to women's singleness.[22] Neither do women speak with close friends about being single: "I would want to be at a really low ebb, just to really bare my soul to them . . . I would have to be at a very low ebb to actually speak, to let people know even the way I am. I am inclined to keep to myself and to keep it inside. . . . people wouldn't know how I felt, the real me" (interview with Caít, age 39).

The research interview is one of the few occasions when women speak about being single. Silencing of singleness talk limits the opportunity for women to explore the narratives in public and private use. For example, women struggle with the conflict between woman identity as defined by ideologies and practices of familism and single identity based on experiential knowledge of the individual benefits and challenges of singleness. Kitty, who is unhappy about the lack of an intimate relationship in her life but yet yearns to "have my own identity," speaks of the tension between autonomous single identity and woman identity as being intimately connected with others: "I would like to be somebody's wife and somebody's mother, but I would also like to be me. With my own life and my own career . . . to have my own identity. But to have somebody to share it with" (interview with Kitty, age 31).

Most of the women interviewed think of themselves as single: it is a conscious, present characteristic that not only shapes others' interactions with them but is part of their knowledge about themselves. Women are attuned to the lack of fit between the rigidity of the social category of singleness and their own personal experience of living as a single woman. Women's narratives reveal this tension and their struggle around their capacity to alter their subject position so that a positive, coherent identity can be achieved. Although many women think of themselves as single, they immediately modify their response, reluctant to foreclose on future possibilities. Women speak about waiting for "the right person" or wanting to have a child, which could alter their single identity: "I do now, but I didn't. That is not to say that I don't want to get married, if I met the right person. But I am quite happy to be single if that is what falls to me" (interview with Kelly, age 36). And women reveal that, even if these possibilities fail to transpire, they have sufficient "confidence" to be single and are "happy" to be single.

Negative Repertoires: Singleness as an Unacceptable Social Identity

The women interviewed use negative and positive repertoires in different combinations. Nevertheless the negative repertoire is more commonly used by less successful singles and those who reluctantly accept their singleness. For these women, singleness as a deviant social identity intrudes into their perception of singleness. A negative repertoire is evident in the characterization of singleness as a deficient personal attribute and the notion that women themselves are to blame for being single. For example, women speak about the types of single women with whom they did not wish to be associated. Labels that they found objectionable and insulting when applied by others to themselves they uncritically apply to other single women. This finding is in contrast to those of Cynthia Burnley, who observes that the single women she interviewed are loath to describe other single women in negative terms (apart, that is, from those they perceived as searching for a partner and who participated in "singles' activities").[23] Burnley's women are sensitive about the negative portrayal of single women as suggested by terms such as "loser," "swinger," "never married," "unmarried," "old maid," and "spinster," and they are also aware that strangers and acquaintances would use these labels about single women like themselves. In contrast, the women I interviewed had little difficulty applying negative terms to single women from whom they wish to distance themselves.

You would get one or two spinsters coming in and they were very, very particular, because they were so used to having everything their own way. I would hate to end up like that, maybe I will, but well . . . in time gone by, they would be pernickety, or they would be looking for attention. (Interview with Fiona, age 34)

In not wanting to be single, Kitty has difficulty accepting other single women. She describes herself as "a watcher of other women."

I personally don't accept myself as being a single woman, so then I wouldn't really accept other single women. I am tired of people watching me and wondering if I am going to get married and I would be as much a watcher of other women and wondering if they were going to meet someone or going to get married. No I don't think it [being single] is a viable alternative to being married. I think a few women who choose to be that way, who have absolutely no interest in meeting someone, just being quite happy just being themselves. For them, yes it is viable, but for those who don't choose it, it is not. (Interview with Kitty, age 31)

Some women distinguish between acceptable and unacceptable singles. Acceptable singles are those who, like themselves, might marry someday, whereas unacceptable singles are "fussy, selfish, choosy, particular, spinsters, women who are staid, old, not living, single women who hate men, old maids, wallflowers, lonely women who are left on the shelf, and women who have something wrong with them." Although she identified herself as one of them, Susan distanced herself from other single people who are "oddballs," had "odd mannerisms," and are "very pernickety." Single women also distinguish between singles with and without intimate partners. For some women, those with partners are not "true" singles, having the privileges and futures of being coupled. Partnered singles are construed as strong, choosing singleness and intimacy, but in "having the best of both worlds" they too are marked as unacceptable and, revealingly, as not authentic single people: "Some people like being single and have . . . a lot of outside interests and they are very strong people and they were determined to be single anyway. Now they may have boyfriends and not live with them. That means they wouldn't be single in the true sense. They wouldn't be single" (interview with Fionnuala, age 44).

Those for whom singleness is difficult are unable to recognize the successful movement away from a negative identity or the negotiation between independence and intimacy that partnered singleness achieves. Bounded by singleness as an unacceptable social identity, such women do not notice the potential of alternative identity accounts.

Singleness as Lack

For most women, singleness as a social category is defined as "not married," "not in a relationship," and "not chosen." For some, this category means that to be single is "being alone" and "lonely."

Spinster, on the shelf, not going to get married. It is a lonely life really. . . .
Being lonely. (Interview with Edel, age 43)

For Mel, womanhood is based on a "natural" imperative to reproduce. She explains her failure to marry as a personal deficiency, that she is lacking in some capacity or attribute. Singleness means

I am different. What is wrong with me that I cannot get married? Looked down on. Women should get married. Women should have children. It is so natural to do so. (Interview with Mel, age 44)

Similarly, Fiona is provoked to think about her gender identity and regards singleness as somewhat "selfish," particularly for women. She finds it difficult to reconcile her single identity with her identity as a woman. Womanhood is self-less, it means "giving" and "sharing" to family and children; any other conception of womanhood is "selfish." Perceiving oneself as selfish causes doubt about one's womanhood.

Being a woman, it was nearly selfish. That I should maybe think of shar-ing something with somebody else and maybe should be giving time to family and children. (Interview with Fiona, age 34)

Stereotypical and negative, self-deprecating representations of singleness are found in women's narratives—similar to those found in the British study. Even when women attempt to challenge negative conceptions, they recognize the tenacity of them and the need to find a way of speaking and thinking differently about singleness.

I suppose, what I would love would be if being single was OK. If society would allow people to be single and I suppose that I could argue that must come from in here first and I probably have a conditioning that makes it difficult even for me to allow single to be OK. So I can't accept it myself. (Interview with Cara, age 39)

Singleness as Loss and Exclusion

Singleness is construed as loss and being excluded from society, and in women's talk it is construed as missing being with others, missing intimacy, and missing motherhood and children. Because, for women, being single is most com-monly thought about as not coupled, absence of a partner is one of the most talked about aspects of singleness among single women themselves. In having to account for being unattached, the single woman has to engage in reflection about whom she is in order to present herself to others: "I don't have much of a social outlet because of the fact that I am single. And I think once you reach a certain age, it is a couples world after that . . . you are fairly isolated because of that" (interview with Fionnuala, age 44). The narratives contain many personal experiences of be-ing excluded from coupled occasions and social gatherings by family, friends, and colleagues in work settings precisely because they are women alone.[24]

Feeling lonely and isolated are mentioned as the main drawbacks to being alone. Most women—even those who say they lead full and satisfying lives, who identify as single women and who plan to be alone—speak about lonely times. The companionship of others cannot be taken for granted by single women. Susan finds that she has to look for companionship all of the time, something she assumes she would not have to do if she had a partner or husband. After her mother died, Fionnuala stopped attending social occasions or night classes and dreads the winter most. She misses the companionship of her mother, someone to come home to at the end of a working day and someone with whom to share events, both remarkable and unremarkable. Although she works full time and lives in a large urban area, she feels lonely and isolated, something she could not have anticipated. No longer a caretaker, she feels she had no personal identity, no sense of who she is.

> It is something that I didn't imagine going to feel like this for the rest of my life. As you get older I suppose that you realize that you don't have any family . . . somebody who would think about you and appreciate your worth and needs for the rest of my life. . . . you realize that you are not part of family anymore and that the family who are your siblings have gone on to make families of their own . . . you don't really have an identity. (Interview with Fionnuala, age 44)

With no intimate, sexual partner, women say they miss the companionship of another adult with whom they could share and talk about daily, routine, mundane activities. Cara misses not only having someone to socialize with but also having someone with whom to talk things through.

> [I miss] not having somebody to do things with. . . . I wouldn't go to the pictures on my own. . . . [I miss] somebody to go on in my everyday life with. If I am having problems at work, figuring out something or somebody, it is great to talk to somebody. It helps you figure it out in your mind. I miss that. (Interview with Cara, age 39)

In these women's talk about their feelings of missing the companionship of adults, other feelings are revealed: feelings of missing one-to-one intimacy, feelings of regret about not having children, and feelings of the loss of attaining woman identity as traditionally defined. Physical contact and sexual intimacy are also missed. Many women speak at length and freely about singleness as absence of intimacy and absence of sexual relationship, which reflects on their sexuality. Apart from talking with a therapist, these women found no opportunity to explore feelings about sexuality.

> I am trying to get the words right for this. I know exactly what I miss most. I think there is something special between a couple, a husband and wife, partners. . . . That there is a bond or a contract, an unwritten contract between two people. You always have somebody, well hopefully anyway, somebody to talk to, somebody to come home to, somebody to

share things with, hide things from. That you have somebody constant in your life. . . . At the end of the day you have somebody to climb into bed with and put your arms around. . . . And yes there are nights when I would go to bed feeling so lonely and would love to be held by somebody. And that is something I would miss the most. Having somebody special in my life. Somebody that I am special to and that are special to me. Just having this person to be there with me. (Interview with Bridget, age 32)

Another woman specifically misses having sex with someone.

I suppose I would very much like to have a physical relationship . . . I think I will have to take practical steps. . . . It would be a dreadful thought to think that for the rest of my life I wouldn't have a physical relationship with somebody . . . I am sexually frustrated . . . I suppose I miss the actual physical act itself, the actual physical sensations and the closeness. The ability to get close to somebody very quickly. (Interview with Cliona, age 37)

Although most women are definite that they would never consider having a child alone, others are ambivalent, unwilling to firmly reject the option. Most miss having the opportunity to have children.

I have gone past, I can't have children now. And my childbearing years from thirty onward were so taken up taking care of my parents that I suppose that I lost out on those years. . . . I adore children. It is the only thing that I regret. I wouldn't care if I never had a man as long as I had kids. (Interview with Fionnuala, age 44)

A number are unwilling to wait for Mr. Right and would consider parenting a child alone.

I would, I would like it actually. It wouldn't be my upbringing and it wouldn't be my family's way at all, but in another couple of years, if I have not got a long-term relationship going, I wouldn't hang on. I would have a child . . . I would just say that I would like to have a child. I wouldn't like to go through life without having a child. (Interview with Brenda, age 31)

Women know how they feel, have thought about their vulnerabilities in independence, and have thought about "the practical steps" that they need to take to live as single women.

Family and Negative Conceptions of Singleness

Often it is attributes of the single woman herself that are the focus of attention. Family and friends often charge that the single woman is "too fussy, too choosy, too particular": "A lot of them would say that I am too fussy, all the time I have been told that I am fussy, but not only by my family and friends" (interview with Brenda, age 31). Fussiness is regarded as a regrettable personal characteristic closely associated with and used an as explanation for the single status. Interestingly, most women accept the label rather than openly challenging the interpretation of themselves as a person who is too choosy, too particular in their search for a partner. The pejorative label of "too fussy" is a judgment, critical of the single status, questioning single women's apparent failure to support the majority form of female social identity, as the married, childbearing, heterosexual woman. The alternative interpretation of woman as chooser is little heard.

Many women mention that because they are single, family members and mothers in particular regard them as incomplete adults, as "girl like." The deprivation of full adult status or personhood is a recurrent theme.

> My mother gives me an awful hard time, and my eldest sister gives me an awful hard time over being single. And I always have a feeling from both of them and probably from other folk as well that I am not complete when I am not married. (Interview with Emer, age 33)

Bridget is not only confused about her single identity but also about "who I really am," about her identity as a woman.

> I don't feel like I am a girl anymore. I don't feel I am a girl. But on the other hand, there is this very strong message telling me that I am and that I am not having relevant experiences which would show otherwise. (Interview with Bridget, age 32)

The single woman perceives that she is less important than married family members. Katie, caring and living with her elderly mother, recounts that her sister has a big family and runs a successful business with her husband. Accordingly, their mother treats her sister with more affection.

> She is the daughter that is doted on and I am the maid. Again my mother has more respect for the one that is married. . . . I definitely feel that it is because my sister is married to a successful man. . . . They don't give me much heed at all. I think a lot of that is because I am single and they don't take much notice of you. You are not worth as much, with my family anyway. (Interview with Katie, age 45)

Despite her caring work, Katie feels she is not "worth as much" because she is not married. Her sisters and brothers pay her very little attention, not inviting her opinion or inquiring after her health and well-being or any other needs that she may have. Narratives reveal that single women are placed in a subordinate relation to families and heterosexual couples: the interests of those who realize familistic, societal norms supersede the interests of single women. Being treated by families as less than adult, as immature, as not deserving attention, support, or care is a consequence of their devalued status.

Positive Repertoires: Independence and Being in Control

While the trials of managing alone form part of the negative repertoire of singleness, this same aspect is valorized in women's narratives when speaking about independence and freedom of choice as the main benefit and privilege of being single. Indeed, the positive repertoires revolve around being independent and having freedom of choice. Perception of self as strong and self-reliant, being mobile, achieving career or educational goals, valuing time to oneself, and engaging in creative and self-development activities are given as positive examples of being single. Women's shared commitment to independence emerged as the most significant aspect of their singleness. Components of independence identified in Tuula Gordon's study were achieving financial independence, taking care of oneself, being in control, having emotional and mental independence, and being alone.[25] For Gordon's participants, establishing independence was hard work; it had to be learned over time and then sustained through developing "symmetrical relationships" with others. Attachment to independence as the most valued characteristic of being single is marked in the narrative accounts. Gordon's participants most commonly use the word "independent" to describe themselves or other single women they know. For them, independence, singleness, and the desire for autonomy are intertwined in women's view of themselves. Colette points to her single lifestyle, which supports her "want for independence."

> I don't have a problem with being single. I think I have an awful lot of advantages with being single. It supports my want for independence. (Interview with Colette, age 37)

For Katie, singleness, independence, and individuality are equated. Katie's view of herself is as a single person who is "very independent." Despite the positive accent on independence, Katie continues to construe singleness as not coupled.

> Oh yes, I am conscious of it [being single]. Being single or being an individual and not part of a couple, I would see myself that way. I would see myself very much as an individual and not part of a couple and I like to be very independent, but it is not always possible. (Interview with Katie, age 45)

A number of women either describe themselves as "strong" or believe that one has to be "strong" to be independent.

> I think you would need to be strong because I mean, I feel that in lots of women there is a huge sense of dependency on a man, or on a partner. . . . You know I think oftentimes it is a sense of vulnerability in women and they just need to latch onto somebody. (Interview with Collete, age 37)

> I suppose I am a strong person . . . I only rely on myself. I am very independent and I don't make a decision based on what someone else may do for me . . . I do it myself. (Interview with Eleanor, age 32)

Having the confidence to be independent and having the confidence to stay single is a recurrent theme. Some women recognize that they have gained the confidence to go on living the single life, even in times of adversity. Bridget described being single as having to deal with "the opposite all the time": she has to constantly deal with her own and others conceptions of woman as coupled and mother. It is an effort to construct a positive single identity in this context, but an effort that is important to make. Attachment to independence partially explains the viability of a single identity and the single lifestyle.

In the context of independence, being without relationship ties is construed as a benefit of the single life. Being in charge of oneself, having developed the capacity for self-reliance, having time to oneself, and being a self-governing individual are aspects of independence that are valued and to which women are attached. Much emphasis is placed on being able to support oneself financially. Women gain confidence from their success at providing for themselves, content that they could buy their own home, car, or holiday abroad, for example. Being independent clarifies a way of being in the world, imbuing a strong positive hue to single identity. Siobhan describes independence as being "complete," a very different conception of singleness as lack, as incomplete.

> To be independent . . . it means being able to stand on your own, not feeling that you are lacking in anything. That you are complete and able to stand on your own, even through strengths and weaknesses and ups and downs. . . . I attach some kind of . . . importance to being on my own and able to stand up and able to manage and get things done, on my own. (Interview with Siobhan, age 37)

Satisfaction with Living Alone

Living alone is perceived as an important aspect of independence. Almost half of the women live alone. Living alone also means that one has to be financially independent, self-reliant, and emotionally self-sufficient. For some, living alone is an "unexpected pleasure." Cara, initially anxious about people breaking in and strange noises at night, found that her worries gradually ceased: "After a while, then it just stopped and I don't know how or why, but it did . . . and I just thought, I love it and I just love living on my own and it was one of the joys that I hadn't anticipated and it is something that has given me more pleasure than anything that I can remember for a long time" (interview with Cara, age 39).

Many of the women talk about how important it is to live by oneself, taking pleasure in one's own space, and to be as one chooses to be. In a study of a "family-oriented" society in the Netherlands, Jenny De Jong-Gierveld and Monique Alberts conclude that the unmarried, divorced, and widowed are lonelier than married people.[26] However, a subgroup of unmarried and divorced people living alone, identified as "creative singles," report fewer feelings of loneliness. Among these, more women compared to men tend to value living alone in positive terms. De Jong-Gierveld and Alberts conjecture that women's capacity for self-sufficiency is greater, perhaps because they possess more internal resources. An orientation to values and practices based on independence is perhaps part of that explanation. In my Irish research, I found that although those who enjoy living alone feel lonely "at times," few would consider giving up living by themselves. Even when financial benefits of sharing would ease the burden of debt, the pleasure of living alone won out. Deciding to live alone is also a statement to oneself, a recognition of a conception of self as "preferring" to be live alone, as "needing" to live by oneself. Recognizing one's preferences and acting upon them, in this instance, living alone, is part of the process of composing an autonomous, single identity.

Being in Control: Refusing Sexual Relationships

Accounts of women's involvement in career and educational development reveal their commitment to nurturing independence and self-development as a priority in their lives. Being in control is crucial to these women. Such women defer marital or reproductive decisions, being more interested in creating options for themselves that ensure a degree of personal independence not available to their mothers. A concern with personal growth, challenging oneself, and having confidence in one's own judgments permeates women's accounts of their working lives, business activities, and educational plans. Brenda describes how she "discovered herself" through being ambitious and testing herself in her career. In her view, she is no longer "shy and reserved" but "confident and ambitious." Fiona, who started her own business on leaving school, and owned her own house and car by the time she was twenty-one, found it difficult to reconcile her enthusiasm for and success in entrepreneurial activity with her sense of herself as a woman. For her, women have a social obligation to unselfishly "give time to family and children," but she wanted to make a commitment to developing and expanding her own business. Doubts about her femininity and capability assailed her. Her account of the resolution is interesting: "It dawned on me. Deal with yourself and your person and what you are happy with and you go with it" (interview with Fiona, age 34).

Fiona realized that she was feeling constrained by social expectations of what it is to be a woman, and "once that was out of the way" she proceeded to become fully engaged in her business development plans. She had to reflect on herself as a person and on what kind of person she thought herself to be so that she could set aside conventional expectations and fulfill her career ambition.

Most of the older, single women in this study are no longer sexually active with another person, some for ten years or more, while a few have never been sexually active with another person. Cliona observes that she is less dependent, less needy when not sexually involved with another: "You are free of wanting another person. Of being a little bit, how would you say it, dependent. Dependency isn't there because there is no need for a person and there is a certain dependency when you need the person . . . there is a freedom, a little bit of freedom" (interview with Cliona, age 37).

Wanting to be a person in "my own right" was another important aspect of independence. If intimate relationships did not allow women to be themselves, women "withdrew," avoiding relationships that would constrain or confine their sense of themselves. Fiona regards relationships with men as inhibiting her self-development: "I suppose in relationships with men, I felt that he'd be keeping you back in some shape or form. . . . I don't like any form of coercion" (interview with Fiona, age 34).

Others talk about previous relationships they severed because they were not recognized as persons in their own right. Unhappy about being perceived as somebody's girlfriend, "I was . . . a non-identity. . . . I want to be a person in my own right, not somebody else's appendage." Her boyfriend paid little attention to her career ambitions and made decisions about their life together without consulting her. "I actually ended the relationship and I remember at the time that friends of ours were absolutely stunned. . . . But I just realized that he really didn't love me and the other thing was that he actually didn't take my studies very seriously" (interview with Anna, age 42).

The evidence from this study is that women significantly value their independence: that it is meaningful to the daily practice of single living. Women who value independence are emphasizing autonomy as a key goal around which they are organize their lives. This goal fundamentally structures their relationships with others and consequently their personal identities. Jennifer Church emphasizes reflection, planning, and self-control as constitutive of self-identity. Valuing independence also has implications for female gender-identity, setting up a "new specification" of what it is to be a woman.[27] If one accepts Carol Gilligan's proposition that women have a different moral orientation than men (toward caring and relationship) and that this bearing "sets it own distinctive developmental path," then achieving woman identity based on single values will be problematic for single women.[28] For women, autonomy, rather than attachment, is portrayed by Gilligan as "the illusory and dangerous quest." In living independently, in saying "I am an independent woman," single women are claiming an autonomous self-hood in the context of their relational, gendered identities as women. Autonomy and relationality are clearly identity issues that single women have to struggle with and resolve.

Impossible Utterances and Actions

Reynolds and Wetherell "suspect that it may be unusual to have to draw on a discursive and ideological space that is so polarized, where the ideological dilemmas raised by the contradictions between the repertoires are so closely linked to the possibilities for who one can be as a person." While other marginalized or excluded groups in society generally have the support of a social movement and lobby groups to counteract stigma, single women "lack a social movement or identity politics around singleness."[29] This is indeed problematic and a phenomenon recognized by a number of scholars of singleness studies who advocate a politics of change around singleness, a project perhaps of interest to feminism.[30]

Reynolds and Wetherell note the discursive strategies open to women negotiating their membership in the "troubled category" of singleness. These include distancing oneself from the category or defining the category through positive conceptions of singleness. Few women in the British study chose the latter option, the denigrating conceptions of singleness being in command. However, women made it clear in their accounts that they are not personally deficient, and they resisted this construction of singleness. Women demonstrated distancing by explaining why they were not true members of the category: they had a boyfriend, or lots of friends, or a good social life; they would like to have married; they are financially independent; they are really different from women who are "spinsters." Distancing is the most common strategy used; the primary task is to disavow membership in the troubled category, in the effort to communicate "a more positive sense of self" to others.[31]

In the Irish study, distancing is used but to lesser extent. Usually these women accept their single designation and are likely to blame themselves for being single as a result of some inherent personal deficiency or inability to maintain long-term relationships. For example, some women say they do not know how to be sexually close to another person. Others cite adverse family background, such as having parents who were alcoholics or having witnessed or having been the victim of domestic violence. Illness, being separated from parents at an early age, or having to assume caring responsibilities early in life are other biographical details presented to explain a personal inability to form a long-term couple-like relationship with another. Other women speak about having no control over their lives, of fate rather than self-controlling destiny. For these, singleness is "something that just happens."[32] A consequence of polarized repertoires on singleness is a difficulty in saying, "I choose to be single." Choosing to be single is an impossible utterance in the context of denigrating or idealized repertoires of singleness. More commonly, women clarify at length that they did not choose to be single. Singleness is regarded as a challenge that can be embraced by some but is beyond the ability of others. A passive, fatalistic account of singleness stands in marked contrast to actively choosing to be single.

Combining independence and intimacy is also a challenge for women. Bridget feels confused by her single identity in that she wants to be "independent" and "I can direct my own life, but I would like to have somebody else in there as well." Bridget wants to be in control of her life, but she also wants human connection in an intimate, sexual relationship. The polarized repertoires of singleness make it difficult for women to be positively single and yet admit to a desire for an intimate relationship. Some women resolve the "intimacy problem" in creative and individual ways, some of which challenge conventional expectations of female behavior. Alternatives to marriage for post-thirty-year-old single women include nonresident, intimate relationships.

> I think a lot of women . . . choose to live singly. . . . I know [two] women
> having relationships with men for maybe six years . . . they each have
> their own apartment and their male partners have their apartment and

they just go back and forward . . . and if you ask them are they single, they say "yes." And that is the way they choose to live their life. I think a lot more women are choosing to do that. (Interview with Nancy, age 36)

For the six women with partners, the presence of an intimate relationship did not change their view of themselves as single women. Being in an intimate relationship brings many personal benefits but does not compromise an independent single lifestyle or self-identity.

> Marriage isn't an option because he already has been married and has a family and it is just not an option. Even if it were from his point of view, I don't think it is something I would fancy. We go out together socially, we get on very well, we have quite a bit in common, but there is a lot of him I couldn't live with . . . I am quite happy the way I am. It would be a huge, huge commitment for me to make now, because there are a lot of things I would have to give up. I have based my life around what I am, what I do and I have tremendous flexibility and I think that would be very hard for a man to take on board. (Interview with Collete, age 37)

Marriage would interfere with Colette's career plans and the mobility and flexibility that she enjoys. For her there is no economic, social, or sexual reason to marry. Social and economic changes in Irish society mean that "it is very easy to establish your own base and live quite comfortably without a partner." Colette had recently built her own home, described herself as "single through choice," and would not give up her single way of life. Being single supports her "want for independence" and gives her "a sense of freedom," while the nonmarital committed sexual relationship fulfils her need for intimacy.

Talking about the Dilemmas of Being Single

A number of women use therapy to talk through and resolve some of the dilemmas of singleness. In therapy, women's concerns focus first on transforming their own attitude toward singleness and then on "making singleness OK" in society. Through psychotherapy, Kitty is learning to deal with her anger and other people's view of her as "written off" because she is not married.

> In doing the work that I do in psychotherapy, I am dealing with those issues quite a lot. So I would hope that in working with those issues that I would be more able to accept it [being single] and live with it and enjoy it even. To try and turn it round for myself. (Interview with Kitty, age 31)

Bridget is angry at others' lack of respect for women who are not coupled, a situation she finds both undermining of women's choices and single women's claims for recognition. Bridget is concerned not only with her own struggles and dilemmas, but also with those of all women whose identity claims and alternative "ways of life" are denied.

So I suppose I am actually angry with that. I feel it is a very ignorant stance to take, very disrespectful and I feel that it is very undermining as well. . . . I see a lot more women who have chosen not to be or maybe not so much as chosen, but are not in relationships and it is very much a way of life and it is a way of life that is undermined . . . many women, including myself, may always live in it. So it is a kind of denial, I suppose, of who we are and how we are living our lives and the value of our lives as seen by others. (Interview with Bridget, age 32)

Singleness as an Acceptable Social Identity

Part of the feminist theoretical debate about conceptions of womanhood has moved somewhere between essentialist/universalist definitions of woman and those poststructuralist arguments that find analysis of discursive practices on identity more useful. Much of this theorizing is an effort to deal with women's agency. What set of factors or conditions motivates one person to embrace change and resist constraints yet allows another to continue to participate in her own oppression, so to speak?

How do we account for the fact that even when confronted with alternative perspectives, some women choose to become liberated or at least to resist patriarchy while others do not? How do we explain why, even when shown the face of their oppression, some women still justify their oppressors?[33]

The development of skills and competencies assists identity transformation. Diana Tietjens Meyers identifies socialization for autonomy competency as key to releasing agency and achieving full personhood for women.[34] Certainly socialization, consciousness-raising, the development of competencies, as well as contact with ideas and alternative ideologies go some distance in theorizing individual identity transformation. Structural elements such as the availability of material resources and the enhancement of legal rights, for example, are without doubt crucial prerequisites to realizing individual autonomy and self-determination. Absence of prerequisites is most evident when a bar or impediment exists, such as in the case of the Irish marriage bar of 1932–73, which formally and legally excluded married women from public service and financial services. The marriage bar limited women's employment opportunities and depressed women's bid for economic independence. Inequalities imposed by class, race, sexual orientation, physical and mental ability, as well as gender, for example, all impact on the person we claim to be and on individual identity. I am not arguing here that such structural constraints or opportunities are ignored but rather that these are combined with a focus on individual capacity for change and the consequences for social transformation. Patricia Huntingdon advises that feminists need to theorize "the activity whereby we assume responsibility for who we become and for cultivating critical consciousness, even as our desires and intentions remain socially influenced and even though we liberate ourselves via the range of critical discourses already available."[35]

For Huntingdon, the concept of self-determination combines the freedom of self-constitution with the constraint of social construction, that is, "the subject whose identity . . . is rooted in the self-critical choices she makes." Self-reflection and self-awareness develop one's capacity to make self-critical choices. These choices inform one's activities and one's relationships, which "produce new habits and capacities" and engender autonomy.[36] Thus the capacity for being oneself, for composing oneself, comes into being.

The response to singleness among single women in this study is varied. Yet each response reflects on the particular woman's own identity, a concern motivated by the deviant social identity of a single woman in a heterosexual, familistic society. The effects of stigmatizing interactions with others precipitate intense awareness that one's own identity claims as an acceptable single women are not validated, a pattern that women commonly observe in their interactions with others. This awareness, this self-reflection in interactions while they are going on, compels women to reinterpret the significance of dominant social identities and find "acceptable" ways of being single women for themselves. In the face of others' view of them as not-women, as not-adult, women compose their own definitions of self that do not rely on their conceptions of woman as wife, as mother, as coupled in sexual intimacy, or as economically dependent within a familial setting; the result is a developing conception of woman as an autonomous, self-defined person. In actively transforming their own identity, in deferring to one's own values, in making distinctive relationship choices, in contesting and resisting patriarchal constructions of womanhood, single women demonstrate their impressive capacity for innovatory action.

What did women have to say about the future viability of singleness as an acceptable social identity? Four responses to the dominant constructions of womanhood and singlehood are noted: compliance, acceptance, resistance, and transformation. For five of the thirty women, the lack of sexual intimacy in their lives defined their single identity as failure, despite impressive personal achievements in other spheres and awareness of the advantages of the single lifestyle. Significantly influenced by heterosexual familistic ideology, their perception of singleness as different and marginalized leads to a sense of personal failure in achieving womanhood. Being caught in the repertoire of single woman as failure limits their capacity for innovative or transformatory action. None is interested in promoting singleness as a basis for continuing self-identity or indeed for social identity. They seek to exchange the stigmatized social identity of singleness for the more valued social identity of marriage. In complying with the dominant conceptions of womanhood, they seek change only for themselves.

In contrast, although there are differences of degree among them, twenty-five women agree that singleness "ought" be an alternative social identity for women. Of these, some single women are characterized by their pragmatic or realistic view of the world. Although very attached to the single lifestyle and accepting of their own self-identity as single, they agree that dominant social identities for women continue to prevail, and they also agree with and accept this conception of womanhood. The stigma of being single continues to have resonance, and resolving tensions concerning woman identity and single identity is not easy. Although Eleanor finds being single difficult and lonely, she is keenly aware of the benefits of independence, accepts the fact of her singlehood, and would be reluctant to exchange her singleness now for a relationship or marriage. Singleness is an alternative identity location for women, in her view, as it is a reality that represents her life and the lives of all her friends.

> Oh yes. It has to be because it is there. There is no what will I do? Will I get married? There is none of that. Myself and my peers, we are all too intelligent to go for the "I want to get married and he'll do." None of us are going to go for that. I think if I waited this long and things haven't worked out, so what? I would definitely be on my own than lonely in a marriage. (Interview with Eleanor, age 32)

For Kelly the single identity is "absolutely" a viable alternative to a married identity, one of a range of alternatives that are being considered by women in contemporary Ireland.

> I feel myself luckier than a lot, I see myself as a lot luckier than a lot of women I know and even a lot of women that I don't know. . . . Yes, I think there are all sorts of alternatives to marriage. (Interview with Kelly, age 36)

Women are aware of the difficulties of claiming singleness as an acceptable social identity. For changes in social identities to be accepted, it is not enough to claim that the identity *ought* to be acceptable; the larger community of others must also agree to the changes. Brenda believes that "things are changing in a lot of ways in Ireland," citing the introduction of divorce and the growing economic independence of women. She has learned much from observing her mother's life, a life spent at home looking after twelve children, unable to drive a car, uninvolved in activities outside the home, and, crucially, having no money of her own. It was a life that Brenda was determined not to live: "She had twelve children and I have felt that she shouldn't have had twelve children. She should have been a career lady. And I can see the mistakes now. . . . I could see her having had a better life" (interview with Brenda, age 31).

Brenda, despite the changing cultural and economic environment, believes that marriage and motherhood cannot be combined with achieving economic independence for women or with the risks, resources, and time required for entrepreneurial activity. While this situation continues to prevail, the single identity "is an alternative in a way but [also] it is not." Brenda is happy to live her life as an independent single woman with an established career, who can take financial risks and experiment with her life plans. However, the problematic issue of composing an acceptable female identity as a single woman remains to be resolved in the future. Katie believes that single women have the opportunity now to make independent personal and lifestyle choices, but it is also evident from her account that the legitimacy of singleness as a social identity has not yet been secured.

> They used to be viewed as kinds of losers. I think that has probably changed now. It is easier to be single now and people can choose to be

single and still to be financially afloat. But I think that they also see single women that remain single, especially women, they see them as very hard-nosed and very well off and very self-centered. A lot of people would think that single professional women are too selfish and too self-centered to get married. And I would say that a lot of people would not like this view that women can choose to get married or not. Women can choose to live with somebody and get married or not. Women can choose to have a family or not. They can make all these decisions now and still keep going. (Interview with Katie, age 45)

Bridget believes that it is easier to be a single woman now than it was twenty years ago and that perceptions of single women have changed from being viewed as "spinsters" and "minders" to include gay women, career women, and women who postpone motherhood. She is aware that the acceptability of singleness is dependent on one's class position. Hers has conferred benefits and opportunities that allow her to be economically independent and self-sufficient, and to remain single if she so chooses.

I suppose I am quite privileged. . . . I did get to college and that I have a job that allows me access to clothes, to holidays, to therapy. So I am privileged to have access to a way of life that is maybe more free and I am not sure that it is like that for all women. (Interview with Bridget, age 32)

She believes that her life is quite different from the life of many economically poorer women, who believe that financial and social security are found in marriage.

Being in a relationship was your means of security and still is for a lot of women and is sought after. And you get dolled up to the nines and you go out and you go out there to "catch." That is the way it is and . . . while I say it is a lot easier [to be single], I think that maybe those women feel that they should be in a relationship in order to complete themselves is quite prevalent. I don't think that is gone. (Interview with Bridget, age 32)

The "new" single identity is womanhood as independent and self-reliant, as exercising the capacity to choose and to determine one's own life path. Single women make unconventional choices and "still keep going." Siobhan believes that she alone is responsible for her life and her happiness; she believes that she is in charge of her own future, to be organized according to what she values most. Her involvement in community and voluntary activities is connected to the sense that she alone is accountable for her own self-development, happiness, and security.

I like to get involved in things for itself, and I think I often feel excluded if I don't involve myself in things. Secondly I think it is something of taking on responsibility for furthering the things in your life or your environment that you think are important. Just on its own as something you should do and is worthwhile doing. (Interview with Siobhan, age 37)

Although singleness means that "you haven't the voice in political terms and being represented and . . . being single is less than best," Mari advocates collective-based change. Committed to making singleness a more acceptable social identity, she argues that one has to remain "on the outside," a place requiring strength and support from others. She and other single women are "at the beginning of a frontier in a way and that we are trying to stand up and be counted as being single." She is concerned that singleness be made visible and embraced as a legitimate alternative to marriage for women.

A focus on the narratives of single women reveals critical resistance to the effects of stigmatizing categorizations underpinned by familist ideologies. Transformative identities are achieved through self-understanding and awareness of the contradictions imposed by narrow conceptions of womanhood and singlehood. The capacity for making autonomous choices in relationships with others, in chosen activities based on one's own values, and in devising a number of innovatory and nonconformist resolutions to combining intimacy with independence is also significant. Taking responsibility for transformatory action and living as a single woman bring the possibility of singleness as an acceptable identity ever closer.

Notes

1. Jill Reynolds and Margaret Wetherell, "The Discursive Climate of Singleness: The Consequences for Women's Negotiation of a Single Identity," *Feminism and Psychology* 13, no. 4 (2003): 489–510.
2. Michèle Barrett and Mary McIntosh, *The Anti-Social Family* (London: Verso Books, 1982), 26.
3. Bella DePaulo and Wendy Morris, "Singles in Society and Science," *Psychological Inquiry* 16, nos. 2/3 (2005): 57–83.
4. Pierre Bourdieu, "On the Family as a Realized Category," *Theory, Culture and Society* 13 (1996): 20, 21, 26, 22.
5. Ibid., 25.
6. Eileen Connolly, "Durability and Change in State Sender Systems: Ireland in the 1950s," *European Journal of Women's Studies* 10, no. 1 (2003): 80.
7. This interview, along with twenty-nine others, some of which are quoted in this essay, was conducted as part of a larger study of single women in Ireland. Interviews were conducted by the author from January 1995 to September 1998. Connolly, "Durability and Change," 1.
8. DePaulo and Morris, "Singles in Society and Science," 58, 57.
9. Anne Byrne and Deborah Carr, "Caught in the Cultural Lag: The Stigma of Singlehood," *Psychological Inquiry* 16, nos. 2/3 (2005): 87.
10. Anne Byrne, "The Socio-Economic Situation of Single Women in Ireland, 1989," National Report, University College Galway, Ireland, prepared for the Commission of the European Communities study, by Jane Millar, *The Socio-Economic Situation of Solo Women in Europe* (Brussels, 1991); Anne Byrne, "Single Women in Irish Sociological Writing," in *Women in Irish Society: A Sociological Reader,* ed. Anne Byrne and Madeleine Leonard (Belfast: Beyond the Pale Publications, 1997); Anne Byrne, "Researching One An-Other," in *Researching Women: Feminist Research Methodologies in the Social Sciences in Ireland,* ed. Anne Byrne and Ronit Lentin (Dublin: Institute

for Public Administration, 2000); Anne Byrne, "Single Women's Identities in Contemporary Irish Society" (PhD diss., University of Limerick, Ireland, 2000); Anne Byrne, "Developing a Sociological Model for Researching Women's Self and Social Identities," *European Journal of Women's Studies* 10, no. 4 (2003): 443–464; Byrne and Carr, "Caught in the Cultural Lag"; Breeda Duggan, "Single Women" (master's thesis, University College Cork, Ireland, 1993); Jane Millar, *The Socio-Economic Situation of Solo Women in Europe* (Brussels: Commission of the European Communities, 1991); Mairead Flynn, "Self-Actualization: A Study of Married and Single Women in the Dublin Area" (master's thesis, University of Dublin, Trinity College, Ireland, 1992).

11. Byrne, "Socio-Economic Situation"; Duggan, "Single Women."
12. Duggan, "Single Women," 66.
13. Flynn, "Self-Actualization."
14. Trevor Purvis and Alan Hunt, "Discourse, Ideology, Discourse, Ideology, Discourse, Ideology," *British Journal of Sociology* 44 (1993): 473–499.
15. Gillian Dunne, *Lesbian Lifestyles: Women's Work and the Politics of Sexuality* (London: Macmillan, 1997), 13.
16. Anne Byrne, "Singular Identities: Managing Stigma, Resisting Voices," *Women's Studies Review* 7 (2000): 13–24 (http://www.medusanet.ca/singlewomen).
17. Reynolds and Wetherell, "Discursive Climate of Singleness."
18. Ibid., 493.
19. Ibid., 496.
20. Ibid., 501.
21. Ibid., 507.
22. Byrne, "Singular Identities."
23. Cynthia Brunley, "Selves, Careers, and Relationships of Never Married Women" (PhD diss., University of Tennessee, 1979).
24. Byrne, "Singular Identities."
25. Tuula Gordon, *Single Women: On the Margins?* (New York: New York University Press, 1994).
26. Jenny De Jong-Gierveld and Monique Alberts, "Singlehood: A Creative or Lonely Experience?" *Alternative Lifestyles* 3, no. 3 (1980): 350–368.
27. Jennifer Church, "Ownership and the Body," in *Feminists Rethink the Self,* ed. Diana Tietjens Meyers (Boulder, CO: Westview Press, 1997).
28. Carol Gilligan, *In a Different Voice: Psychological Theory and Women's Development* (Cambridge, MA: Harvard University Press, 1982), 48; Marilyn Friedman, "Autonomy and Social Relationships: Rethinking the Feminist Critique," in Meyers, *Feminists Rethink the Self,* 43.
29. Reynolds and Wetherell, "Discursive Climate of Singleness," 502.
30. Byrne and Carr, "Caught in the Cultural Lag," 84–91.
31. Reynolds and Wetherell, "Discursive Climate of Singleness," 502, 505.
32. Byrne, "Singular Identities."
33. Patricia Huntingdon, "Towards a Dialectical Concept of Autonomy: Revisiting the Feminist Alliance with Poststructuralism," *Philosophy and Social Criticism* 21, no. 1 (1995): 37–55.
34. Diana Tietjens Meyers, *Self, Society, and Personal Choice* (New York: Columbia University Press, 1989).
35. Huntingdon, "Towards a Dialectical Concept," 43.
36. Ibid., 50.

CHAPTER 2

Virgin Mothers

SINGLE WOMEN NEGOTIATE THE DOCTRINE OF MOTHERHOOD IN VICTORIAN AND EDWARDIAN BRITAIN

————➤●◀————

EILEEN JANES YEO

Single women faced hard times in Victorian and Edwardian Britain. Their supposed opposite, married mothers, occupied the highest place on the ideological pedestal and were held fast in that position by powerful forces, or by a proliferation of discourses, coming from many directions. This chapter begins by evoking the strength of the doctrine of motherhood before going on to explore some important intellectual and representational resources that single, childless women of the middle and upper classes employed to challenge negative stereotypes of themselves. Of course motherhood was more than just ideology. It was also deeply inscribed in feminine desire. I next review the strategies that some single women devised for coping with their own psychic longing to become mothers. Finally, I consider some of the contradictions that followed from the impressive steps single women took to create a dignified and fulfilling place for themselves both in the public and private spheres, in their external and internal worlds.

The Doctrine of Motherhood

The power of the doctrine that femininity was motherhood can be gauged by the strength of the cultural voices that sang its praises. Virtually the whole range of dominant institutions and systems of knowledge, namely, church, state, class, religion, medicine, and science, joined the chorus. Earliest and most familiar would probably be the spectrum of Protestant groupings, ranging from the Anglican Church through the Nonconformists, who shared the evangelical view of women as being especially in tune with religion and morality, and divinely suited to act as spiritually redemptive wives and mothers, especially as angels in the home. The work of Lenore Davidoff and Catherine Hall has shown how central motherhood was to the formation of the middle class, whose members contrasted the superiority of their own Christian family life with the vanity and frivolity of the fashionable ladies of the upper classes or with the ignorance and vice of the working class, especially negligent working mothers.[1]

State policy in the first half of the nineteenth century also utilized these ideas and tried to move women workers from the public labor force into the home, where they would not only redeem their families but also rescue their social class by wooing their menfolk away from public houses and political agitation.[2] In the second half of the nineteenth century, eugenic science reinforced state attitudes, and by the turn of the twentieth century the state regarded women primarily as producers for the race. Although women did not have citizenship rights, they were nonetheless important, in their capacity as mothers, to the survival of the nation and the empire.[3]

Medicine and science added their authoritative knowledge to the understanding of women as mothers of the race. In the eighteenth century, Scottish male midwives like Dr. William Hunter, who developed obstetrics and gynecology, had rejected the necessity of a female orgasm to produce conception. They redefined women as passive reproductive systems, as receptacles capable, for example, of being artificially inseminated; Hunter carried out the first such procedure in 1776.[4] By the mid-nineteenth century, the medical profession was developing into its modern form and in the process diagnosed (or created) a plethora of women's diseases that were caused by malfunction of the reproductive system and that only medical men were capable of curing.[5] Single women were fated to suffer the shriveling of their wombs through disuse and to become masculinized hags. This is such familiar territory that I will say no more about it and move on to take note of evolutionary and eugenic science. The Darwin family has a lot to answer for. Evolutionary biology, as developed by Charles Darwin, emphasized survival of the fittest populations and thus ratified women's role as population producer, while his cousin, Sir Francis Galton, developed eugenics, the science of race improvement, in which again women's primary function was reproductive.[6]

It should be apparent by now that a formidable phalanx of cultural authorities were arrayed against single, childless women in Victorian and Edwardian Britain. Unmarried mothers were even worse transgressors. They were considered the lowest of the low, seen as Eve-like temptresses (for example, by the Poor Law Inquiry Commission), and lumped with prostitutes.[7] To compound matters, the mixture of anxiety around the 1848 revolutions and the 1849 cholera epidemic, followed by the 1851 census (mirrored in 1861), showed a pool of adult spinsters and precipitated single women into the center of national debate. Alarmists called them "surplus," "redundant," or "superfluous." Insult became the name of the game: the notoriously misogynist *Saturday Review* announced that since "married life is a woman's profession," those who remained single had "failed in business."[8]

Some of the solutions proposed for the "surplus woman problem" were as offensive as the way of defining the supposed problem. W. R. Greg, for example, in his article "Why Are Women Redundant?" urged that single women become marital exports to the colonies, where they could find a good supply of willing mates. Or else they could take a lesson from successful courtesans at home and learn how to make themselves more attractive to men.[9] His article was a kind of cultural magnet attracting a large number of responses in the periodical press and thus creating a public issue if not a moral panic.[10] The topic of dignified public work for single women was exceedingly problematic at the time. Even language was an obstacle. Whereas a public man denoted a citizen with political rights and powers, a public woman meant a prostitute.[11]

At the close of the century, the eugenic alarm that accompanied the British army's near defeat in the Boer War (1899–1902), and the revelations about the poor physical condition of many army recruits, intensified the spotlight on racial efficiency and deterioration, and linked these to the performance of women as mothers. In this climate of opinion, emerging sexology, particularly as proposed by Havelock Ellis and Iwan Bloch,[12] found it easy to label any deviation from heterosexual maternity as unnatural and sometimes conflated single womanhood with the "perversion" of same-sex love (which they called sexual inversion), a kind of treason to the future of the race.

Subverting the Doctrine of Motherhood

Single women did not take this cultural assault lying down. They actively devised strategies to counter conventional understandings of femininity and created representations and activities that would allow them to lead dignified and useful lives. The women I discuss in this section were all active in campaigns and institutions that aimed to widen women's sphere, and all wrote extensively about their beliefs and work. They knew each other, and some worked together closely, like Mary Carpenter and Frances Power Cobbe for a short time in child rescue, and Barbara Leigh Smith and Bessie Rayner Parkes for longer in the Langham Place group, a powerful engine of midcentury feminism. Later, women like Charlotte Despard and Frances Swiney became activists in the turn-of-the-century women's suffrage movement. Many published in the periodical press, especially in the *English Woman's Journal* (later *Englishwoman's Review*).[13] They represented a spectrum of religious belief, with family backgrounds ranging from Evangelical Protestantism to radical Unitarianism, which included rejecting the divinity of Christ. Their own beliefs developed to cover an even wider span, from Roman Catholicism at one pole to Theosophy at the other.

Historians have already perceptively explored their campaigns for greater educational and occupational opportunity, although often underplaying the theological positions that sometimes underlay their arguments.[14] For example, Emily Davies, who founded Girton College in Cambridge, rested her case for an equal curriculum on theological equality between the sexes, as "God had created man and woman in his own image," while even freethinking Barbara Bodichon started her book *Women and Work* with the assertion that God made work the main feature of the human condition for both man and woman: "To do God's work in the world is the duty of all, rich and poor, of all nations, of both sexes. No human being has a right to be idle." Yet not every occupation was suitable for women. Even Bodichon believed that women would not be attracted to professions like the army, law, or politics, which were based on conflict and controversy, while Bessie Rayner Parkes insisted that women must not work

alongside men and must be supervised by "older women" in a replica mother/
daughter relationship.[15]

Here I explore more thorny ground and focus on motherhood, at once the
dominant definition of femininity, but seemingly off-limits to single women. I
examine two strategies, virgin motherhood and a feminist version of the sexual
communion of labor, which activists employed to stretch the construct of motherhood to fit single women and justify their public work.[16] Historians have noted the
identity of the social mother before but have usually dated its emergence from the
turn of the twentieth century rather than located its real birth date fifty years earlier, as part of the attempt to dignify single women. Of all the strains of feminism
in the midcentury period, including equal rights feminism and campaigns about
prostitutes and sex, maternal feminism was the species that was least threatening
or destabilizing to convention and therefore most permitted to survive and grow.
Later, at the turn of the twentieth century, feminists had to engage with the dominant paradigms of the day, namely, evolution and eugenics, and gave a radical
biological and theological shape to their earlier constructs. This tendency to sub-
vert dominant discourses should not surprise us. Few historical men and women,
regardless of how brave, have created immaculately new revolutionary identities.
Even Karl Marx called attention to the way in which male radicals often adopted
historical identities to dignify their cause and used "time-honoured disguise and
. . . borrowed language."[17] For women wishing to remain respectable while creating new opportunities for themselves, the pressure was heavier still to live in and
against resonant rhetorics and representations.

In the mid-nineteenth-century cultural moment, when Christianity was still
a powerful language of authority and when most of the women studied here were
religiously committed, it is no surprise to find them searching the Christian repertoire for liberating resources. Despite the rabid anti-Catholicism of British culture,
feminists discovered some of the most useful symbols, ideas, and institutions in
the Roman Catholic faith. Rather than repudiating the doctrine of motherhood,
they recuperated the Madonna and the unmarried female saints, who had been
largely dethroned at the Reformation, and refashioned the conception of motherhood to fit the single woman.[18] Irish Evangelical Protestant Frances Power Cobbe
(1822–1904), who never married, refused the protection of her landowner brother,
and insisted on working to support herself, argued that Catholicism gave a value
to the single woman that Protestantism denied. She protested that the "the Protestant 'Old Maid' has been for centuries among the most wretched and useless of
human beings."[19]

In the Madonna, Protestant feminists found a role model of a woman who
had become a splendid mother without undergoing full biological maternity.
With the help of Catholic tradition, feminists now placed alongside the Protestant image of the married mother an icon of a virgin, moral, or social mother
doing self-sacrificial work with the poor and needy in the public world. Unitarian minister's daughter Mary Carpenter (1807–1877), after referring to a sermon
on "the Glory of the Virgin Mother," urged single women "who are mothers in
heart, though not by God's gift on earth" to work in the juvenile reformatory

movement and thereby "bestow their maternal love" on "those wretched moral orphans, whose natural sweetness of filial love has been mingled with deadly poison."[20] As moral mothers, single women were empowered to help in creating the "caring professions," especially in the health and social service fields and particularly to work with women, children, and adolescents at risk in other social classes. One of the early occupations was that of "matron," usually a virgin mother who presided over a residential institution called a "home," from the mid-nineteenth century onward.[21]

The Catholic monastic tradition also gave resources for dignifying single women's social work, and Anglican sisterhoods of various kinds reappeared for the first time since the Reformation. It was this systematized, large-scale social welfare effort rather than any interest in the ritual or "emotional side of religion" that attracted Bessie Rayner Parkes (1829–1925) and impelled her to convert from Unitarianism to Catholicism. She also wrote disparagingly about Catholicism's intellectual allure:

> I do not suppose that the Roman Church has any woman intellectually equal to Florence Nightingale; but it has 17,000 Sisters of Charity all over the world. I should never go to an Order to find a woman of wide and high cultivation and originality. But I should find efficient and devoted workers by the hundred. Is the individual sacrifice worth the cost? Considering the deal of trouble the Devil makes in the world, I think it is; though I am quite aware that *it is* a sacrifice of a certain kind of individual growth and excellence.[22]

Another way of revamping motherhood was to make it metaphysical and thus more powerful than any biological or social relation. Using this approach, Evangelical Anglican Josephine Butler (1828–1906) gave an account of the life of Saint Catherine of Siena that sanctioned an active public role for women. Butler, highly connected in gentry circles (she was the niece of Earl Grey of Reform Bill fame), was a married mother whose husband, the Rev. George Butler, clearly thought her a prophet or a saint and allowed her a latitude unusual for an Evangelical wife. Interpreting Catherine's life, Butler extended and spiritualized all the family relations in which respectable femininity was located: Catherine was Daughter of God and the Church, and she was mother "of the great family for whom she elected to live—humanity."[23]

These spiritual relations in Catherine's life overrode all duty to the biological family and all social convention about the role of women. In an early dream, Catherine saw herself with a baby at her breast and felt great happiness. But over this touching scene, "the celestial wooer prevailed," and Christ married her instead. Informing her parents that she would not marry in the conventional way, they built her a cell in the family home where she could remain among them but live as a hermit. In another dream, when she resisted God's command to go into the public world, insisting "my sex is an obstacle," God assured her that "I pour out the favor of my spirit on whom I will. With me there is neither male nor female, neither plebeian nor noble but all are equal before me."[24] Following God's instruction, Catherine committed a cardinal sin against Victorian femininity by speaking in public. And she sinned in the most spectacular way by lecturing the chief cardinal on earth, the pope.

Protestant feminists also tried to make the godhead more feminine and maternal in order to give human women the authority to be more active in public life. Anglican Anna Jameson, the art critic whose parlor lectures gave radical content to the phrase "the communion of labor," had argued that the Madonna was needed because earlier ideas of Christ as both masculine and feminine had split apart, necessitating a return of the repressed element.[25] An exasperated Cobbe also complained that "we have heard enough of man's thought of God—of God first as the King, the 'Man of War,' the demiurge, the Mover of All things and then, at last, since Christian times, of God as the Father of the World. . . . But the woman's thought of God as 'the Parent of Good Almighty,' unites in one the father's care and the mother's tenderness that we have never yet heard."[26] Butler too invoked "the Great Father-Mother, God."

Although God was androgynous, Cobbe, who developed her beliefs in a nondenominational theistic direction, insisted that human men and women had different, equivalent, and complementary natures. Both natures were needed to make a full humanity and produce what she called a "stereoscopic view." This unity could only come about through the "communion of labor," that is men and women working together on divided tasks in every area of public as well as private life. This feminist version of communion challenged the Ruskinian idea of woman in the home complementing man in the public sphere. The kind of complementarity that Cobbe had in mind was conveyed by her coupling of opposites: "We want her sense of the law of love to complete man's sense of the law of justice. We want her influence inspiring virtue by gentle prompting from within to complete man's external legislation of morality. And, then we want woman's practical service. We want her genius for detail, her tenderness for age and suffering, her comprehension of the wants of childhood to complete man's gigantic charities and nobly planned hospitals and orphanages."[27] Love was to complete justice; inner spirit to complement external law. Intuition was to supplement abstract intelligence; attention to the individual and the particular to enhance the capacity to plan large-scale institutions and systems.

The medical field shows how this prescription was to work in the public world. One mutually approved communion arrangement was the relation between increasingly professional medical men and new-style Nightingale nurses. A kind of surrogate family could be created on the hospital ward, where the nurse-mother would do the sanitary and moral healing while the doctor-father did physical curing.[28] Another permissible example was the relation between women health visitors and public health doctors. The medical journal the *Lancet* praised sanitary visitors to the homes of the poor; such visitors could "proselytise in quarters where masculine and rougher apostles could scarcely gain a hearing."[29] Women doctors had trouble with this communion formula, however, and were blocked by the *Lancet* on the grounds that complementarity was being violated: "the moment she affects the first or leading *role* in any vocation she is out of place, and the secondary, but essential part of helpmeet cannot be filled."[30] Medical women like Sophia Jex-Blake then created a new version of complementarity, insisting that women doctors should treat women and children, while male doctors should attend to men.[31] This formula shaped women's medical practice until Dr. Elsie Inglis, another single woman, broke the taboo in World War I by proposing hospitals completely staffed by women for the soldiers at the front.[32] This was an offer that the British government was only too delighted to refuse but which was taken up by the French and the Croatians.

As the nineteenth century drew to a close, the growing dominance of evolutionary paradigms in some cases even replaced religious authority, and the concept of complementarity became biologized. Pioneer sociologist Patrick Geddes and J. Arthur Thomson, who had both trained as biologists, created a version of evolution in which the law of love rather than competition drove the process.[33] But they also discovered, throughout the natural and social worlds, an anabolic tendency toward constructive nurturing complemented by a katabolic metabolism that actively consumed energy. By regarding "woman as the relatively more anabolic, man as the relatively more katabolic," and by insisting that both were necessary to all life, the Geddes school gave a biological dimension to the idea of the sexual communion of labor—which they radicalized in the end. At first, Geddes and Thomson had produced a conventional idea of the female of the species solely as a biological mother, together with the notorious verdict that sex differences "decided among the prehistoric Protozoa cannot be annulled by Act of Parliament." [34]

After having been ridiculed and educated, however, by feminists like Olive Schreiner, whose *Women and Labour* (1911) they praised as "full of power and insight," Geddes and Thompson ended up proposing a much more fluid and dynamic process. In their 1914 volume titled *Sex,* they argued that although sexual difference was a law of nature, its full nature was not yet known. They called for a distinction between what was due to nature or to "nurture (food, atmosphere, surrounding, education, exercise, habits, etc.)," and they insisted that women were best placed to reveal the answers: "who can tell what men or women can do effectively until a fair trial is made? Social evolution is an experimental art. And one quite unworkable plan is that man should prescribe what the lines of woman's evolution are henceforth to be."[35] Now they extended the idea of motherhood into "civic matriarchy," which no longer depended only on biological motherhood but on the introduction of the feminine principle into public life.

Interestingly, these biologists subscribed to a version of evolution that was also penetrating a religion that proved very attractive to feminists at the time, namely, theosophy. Theosophy was a hybrid faith that rejected dogma but invited seekers, "without distinction of race, creed, sex, caste or colour," to distill the common essence from all the world's religions. Most adherents, like Charlotte Despard (1844–1939), leader of the Women's Freedom League (which attracted Scottish medical women like Elsie Inglis), continued with the idea of a dual Godhead. Despard indeed saw the ultimate aim of the women's movement as reinstating a masculine/feminine humanity, but with a maternal side that conformed to the law driving the evolution of the vegetable, animal, and human world: "the law both of physical and spiritual life is sacrifice and that, in the higher spheres, manifests as love."[36]

The more radical feminists posited stages of metaphysical evolution starting with a mother age, which also characterized Geddes and Thomson's biosocial evolutionary schema. Frances Swiney (1847–1922), the wife of a Tory major general, a militant suffragist, and founder of the League of Isis (1909), in her book *The Cosmic Procession; or, The Feminine Principle in Evolution* (1906), argued that the Elohim of Genesis was really the Supernal Mother ("from the womb of the I Am all things came") and that the Holy Ghost was also a feminine principle. However, the institutional church brought about a masculine stage when, in the fourth century, the church fathers pronounced the Trinity to be definitively male. For Swiney, even Christ the Son, the perfection of the male dimension of humanity, marked only a transitional phase, to be superseded by the final reign of the feminine: "in the consummation of all things the Father and the Son are reabsorbed, or return to the primal source. They enter into Zion, so that the Three may be One in the perfect fullness of the Divine Feminine."[37] For Geddes and Thomson too, the mother age was followed by a patriarchal period, which had reached its present mechanical industrial apogee and was characterized by materialism and competition. This epoch now needed to be moved to a yet higher stage by woman's effort as the "inspirer and eugenic mother, as instinctive synthetist, as educationalist, as orderly home-planner and citizen; and, by her guidance of consumption, directing industry and skill, ennobling utility into art."[38]

Longing for Motherhood

Although many feminists used an identity as virgin or social mother as a pathway into public life, some also yearned for more intimate and ongoing one-to-one mothering relationships in their private lives. It was inevitable that a doctrine so powerful as motherhood should also resonate in the psyche. For psychoanalysts such as Carl Gustav Jung and Melanie Klein, the mother figure is perhaps an even more powerful presence than the father, for she is the child's earliest experience of a giver of life and nurture and also the potential withholder of care and thus the possible agent of death.[39] For some women, motherhood was at the unchallenged center of the stage, especially when no man was so intensely present as to activate other characters, like the Freudian father, in the family psychodrama.

For others the opposite was true. Mary Carpenter was close to her father, who groomed her for an independent life as a teacher. She sank into a two-year-long depression when he died but bounced back partly by conflating him with God the Father and thus keeping him forever present. She hinted at a relationship with a man but left it to God to authorize it, which He never did, but instead urged a life of social work with the neediest children. Even very late in life, the sight of her nephew holding his child recalled for Carpenter "the feeling of my father's arm around me. . . . It quite drew tears from my eyes when I looked down the vista of the years."[40] Her experience of social mothering comes later and closes this section.

Elsie Inglis (1864–1917), a pioneer Scottish doctor and women's suffrage activist, was also deeply attached to her father, an eminent civil servant in the Raj, whom she seemed able to wind round her little finger. Her sister claimed there was no family jealousy of the relationship: "Elsie and he were comrades, inseparables from the day of her birth."[41] When her mother died, Elsie's devotion to father became even more intense, and in time she recruited her father and his powerful connections to help with her plan to displace Sophia Jex-Blake's medical school with one of her own, a project that succeeded in 1889. But still she longed for motherhood, and despite her formidable presence in public life, she was a relentless needlewoman, embroidering little flannel garments for nieces and nephews: "the babies as they arrived in the family met with her special love."[42]

Inglis wrote an unpublished novel titled "The Story of a Modern Woman," in which the main character, Hilgegaard Forrest, is thirty-seven and unmarried. Hilgegaard has had a happy childhood full of family and friends, but "one by one these are taken from her." One Christmas, as Hilgegaard is remembering the joyous past, she is visited by several friends, each of whom is "feeling the depression of a lonely woman." Hilgegaard says to them, "Christmas is a hard time with all its memories. I think I have found out what we lonely women want. It is a future. Our thoughts are always turning to the past. There is not anything to link us on to the next generation. You see other women with their families—it is to the future that they look. However good the past has been, they expect more to come, for their sons and their daughters. Their life goes on in other lives." After an accident in which she nearly drowns, Hilgegaard has an epiphany and throws herself into causes that involve "children who need her love and care and makes them her hostages for the future."[43]

The women I've discussed in this chapter present a rich tapestry of experiences with maternal longing. Some of them articulated a wish to be mothered and, at the same time, tried to become social mothers. Cobbe's delicate mother gave birth to her relatively late in life, sustained an injury that disabled her soon after, and died when Frances was a young adult. Cobbe seemed to carry a linked burden of guilt for her mother's death and idealization of the quality of the love between her mother and herself (perhaps a way of justifying the relationship and its unfortunate outcome). She spoke of her mother as "the one being in the world whom I truly loved . . . the only one who really loved me."[44] When her father died, Cobbe left the protection of the family estate, supporting herself from a small inheritance, her writing, and the Anglo-American lecture circuit. At first she acted as a virgin mother in her regular volunteer work with female juvenile delinquents and then with workhouse girls, but eventually, because animals were more her passion (and perhaps her substitute children), she took up the campaign against scientific cruelty in the antivivisection movement. She never married in the heterosexual sense but formed the second important relationship of her life with the sculptor Mary Lloyd, another animal lover. Lloyd enabled Cobbe to work productively and to reexperience her mother's love in "a friendship which has been to my later life what my mother's affection was to my youth."[45] Cobbe also sometimes played the role of a jealous spouse in this complex partnership, which lasted thirty-four years, "until death did them part."[46]

Bessie Rayner Parkes married but seemed to be more in love with her mother-in-law than with her invalid husband. Indeed many strands of motherhood were tangled together in this relationship. Bessie was the product of an unhappy marriage, and her parents managed best when they lived apart. Her father was a member of Parliament and kept a house in London, while Bessie stayed in her mother's Birmingham house, which she found lacking "in real happiness." After years of women's reform activity among the Langham Place set, at the age of thirty-eight Bessie "fell in love" with Eugene Belloc, who had recently suffered a nervous breakdown. In his mother she found the mother she had always craved, whose house was "a paradise of joyous lightness and buoyancy." Told by doctors that she could not have children, Bessie might have wanted to offer Eugene "the affection of a mother, as well as that of a wife," a "sacrifice" that his mother thought "too much to ask."[47] But the doctors were wrong. Bessie conceived almost immediately and quickly gave birth to two children, after which she virtually retired from British public life to attend to her demanding family duties.

Bessie's closest collaborator during the Langham Place years was Barbara Leigh Smith (1827–1891), who like other women tried to satisfy a longing for biological children by the putative adoption of relatives or attractive outsiders. The daughter of another Unitarian MP, Barbara had had an unconventional and ultra-radical upbringing. Her mother, Anne Longden, a milliner's apprentice who on principle had never married the father of her children, Benjamin Leigh Smith, died young. Benjamin then brought up the children in a more hands-on way than was conventional for a father of the period—for example, he had a special carriage constructed large enough so that he could take all his five children out on excursions together—and he hired unusual tutors, such as the Swedenborgian schoolmaster from Robert Owen's New Lanark experiment.[48] Barbara's father not only gave her intellectual capital but settled a large allowance on her at age twenty-one, which made her the only woman discussed here who was wealthy in her own right.

After having flirted with the idea of a ménage à trois with the publisher John Chapman and his wife, Barbara was packed off for foreign travel by her family, and in Algeria she met the eccentric Positivist doctor Eugene Bodichon, whom she married in 1857. Their marriage was unusual in that it allowed her to live as a married woman in Algiers or a single woman in England at different times of the year. But whatever the peculiarities of the union, her longing for a biological child remained profound but unfulfilled. She tried to become pregnant but without success. At age thirty-seven she wrote, "did you hear of the storks building on my studio top in Algiers? I hope it is a good omen."[49] In the end, she did for others what Anna Jameson had done for her, namely, she acted as an empowering mother figure, helping gifted young women to make independent lives for themselves.[50] Her most intense involvement was with Hertha Marks Ayrton, the distinguished mathematician.

Anna Jameson (1794–1860) had a less happy experience of putative adoption. She carried many familial burdens, indeed, she financially assisted many family members. She supported her ineffectual father, and when he died she looked after her mother and four sisters.[51] In 1825, after five years of his persistent courtship, she married Robert Jameson, who seemed capable only of long-distance affection: "at a distance," wrote her niece, "he was the most devoted and admiring of husbands, but in the privacy of the domestic circle, cold, self-absorbed and unsympathetic."[52] The marriage was unhappy, and they lived separately for many years. Eventually it ended in the "most painful and humiliating" way, when Robert died not only owing Anna money but leaving a bequest to another, married, woman. Anna did not contest his will, although it left her in virtual penury, because she did not want "his memory and my own domestic misery to be dragged into a court of justice."[53] For Anna these experiences left a residue of bitterness about men. Writing to her friend Ottilie von Goethe, daughter-in-law of the poet, she complained of the obsessive need to be loved by men that filled Ottilie's letters: "I find not one word of any of your children, and a great deal about those horrid men who have destroyed your happiness and mine, what pain, what fear, what shame overpowered me!"[54]

Anna Jameson sought personal happiness not only in work but in an intense relationship with her niece Geraldine Bates. Keeping an eagle eye on Geraldine's upbringing, Anna became increasingly critical of her sister and brother-in-law as parents, until, in 1842, she took the child over: "she is with me now and her education takes up much of my day. . . . I do [not] think she will be a genius or very distinguished and famous, but she will be a happy being, and I will try to give her the means of independence." Basically Anna adopted Geraldine as her apprentice: "I had the happy sense," Geraldine recalled, "of feeling that I was my aunt's assistant in her important work, and was at her side constantly to trace, to draw, to note, as occasion might require." The requirements ranged "from the details of a drawing to the making of that cup of tea which is always an Englishwoman's consolation."[55] In 1846 Anna wrote, "I have now undertaken to be a mother to Geraldine"; she even called the girl Jameson on their travels,[56] although evidently not with the complete consent of her parents. By Anna's account in 1848, "I have given up all guidance and authority; or rather from a foolish weakness on the part of her father and mother; it has been taken from me"; in 1849 they "let her manage her own affairs and I have ceased in any way to interfere. I am and have always been dissatisfied, but can *do* nothing!"[57]

An unkinder cut was still to come. At age sixteen, during one of their Italian trips, Geraldine fell in love with Scottish artist Robert Macpherson. She later married him and moved outside the pale of Anna's maternal fantasy forever. Geraldine's memoirs of her aunt, shaded by a clear tinge of guilt, described this process in a moving way:

> In the very moment when providence seemed to have given to Mrs. Jameson a child who might cherish and comfort her for years and make up to her a little for adversities of fate—at the time when she began to get

a little real pleasure and aid from the girl to whom she had been a second mother all her life, another great disappointment was already preparing for her. I cannot but feel, with a remorseful pang, how bitter it must have been to her to see the child she had so cherished desert her so summarily. It is the course of nature, as people say, and it is only by the teaching of years that we perceive how hardly the loves and joys of our youth often fall upon those from whom the tide of our own personal life and story carries us away. Mrs. Jameson, of course, no more than any other in her position, would willingly have kept her niece unmarried in order to make of her a permanent companion; but the speedy conclusion of this companionship startled her and, I fear, must be counted among the disappointments of her life.[58]

Anna then commuted her mothering to supporting other young women around the Langham Place circle, whom Geraldine called "half daughters, half disciples to her, and to whose affection the motherly side of her nature never failed to respond." Interestingly, whether to reproduce or to distance the experience of mothering Geraldine, Anna did not call these young women her daughters but "her nieces."[59]

For Mary Carpenter, the balance between social and adoptive mothering seemed to have been the reverse, once certain obstacles were overcome. The 1854 Juvenile Offenders Act, for which she had lobbied, enabled her to open her Reformatory School at Red Lodge House, which housed girls who had already tangled with the law and which aimed to give them the experience of a home and moral mothering. Things did not go well. The girls were unused to the discipline, and the older girls were sexually experienced and unable to settle into the rules, which were read almost like a riot act to each inmate as she entered. The nadir was reached in 1857, when three absconders were put in prison, and one came out pregnant, supposedly after a liaison with the governor of the jail.[60] If the juveniles were unruly, the staff was equally unable to combine the qualities of real concern with firmness. Yet when the resourceful Mrs. Johnson took charge in 1859 and the community began to calm down, Mary Carpenter was intensely jealous of her wresting control.

Fortunately, by then Mary had another focus. In 1858 she had adopted a five-year-old girl, Rosanna Powell, whose widowed mother had disappeared and stopped payments to the domestic missionaries, the Foxons, entrusted with her care. They tried to place Rosanna in Red Lodge. Without fully examining the circumstances, Mary said that "God put it into my mind that I ought to be a mother to the little thing." She asked Rosanna, "Do you think you could live with me in this house and love me, and be happy?" For better or worse, Rosanna said yes.[61] Rosanna was not a distraction for long, although Frances Power Cobbe, when serving as the ascetic Mary's assistant, found Rosanna very irritating, just as Mary resented Frances's pampered Pomeranian dog. Rosanna was soon of an age to go to boarding school and after that to embark on foreign travel to finish her education, which freed Mary for her social work not least in India.

A more real threat appeared in 1860, when Rosanna's birth mother wrote to the missionary demanding back her child. The mother then brought an action against Foxon for child stealing, which did not succeed but enlisted the sympathy of bystanders, who raised enough funds to enable the mother to travel to Bristol to get her daughter back. She evidently confronted Mary but backed down in the face of Mary's storm of accusations that she had abandoned the child and the evidence that Mary was bringing the child up as her own. The birth mother supposedly said that Miss Carpenter was a true friend and that little Rosanna would be better cared for than ever she could manage, and then went away forever.[62] When Rosanna finished her education, she returned to Bristol to keep house for Mary. One June morning in 1877 she came for the housekeeping keys to find that Mary had died peacefully during the night. Mary left her "adopted daughter" an annuity for life, a third of all her glass and china, as well as all books, pictures, and Indian treasures "not otherwise bequeathed." Rosanna was to be found as a single woman in London in 1919—so that one spinster, so to speak, had begotten another.[63]

Some Contradictory Consequences, Past and Present

In a period and culture that seemed to offer no approved role for single women outside that of dutiful daughter or attentive maiden aunt, the women I've discussed bravely carved out other pathways for themselves. But their lines of advance contained restrictions, which are also important to map. First, their probably necessary stress on chastity robbed them of any chance of sexuality in a culture that became, at least at its advanced edges, at the end of the nineteenth century, more relaxed and even positive about women's sexual pleasure, at any rate within a framework of marriage and procreation. In an earlier period, to get around the understanding of a public woman as a prostitute and also to combat accusations of selfish shirking of feminine duty, publicly active single women employed chastity and sacrifice as bywords in their vocabulary. Cobbe, for example, insisted that single women were not propelled by "selfishness" but that "self-sacrifice even more entire than belongs to the double life of marriage is the true law of celibacy."[64]

The asceticism of a life dedicated to sacrificial duty probably did not suit all. Cobbe, for example, liked fine wine and a good cigar and could not bear living within Carpenter's anorexic regime. As sexologists, evolutionists, and then psychoanalysts began to value women's sexual pleasure for the first time in one hundred years, some single women felt they were missing out, as a rather opaque article in the *Freewoman,* titled "The Spinster," suggested. The author, a single woman herself, argued that persons in her situation, deprived of pleasure and fulfillment, became like moral police, closing down the delights of others: the spinster "remains at once the injured and the injuring. Society has cursed her and the curse is now roosting at home."[65] With the sexologists now recognizing but interdicting lesbianism as pathological, there was also great difficulty in exploring more flexible sex and gender roles. Some very outré voices, such as those writing for the periodical *Urania*, enjoined women to refuse categories of femininity and masculinity altogether and to decenter motherhood, but this was very much a message from beyond the pale.[66]

By positioning herself so firmly on the side of the chaste angels, the single woman contributed, even if unintentionally, to reinforcing the immorality of her supposed opposites, the prostitute and the unmarried mother. Single mothers persisted as an outlaw category right up until the second wave of the women's liberation movement starting in the 1960s, and arguably even now, in some quarters, they remain trapped in what is still regarded as a linguistic sin bin. The need for rectitude sometimes inhibited sisterhood with women from classes and cultures with different values. I have written elsewhere about the tremendous emphasis that social mothers placed on truthfulness and their horror of lying, and the problems these priorities caused in their relations with working-class women, who often seemed to prize an accommodating disposition and sisterly support and were more relaxed about absolute truth.[67] Just as social motherhood could accentuate rather than bridge social distance, so too single women often positioned themselves as big sisters guiding their deficient little sisters on the right path. Basically this version of sisterhood reproduced inequality rather than transcending it.

Equally long-lived was another consequence of the doctrine of sacrifice—the legacy of low pay for women in the caring professions. To establish the sacrificial nature of their social service, single women tended to resist the taint of filthy lucre and performed their regular work either unpaid or for a small salary. Until after the Second World War, their initial insistence that they were not jeopardizing the domestic motherhood of the married woman but simply adding a new role of virgin motherhood to the canon of respectability also helped keep a marriage bar in place in many professional occupations, where a woman had to resign when she married. The need for caring professionals in the postwar welfare state pushed the marriage bar finally out of the way, but it also established a new category of worker who received less than equal treatment, the part-time worker. These contradictions need to be exposed but do not diminish the achievements of the single women themselves. Like all women, single women were caught in constraints not always of their own making. Their movement in new directions, if they did not want to step beyond the pale of respectability, entailed real limitations as well as avenues of advance. But then, as the poet William Blake once put it, "without contrarieties, there is no progression."

Notes

1. Leonore Davidoff and Catherine Hall, *Family Fortunes: Men and Women of the English Middle Class, 1780–1850* (London: Hutchinson, 1987), 18; Eileen Janes Yeo, *The Contest for Social Science: Relations and Representations of Gender and Class* (London: Rivers Oram, 1996), 23–24. Of course the prescriptive model was not always the middle-class reality; see Eleanor Gordon and Gwyneth Nair, *Public Lives: Women, Family, and Society in Victorian Britain* (New Haven, CT: Yale University Press, 2003), chap. 6, for a lively picture of single women in Glasgow.

2. Sophie Hamilton, "Images of Femininity in the Royal Commissions of the 1830s and 1840s," in *Radical Femininity: Women's Self-Representation in the Public Sphere,* ed. Eileen Janes Yeo (Manchester: Manchester University Press, 1998), chap. 3.

3. Anna Davin's classic article "Imperialism and the Cult of Motherhood," *History Workshop* 5 (Spring 1978), first drew attention to this theme; also Carole Pateman, "Equality, Difference, Subordination: The Politics of Motherhood and Women's Citizenship," in *Beyond Equality and Difference,* ed. Gisela Bock and Susan James (London: Routledge, 1992), chap. 1. See too, Gisela Bock and Pat Thane, eds., *Maternity and Gender Policies: Women and the Rise of the European Welfare States, 1880s–1950s* (London: Routledge, 1991); and Seth Koven and Sonya Michel, eds., *Mothers of a New World: Maternalist Politics and the Origins of Welfare States* (London: Routledge, 1993).

4. See Angus McLaren, "The Pleasures of Procreation: Traditional and Biomedical Theories of Conception," in *William Hunter and the Eighteenth-Century Medical World,* ed. W. F. Bynum and Roy Porter (Cambridge: Cambridge University Press, 1985), 323, 337–339; also Eileen Janes Yeo, "Medicine, Science and the Body," in *Gender in Scottish History, 1700 to the Present,* ed. Lynn Abrams, Eleanor Gordon, Deborah Simonton, and Eileen Janes Yeo (Edinburgh: Edinburgh University Press, 2006), 141–144.

5. Yeo, *Contest for Social Science,* 133, 206. There is a huge interdisciplinary literature about medicine and femininity, starting with Barbara Ehrenreich and Deirdre English, *For Her Own Good: 150 Years of the Experts' Advice to Women* (Garden City, NY: Anchor, 1979); and more recently psychologist Jane Ussher, *Women's Madness: Misogyny or Mental Illness?* (New York: Harvester, 1991).

6. Yeo, *Contest for Social Science,* 189, 193–194.

7. Hamilton, "Images of Femininity," 86, quotes one magistrate telling the commissioners that the law allows "a woman of dissolute character to pitch upon any unfortunate young man, who she has inveigled into her net, and swear that child to him."

8. "Queen Bees or Working Bees?" *Saturday Review,* 12 November 1859; for the best discussion of the surplus woman "problem," see Martha Vicinus, *Independent Women: Work and Community for Single Women, 1850–1920* (London: Virago, 1985), chap. 1; also Janet Fink and Katherine Holden, "Pictures from the Margins of Marriage, Representations of Spinsters and Single Mothers," *Gender and History* 11 (1999): 2.

9. William Rathbone Greg, "Why Are Women Redundant?" *National Review* 14 (1862): 446, 452.

10. See Denise Quirk, "The Empire of Opinion: Feminism, Gender and Cultural Authority in Victorian Britain" (PhD diss., Rutgers University, 2005), chap. 3, for a discussion of the press response to Greg.

11. Eileen Janes Yeo, "Will the Real Mary Lovett Please Stand Up? Chartism, Gender and Autobiography," in *Living and Learning,* ed. Malcolm Chase and Ian Dyck (Aldershot, UK: Scolar Press, 1996), 167–174.

12. Both were insistent on essential differences between the sexes: Havelock Ellis, *Man and Woman: A Study of Human Secondary Sexual Characters,* 6th ed. (1894; repr., London: A. and C. Black, 1930) and his work on sexual inversion in *The Psychology of Sex,* vol. 2 (1897; repr., Salem, NH: Ayer, 1994); Iwan Bloch, *The Sexual Life of Our Time in Its Relations to Modern Civilization,* trans. of 6th ed. (London: W. Heinemann, 1908), which made the notorious conflation between feminism and sexual inversion. See too Lucy Bland and Laura Doan, eds., *Sexology in Culture: Labelling Bodies and Desires* (Cambridge, MA: Polity Press, 1998).

13. For the *Journal* and Langham Place, see Jane Rendall, "'A Moral Engine?' Feminism, Liberalism and the English Woman's Journal," in *Equal or Different: Women's Politics, 1800–1914*, ed. Jane Rendall (Oxford: Basil Blackwell, 1987).

14. Barbara Caine, *Victorian Feminists* (Oxford: Oxford University Press, 1992), is sensitive to religion; also Phillipa Levine, *Victorian Feminism: 1850–1900* (Tallahassee: Florida State University, 1987), chap. 3; Quirk, "Empire of Opinion."

15. Bessie Rayner Parkes, "What Can Educated Women Do?" *English Woman's Journal* 4 (January 1860): 296; Barbara Bodichon, *Women and Work* (London: Bosworth and Harrison, 1857), 6–7; Emily Davies, *The Higher Education of Women* (1866; repr., New York: AMS, 1973), 22–23.

16. Yeo, *Contest for Social Science*, 122–135. Of course there were some feminists, such as Harriet Taylor Mill (d. 1851), who proposed an equality of human capacity between men and women and who underplayed sexual difference. On the whole, however, later feminists hedged the issue by saying that woman's full potential was not yet known because her nature had been deformed by social and cultural conditioning (ibid., 138–139).

17. Karl Marx, "The Eighteenth Brumaire of Louis Bonaparte," in *Selected Works*, by K. Marx and F. Engels (1869; repr., Moscow: Foreign Languages Publishing House, 1962), 1:247. I explore this issue at greater length in Yeo, *Radical Femininity*, 6–15.

18. I discuss the use of Catholic elements more fully in Eileen Janes Yeo, "Protestant Feminists and Catholic Saints in Victorian Britain," in Yeo, *Radical Femininity*, chap. 5.

19. Frances Power Cobbe, "Social Science Congresses and Women's Part in Them," *Macmillan's Magazine*, December 1861, 90.

20. Mary Carpenter, "Women's Work in the Reformatory Movement," *English Woman's Journal* 1 (1858): 291–292.

21. See my discussion of "homes" in Yeo, *Contest for Social Science*, 124–126.

22. Bessie Rayner Parkes Papers, box 10, item 36, n.d., Girton College, Cambridge.

23. Josephine Butler, *Catherine of Siena*, 3rd ed. (London: Horace Marshall, 1894), 36. For Butler, see Anne Summers, *Female Lives, Moral States: Women, Religion and Public Life in Britain, 1800–1930* (Newbury, UK: Threshold Press, 2000); Jane Jordan, *Josephine Butler* (London: John Murray, 2001).

24. Butler, *Catherine of Siena*, 66, 36, 46.

25. Anna Jameson, *Legends of the Madonna as Represented in the Fine Arts*, new ed. (London: Longmans, 1891), xlx. Kimberley van Esveld Adams, *Our Lady of Victorian Feminism: The Madonna in the Work of Anna Jameson, Margaret Fuller, and George Eliot* (Athens: Ohio University Press, 2001), chaps. 4 and 5.

26. Cobbe, "Social Science Congresses," 91–92.

27. Ibid., 92.

28. Anne-Marie Rafferty, *The Politics of Nursing Knowledge* (London: Routledge, 1996), chap. 2.

29. *Lancet*, 19 April 1862; see Rafferty, *Politics of Nursing Knowledge*, 31, 40.

30. *Lancet*, 17 August 1878, 227, argued that only nurses could be both helpmeets and social mothers: "it is woman's prerogative to nurse, whether the helpless being at her mercy be an infant, or an adult reduced to the level of childhood by disease. Women cannot desert the position of nurses of the sick unless they also abandon the rearing and tending of the young." See Anne Crowther, "Why Women Should Be Nurses and Not Doctors" (2002), http://www.ukchnm.org/seminars01.php (accessed 16 April 2007).

31. Sophia Jex-Blake, *Medical Women: A Thesis and a History* (Edinburgh: Oliphant, Anderson, and Ferrier, 1886), 7. See Yeo, "Medicine, Science and the Body," 148–152,

154; for women doctors adopting a "difference" strategy of advance, see A. Witz, *Professions and Patriarchy* (London: Routledge, 1992).

32. Lena Leneman, *In Search of Life: The Story of Elsie Inglis and the Scottish Women's Hospitals* (Edinburgh: Mercat Press, 1994); M. Todd, *Life of Sophia Jex-Blake* (London: Macmillan, 1919), 479–480, tells how Jex-Blake refused to set up a hospital in Sarajevo during the 1870s lest by treating men she damage the chances of medical women.

33. Patrick Geddes and J. Arthur Thomson, *Evolution* (London: Williams and Norgate, [1911]), 246–247; Patrick Geddes and J. Arthur Thomson, *Sex* (London: Williams and Norgate, 1914), 232–234.

34. Geddes and Thomson, *Evolution,* 267, 270–271, for a stark gender contrast between katabolic and anabolic. See Geddes and Thompson, *Sex,* 208, for the more nuanced version quoted in this paragraph.

35. Geddes and Thomson, *Sex,* 213, 239.

36. Charlotte Despard, *Theosophy and the Woman's Movement* (London: Theosophy Publishing Society, 1913), 48, 16, 45; Andro Linklater, *An Unhusbanded Life: Charlotte Despard, Suffragette, Socialist, and Sinn Feiner* (London: Hutchinson, 1980).

37. Frances Swiney, *The Cosmic Procession; or, The Feminine Principle in Evolution* (London: Ernest Bell, 1906), 126, 99–100, xi. See D. Burfield, "Theosophy and Feminism: Some Explorations in Nineteenth-Century Biography," in *Women's Religious Experience,* ed. Pat Holden (London: Croom Helm, 1983).

38. Geddes and Thomson, *Sex,* 244.

39. Carl Gustav Jung, "Psychological Aspects of the Mother Archetype," in *The Archetypes and the Collective Unconscious* (1938; repr., London: Routledge, 1991); Hannah Segal, *Introduction to the Work of Melanie Klein* (London: Heinemann, 1973), gives the clearest exposition of Klein's ideas.

40. Joseph Estlin Carpenter, *The Life and Work of Mary Carpenter,* 2nd ed. (1879; repr., Montclair, NJ: Patterson Smith, 1974), 52, 84, 381.

41. Eva Shaw McLaren, *Elsie Inglis: The Woman with a Torch* (London: SPCK, 1920).

42. Lady Frances Balfour, *Dr. Elsie Inglis* (London: Hodder and Stoughton, n.d.), 47.

43. As quoted in McLaren, *Inglis,* 20.

44. Frances Power Cobbe, *The Life of Frances Power Cobbe,* (Boston: Houghton Mifflin, 1894), 1:88.

45. Ibid., 2:359.

46. See Lori Williamson, *Power and Protest: Frances Power Cobbe and Victorian Society* (London: Rivers Oram, 2005), 85–89, for a sensitive discussion of the nature of female companionship and the impossibility of ever knowing whether Cobbe's relationship with Lloyd was fully sexual.

47. Marie Belloc Lowndes, *I Too Have Lived in Arcadia* (London: Macmillan, 1941), 74; the author is Bessie's daughter.

48. For her early life, see Sheila Herstein, *A Mid-Victorian Feminist: Barbara Leigh Smith Bodichon* (New Haven, CT: Yale University Press, 1985), chap. 1; Hester Burton, *Barbara Bodichon, 1827–1891* (London: John Murray, 1949), 36.

49. As quoted in Burton, *Bodichon,* 138.

50. Burton, *Bodichon,* 207ff.; Herstein, *Bodichon,* 184ff.; Rendall, "A Moral Engine?" 114, for relations with Jameson.

51. She worked intermittently as a governess and then became an art critic and the type of "literary lady" who received "a large share of the easy ridicule of the inconsiderate" for "emancipating themselves from common ties. How many among them have been

the support and stay of their families, the bread-winner upon whom many helpless or disabled relatives depended, it is not for me to say"; George Henry Needler, ed., *Letters of Anna Jameson to Ottilie von Goethe* (Oxford: Oxford University Press, 1939), 179–180. The most recent biography is Judith Johnston, *Anna Jameson: Victorian, Feminist, Woman of Letters* (Aldershot, UK: Scolar, 1997).

52. Geraldine Macpherson, *Memoirs, of the Life of Anna Jameson* (London: Longmans Green, 1878), 98.

53. Anna Jameson to Ottilie von Goethe, 20 October 1854, in *Letters* (ed. Needler), 197.

54. Anna Jameson to Ottilie von Goethe, 27 June [1836], ibid., 44.

55. Macpherson, *Memoirs*, 133.

56. Clara Thomas, *Love and Work Enough: The Life of Anna Jameson* (London: University of Toronto Press, 1967), 174.

57. Anna Jameson to Ottilie von Goethe, [1848], in *Letters* (ed. Needler), 162; Anna Jameson to Ottilie von Goethe, 8 February 1849, ibid., 164.

58. Macpherson, *Memoirs*, 242–243.

59. Ibid., 310, 209.

60. Jo Manton tells this story of misrule in *Mary Carpenter and the Children of the Street* (London: Heinemann, 1976), chap. 9.

61. Bristol Record Office, 126193/2, records of Mary Carpenter, Red Lodge Journal, September 1858.

62. Bristol Record Office, 126193/1, Scrapbook of Miscellaneous Papers, which also holds a copy of Mary Carpenter's will.

63. Conveyance for the Red Lodge, Bristol, 25 March 1919, Bristol Record Office, 5535/59; Rosanna's annuity was linked to the property, and thus she was involved in its sale. Thanks to Alison Brown, the archives officer, for help in tracking Rosanna.

64. Cobbe, "Social Science Congresses," 90.

65. "The Spinster, by One," *Freewoman*, 23 November 1911, reprinted in Sheila Jeffreys, ed., *The Sexuality Debates* (London: Routledge and Kegan Paul, 1987), 602.

66. See Alison Oram, "'Sex Is an Accident': Feminism, Science and the Radical Sexual Theory of Urania, 1915–40," chap. 13, in Bland and Doan, *Sexology*.

67. Yeo, *Contest for Social Science*, 272–278.

CHAPTER 3

Social and Emotional Well-Being of Single Women in Contemporary America

DEBORAH CARR

The harmful consequences of singlehood for contemporary American women's physical, emotional, social, and economic well-being have been widely documented and debated.[1] The observation that being single is a less desirable status than being married has been trumpeted in recent popular books, including Linda J. Waite and Maggie Gallagher's *The Case for Marriage,* Sylvia Ann Hewlett's *Creating a Life,* and Danielle Crittenden's *What Our Mothers Didn't Tell Us,* and has guided the implementation of pro-marriage social policies, including "covenant marriage," and economic and tax policies that favor married couples.[2]

Despite pervasive beliefs that marriage enhances the quality of American women's lives, past empirical research on the protective effects of marriage has several limitations that may undermine its persuasiveness. First, "marriage" is narrowly conceptualized and refers to one's legal status only. The nature and quality of one's marriage are seldom considered: the assumption is that all marriages are "good" marriages. Similarly, "single" women often are treated as a monolithic and homogeneous group, yet this large and heterogeneous group actually includes formerly married women (i.e., divorced, separated, or widowed), never-married heterosexual women residing with a romantic partner, lesbians, and women with no romantic partner. Second, the purported benefits of marriage (relative to singlehood) are conceptualized in fairly narrow terms and reflect traditional notions of marriage in which husbands perform "instrumental" roles and women specialize in "expressive" tasks.[3] Women are presumed to benefit financially from their husbands' paid employment, while men receive emotional and physical health benefits from their nurturing wives. Other aspects of marriage and social life, such as sexual intimacy, or the extent to which spouses receive emotional support from others, often are ignored.

Third, most research presumes that the meaning, desirability, and necessity of marriage are stable over both historical and personal time. However, as the advantages traditionally associated with marriage have eroded over the past half century, the disadvantages typically associated with singlehood have eroded in tandem. For example, women's educational and occupational opportunities have expanded dramatically over the past four decades; thus women's economic need for marriage has declined considerably, and women's ability to support themselves without a spouse has increased.[4] At the same time, advancements in reproductive technologies—such as in vitro fertilization—enable unpartnered women (and lesbian couples) to have a biological child outside of the traditional heterosexual marital relationship.[5]

Cultural and normative shifts in the value of marriage vis-à-vis other forms of social relationships, such as cohabitation, friendships, and gay relationships, also have occurred in the last four decades. The proportion of Americans who cohabit before (or in place of) marriage has increased steadily over the past three decades, and the majority of newlyweds today lived with their spouse before marriage.[6] Nearly universal acceptance of premarital sexual relations today means that marriage is no longer a prerequisite for establishing and maintaining an intimate romantic partnership.[7] The importance and beneficial effects of marriage also may shift over the personal life course; single women's adaptations are neglected in extant studies of marriage and well-being. Few studies of the benefits of marriage (and the stressors of singlehood) acknowledge that adults adjust to the opportunities and constraints facing them; unmarried women may make choices and carve out lives for themselves that mesh with and enhance their role as a single woman.

In this chapter, I question the pervasive assumption that marriage enhances women's well-being and examine whether currently married, cohabiting, never-married, and formerly married women differ significantly in their psychological health. I also evaluate four possible explanations for the observed linkage between marital status and psychological well-being: (1) availability of social and emotional support from friends; (2) satisfaction with one's sexual life; (3) one's particular sexual orientation; and (4) personal beliefs about the desirability and necessity of marriage. Finally, I examine the extent to which the psychological consequences of marital status vary over the life course and across birth cohorts. I use data from the Midlife Development in the United States (MIDUS) study, a sample survey of more than three thousand Americans ages twenty-five to seventy-four in 1995, to address these aims.

Single Women in America: Who Are They?

The United States is unquestionably a pro-marriage society. Cultural images, public policies, and personal attitudes elevate the status and value of heterosexual marriage relative to single life in the United States today.[8] Even popular "reality" television shows, situation comedies, and films owe a posthumous screenwriter's credit to Jane Austen, as their final scenes often fade to a dreamily enamored heterosexual couple at (or on their way to) the altar.[9] Although marriage persists as a cultural ideal, single adults—and particularly single women—comprise a sizable, heterogeneous, and rapidly growing sector of the United States population. In 2000, roughly one-half of the fourteen million adult women in the United States were married, and an equal proportion were unmarried. According to official U.S. Census statistics, the terms "single" and "unmarried" women may include never-married women who live alone, never-married women who cohabit with a romantic partner, and divorced, separated, or widowed persons who formerly were married. Moreover, the "never-married" subgroup is highly diverse: some are unmarried by choice; others view themselves as "temporarily" single and are waiting to find a spouse; others, still, are legally prohibited from marrying because they and their partner are of the same sex.[10]

The proportion of women in the United States who are currently single has increased steadily over the past five decades for several reasons. First, women are delaying marriage, remaining single well into their thirties and even forties. In the 1950s and early 1960s, American women married at age twenty-one on average. Today, the average woman marries at age twenty-five, and this age creeps up steadily as a woman's educational attainment increases.[11] This delay in marriage is due in part to young women's desire to complete their education before marrying. Yet delayed marriage also is due to an increased acceptance of premarital sexual relations and a concomitant rise in cohabitation rates; more than 60 percent of recent newlyweds lived with their partner before marrying.[12] As a result of these patterns, a statistical snapshot of the United States reveals a higher proportion of "never-married" women than ever before.

Second, divorce rates increased steadily and then plateaued during the last four decades of the twentieth century, reflecting a greater acceptance of divorce, a rise in the ideology of individualism, and increases in women's economic independence.[13] In 2000, roughly 20 percent of women ages thirty-five to fifty-nine were divorced or separated, whereas in 1950 just 5 percent of same-age women were divorced or separated. Third, the gender gap in mortality has increased steadily throughout the twentieth century, whereby men now die seven years younger than women. The gender gap in mortality reflects historical shifts in the causes of death; leading causes of death today—particularly cancer and heart disease—disproportionately strike men.[14] As a result, many more women than men are widowed. Among men and women ages sixty and older in 2000, just 11 percent of men yet 40 percent of women were widowed.[15] Widowed and divorced women are far less likely than their male peers to remarry, reflecting a gender imbalance in the older population, coupled with men's tendency to marry women two to three years younger than themselves. Interestingly, just 46 percent of women but 75 percent of men ages sixty and older were married in 2000.[16] Although singlehood today is relatively common, and even normative for some age strata, both social scientists and casual observers characterize single women as less happy, well-adjusted, and fulfilled than their married peers.[17] The overarching aim of this chapter is to interrogate the assumption that married women are better off and to uncover the reasons behind this pervasive and widely accepted belief.

The Psychological Well-Being of
Married and Unmarried Women

Married women in the United States today typically experience better psychological and physical health, sexual satisfaction, and economic stability than their unmarried peers do.[18] However, explanations for why and how marriage enhances (and singlehood undermines) well-being are incomplete. Most studies of marriage and well-being follow one of two tracks: identifying the distinctive aspects of marriage that benefit women and men, and examining whether marriage affects psychological well-being, or vice versa.

Gender differences in the benefits (and strains) of marriage have been explored extensively. Feminist writings, exemplified in Jessie Bernard's (1972) *Future of Marriage*, have argued that traditional marriages—in which men specialize in performing the "breadwinner" role and women are responsible for childbearing and childrearing—benefit men more than women. Although "his" marriage brings a man health, power, and life satisfaction, "her" marriage subjects a woman to stress, dissatisfaction, and loss of self.[19] Men are purported to suffer more than women when single or upon the loss of a spouse because they have more to lose. Recent empirical studies counter, however, that marriage benefits *both* women and men, yet in different ways.[20]

Women typically benefit economically from marriage and remarriage, whereas men receive rich social and emotional rewards. Women are more likely than men to experience economic hardship (and consequently, psychological distress) upon either divorce or widowhood.[21] Because women typically shoulder the responsibility for childrearing in traditional marriages, they exit the labor force (or reduce their work hours) when children are young, and so they experience both the absolute loss of personal earnings and the loss of skills that enable their smooth reentry into the work force.[22] Forsaking one's career to care for one's family also takes a direct toll on a woman's self-acceptance and optimism about her future career prospects.[23]

For men, in contrast, marriage provides social, emotional, and health-enhancing support. For instance, men are more likely than women to engage in reckless health behaviors such as smoking or drinking over the life course, and these patterns are most acute among men who do not have wives to curb their unhealthy behaviors.[24] Men also are more likely to lack close confiding relationships with persons other than their spouses.[25] Women tend to provide more emotional support to their spouses than do men for women, so the absence or loss of a spouse may create a greater emotional void in men's lives. For these reasons, the married are generally characterized as having better psychological health than the single, divorced, or widowed, and these benefits are greater for men than for women.

Yet research on the protective effects of marriage typically contrasts married and "unmarried" adults, and neglects the distinctive and heterogeneous experiences of never-married versus formerly married (i.e., separated, divorced, or widowed) persons. For divorced or widowed women, the loss of a husband's income, his contributions to the maintenance of the home, and emotional and sexual intimacy may represent a distressing transition that warrants readjustment after a period of grief or psychological distress.[26] Never-married women, in contrast, have not experienced a potentially distressing change in marital status, and most are self-sufficient in terms of both financial security and maintaining a home.[27] Moreover, whereas divorced and widowed women may experience "desolation" or a decline in social engagement and increase in social isolation after the loss of their partner, single women often have long-established, enduring patterns of social interaction that protect them against psychological distress.[28] To more fully document the linkage between marital status and psychological well-being, I contrast the distinctive emotional experiences of never-married, formerly married, currently married, and currently cohabiting women.

A second line of inquiry examines whether marriage actually provides psychological benefits, or whether the emotionally and physically healthy are more likely to marry, remain married, or remarry following widowhood or divorce. The "social selection" hypothesis holds that the observed statistical relationship between marriage and well-being is due to distinctive characteristics of those who marry (or remarry), such as emotional well-being, good physical health, positive health behaviors, desirable personality traits, and rich socioeconomic resources.[29] For the most part, recent empirical findings have supported the social causation perspective, that is, marital status causes psychological well-being rather than the reverse.[30]

Examinations of gender differences in the psychological consequences of marriage and singlehood, and evaluations of the social selection versus social causation hypotheses, are important, yet they do little to advance understanding of the linkages between marital status and well-being, particularly in an era when gender-typed social roles in marriage are beginning to blur, and social changes in values and attitudes have created a context in which the meaning and desirability of marriage have shifted.[31] The linkage between marital status and women's well-being may reflect a broader range of influences, including personal evaluations of the importance of marriage as a social institution; social support from persons other than one's spouse or romantic partner; sexual orientation, given that most lesbians are unable to marry even if they wish to do so; and changes in the meaning and desirability of marriage over both historical time and personal time.

The Importance of Marriage as a Cultural and Personal Ideal

Marriage represents the attainment of a cherished and (arguably) compulsory cultural ideal; conforming to a widely held ideal, in turn, may enhance psychological well-being. The experience of marriage (and romantic love) is idealized in modern Western cultures and is conceptualized as a transcendent state that marks the completion of a quest for one's intended other.[32] Developmental psychologists argue further that marriage is a necessary precondition for healthy emotional adjustment in adulthood. Marrying and having children are considered critical "developmental tasks," or anticipated and normative life stages, for young adults.[33] Erik Erikson's stage model of successful adult development proposes that young adults must resolve the challenge of intimacy versus isolation; the former involves the establishment of an enduring, committed, and emotionally intimate relationship with a romantic partner.[34] Failure to resolve this crisis prevents young adults from progressing to the next developmental stage, and thus one's emotional maturation is stalled.

The formation of a lasting romantic relationship is considered a critical source of women's emotional adjustment and maturity, and a more powerful source of identity than it is for men. The psychologist Jean Baker Miller has argued that women define themselves through relationships with others: "women's sense of self becomes very much organized around being able to make and then . . . maintain relationships. . . . Eventually, for many women the threat of disruption of connections is perceived not as just a loss of a relationship but as something closer to the loss of the self." Consequently, the "failure" to establish or maintain an enduring romantic relationship may threaten women's sense of identity, emotional security, and competence.[35]

Remaining single—or dissolving a marriage—also may have psychological costs for women because it signifies the failure to achieve a goal that is strongly endorsed by social norms and institutions. Conforming to social expectations—such as marrying and remaining married—may provide psychological rewards via two pathways. First, conforming to widely held expectations may bring social approval or subtle rewards from significant others. Social approval, in turn, may foster positive views of the self. Second, the individual may internalize societal norms and expectations: "the individual thus becomes his [or her] own judge, approving or disapproving of his behavior in terms of internal standards."[36] The discordance between one's own experiences and either the expectations of others or of one's self is a powerful (negative) predictor of psychological well-being. A discrepancy between one's current situation and the situation to which one aspires is associated with depression and self-criticism, whereas a discrepancy between one's current situation and the expectations imposed by others may create anxiety.[37]

The societal expectation that marriage is a desirable and normative life transition has a further consequence for unmarried persons: they may be stigmatized and judged negatively by others. A burgeoning literature on single stigma, or singlism, reveals that the failure to marry is viewed as indicative of a moral or character flaw, and as such, single persons are subject to stereotyping, prejudice, and both interpersonal and institutional discrimination.[38] Surveys and quasi-experimental studies reveal that single women are evaluated as less attractive, moral, emotionally stable, loyal, responsible, and dependable than their married peers and also are more likely to report that they have been subject to interpersonal discrimination and mistreatment.[39] Individuals who are mistreated or stigmatized by others may internalize the belief that they are unworthy or undesirable and may develop a compromised sense of self-esteem as a result.[40]

Despite widespread denigration of singlehood and both attitudinal and behavioral support for marriage (more than 90 percent of American adults still marry), some individuals may be less committed to the marriage ideal and may believe that singlehood is an equally desirable state. For these individuals, remaining single may represent a conscious life choice at best—and at worst an undesired status, but one that is not evaluated as inferior to being married. Past research on the psychological consequences of marriage has not addressed the possibility that marriage is a less cherished and compulsory goal for some; the neglect of this factor may overstate the psychological costs of singlehood. Thus, I examine whether the psychological costs of singlehood attenuate when attitudes about the desirability of marriage are considered.

Sexual Orientation

The goal of marriage is simply unattainable for most American gays and lesbians, regardless of their preferences for such a union. I know of no studies of marital status differences in psychological health that have acknowledged that gays and lesbians are included in their samples of unmarried individuals and that the linkage between singlehood and psychological health may in part reflect the experiences of gay individuals. According to recent estimates, between 3 and 10 percent of the United States population self-identifies as homosexual or bisexual, and most of these individuals have either never married or are cohabiting with a romantic partner.[41] Although this proportion is small enough so that it cannot account fully for the link between singlehood and psychological well-being, sexual orientation may be one pathway that partially accounts for the psychological disadvantage of the never married. Gays and lesbians face distinctive stressors, including homophobia, discrimination, and the lack of public acknowledgment of their romantic relationships—especially when the relationship dissolves.[42] Consequently, I examine whether the linkage between singlehood and psychological well-being attenuates when sexual orientation is controlled.

Social Support and Sexual Intimacy

Marriage is believed to enhance psychological health by providing sexual and emotional intimacy. Married women typically report higher levels of sexual satisfaction than their unmarried peers, reflecting the fact that married women have continuous and proximate access to a committed, exclusive, and long-term sexual relationship.[43] Surprisingly, researchers have not investigated systematically whether sexual satisfaction accounts for unmarried women's disadvantaged psychological health. In this chapter, I investigate whether the marriage gap in women's psychological health is attributable to differences in married and unmarried women's satisfaction with their sexual lives.

Although unmarried women may not have regular access to a sexual partner and confidante, they may adapt by actively pursuing and maintaining platonic friendships and relationships with other relatives and romantic relationships with a nonmarital partner. The substitution theory of relationships holds that in the absence of a spouse or children, unmarried individuals will turn to more remote kin, such as siblings or parents. When these relatives are not available, other close relationships, such as friends, are substituted.[44] Because their social networks are often more expansive and diverse than those of their married peers, never-married women have been found to be more socially integrated than other women—based on an "isolation index" assessing frequency of visits with neighbors, number of friends living in the neighborhood, and feelings of being part of their communities.[45]

For never-married and formerly married women, friendships may provide many of the same emotional rewards as marriage. Research on social support shows persuasively that having a single confidante is of greater value in addressing an individual's emotional needs than having several superficial friendships or a tenuous and troubled marital relationship.[46] Friendships are particularly rewarding and intimate for women; thus the psychological disadvantage experienced by unmarried women may be less pronounced when social and emotional support from friends is considered.[47] I therefore explore whether the psychological disadvantage associated with singlehood persists when I adjust for an unmarried woman's contact with and emotional support from friends and neighbors, and her satisfaction with a sexual relationship.

Do the Benefits of Marriage Change over Historical and Personal Time?

Research on the protective effects of marriage is based on the implicit assumption that the meaning and psychological consequences of marriage are constant over historical time and personal time. However, historical shifts in the meaning, desirability, and necessity of marriage may have created a context in which marriage may affect psychological health differently for different birth cohorts.

A birth cohort is a group of individuals born at the same point in history and who "experience the same event within the time interval."[48] Given their shared age at a given point in history, members of a birth cohort face similar opportunities and constraints as they pass through the life course. For instance, women's educational attainment, labor force participation, and earnings relative to men have increased steadily over the past fifty years.[49] Thus, current cohorts of young women are far more likely than their mothers to have achieved economic independence and may be less compelled to marry (or remain married) for purely economic reasons.

Members of a birth cohort also share a unique cultural lens or a "set of cognitive and evaluative beliefs about what is or what ought to be."[50] A cohort is most likely to develop a set of beliefs that are distinct from those of preceding cohorts during periods marked by rapid social changes, such as stark changes in gender roles in the home and workplace over the past forty years.[51] The Baby Bust (b. 1960–1970), Baby Boom (b. 1944–1959), and Silent Generation (b. 1931–1943) birth cohorts may hold very different motivations and preferences for marriage. As noted earlier, gender role shifts in the family and workplace—combined with delayed and decreased fertility—mean that the functional bases for marriage are less acute for members of younger cohorts relative to those of older cohorts.[52] Increasing acceptance of nontraditional family forms, such as cohabitation, and changing attitudes toward the acceptability of nonmarital sex have created a context in which young women and men today may receive many of the benefits of marriage without actually entering a legal union.[53] Moreover, although marriage was once perceived as a permanent bond broken only by death, it is now viewed as a potentially temporary bond that could be severed through separation and divorce. For these reasons, singlehood and marital dissolution may pose fewer psychological costs to members of the Baby Boom and Baby Bust cohorts than for those persons who came of age in the 1940s and 1950s.

Expectations for married life also have changed, however, and may make marital dissolution more difficult for members of younger birth cohorts. Greater gender-based equality in both the home and workplace today means that women and men no longer seek out a "helpmate" to fulfill the instrumental and expressive marital roles traditionally performed by members of the opposite sex.[54] Rather, the bases of spouse selection today are more likely to include individual preferences (rather than a choice endorsed or selected by parents or community members), love, shared interests, and the idealized notion of a "soul mate."[55] When the marriage ends, then, the divorced or widowed survivor must grapple with both the loss of a partner and the recognition that their idealized union has failed. For these reasons, members of the younger birth cohorts may be affected more powerfully by the loss of partner, whether through divorce or widowhood.

The psychological consequences of marriage also may vary at different stages in the life course. First, most Americans believe that there is an "appropriate" time line for making important life transitions, such as marriage. A person who has not yet married by their fifties is committing a more powerful normative violation than is a person in their twenties who has never married; being out of step with one's peers and with prevailing expectations may take a psychological toll.[56] Moreover, structural constraints often make it particularly difficult for women to marry at older ages. The imbalanced gender ratio at older ages, combined with men's preferences for younger partners, may preclude older women from marrying, even if they are positively disposed to the idea.[57] Consequently, singlehood may be particularly distressing to older women.[58]

Second, the need and desire for a spouse may wax and wane over the life course; midlife and older adults are less likely to require either the homemaking or breadwinning services of a partner. Boundaries demarcating traditional gender-typed roles in marriage become blurred as adults age. Midlife and older adults are no longer responsible for the daily care of young children, a task that falls largely to women in young and mid-adulthood.[59] The onset of physical health problems may render older adults less able to manage the specialized homemaking, home maintenance, or breadwinning roles that they performed earlier in the life course.[60] Consequently, for midlife and older adults the absence of a spouse may pose less of a challenge than it does for younger adults, who are more likely to be grappling with the current and competing demands of paid employment and childrearing.

To evaluate the proposition that marital status may affect psychological health differently across birth cohorts and life stages, I examine whether the linkage between marital status and psychological distress, self-esteem, and depressive symptoms is significantly different for women of three different birth cohorts (and life course stages): Baby Bust (b. 1960–1970, age thirty-five and younger in 1995), Baby Boom (b. 1944–1959, age thirty-six to fifty-one in 1995), and Silent Generation (b. 1931–1943, age fifty-two to sixty-four in 1995) cohorts.

Emotional Well-Being of Single Women in the Contemporary United States: Empirical Evidence Data and Analytic Plan

My objective is to investigate whether never-married, cohabiting, and formerly married women differ from currently married women in their reports of depressive symptoms, psychological distress, and self-esteem. (Table 3.1 provides further detail on each of the three well-being measures.) I examine data from the Midlife Development in the United States (MIDUS) survey, a random sample survey of more than three thousand men and women ages twenty-five to seventy-four in 1995.[61] The analyses explore whether women's psychological health is shaped by their marital status and the reasons why women's marital status affects their current well-being. Specifically, I consider four potential pathways that may account for the widely documented linkage between marriage and women's well-being: friendships, including frequency of visits with friends and availability of emotional support from friends; sexual orientation; satisfaction with one's sex life; and adherence to the cultural view that marriage is more desirable than singlehood.

First, I conduct bivariate analyses to identify variations in women's psychological well-being by marital status. Second, I evaluate the extent to which marital status differences in psychological well-being persist after I adjust for possible confounding or "selection" characteristics. Selection characteristics refer to those personal characteristics that affect the likelihood that one ever marries or remains married, such as early life health, educational attainment, and race. Past studies have revealed that African Americans, persons with poor physical health, and persons with lower levels of education and occupational status are less likely to marry and more likely to divorce or become widowed, compared to whites, persons with excellent physical heath, and highly educated persons.[62] I control for these potential selection characteristics in my analysis because they also are well-documented influences on one's psychological health.[63] Statistical models that do not adjust for these characteristics could overstate the negative psychological consequences of singlehood. Third, I evaluate whether marital status differences in psychological well-being persist after I adjust for each of the potential pathway variables described earlier (i.e., friendship, sexual orientation, sexual satisfaction, and attitudes toward marriage). Finally, I evaluate whether the relationship between marital status and psychological well-being varies for three distinctive cohorts of women: Baby Bust (b. 1960–1970), Baby Boom (b. 1944–1959), and Silent Generation (b. 1931–1943) women. An overarching theme of this chapter is that the meaning and desirability of singlehood (and marriage) shift both over historical time and over the personal life course. As such, both the emotional benefits and disadvantages of marriage and singlehood may vary based on one's birth cohort or generation.

Bivariate Results

The bivariate analyses (shown in table 3.2) provide a statistical portrait of each of the four marital-status groups: currently married, cohabiting, never-married, and formerly married (i.e., separated, divorced, or widowed) women. Asterisks denote whether a marital status category differs significantly from the

TABLE 3.1   *Scales used in analysis*

Psychological distress ($\alpha = .87$)	During the past 30 days, how much of the time did you feel: • so sad nothing could cheer you up • nervous • restless or fidgety • hopeless • that everything was an effort • worthless Response categories range from 1 (none of the time) to 5 (all of the time).
Self-acceptance ($\alpha = .62$)	• I like most parts of my personality. • When I look at the story of my life, I am pleased with how things have turned out so far. • In many ways I feel disappointed about my achievements in life (reverse coded). Response categories range from 1 (strongly disagree) to 7 (strongly agree).
Depressive symptoms in the past 12 months	A diagnosis of Major Depression requires a period of at least two weeks of depressed mood most of the day, nearly every day, and at least four other symptoms typically found to accompany depression, including problems with eating, sleeping, energy, concentration, feelings of self-worth, and suicidal thoughts or actions.
Positive emotional support ($\alpha = .88$)	• How much do your friends really care about you? • How much do they understand the way you feel about things? • How much can you rely on them for help if you have a serious problem? • How much can you open up to them if you need to talk about your worries? Response categories range from 1 (not at all) to 4 (a lot).
Frequency of contact with friends	• How often are you in contact with any of your friends—including visits, phone calls, letters, or electronic mail messages? Response categories range from 1 (never or hardly ever) to 8 (several times a day).
Sexual orientation	How would you describe your sexual orientation? • Heterosexual (sexually attracted only to the opposite sex). • Homosexual (sexually attracted to only your own sex), or bisexual (sexually attracted to both men and women).
Satisfaction with one's sex life	How would you rate the sexual aspect of your life these days? Response categories range from 0 (worst possible situation) to 10 (best possible situation)
Attitudes toward marriage ($\alpha = .85$)	Indicate how strongly you agree or disagree with each of the following statements. • Women can have full and happy lives without marrying. • Men can have fully and happy lives without marrying.

TABLE 3.2 *Descriptive statistics by marital status, women of the MIDUS survey*

	Total sample	Currently married	Cohabiting	Never married	Formerly married
Dependent variables					
Depression (two-week spell) in the past year	.17 (.37)	.14 (.34)	.17 (.38)	.21* (.41)	.21*** (.41)
Psychological distress in the past two weeks	1.63 (.67)	1.57 (.64)	1.67 (.64)	1.73** (.69)	1.70*** (.73)
Self-acceptance	5.40 (1.19)	5.53 (1.15)	5.44 (1.32)	5.27*** (1.21)	5.19*** (1.19)
Independent variables					
Selection characteristics					
Mental health was fair/poor at age 16	.09 (.28)	.07 (.25)	.13* (.34)	.14*** (.35)	.093 (.29)
Physical health was fair/poor at age 16	.04 (.21)	.04 (.19)	.05 (.22)	.07* (.25)	.05 (.22)
Current physical health (10 = best; 0 = worst)	7.35 (1.72)	7.40 (1.66)	7.29 (1.75)	7.30 (1.73)	7.29 (1.82)
Demographics					
Age	47.16 (13.29)	46.71 (12.80)	37.34*** (9.96)	37.92*** (11.99)	52.99*** (12.08)
Race (1 = black; 0 = white or other)	.14 (.35)	.11 (.31)	.18* (.39)	.28*** (.45)	.16** (.37)
Educational attainment					
Less than 12 years	.09 (.29)	.08 (.27)	.09 (.28)	.08 (.27)	.12** (.33)
12 years	.31 (.46)	.34 (.47)	.34 (.48)	.17** (.38)	.30 (.46)
13–15 years	.33 (.47)	.31 (.46)	.39 (.49)	.26 (.44)	.37* (.48)
16 or more years	.28 (.45)	.28 (.45)	.18 (.39)	.49*** (.50)	.21** (.41)

(continued)

Table 3.2. (continued)

	Total sample	Currently married	Cohabiting	Never married	Formerly married
Current/most recent occupation					
Upper white collar	.26 (.44)	.25 (.43)	.18 (.39)	.40*** (.49)	.25 (.43)
Lower white collar	.29 (.45)	.29 (.45)	.39* (.49)	.25 (.43)	.29 (.45)
Blue collar	.07 (.25)	.07 (.25)	.11 (.31)	.04 (.20)	.07 (.26)
Full-time worker, current/last job	.51 (.50)	.44 (.50)	.67*** (.47)	.68*** (.40)	.49 (.25)
Own income (natural log)	8.77 (2.01)	8.53 (2.08)	9.29*** (1.70)	9.42*** (1.66)	8.94*** (1.98)
Income missing/DK	.05 (.22)	.05 (.21)	.02 (.16)	.05 (.21)	.07 (.26)
Emotional support					
Frequency of visits with friends (8 = highest)	5.75 (1.68)	5.59 (1.23)	5.40 (1.91)	6.11*** (1.53)	5.96*** (1.69)
Positive emotional support from friends (4 = highest)	3.34 (.67)	3.33 (.65)	3.35 (.72)	3.39 (.68)	3.33 (.65)
Sexuality					
Lesbian or bisexual	.02 (.15)	.01 (.09)	.07*** (.26)	.09*** (.29)	.02 (.12)
Satisfaction with current sex life (10 = highest)	5.19 (3.23)	5.99 (2.84)	7.10*** (2.63)	4.46*** (2.94)	3.61*** (3.42)
No report of sexual satisfaction (1 = missing)	.05 (.21)	.02 (.14)	.01 (.11)	.05** (.22)	.09*** (.29)
Cultural evaluation of marriage					
Believes singlehood is acceptable (7 = greatest acceptance)	5.64 (1.54)	5.58 (1.57)	5.97* (1.26)	5.96*** (1.23)	5.58 (1.61)

(continued)

Table 3.2. (continued)

	Total sample	Currently married	Cohabiting	Never married	Formerly married
Percentage in marital status category	100	56	4.6	11	29
N	1,785	1,000	82	189	514

Source: MIDUS survey, 1995.

Notes: Two-tailed t-tests were conducted to evaluate marital status differences, where "currently married" is the reference group. Unstandardized regression coefficients and standard errors are presented.
* $p > .05$; ** $p > .01$; *** $p > .001$.

"currently married" (reference category) in terms of important psychological, demographic, and socioeconomic characteristics.

Never-married and formerly married women fare worse than their married peers in all three dimensions of psychological health. They are significantly more likely to have experienced a two-week spell of depression in the past year (21 percent versus 14 percent for currently married women), and they report significantly more psychological distress. Never-married women have significantly lower self-acceptance scores than either married or cohabiting women, yet they still fare better than separated, divorced, or widowed women.

Women with poor physical and mental health during their adolescent years are less likely than healthier women to marry in the first place. Never-married women are significantly more likely than their married peers to report that they were in poor mental and physical health at age sixteen. Although married women enjoy better physical and mental health than single women, unmarried women enjoy richer work lives and higher personal earnings. Never-married and cohabiting women are significantly more likely than the married to be working full time for pay, and they (and formerly married) also report significantly greater personal income than married women. Never-married women are far more likely than all other women to have at least a four-year college degree and to work in an upper-level white-collar (i.e., professional or managerial) occupation. These findings are consistent with data spanning more than a century, which show that never-married women are particularly successful in terms of their own educational and career pursuits.[64]

Unmarried women have an additional resource that distinguishes them from married women: more frequent social contact with friends. Both never-married and formerly married women report more frequent visits with friends, suggesting that unmarried women are adaptive and will find ways to fulfill their social needs—even if outside of marriage. However, women do not vary widely in terms of the emotional support they receive from friends, regardless of marital status.

The sexual lives of unmarried women also differ starkly from those of married women. Women who have never entered a legal union (i.e., the never married and cohabiting) are significantly more likely than married women to be gay or bisexual. Nine percent of never-married women and 7 percent of cohabiting women report that they are lesbians or bisexual. Interestingly, the three groups of unmarried women vary widely in terms of how satisfied they are in their sexual relationships. Cohabiting women report significantly greater sexual satisfaction than married women do, yet women without regular access to a sex partner (i.e., the never married and formerly married) report much lower satisfaction with their sex lives. Women without regular access to a sexual partner also are the most likely to simply skip the sexual satisfaction question; 5 percent of never-married and 9 percent of formerly married women did not answer the question. They may feel that they cannot evaluate the quality of their sex life if they do not have a regular partner.

Unmarried women report much greater acceptance of singlehood than do married women; this may reflect the process of "dissonance reduction." People tend to report attitudes and cognitions that mesh with their current behaviors in order to avoid the uncomfortable feeling of cognitive dissonance.[65] Unmarried women may find it distressing to strongly endorse a social institution that they are not a part of, whereas married women may enhance their sense of self-worth by elevating the importance of their marital relationship.

Multivariate Analyses

Does marital status affect psychological well-being? The next objective is to evaluate whether the marital status differences in psychological health documented in the bivariate analysis persist when social selection and socioeconomic status characteristics are adjusted. Does marital status affect psychological well-being? A summary of regression coefficients is presented in table 3.3. Model 1 in table 3.3 presents the unadjusted effects of marital status on the three psychological well-being indicators, and model 2 presents the effects after adjusting for demographic, health, and socioeconomic status characteristics. The results in model 2 reveal that never-married and formerly married women still fare worse than the married in terms of both elevated psychological distress ($b = .12$ and .14, respectively) and lower self-acceptance ($b = -.30$ and $-.33$, respectively), after selection characteristics are adjusted. Formerly married women are more than twice as likely as married women to have had a recent depressive spell.

Why and how does marital status affect psychological well-being? To identify the causal pathway(s) linking marital status to distress, self-acceptance, and depression, I estimate regression models that adjust for social selection characteristics and each of the following pathway variables: attitudes toward marriage, frequency of visits with friends, emotional support from friends, sexual satisfaction, and sexual orientation. If the effect of marital status declines or is no longer statistically significant after a potential mediator is added to the regression model, then the link between marital status and well-being is at least partially attributable to that mediator.

The results in rows 3–8 of table 3.3 show how the linkage between marital status and psychological well-being attenuates when possible pathway variables are controlled. Surprisingly, not attitudes toward marriage, relationships with friends, nor sexual orientation explains the linkage between marriage and psychological well-being.[66] Neither the size nor statistical significance of the marital status coefficients changes appreciably in these models. However, satisfaction with one's sexual life fully accounts for never-married women's disadvantage in terms of psychological distress and self-acceptance, and nearly "explains away" the disadvantage reported by formerly married women. However, sexual satisfaction does not account for formerly married women's elevated risk of depression, although this risk declines slightly (from 2.1 to 1.9) after sexual satisfaction is controlled.

Next, I evaluated whether the effect of singlehood on psychological health differed for women of the Silent Generation, Baby Boom, and Baby Bust cohorts. Surprisingly, the analyses revealed that never-married women enjoy similar levels of self-acceptance, regardless of their generation and life stage. In contrast, the self-esteem levels of formerly married women (i.e., divorced or widowed) varied based on their cohort and/or life stage. Among formerly married women, self-esteem levels are lowest among the Baby Boom and Baby Bust generations; this may reflect the fact that older women anticipate becoming widowed, and thus losing a spouse may not take the toll that it does on younger women. Moreover, older women may have had more time to adjust to their changed marital status. Marital dissolution also may be particularly difficult for those generations of women who were socialized to believe that their life partner should be a unique and idealized soul mate rather than a helpmate.[67]

Discussion

In this essay I have investigated the pathways linking marital status to psychological well-being among American women in the late twentieth century. Three important patterns emerged from the analysis. First, unmarried cohabiting women do not differ from their married peers in terms of the three psychological outcomes, after social selection and socioeconomic status are controlled. Second, level of satisfaction with sexual intimacy is the most powerful explanation for the psychological health disadvantage among unmarried women. Third, I found weak support for the proposition that the psychological consequences of singlehood vary by life stage or birth cohort.

Cohabiting women are similar to the currently married in terms of self-acceptance, psychological distress, and depression risk, after social selection characteristics are taken into consideration. Previous studies have portrayed cohabiting unions as less stable and less satisfying than legal marriages: Waite and Gallagher observe that "cohabitation is a halfway house for people who do not want the degree of personal and social commitment that marriage represents," whereas Booth and colleagues characterize cohabitants as persons who will go on to have poorer-quality marriages and higher rates of marital dissolution than their peers who did not cohabit before marriage.[68] However, these claims are based largely

TABLE 3.3 *Summary of regression analyses: Effect of marital status on women's psychological well-being, after adjusting potential pathway variables*

| | OLS regression | | | | | | | | Logistic regression | | | |
| | Psychological distress | | | | Self-acceptance | | | | Depressive spell, past 12 months | | | |
	Never married	Formerly married	Cohabiting	Adj. R2	Never married	Formerly married	Cohabiting	Adj. R2	Never married	Formerly married	Cohabiting	Chi-sq.; DF
Model 1. Unadjusted effects of marital status	.16** (.05)	.13*** (.04)	.02 (.08)	.01	−.26** (.09)	−.34*** (.06)	−.09 (.14)	.02	1.65*	1.69***	1.29	15.7; 3
Model 2. Adjusting for selection, socioeconomic status, and demographic characteristics	.12* (.05)	.14*** (.03)	.01 (.07)	.19	−.30*** (.09)	−.33*** (.06)	.02 (13)	.13	1.23	2.09***	.94	148; 16
Model 2 + cultural evaluation of marriage	.12* (.05)	.14*** (.03)	.02 (.07)	.19	−.31*** (.09)	−.33*** (.06)	.01 (.13)	.13	1.23	2.10***	.93	148; 17
Model 2 + frequency of visits with friends	.13** (.05)	.15*** (.04)	.01 (.07)	.20	−.34*** (.09)	−.37*** (.06)	.03 (.13)	.14	1.23	2.09***	.64	148; 17

Model 2 + emotional support from friends	.13* (.05)	.14*** (.03)	.02 (.07)	.21	-.32*** (.09)	-.34*** (.06)	-.01 (.13)	.16	1.23	2.10***	.94	148; 17
Model 2 + sexual orientation	.12* (.05)	.14*** (.03)	.02 (.07)	.19	-.31*** (.09)	-.33*** (.06)	.01 (.13)	.13	1.21	2.10***	.93	148; 17
Model 2 + satisfaction with sex life	.05 (.05)	.06 (.04)	.04 (.07)	.22	-.11 (.09)	-.14* (.06)	-.05 (.13)	.17	1.12	1.89***	.97	154; 18
Model 2 + all five potential pathway variables	.06 (.05)	.07 (.04)	.05 (.07)	.23	-.12 (.09)	-.18** (.06)	-.06 (.13)	.20	1.08	1.86***	.96	155; 22

Source: MIDUS survey, 1995.

Notes: N = 1,785. Unstandardized regression coefficients, standard errors, and adjusted R2 values are presented for OLS regression models. Odds ratios and chi-square statistics are presented for logistic regression models.

* $p > .05$; ** $p > .01$; *** $p > .001$.

on research conducted with generations of adults who cohabited in the 1970s and 1980s. Cohabitation is a much more common and widely accepted practice today and has become a rite of passage for most young women and men. More than half of all women who married during the earlier 1990s had cohabited before their marriage.[69] Rather than a refuge for those who lack the economic or emotional resources to marry, cohabitation has become an accepted life course stage between dating and marriage that provides many of the same emotional and sexual rewards as legal marriage.[70]

An unanticipated yet intriguing finding was the extent to which sexual satisfaction "explained away" the psychological disadvantage of unmarried women. When sexual satisfaction was controlled, the psychological disadvantage associated with being never married or formerly married either attenuated considerably or was accounted for fully. Although friends and relatives may provide many of the important social and instrumental benefits of marriage, sexual intimacy may be a unique attribute of the marital (or cohabiting) relationship. Marriage, and romantic relationships more generally, have been characterized in terms of the presence or absence of three critical components: emotional intimacy, commitment, and passion.[71] In Sternberg's (1988) "triangular model of marriage," the most satisfying and enduring unions encompass all three components; marriages that lack sexual passion are believed to be conceptually similar to close and enduring friendships.

My analyses also showed that the psychological consequences of marital dissolution (i.e., divorce and widowhood) were less deleterious to women in the oldest birth cohort than to those in the younger two cohorts. This finding may reflect several factors. First, marital dissolution—usually through widowhood—is an anticipated social transition for older women. Because women are more likely than men to outlive their spouses, they experience anticipatory socialization by watching their peers adjust to the loss of a spouse.[72] Thus, older women are better equipped and prepared for the loss of spouse. In general, anticipated life transitions are less distressing than unexpected ones.[73] Second, the younger cohorts may have a more idealized view of marriage, given that younger cohorts are more likely than older generations to have received minimal input from family or community members in the choosing of a partner and more likely to have envisioned their life partner as their one and only "intended."[74] The dashed expectations of the younger two generations may contribute to their lower self-esteem.

Surprisingly, never-married women across three very different generations—Baby Bust, Baby Boom, and the Silent Generation—had similar levels of psychological well-being. Although the economic and instrumental benefits of marriage have shifted over the past half century, making marriage less of a practical necessity, cultural norms still encourage and elevate the pursuit of an enduring romantic relationship with one's "intended other."[75] Popular culture in the early twenty-first century, exemplified in the recent spate of "reality" television shows portraying young adults' very public pursuit of spouses, underscores the pervasiveness of the cultural message that marriage is still a sought-after and irreplaceable goal for healthy heterosexual women.[76]

Limitations

The analysis presented in this chapter has several limitations and omissions that should be pursued in future studies. First, I considered a limited range of outcome measures. Future analyses should consider whether the physical health and economic advantages associated with marriage and singlehood shift across birth cohorts and over the life span. Other indicators of negative psychological health, including substance abuse, anxiety, or loneliness, as well as positive indicators such as personal growth and autonomy also should be considered. Second, marital status was conceptualized here as a social role; I did not directly address the possibility that divorce and remarriage also may be conceptualized as stressful life events. The psychological distress associated with divorce and widowhood is typically most acute shortly after one's transition from married to formerly married occurs. For instance, although most widowed persons experience a spell of depressed mood, these effects are usually limited to the first twelve months following loss.[77] Future studies should examine whether the formerly married differ from the never and currently married along important psychological characteristics at different time points after their transition.

Finally, because the MIDUS data are cross-sectional, it is not possible to ascertain definitively whether the consequences of marriage differ across birth cohort or the life span—although both possibilities are equally plausible. Future replications of this study should rely on multi-wave multi-cohort data. Such efforts will be valuable; marital values, attitudes, and behaviors are molded by historical and social-legal context. Gergen and others have observed that the cultural consensus about gender and marriage has "deteriorated" in recent years and that current cohorts of young adults are "redefining cultural rules about being spouses."[78] As cultural rules shift, both expectations for and the rewards associated with singlehood, marriage, and other relationship forms may shift accordingly.

Notes

1. Bella DePaulo and Wendy Morris, "Singles in Society and Science," *Psychological Inquiry* 16, nos. 2–3 (2005); Linda J. Waite, "Does Marriage Matter?" *Demography* 32 (1995): 483–506.

2. Linda J. Waite and Maggie Gallagher, *The Case for Marriage: Why Married People Are Happier, Healthier, and Better off Financially* (New York: Doubleday, 2000); Sylvia Ann Hewlett, *Creating a Life: Professional Women and the Quest for Children* (New York: Miramax, 2002); Danielle Crittenden, *What Our Mothers Didn't Tell Us: Why Happiness Eludes Modern Women* (New York: Touchstone, 2000); Laura A. Sanchez, Steven L. Nock, and James D. Wright, "The Implementation of Covenant Marriage in Louisiana," *Virginia Journal of Social Policy and the Law* 9 (2000): 192–223.

3. Talcott Parsons, "Sex Roles in the American Kinship System," in *Family, Socialization, and Interaction Processes,* ed. Talcott Parsons (New York: Free Press, 1955), 324–328.

4. Deborah Carr, "The Psychological Consequences of Work–Family Tradeoffs for Three Cohorts of Women and Men," *Social Psychology Quarterly* 65 (2002): 103–124.

5. Jeremy Rifkin, "The Biotech Century: Human Life as Intellectual Property," *Nation* 266 (1988): 11–19.

6. Judith A. Seltzer, "Cohabitation in the United States and Britain: Demography, Kinship, and the Future," *Journal of Marriage and Family* 66 (2004): 921–928; Pamela J. Smock, "Cohabitation in the United States: An Appraisal of Research Themes, Findings, and Implications," *Annual Review of Sociology* 26 (2000): 1–20.

7. Arland Thornton and Linda Young-DeMarco, "Four Decades of Trends in Attitudes toward Family Issues in the United States: The 1960s through 1990s," *Journal of Marriage and Family* 63 (2001): 1009–1037.

8. DePaulo and Morris, "Singles in Society and Science"; Betsy Israel, *Bachelor Girl: The Secret History of Single Women in the Twentieth Century* (New York: William Morrow, 2002).

9. Cheryl Wetzstein, "Reality Check for Marriage," *Washington Times,* 29 May 2001.

10. DePaulo and Morris, "Singles in Society and Science."

11. U.S. Bureau of the Census, *Marital Status: 2000* (Washington, DC: U.S. Government Printing Office, 2003).

12. Linda Lyons, *The Future of Marriage, Part 2* (Washington, DC: Gallup Poll, Gallup Tuesday Briefing, 2002).

13. Larry Bumpass, "What's Happening to the Family? Interactions between Demographic and Institutional Change," *Demography* 27 (1990): 483–498.

14. Abdel R. Omran, "The Epidemiologic Transition: A Theory of the Epidemiology of Population Change," *Milbank Memorial Fund Quarterly* 29 (1971): 509–538.

15. U.S. Bureau of the Census, *Marital Status: 2000.*

16. Ibid.

17. DePaulo and Morris, "Singles in Society and Science."

18. Waite and Gallagher, *Case for Marriage.*

19. Jessie Bernard, *The Future of Marriage* (New York: Bantam, 1972).

20. Waite and Gallagher, *Case for Marriage;* Robin W. Simon, "Revisiting the Relationships among Gender, Marital Status, and Mental Health," *American Journal of Sociology* 107 (2002): 1065–1096.

21. Karen C. Holden and Pamela J. Smock, "The Economic Costs of Marital Dissolution: Why Do Women Bear a Disproportionate Cost?" *Annual Review of Sociology* 17 (1991): 51–78.

22. Daphne Spain and Suzanne M. Bianchi, *Balancing Act: Motherhood, Marriage and Employment among American Women* (New York: Russell Sage Foundation, 1996).

23. Carr, "Psychological Consequences of Work–Family Tradeoffs."

24. Sidney Zisook, Stephen R. Shuchter, and Mary Mulvihill, "Alcohol, Cigarette, and Medication Use during the First Year of Widowhood," *Psychiatric Annals* 20 (1990): 318–332.

25. Toni C. Antonucci, "Social Support and Social Relationships," in *Handbook of Aging and the Social Sciences,* ed. Robert H. Binstock and Linda K. George, 3rd ed. (San Diego, CA: Academic Press, 1990), 205–226; Arnold Peters and Aart C. Liefbroer, "Beyond Marital Status: Partner History and Well-Being in Old Age," *Journal of Marriage and the Family* 56 (1997): 687–699.

26. Deborah Carr and Rebecca Utz, "Late-Life Widowhood in the United States: New Directions in Research and Theory," *Ageing International* 27 (2002): 65–88; Simon, "Revisiting the Relationships."

27. Tuula Gordon, *Single Women on the Margins?* (New York: New York University Press, 1994).

28. Jaber F. Gubrium, "Marital Desolation and the Evaluation of Everyday Life in Old Age," *Journal of Marriage and Family* 36 (1974): 107–113; Anne E. Barrett, "Social Support and Life Satisfaction among the Never Married: Examining the Effects of Age," *Research on Aging* 21 (1999): 46–72.
29. Arne Mastekaasa, "Marriage and Psychological Well-Being: Some Evidence on Selection into Marriage," *Journal of Marriage and Family* 54 (1992): 901–911.
30. Nadine F. Marks and James D. Lambert, "Marital Status Continuity and Change among Young and Midlife Adults: Longitudinal Effects on Psychological Well-Being," *Journal of Family Issues* 19 (1998): 652–686.
31. William Axinn and Arland Thornton, "The Transformation in the Meaning of Marriage," in *Ties That Bind: Perspectives on Marriage and Cohabitation,* ed. Linda Waite, Christine Bachrach, Michelle Hindin, E. Thomson, and Arland Thornton (New York: Aldine de Gruyter, 2000), 147–165; Spain and Bianchi, *Balancing Act.*
32. Anthony Giddens, *The Transformation of Intimacy: Sexuality, Love, and Eroticism in Modern Societies* (Stanford: Stanford University Press, 1992).
33. Robert J. Havighurst, *Developmental Tasks and Education* (New York: David MacKay, 1972).
34. Erik Erikson, *The Life Cycle Completed* (New York: W. W. Norton, 1982).
35. Jean Baker Miller, *Toward a New Psychology of Women,* 2nd ed. (Boston: Beacon Press, 1986), 83; Carol Gilligan, *In a Different Voice: Psychological Theory and Women's Development* (Cambridge, MA: Harvard University Press, 1982).
36. Jay Jackson, "Structural Characteristics of Norms," in *Role Theory: Concepts and Research,* ed. Bruce J. Biddle (New York: Wiley, 1966), 113–126, 125 (quote).
37. Deborah Carr, "The Fulfillment of Career Dreams at Midlife: Does It Matter for Women's Mental Health?" *Journal of Health and Social Behavior* 38 (1997): 331–344; E. Tory Higgins, "Self-Discrepancy: A Theory Relating Self and Affect," *Psychological Review* 94 (1987): 319–340.
38. Anne Byrne and Deborah Carr, "Caught in the Cultural Lag: The Stigma of Singlehood," *Psychological Inquiry* 16, nos. 2–3 (2005): 84–91; DePaulo and Morris, "Singles in Society and Science."
39. Wendy Morris, Bella DePaulo, and L. C. Ritter, "Perceptions of People Who Are Single: A Developmental Life Tasks Model," manuscript, 2006; Byrne and Carr, "Caught in the Cultural Lag."
40. Charles H. Cooley, *Human Nature and the Social Order* (New York: Free Press, 1956).
41. Edward O. Laumann, John H. Gagnon, Robert T. Michael, and Stuart Michaels, *The Social Organization of Sexuality: Sexual Practices in the United States* (Chicago: University of Chicago Press, 1994).
42. Carmen Vázquez, "Appearances," in *Homophobia: How We All Pay the Price,* ed. Warren J. Blumenfeld (Boston: Beacon Press, 1992), 157–166; Linda Greenhouse, "Gay Rights Laws Can't Be Banned: High Court Rules," *New York Times,* 21 May 1996, A1ff; Richard A. Friend, "Older Lesbian and Gay People: A Theory of Successful Aging," *Journal of Homosexuality* 23 (1990): 99–118.
43. Scott M. Stanley and Howard J. Markman, "Assessing Commitment in Personal Relationships," *Journal of Marriage and Family* 54 (1992): 595–608; Waite and Gallagher, *Case for Marriage.*
44. Robert L. Rubinstein, "Never Married Elderly as a Social Type: Re-evaluating Some Images," *Gerontologist* 27 (1987): 108–113; Ethel Shanas, "The Family as a Social Support System in Old Age," *Gerontologist* 19 (1979): 169–174.

45. Alfred P. Fengler, Nicholas L. Danigelis, and A. Grams, "Marital Status and Life Satisfaction among the Elderly," *International Journal of Sociology of the Family* 12 (1982): 63–76.

46. Antonucci, "Social Support and Social Relationships"; James S. House, Karl Landis, and Debra Umberson, "Social Relationships and Health," *Science* 241 (1988): 540–545.

47. Janice G. Raymond, *A Passion for Friends: Toward a Philosophy of Female Affection* (Boston: Beacon Press, 1986).

48. Norman B. Ryder, "The Cohort as a Concept in the Study of Social Change," *American Sociological Review* 30 (1965): 845.

49. U.S. Bureau of the Census, *Statistical Abstract of the United States: 1996,* 116th ed. (Washington, DC: Government Printing Office, 1996).

50. James S. House, "Social Structure and Personality," in *Social Psychology: Sociological Perspectives,* ed. Morris Rosenberg and Ralph H. Turner (New York: Basic Books, 1981), 543.

51. Karl Mannheim, *Essays on the Sociology of Knowledge* (London: Routledge and Kegan Paul, 1952), 291.

52. Susan Cotts Watkins, Jane A. Menken, and John Bongaarts, "Demographic Foundations of Family Change," *American Sociological Review* 52 (1987): 346–358.

53. Thornton and Young-DeMarco, "Four Decades of Trends."

54. Gary S. Becker, *A Treatise on the Family* (Cambridge, MA: Harvard University Press, 1981).

55. Axinn and Thornton, "Transformation in the Meaning of Marriage"; Bumpass, "What's Happening to the Family?"; David Popenoe and Barbara Dafoe Whitehead, *The State of Our Unions 2002* (New Brunswick, NJ: National Marriage Project of Rutgers University, 2002).

56. Richard A. Settersten and Gunhild Hagestead, "What's the Latest? Cultural Age Deadlines for Family Transitions," *Gerontologist* 36 (1996): 178–188.

57. U.S. Bureau of the Census. *65+ in the United States,* P23–190 (Washington, DC: Government Printing Office, 1996).

58. X. P. Montenegro, *Lifestyles, Dating, and Romance: A Study of Midlife Singles* (Washington, DC: American Association of Retired Persons, 2003), suggests that older women are increasingly likely to date and marry men younger than themselves, however.

59. Shelley Coverman and Joseph F. Sheley, "Changes in Men's Housework and Child-Care Time," *Journal of Marriage and Family* 48 (1986): 413–422.

60. Maximilane E. Szinovacz and Paula Harpster, "Couple's Employment/Retirement Status and the Division of Household Tasks," *Journal of Gerontology: Social Sciences* 49 (1994): 125–136.

61. Orville Gilbert Brim, Carol D. Ryff, and Ronald C. Kessler, "The MIDUS National Survey: An Overview," in *How Healthy Are We: A National Study of Well-Being at Midlife,* ed. Orville Gilbert Brim, Carol D. Ryff, and Ronald C. Kessler (Chicago: University of Chicago Press, 2004), 1–36.

62. Mastekaasa, "Marriage and Psychological Well-Being"; Waite and Gallagher, *Case for Marriage.*

63. John Mirowksy and Catherine E. Ross, *Social Causes of Psychological Distress,* 2nd ed. (New York: Aldine de Gruyter, 2003).

64. Gordon, *Single Women on the Margins?*

65. Leon Festinger, *A Theory of Cognitive Dissonance* (Stanford: Stanford University Press, 1957).

66. Additional analyses revealed that sexual orientation accounted for a large proportion of the mental health disadvantage experienced by never-married men. This finding reflects the fact that (in the MIDUS data) gay and bisexual men have significantly higher levels of distress, lower levels of self-acceptance, and a greater risk of depression than do straight men ($p \leq .001$). In contrast, gay and straight women do not differ significantly in terms of any of the four outcomes.

67. Bumpass, "What's Happening to the Family?"; Popenoe and Whitehead, *State of Our Unions 2002.*

68. Waite and Gallagher, *Case for Marriage,* 42; Alan Booth and David Johnson, "Premarital Cohabitation and Marital Success," *Journal of Family Issues* 9 (1988): 255–272; Susan L. Brown and Alan Booth, "Cohabitation versus Marriage: A Comparison of Relationship Quality," *Journal of Marriage and Family* 58 (1996): 668–678.

69. Seltzer, "Cohabitation in the United States and Britain."

70. Smock, "Cohabitation in the United States."

71. Robert J. Sternberg, "Triangulating Love," in *The Psychology of Love,* ed. Robert J. Sternberg and Michael J. Barnes (New Haven, CT: Yale University Press, 1988), 119–138.

72. A. Martin Matthews, *Widowhood in Late Life* (Toronto: Buttersworth, 1991).

73. Peggy A. Thoits, "Dimensions of Life Events That Influence Psychological Distress: An Evaluation and Synthesis of the Literature," in *Psychosocial Stress: Trends in Theory and Research,* ed. Howard B. Kaplan (New York: Academic Press, 1983), 33–103.

74. Giddens, *Transformation of Intimacy.*

75. Ibid.

76. Israel, *Bachelor Girl.*

77. Carr and Utz, "Late-Life Widowhood."

78. Kenneth Gergen, *The Saturated Self: Dilemmas of Identity of Contemporary Life* (New York: Basic Books, 1991), 5.

CHAPTER 4

Widows at the Hustings

GENDER, CITIZENSHIP, AND THE
MONTREAL BY-ELECTION OF 1832

BETTINA BRADBURY

The poll had been open for six days when
Marguerite Paris, the widow of a laborer, stepped up to proclaim her vote. Speaking loud enough for the male officials at the poll to hear, she publicly declared that the Patriot candidate, Daniel Tracey, was her choice in the by-election under way in Montreal West, Lower Canada.[1] It was May 1, 1832. The day before, officials had moved the poll from the hall of the American Presbyterian Church—an alien place for French-speaking, Roman Catholic Montrealers like Marguerite to enter—to a house behind it belonging to one of the Donegani brothers, supporters of the Patriot reformers.[2] Surely even this illiterate widow knew that the hustings were particularly dangerous ground during this election? The newspapers of this colonial city had reported fighting from the first day the poll opened. Even Montreal's many citizens, who, like this widow, could neither read nor write, would have known about the disorder at the hustings. Just the day before she voted, the *Montreal Gazette,* the unabashed champion of businessman and establishment candidate Stanley Bagg, had reported the "most disgraceful riots and disturbances." "Several of our most respectable citizens have been most violently assaulted; beaten and otherwise maltreated."[3] The same day, *La Minerve,* equally unwavering in its advocacy of Daniel Tracey, the fiery Irish editor of the *Vindicator,* as the Patriot candidate, had described the insults and violence of drunken bullies who had seriously injured three of his supporters.[4]

In deciding to vote, the widow Marguerite Paris was stepping into a public space that was physically dangerous and politically and culturally contested. It was watched and commented on by the journalists of the city's highly partisan newspapers, and it was occupied by men and some women of all ethnic, religious, and class backgrounds. Even approaching the poll would later be described as a perilous act.[5] This danger did not deter widows like Marguerite. Nor, it seems, had she and other women of the colony absorbed the understanding that politics and the public sphere were for men alone, although historians have argued that such ideas were increasingly prevalent across the Western world by this period.[6]

This particular election is well known to Canadian historians for its length, its violence, and its occasion as a major flash point in the deteriorating relations between the predominantly French-speaking and Catholic Patriots who controlled the elected Assembly and the Conservative pro-governor British group—the Tories—who dominated the appointed Legislative Council and the Executive of the colony of Lower Canada, later the Province of Quebec. The Patriots, like so many bourgeois reformers elsewhere, sought to increase the power of elected representatives. Their struggle was against the intransigence of colonial officials and their supporters, popularly known as the English Party. In retrospect the by-election of 1832 appears as an urban microcosm of the rebellions that pitted Patriot supporters against local militias and the British army in 1837 and 1838. And it is in this light that most historians have analyzed it. The conflict has therefore been interpreted mostly through the lens of ethnicity, linked partially to class positions, and viewed as essentially a contest between English Tories and French-Canadian Patriots and as a key moment in the making of Quebec nationalism.[7]

The by-election in Montreal West was a key moment in the production of divergent imaginings of nation in this colony that included a shrinking indigenous population, the descendants of the Canadiens conquered by the British in 1760, and growing numbers of English-speaking and other migrants.[8] It was also a critical event in the contestation of colonial rule. And as in all such imaginings of identity and nation, understandings of gender, class, and ethnicity interacted to shape and reshape practices and interpretations of the event. The experiences of women, who like Marguerite Paris voted in the elections of Lower Canada in general and in this by-election in particular, also offer historians a different thread in the burgeoning literature on gender, citizenship, and the changing contours of the public sphere. Historians of France, the United States, England, and Canada have explored the masculinization of citizenship in the wake of democratic revolutions and the opening up of suffrage to a broader range of males. This chapter joins literature concerned with the re-gendering of the public and private in the late eighteenth and nineteenth centuries and the growing body of literature exploring the complicated story of women's involvement in multiple publics, in the print media, in religious activism, and in politics. More specifically, this chapter is a response to Jane Rendall's plea that historians pay more attention to the ways some nineteenth-century women exercised their franchise rights; it is a microhistory of women's participation in this particular by-election in a colony in which women's active participation in politics was not unusual and was recorded in extant documents. It thus also adds to studies of women voters in other eighteenth- or nineteenth-century jurisdictions.[9]

It is possible to look in some detail at voting women in Quebec's history because some poll books that carefully recorded election details have survived. These show that some 226 women sought to vote in this by-election alone. Nor were the numbers of women voting in this political contest unique. Earlier that month over 70 women voted in the by-election to determine representatives for the other half of Montreal. Furthermore, Nathalie Picard has shown that women voted in at least fourteen other districts in the British colony of Lower Canada between 1791 and 1849. Many poll books are not available, but evidence suggests that the numbers of women voting increased over time.[10] And knowledge of their actions spread beyond the colony's boarders. Long before the 1832 by-election, in June 1820, a newspaper in the colony of New Brunswick reprinted a Montreal newspaper's editorial deriding the "spiraling influence of women in Lower Canadian politics" and predicting the dangers of a "petticoat polity" should women continue to vote.[11]

Quebec historians have recognized that this by-election was as an important moment in the reshaping of women's rights in Lower Canada. During the 1980s, the antinationalist historian Fernand Ouellet briefly suggested that Patriot leader Louis-Joseph Papineau had decided to disenfranchise women shortly after this election because too many women had voted for the Conservative candidate. In their pioneering synthesis of Quebec women's history, the Collectif Clio briefly linked the legislative attempt to prevent women from voting in 1834 to changes curtailing dower rights in 1840 as evidence of the defeat of women's traditional or ancient rights in the face of "nineteenth-century logic" and the spread of capitalism spearheaded by British interests.[12] More recently, the shifting understandings of gender that informed the political decision to explicitly exclude women from voting have been highlighted by both Alan Greer and Nathalie Picard. They have tied women's disenfranchisement in the colony to the larger gendering of politics that characterized the late eighteenth and early nineteenth century across much of the Western world. Greer deftly attributes women's loss of the vote to the spread of Rousseauian understandings of the naturalness of sexual difference and of separate spheres of ideology especially among the Patriots.[13] Yet Greer rather quickly consigns women to the home and domesticity, and too readily accepts the rhetoric of separate spheres as shaping women's lives. If understandings about separate spheres for men and women, and about politics as a male domain, were as powerful as he implies, then the presence of women such as Marguerite Paris or Emilie Tavernier at the poll in 1832, women's attendance at the Legislative Assembly, or the passionate interest that the women in the family of Patriot leader Louis-Joseph Papineau displayed in politics is difficult to explain.[14]

In what follows I take another look at this by-election, approaching it initially through the experiences of some of the widows who attempted to vote in April and May of 1832, and then exploring the links between this election and the decision to exclude women from voting taken by politicians first in 1834 and then successfully in1849.[15] After a detailed look at the characteristics of voting women, I analyze, in the second part of the chapter, the ways that understandings of class, ethnicity, gender, and citizenship were produced in the print media of the city. In the third section I concentrate on several of the outcomes of the election. One is the evidence given to the Patriot-dominated House of Assembly committee that in late 1832 and early 1833 called on numerous witnesses to recount their experiences of the election. Here I look in some detail at the significant role played by one Montrealer, its future mayor, Jacques Viger, in producing knowledge about women's involvement in the election for the committee.[16] The second is the brief debate, in the same Assembly, that led to the attempt to prevent women from voting in 1834 and to their successful exclusion in 1849.

Widows and Other Women at the Hustings

Marguerite Paris and Emilie Tavernier were 2 of 141 widows who walked up to the polling place and attempted to vote in the 1832 Montreal West by-election. A much smaller number of wives and single women also sought to exercise their citizenship rights. Women made up 14 percent of the citizens seeking to express their political choice in this tumultuous by-election, which, according to Nathalie Picard, was the highest proportion of women involved in any of the Lower Canadian elections for which she was able to locate the poll books.[17]

As residents of Lower Canada, these women could imagine taking part in elections because the law did not explicitly prevent them and because other women had taken advantage of this right in various elections over the years since 1791. That year, the constitutional act that established the first elected Legislative Assembly and set out the property requirements for eligibility had described voters as "persons." Only political candidates were referred to specifically by the pronoun "he." Persons admitted to vote had to be twenty-three years old, a "natural citizen or subject of her Majesty," and most importantly, to possess or rent land above a specified value. In these early decades of the nineteenth century, urban voters had to own a home or a plot of land with an annual revenue

TABLE 4.1. *Women at the polls in the Montreal West by-election of 1832*

	Widows	Married	Single and not listed	All women (n)	
No contestation	50%	12%	27%	40%	90
Oath required	36%	42%	37%	37%	84
Contested, no oath indicated	6%	19%	20%	12%	0
Disqualified	8%	12%	12%	9%	46
Withdrew	0%	15%	3%	3%	6
Number presenting at the polls	141	26	59		226
Number who voted	130	19	50		199
Percentage allowed to vote	92%	73%	85%	88%	
Percentage of female voters	65%	10%	25%		
Percentage of voting women who were listed as landowners	63%	84%	62%	65%	128

Sources: Bibliothèque et Archives Nationales du Québec–Montréal (BANQM), poll book, Montreal West by-election, 1832; Nathalie Picard, "Database of Women Voters."

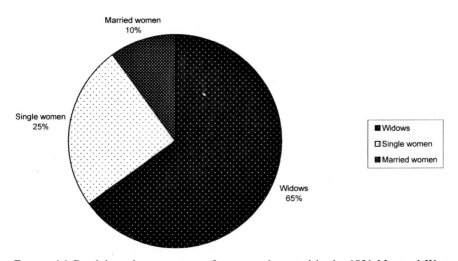

Figure 4.1 Breakdown by percentage of women who voted in the 1831 Montreal West by-election.

worth £5 11s. 1.5d. local currency or have lived as a tenant for twelve months prior to the election in a dwelling for which they had paid a minimum annual rent of double that amount, £11 2s. 2.5p.[18] This franchise was much broader and more inclusive than in England, or than in some of the other colonies of British North America.[19] Catholics could vote, and after 1831 so could Jews. Just south of Montreal, across the Saint Lawrence River, at least twenty-seven First Nations women from Caughnawaga voted in the 1825 election in Huntingdon County, where they helped elect Austin Cuvillier, then a candidate for the Parti Canadien, the precursors to the Patriots.[20]

Local legislation rooted in British constitutional government gave women rights as British subjects in the colony. The Custom of Paris, the French body of law retained for all civil matters after the British conquest, determined women's property and inheritance rights. Like the civil law of much of Europe and unlike the English common law prevailing in most of the states and other colonies of British North America, marriage created community property that was shared equally by man and wife but administered by the husband. If wives became widows, half of that shared property became theirs. They also had the right to use half of their husband's inherited real property or land he owned prior to his marriage as their dower. This then passed on to any children. Widows thus had a greater likelihood of access to property than they did in common law jurisdictions. One English visitor considered these laws the reason "that the fair sex have such influence . . . and even an air of superiority to the husband."[21] English merchants railed against the way these rules deprived men of what they understood as their rights to freely accumulate property, and soon after the British conquest they were influential in securing legislation that gave all men and women freedom of willing, although this freedom could not overturn a widow's right to dower. Migrants from elsewhere also quickly learned to use notaries to make marriage contracts that either established separate property for each spouse or gave husbands power closer to that found in English common law.[22]

Under the broadest interpretation of election law, women should have been able to vote if they owned or rented property of the required value in their own name. This group included widows and single women who had inherited or purchased property, and wives who had kept their property separate at marriage by making a marriage contract to that effect. In practice, allowing women to vote varied from region to region and election to election.[23] For women it was a dubious, contested right. Returning officers had significant power to rule on questions of eligibility. The returning officer ran the election, named the clerk to assist him, arranged for notice of the election to be posted, determined where the poll would be, requested that magistrates provide constables to keep order if necessary, oversaw the taking of oaths, entered all the information in the poll book, and oversaw and judged candidates' objections to a person's vote. Patriot supporter and future Montreal mayor Jacques Viger later told members of the House of Assembly investigating the Montreal West by-election that, as returning officer for the Montreal East by-election, he had systematically refused the vote of all married women. He also turned away all "persons in a state of inebriety." Although Viger likened wives, with their lack of independence, to drunks, who were generally considered easily influenced, he did not contest the right of widows and single women to vote. They had constituted over 9 percent of the voters in that by-election.[24]

Violence and conflict continued during most of the twenty-three days that the poll was open. Election laws had been inherited from the open voting methods of England and then modified somewhat by local legislation. Officials chose the polling places, candidates addressed the crowd, and voters proclaimed their choices verbally. When one hour passed without anyone seeking to vote, the election was declared over and the leading candidate had won. Blocking opponents from the poll was therefore one way to attempt to secure victory for the man who had the most votes at any one time.[25] Candidates and their supporters could verbally challenge the right to vote of those choosing their opponent. Wearing ribbons, cockades, and badges was illegal, as were hurling verbal insults, blocking the poll, fighting, and buying drinks.[26] Nighttime assemblies in the predominantly male spaces of taverns and public places in which the champions of each candidate sought to recruit voters spilled into daytime jostling and jeering. In the rough politics of open voting, both sides engaged in verbal and physical intimidation. Violence became so much a part of this election that the newspapers made a special point of remarking on the occasional peaceful day. They also reported on each day's tally. Such published counts gave the wider citizenry the knowledge of who was ahead, much as opinion polls do today. In these nineteenth-century contests, the election campaign, the actual voting, and the publication of people's choices were concurrent, a potent mix that fueled violence.

In this election, Stanley Bagg, the candidate closely linked to the colonial establishment, had the power to shape the running of the election in ways that

FIGURE 4.2 Charles William Jefferys, *Papineau Addressing a Crowd*, ca. 1901–1910. Watercolor over pencil on commercial board. Jefferys was a painter, illustrator, writer, and educator who wrote and illustrated numerous books of Canadian history during the 1920s and 1930s to teach history and foster nationalism, especially among schoolchildren. Note the absence of women in his representation of the crowd at the hustings, which parallels newspaper reports of the time, and the way he uses hats to show the class and ethnic differences among the men present. Courtesy Library and Archives Canada, Accession No. 1972–26–759.

Tracey could not. That the poll opened in a Protestant church hall in this city in which Catholics were a majority and most Patriot supporters were Catholic was one powerful sign of his influence. As the election continued, he and his supporters drew on their close links to the justices of the peace, swearing in additional constables from among his supporters to maintain the peace. Some of these constables had been the very "bullies" who had intimidated Tracey supporters. On the second to last day of what turned out to be the longest election in the colony's history, as tempers and intimidation reached new heights, pro-Bagg magistrates called on the British troops garrisoned in the city. By the end of that day, three men in the crowd, all Canadiens, had died at the hands of the soldiers. Canadiens quickly renamed the street the rue du Sang—the street of blood.[27]

All this was in the future when Marguerite Paris proclaimed her vote on May 1—a relatively peaceful day, as newspapers would later report. The poll opened at 8:00 AM. Tracey was well ahead with 296 votes to Bagg's 220. When Paris stepped up to voice her choice, Stanley Bagg contested her right to vote. This laborer's widow was thus required to publicly affirm the authenticity of her claim to citizenship rights. She swore on oath that she did indeed possess the requisite property qualifications. Her vote was accepted. The male polling clerk inscribed her name in the poll book, indicated that she lived on Vallée Street in the Saint Lawrence ward, put a tally mark under Tracey's name, and noted that Bagg had contested her right to vote. The returning officer, Mr. St. George Dupré, then signed his name beside this entry.[28]

Women who considered voting could anticipate a series of contestations. The first was the very question of whether as women they should go to the poll, for the idea that such engagement in politics was improper for women had its supporters in the colony. Early in the 1820s an article in the *Montreal Gazette* had dismissed women's participation as voters as "absurd and unconstitutional." Shortly after the election, the same newspaper, the mouthpiece for the pro-British Bureaucratic Party, reproduced the statement of an English novelist, Mrs. Hemans, that a woman could "never with consistency appear in the forum or the pulpit—in the senate or at the poll . . . without disparagement of her sexual character." In direct contrast, a petition from Quebec electors in 1828 stressed women's intellectual equality with men, arguing that to vote was not a natural right of either men or women but was based on their qualifications. The petition was reproduced approvingly in an article in *La Minerve*, which argued that widows with the proper qualifications were in all ways equal to men.[29] The year before, *La Minerve* had lauded voting by Patriot women in the previous election and reported favorably that they had crowned their winning candidate with flowers.[30]

A woman's presence at the poll was sufficiently contested that such a move might risk tarnishing her respectability. Yet women went in great numbers. On the way to vote, some must have braved the derision of their candidates' opponents. Women could anticipate the humiliation of the returning officer denying their right to vote if he suspected they were not qualified or if he had decided that women should not vote. Or, like Marguerite Paris, they might be forced to defend the authenticity of their claim against a challenge from their candidate's opponent and be required to swear an oath attesting to their eligibility. Days later, as the 1832 election drew to an end, the returning officer requested that Montreal's chief of police provide "six Constables with long Constable's staves," to prevent anyone from getting too close to the Hustings, unless they wished to vote or were accompanying ladies.[31] In this protective move he both recognized women's presence and furthered the understanding that women voters were unlike male ones.

Marguerite Paris was not alone in having to publicly affirm that she possessed the necessary qualifications to vote. Six of every ten women who dared to present themselves at the hustings during this election were either called on by the opponent of their candidate to swear to their qualifications or were not allowed to vote. Women were much more likely to be disqualified and contested than were men. More than one in every five women were disqualified or refused to swear an oath and withdrew.[32] The proportion of men who were disqualified or withdrew was less than half that of women.[33] Ambiguity about the propriety of women at the poll legitimated aggressive challenges to their claims, as did the suggestion, voiced periodically in the press and later, that women were sought after by candidates because they were susceptible to being told how to vote. They were considered, along with cripples, drunks, and other categories of Montrealers, as lacking independence and autonomy. How individual women were treated at the poll depended on a complex mix of political expediency, personal networks, and gendered treatment in which some men sheltered some women as they entered the hustings, while others engaged in hostile questioning.

In these contestations at the poll, women were not treated as a single category. Widows faced fewer challenges or showed greater tenacity than married and single women. None withdrew, fewer were required to swear an oath, and a greater proportion ended up voting than other women. As women no longer obviously under the patriarchal power of fathers and husbands, their claim to vote on the basis of independence and ownership of property had greater resonance than that of single women or of wives whose property was separate from that of their husbands. At the poll, what mattered was whether women were known to hold property or would swear that they did. Thus, although half the widows were able to vote without any questioning of their right, only a quarter of the single women received such treatment and half again that proportion of the wives.

The poll book records no challenge to the vote of the widow Emilie Tavernier. She confirmed her family's close political ties to the Patriots by choosing Tracey on May 9, the twelfth day of the election. Her brother, François Tavernier, was an ardent supporter of Papineau and the Patriots. He had been her official guardian between the time her father died, leaving her an orphan at the age of fourteen, and her marriage to Jean-Baptiste Gamelin in 1823. Indeed at some point during the election François was arrested and charged with assaulting a Bagg supporter.[34] Emilie's recently deceased cousin Joseph Perrault, with whom she had been raised, had been elected as a member of the Assembly and a supporter of the Parti Canadien, the precursor to the Patriots. She also had close family links among some of the notable Canadien families who had broken with Papineau and thrown their support behind Bagg and his Tory supporters. Strong family connections, property, and her reputation as a devout Catholic widow working with the poor and elderly of the city likely guaranteed her immunity from harassment.

Emilie Tavernier become a widow in 1828 after just five years of marriage with the much older local merchant Jean-Baptiste Gamelin. One year later her only surviving son died. Although their marriage contract had provided that the two spouses' property should remain separate, it had also stipulated that should the surviving partner outlive any offspring, he or she could dispose of all the other's property as full owner.[35] Emilie faced widowhood with three small properties, which gave her the means to do what became her passion and eventually her profession—provide material, physical, and spiritual support to the poor. During her childhood and her short time as a wife she had always provided meals and support to the poor of the city, who learned that hers was a door they could knock on when hungry. After Jean-Baptiste's death she threw herself into this work. She was at the heart of many of the new ventures that the city's bourgeois Catholic women were organizing to care for orphans and the sick, and to help girls from the country seeking domestic work, and to redeem prostitutes. Her prime concern, however, was sick and elderly women. In 1829 she took four frail widows into her home on Saint Antoine Street. Needing more space, she soon arranged to use a larger building in the Saint Lawrence suburb, where so many of her family and relatives lived.[36]

At the time of the election she had recently moved these elderly and infirm widows yet again, this time into a larger building that she rented in the Saint Lawrence suburb, at the corners of Saint Lawrence and Saint Philippe streets. This dwelling was large enough to house herself and up to twenty women. She and the friends, relatives, and other women who were assisting her in this work and in organizing other charitable enterprises regularly traversed the streets of the city. They collected food, clothing, and money for their poor from the city's citizens and visited others in their homes.[37] The streets of the city were familiar to them, and Emilie and her colleagues would have been well-known figures on the streets. Catholicism, like Protestantism, translated readily in this period "into a claim to enter the public world and contribute to the work which needed to be done," giving such women "license to enter the public arena" in "purposeful and empowering ways."[38] The electoral district of Montreal West covered the western half of the city, stretching from Saint Lawrence Street to the city's western boundary and south to the river.[39] Although it already had a sizable English-speaking population, this western section of the city was still the home of many of the Canadien families who traced their histories back centuries. Located within its borders were the homes and institutions that were part of Emilie's history and networks in the city. These included the home to which Emilie and her cousin Agathe Perrault had moved after Agathe's mother, who raised Emilie, died in 1822. The home she had shared with Jean-Baptiste Gamelin during their brief marriage as well as that of her brother were both located on the same street. Here too were all the shelters for the elderly she had run in recent years.

A few days before Emilie Tavernier chose to vote, the poll was moved for the third time. The new poll was located in a fire pump building between the Bank of Montreal and a building occupied by the church wardens of the huge parish of Notre Dame on the northwest corner of the Place d'Armes.[40] For a devout Catholic like the widow Emilie Tavernier, this more public and less Protestant space must surely have been a preferable place to exercise her vote than the earlier two locations. It was close to the new Catholic parish church, which was still under construction. Before her husband's death they had shared a keen interest in this project.[41] It was also a bit closer to her shelter for women on Saint Philippe Street, some six blocks north, than the earlier poll had been.

Some fifty-five people sought to vote the same day as Emilie Tavernier, the widow Gamelin. Ten of them were women. The fifth voter after the poll opened that morning was a widow; so was the eighth. Twenty-one men in a row then marched up to voice their choices. One Tracey supporter retired when his vote was objected to by Bagg. A male laborer's vote was contested. He left but came back later and voted. The nine men just ahead of Widow Gamelin all chose Stanley Bagg. Then the profoundly male face of the voters changed. Felicité Barbeau, a married woman, chose Stanley Bagg. Daniel Tracey demanded that she swear on oath that she did indeed own property. Two unmarried sisters, Charlotte and Margarite Leduc, both chose Tracey and faced the objections of his opponent. Over the rest of the day four more women voted. Only Emilie's vote went uncontested.

The gender composition of voting citizens varied from day to day over the course of the election. Few women had presented themselves at the hustings in the early days of voting. By the fourth day, however, the male face of the electorate was diluted. Every day between April 28 and May 9, between 13 and 29 women came to the poll. The peak day of female involvement occurred the day after Marguerite Paris's vote. Women must have been highly visible as electors that day, for they represented over a quarter of those endeavoring to express their political choice. Some women voted alone. Others, like Emilie Tavernier, voted with a small cluster of other women. They came from all parts of the electoral district—from the commercial streets of the old city and from the rougher streets of the suburbs of Saint Lawrence and Saint Joseph. Some were neighbors. In this relatively small colonial town, many would have known each other.

Every day from then on women came. When the press mentioned women, they represented them as the dupes of the candidates. Historians have not sufficiently critiqued the gendered underpinnings of such claims. The patterns of their voting and their family histories make it hard to imagine that all or even many of the women voted against their will. Few wives voted at the same time as their husbands, or daughters with their fathers. Politics permeated the culture of the colony and especially of Montreal, the city in which the differences of language, religion, and culture between old and new colonizers were so apparent especially to visitors. Politics was hardly a foreign world, or a domain of men, for many of these women. Nathalie Picard has pointed out that many came from Quebec families with a long tradition of women voting. Evidence of this tradition in Emilie Tavernier's own extended family is striking. The aunt who had raised her, Marie-Anne Tavernier Perrault, voted as a widow in 1820, as did Barbe Castagnez, Emilie's brother's wife and her close friend. In the election of 1827 her cousin Agathe Perrault, the widow of Maurice Nolan, voted for Louis-Joseph Papineau and Robert Nelson in the Montreal West election. Agathe voted again in 1832, three days after her cousin Emilie, also choosing Tracey.[42]

The Quebec historian Fernand Ouellet has argued that the women who voted in Lower Canadian elections seem "to have followed the major trends." He suggests that this means they were "swayed by pressure from the candidates."[43]

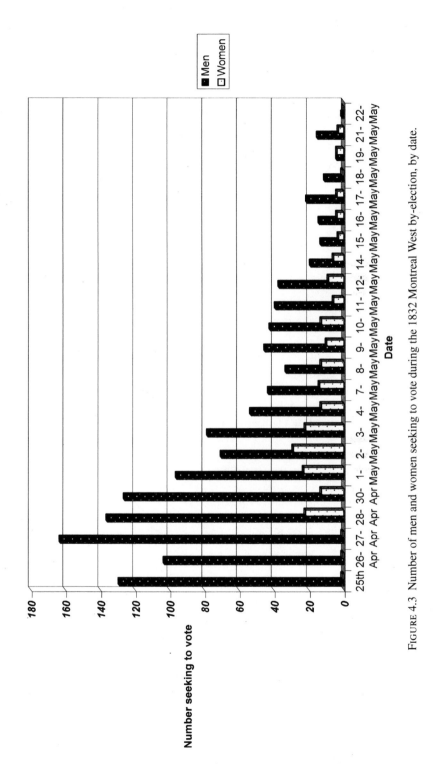

FIGURE 4.3 Number of men and women seeking to vote during the 1832 Montreal West by-election, by date.

Such analysis downplays the cultural importance of political conflicts in this period. It allows no place for women embracing familial traditions of passionate involvement in politics. It is hard to imagine that either Emilie Tavernier or Agathe Perrault would have been "swayed" by any arguments Tory candidates might make. Their families were so intimately involved in the emerging Patriot movement that their minds would have been made up long before an election. Nor does it seem likely that even a fairly poor widow like Marguerite Paris would have been tempted by money or other offers to vote against the party so strongly supported by the largely Canadien "craftsmen, farmers, carters, and day-labourers" in the Saint Lawrence suburb who were her neighbors and relatives.[44] Women supportive of the Patriots might be influenced to vote for their candidate, but it is highly unlikely they could be swayed in the opposite direction.

Similarly, given the growing identification of the Patriots with a nationalism that embraced Irish supporters but represented the British as coterminous with the ruling elite, there was little space for English-speaking widows to imagine not voting for the group identified with imperial rule. Anna Foster's "gentleman" husband died just one year after their marriage in 1823. In 1827 she was one of ninety widows who voted in the Montreal West election that had pitted the Parti Canadien candidates Louis-Joseph Papineau and Robert Nelson against the establishment candidates Peter McGill and John Delisle. The latter were her choice then, as was true of most of the widows with English names. When she voted on May 16, 1832, she again chose the establishment candidate, Stanley Bagg. In such heated times, public, open voting ensured that if reluctant women were encouraged to vote, it would be by those whose politics they shared. Personal politics—forged in the crucibles of family discussions, family and ethnic culture, and class interests and empire—would have shaped most women's allegiances more than a candidate's rhetoric or money would have, and long before the women reached the poll.

Nevertheless, in the aggressive attempts of supporters on each side to ensure victory, candidates courted supporters with free drinks, dinners, and promises. They received them in the taverns and hotels of the city and sought them out on the streets and in their homes, despite legislation that fined those seeking to influence voting.[45] The resulting intrusion of politics into domestic space would be signaled afterward by one leading figure in the election as evidence of an election gone awry. As a young man, the Montreal merchant Austin Cuvillier, who was married to Emilie Tavernier's cousin Marie-Claire Perrault, had been a critic of colonial policy and a committed member of the Parti Canadien, the precursors to the Patriots. In the years leading up to the 1832 election, however, he and other more moderate nationalists had increasingly distanced themselves from the politics of the Patriot Party, finally breaking completely.[46] The fissure widened to a chasm when some five hundred Montrealers met to determine who should be nominated to run in this by-election. Speaking in English, eventually to cries of "Parlez français," Cuvillier had publicly nominated Stanley Bagg. He recommended support for Bagg "as a very respectable man" who had been long established in the colony. Drawing on widely circulating stereotypes of the Irish and evoking well-known incidents in Tracey's short history in the colony, Cuvillier dismissed Tracey as an inappropriate choice—too violent and too prone to attacking "the private character of individuals."[47]

Cuvillier's new support of the colonial elite made him the prime target of Patriot scorn during this election. Patriots berated him on every possible occasion during the election and in its acrimonious aftermath. When his wife, Marie-Claire Perrault, sought to vote for Stanley Bagg on May 19, Patriots responded to her not as any woman but as the wife of a Canadien who had chosen to defect from the "national" party.[48] Assimilating domestic and political subterfuge, *La Minerve* questioned the validity of the separation of goods that this auctioneer and his wife had arranged some time between their 1801 marriage and 1817. This possibility of separate property ownership by husband and wife as offered by the Custom of Paris was one that growing numbers of men in economically volatile positions such as Cuvillier's took advantage of to protect some of their property from creditors. *La Minerve* impugned Cuvillier's abilities as family provider and businessman by discussing his bankruptcy and mused more broadly on the implications of separate property for a husband's marital authority. Could two spouses vote if they were properly separate as to goods? If the Cuvilliers' separation was not valid, "does she have the right that she was allowed to exercise?" If they were really separate as to property, why had she paid some of his creditors? In addition, this occasion became one for impugning the independence of the returning officer, understood by all Patriots to be controlled by Bagg and his supporters. Such tricky legal questions, the article suggested, were best left to jurists, but the "Returning Officer did not find this a tricky question. He decided Mme C. should vote without hesitation."[49] In its commentary, *La Minerve* linked voting by wives, rather than women in general, to broader questions of domestic and political disorder in the colony and to the disruptions caused by choices such as separate property, which could be represented as English in origin and of dubious propriety.

More women voted in this by-election and, despite the violence and the repeated contestations of their votes, they constituted a higher proportion of voters than in any other election for which the poll books have survived.[50] Whether they came willingly of their own initiative, reluctantly, or were bribed to do so, they stepped out publicly to assert their political choices in considerable numbers. And if they possessed the required qualifications, they voted. Furthermore, a significant proportion of the women whose property evaluations qualified them to vote seem to have done so. Historians have estimated that somewhere between one in four and one in eight family heads could vote in Lower Canadian elections. About 60 percent of male household heads voted in the two Montreal by-elections of 1832. Contemporary sources make it a challenge to venture similar estimates for women. Because the majority of voters were widows, I have made three rough measures of the extent to which widows who were eligible to vote in this particular by-election and the one the same year in the other half of the city did so. Each measure suggests high rates of engagement. The first is based on the cohort of women who married in Montreal between 1823 and 1826, whose lives I have been tracing as they made the transition from wife to widow. Around one in three of the women who were already widowed in 1832 and had not remarried voted in the by-elections of that year. Comparing the proportion of propertied widows who voted in both by-elections to the number of such women listed in an enumeration of property owners made later that year for the first anticipated Montreal city election suggests that nearly all eligible propertied widows voted. Third, a comparison of the number of widows enumerated as household heads in the 1831 census and the number of voting widows suggests that nearly half the city's widowed female heads of household exercised their political rights in one of these two 1832 by-elections. Somewhere between a third and nearly all of the relatively privileged widows of Montreal who possessed the qualifications to vote were willing to brave the public space and disorder of the hustings to elect either the Patriot or Tory candidate.[51]

Most of these female voters were property owners.[52] In this city in which the vast majority of families rented their homes, women's claims to vote were more rooted in property owning than were those of men. Yet because of the low franchise requirements, fairly meager holdings legitimated some widows' public voice in addition to offering them a source of security in their widowhood. A voting widow such as Marguerite Paris could hardly be further removed from the hypothesis proposed by the political scientist Diane Lamoureux that most female voters in Lower Canada would have been the owners of seigneuries.[53] The property on which Paris staked her claim as a citizen was her small, one-room wooden house and lot on Vallée Street in the Saint Lawrence ward. She and her laborer husband Joseph Guilbault had succeeded in purchasing it through their joint labors during their marriage, and thus it formed part of the community property created by marriage and on which she had a claim as his widow. It had provided her and her daughter, Marie-Marguerite, with shelter during her two years of widowhood at a time when their moveable possessions were minimal. Jacques Viger valued it for taxation purposes at an annual revenue of just £7 or worth about £116 later in 1832. This valuation was close to the minimum necessary to vote in both municipal and colony-wide elections. Amable Leduc, a carter's widow who voted in the Montreal East by-election that year, had property that was assessed even lower. Hers was estimated to have an annual revenue of only £6 or a total value of £100, the lowest possible threshold for voting.[54]

Privileged as these widows were relative to widows without property, income, or support, their modest properties pale beside the value of those of the city's largest male landowners or those of the wealthiest widows. Eleven widows, all with land assessed at a revenue of over £100 or around $333 a year, owned nearly half the total value of all the widows' properties that were evaluated. These wealthy widows included several who expressed their political choices during the by-election. The widow Oakes owned two properties assessed as worth over £300 annually in revenue. The widow Anne Platt, who was active in the Montreal land market, owned two properties on the major thoroughfares Saint Paul and Notre Dame streets, in the western section of the old city; they were worth some £180 annually. Both women voted for the establishment candidate Stanley Bagg. So did Anna Foster, as we have seen, and Sarah Campbell. Married between 1823 and 1826 to a "gentleman" and a merchant, respectively, they, like Emilie Tavernier, were not affluent. Their property would not compare with that of the city's wealthiest widows, but they lived in some comfort. Sarah Campbell must have paid over £11 annually to rent her home on Bonaventure Street. This amount would have procured her respectable housing.

Marguerite Paris's husband had been a laborer. The deceased husbands of some of the other widows of modest means who voted in the 1832 by-elections had been masters and craftsmen in the artisanal trades that were so important to the city's economy. Sarah Harrisson, the tinsmith's widow who voted within two months of her husband's death, was described as renting the property on Saint Paul Street where she lived. Although she lived on this expensive street and had been promised $1,000 outright instead of a dower, her husband was buried in the poor ground of the Protestant cemetery.[55] Mary Howard was the widow of a shoemaker, whereas Emilie Monjean, who voted in Montreal East, was the widow of a master painter who had promised her a middling dower of £100 or $333 in their marriage contract. Her house on Sanguinet Street in the Saint Lawrence suburb was valued at more than twice the worth of Marguerite Paris's at a capital value of around £250, a reminder of the large social and economic gap between a successful master craftsman's widow and that of a laborer.[56] For widows, as for the wider population, the relatively low level of the franchise permitted those of modest means, especially those who had invested in real property, to have a say in elections. Yet Marguerite Paris was an exception among laborer's widows. Most had no property to soften the challenge of widowhood, let alone to provide citizenship possibilities.

Gender, Citizenship, and Election Coverage in the Press

All in all, nearly two hundred women successfully performed the act of citizenship by walking through supportive and hostile crowds during the Montreal West by-election, swearing to their legitimacy as voters, and calling out the name of the candidate of their choice. Over sixty did so in the earlier by-election in Montreal East. Yet in the day-to-day election reports published by Montreal dailies, the presence of these women at the poll is rarely mentioned. When women are referred to, it is usually to discredit the masculinity and behavior of the opposing side or to deride a party's inability to find more appropriate electors. With the exception of the discussion of Mme Cuvillier's vote in *La Minerve*, newspaper reports never named individual women voters.

Conflicting political visions of citizenship that built on and conjured up divergent forms of masculinity and nation take up much more space in the newspaper reports of the election than do hints at gender disorder. In its support of Stanley Bagg and the established order, the *Gazette* claimed a vision of masculine citizenship rooted in independence, industry, integrity, respectability, honor, class hierarchy, and benevolence toward the poor. They stressed that Bagg had been in the colony since his childhood and lauded his contributions to agriculture and commerce and his loyalty to his king, country and the constitution—political language that Cecelia Morgan has shown also represented all that was "both

British and manly" about Upper Canadian Conservatives at the same time.[57] Conservatives belittled their opposition, representing Tracey and his largely Catholic supporters as uncontrolled, dishonest, and desperate—the kinds of rowdy, violence-prone, lower-class men who did not deserve to exercise the vote and who could be easily swayed by the words of eloquent but misguided superiors just as they were by their priests. These dismissals of his supporters frequently represented them as unruly Irishmen rather than Canadiens, implying, for example, that many had recently arrived and had been dependent on charity to get through the winter, charity given by just the kind of men they were opposing. The clothes on their bodies were read to critique the breadth of the franchise and justify contesting their votes: "The appearance of the great majority is sufficient to cast a doubt upon their claim." Mistreatment of women was claimed as further evidence of their misguided manliness: "Mr. Bagg's friends, particularly the ladies, when at the poll, are hooted and hissed at nay, even Mr. Bagg himself has been assaulted and otherwise mistreated." Here surely was proof that "Tracey and his friends have disgraced themselves by their conduct so unworthy of BRITISH subjects, enjoying a free constitution."[58]

In the equally fanatical criticism of "la Bureaucratie," published daily in *La Minerve,* women's presence at the poll was linked with that of cripples, the elderly, and the infirm as evidence that Bagg had few voters left in reserve and was getting desperate.[59] Women's presence, by implication, could only mean that they were dragged to the poll. Patriot supporters claimed to be working for the "public interest," the "public good," and the "rights of the people." The people, in the columns of *La Minerve,* were not only Canadiens. At this time, the Irish and frequently Americans as well were explicitly embraced as supporters. Theirs was, at this point, a nationalist vision that embraced all those who espoused the cause of the people, of the Canadiens.[60]

The citizens described in the newspapers were thus ascribed ethnic characteristics and were resolutely male. Despite the obvious presence of women at the poll, women as a category had little place in the competing understandings of citizenship articulated in the public sphere of assemblies and newspaper reporting and pamphlet writing. In this formative period of Lower Canadian politics, as in the revolutionary politics of the eighteenth-century American colonies or France, or the constitutional politics of England, the citizen whose qualities were in the process of being elaborated discursively by Patriots and Tories alike could only be male. The reason, imagination, and independence that historians have identified as key characteristics of the individual constructed in emerging liberal theory were the very opposite of the emotionality and dependence accorded to females or ascribed to political opponents.[61] Widows and other women could vote, but the gendering of politics as masculine limited their visibility in the press.[62]

The one major exception to this narrative is important. The public debate about the right of Austin Cuvillier's wife to vote, discussed previously, points to the significance of loyalty as a critical theme in this election. Patriots willingly integrated Irishmen like Tracey and his "compatriots, our adopted brothers," into their fold. They were understood to embrace similar political goals and to readily embrace a nationalism being built in opposition to the unjust implementation of British colonial rule. Much more troubling were Canadiens, like Cuvillier, who had "fallen into the trap" of supporting the Bureaucracy, who had turned "Brutus" on their people. In the public rhetoric of the election, as reported in the columns of the press, Patriots wavered between derision and anguish over how such men could be brought back into a party that sought to speak for all Canadiens. During public anguish over transgressions from the boundaries of the imagined nation they were building, Austin Cuvillier was the name most frequently mentioned. That his wife tried to vote and that their marital and monetary affairs were suspect signaled both Cuvillier's perfidy and the unmanly way Stanley Bagg neglected no strategy to muster as many votes as possible.[63] These lapses also further diffused the understanding that it was the Tories who relied on women as voters and further delegitimized women at the hustings.

Viger's Gaze: Producing Knowledge about Citizens

Widows and other women clearly voted. Yet in the public press, citizens are largely presented as masculine. Women's presence denotes improper election behavior or desperation for votes—an outlook supportive of Greer's argument that in the 1830s, the understanding that politics was male was sufficiently widespread to justify women's exclusion from the vote. Yet neither Greer nor other historians have adequately explained why politicians decided in 1834 that the time had come to prevent women from taking to the hustings. True, similar legislation had already been passed in some U.S. states, in England, and would eventually be passed in most of the other colonies of British North America. Fernand Ouellet has suggested that the 1832 election played a role. His explanation that Papineau was upset because too many women had again voted for his opponent seems insufficient. Yet in transforming Papineau into the sole author of the bill and in rooting the explanation in the actual act of women voting rather than in any general set of ideas as the cause, Ouellet inadvertently raises an important question. How did anyone know the number of women who voted for each candidate? The Montreal newspaper the Gazette speaks disparagingly of Patriot leader Louis-Joseph Papineau's lurking around the poll, and especially of his close surveillance during the coroner's subsequent investigation into the murders that would bring the election to an end.[64] Yet it is hard to imagine that he was keeping count of the votes for each candidate by sex. The daily tallies in the newspapers were never broken down by the gender of the voter. Furthermore, if there is a connection between this election and the 1834 bill, why and how did women's vote, so invisible in the print media during the election, become visible?

Jacques Viger, Papineau's cousin, is central to these questions. At the time of the 1832 by-election Viger would have been in his midforties. No Montrealer could have known the city's streets and people better than he did. No one showed a greater interest in accumulating such knowledge. Whereas his more famous cousins focused on the future of Canadiens at the level of the colony, his passion was the city—its past, its people, and its future. In 1813, he was named surveyor of the highways, streets, lanes, and bridges of Montreal. In 1825, he published a document outlining the improvements that could be made to the laws dealing with city's roads. That same year he was one of two census commissioners for the whole island of Montreal. In that capacity, as Jean-Claude Robert suggests, "all the details of his fellow citizens' lives were known to him." Three years later, he drew on his intimate knowledge of the social geography of the city to advise his Patriot politician cousins, L. J. Papineau and Denis-Benjamin Viger, on how best to allocate boundaries for the wards of the town and set the property qualifications low enough to ensure a Canadien majority in upcoming city elections. As politicians prepared a bill to incorporate Montreal, it was Viger who set out to assess the value of all property holdings in anticipation of the city's first election that was predicted for the month of June.[65] Early in April 1832, as stated previously, he had acted as returning officer in the Montreal East by-election. And when a municipal election was finally held in 1833, he was chosen as the city's first mayor.

During the twenty-two days of the 1832 by-election that the poll was open, Jacques Viger was observing and practicing his "habit of collecting matters of history." His testimony to the House of Assembly after the election shows him playing multiple roles and in diverse locations. He went to the hustings on most of the election days. He acted as an intermediary between Papineau and his political adversaries. He repeatedly encouraged Benjamin Delisle, the high constable of the District of Montreal, to produce an accurate list of the constables sworn in and of those who were summoned but refused to appear. He eavesdropped on the whispered conversations of Bagg's Tory supporters about hiring and paying bullies, he asked questions, and he offered advice.[66]

Jacques Viger took on the role of official voyeur as he fixed his gaze on the electoral behavior of the people of the city he loved. Like a growing number of men of his times, Viger sought to made sense of the world through counting and categorizing. One of his ways of mastering this unruly political event in which he had no official capacity was to watch closely, to listen, and to intervene. Another was to have detailed information about people's voting at his fingertips. He did this, as he explained later to Austin Cuvillier, by transcribing daily the details from the poll book until he had produced his own "entire copy" from one made by "a writer in the Police Office of the Prothonotaries at Montreal." He then made additional transcriptions of the entire poll book, organizing each one differently so that he could see at a glance how and when every Montrealer had voted and could identify voters by their ethnicity and sex.[67]

The statistics produced from Viger's analyses and transcriptions of this poll book have served as the basis of most of the published accounts of this election.[68] More interesting are his transcriptions, for they allowed him to answer many questions that Patriot politicians later had about the running of the election. One in particular highlights his interest in the issue of women voting. In the front of the leather volume containing his copy of the poll book, on smaller paper, is inserted an alphabetical list of all the men and women who presented themselves at the hustings. On this list, he wrote the names of those who voted for Tracy in black, those for Bagg in red, and those who were disqualified in blue. Widows and wives are cross-indexed by both their married and maiden names, although following Canadien custom Viger makes the primary reference for most women their maiden name. With his color-coded list, Viger could check at a glance how each citizen had voted. In the days of open voting, this ability is not as shocking as it now seems. It was, however, extremely useful to a man intent on knowing his city, its citizens, and their politics.[69]

In his transcription of the larger poll book he assigned every person who attempted to vote a number and an ethnicity, drawing for the latter on the sets of categories that dominated the discourse of this election. Despite the significance of Scots to the Anglo community in Montreal, this ethnicity was not one that he ascribed. For the purposes of this election he divided the ward's voting citizens into Canadiens, Americans, the Irish—those understood as Patriot supporters—and the "English and others." As he copied and added details on each citizen, Viger changed his pen each time the voter was a woman. In the pages of this volume, the women, so barely visible in newspaper narratives of election events, jump off the parchment, their names inscribed in red rather than black ink. Beside the name of any married man or woman whose spouse voted he indicated, also in red, what their polling number was. This color coding was part of his method of ensuring accurate counts. It also rendered the number of women voters, and their daily presence, highly visible. It was through his careful counting, based on these transcriptions, and his frequent observation of the poll that he legitimated his expertise at the investigations that followed the election.

From Red Ink, Redcoats, and the Street of Blood to Male Citizens

In his leather-bound volume, Viger, with his red ink, marked out female voters as different kinds of citizens. On the streets of the city the shedding of Canadien blood brought this tumultuous election to a close, hardening the identification between Patriots and Canadiens and erasing for a while the significance of the presence of widows and other women at the hustings. On May 21, after twenty-two days of voting, Daniel Tracey was three votes ahead of Stanley Bagg. It had been another conflictual day. Tempers were high, and each side was using its power to try to shape the outcome. Tracey's supporters attacked their opponents with the weapons they had at hand. Umbrellas and stones from the newly macadamized roads are those most frequently mentioned. Bagg's powerful supporters among the city magistrates called in more constables and the troops. British soldiers and the cannons were set up at a discreet distance from the hustings. Jostling with sticks and stones continued. At some point the Riot Act appears to have been read, although when and where would be much disputed in the weeks and months that followed.

After the poll closed the soldiers shot into the crowd and killed three Canadien men. The news of these murders by British soldiers reverberated across the colony, exacerbating the tension between those seeking political change and the supporters of the status quo. The invective that already marked the journalism of the two city newspapers most closely associated with each side reached new heights, carving harder lines of ethnic difference and hatred between both sides and telling two very different tales of the day's events. The *Montreal Gazette* laid the blame squarely and disparagingly on "Mr. Papineau, and his political adherents resident in Montreal," casting Tracey as their dupe, as someone chosen in order to "invite the Irish violently to uphold their course."[70] In *La Minerve,* Duvernay reported that Bagg's partisans approached the corpses laughing, "watching with ferocious joy the canadien blood that flowed in the street," shaking hands, congratulating each other, and regretting that they had not decimated the Canadiens. Soldiers were said to have been rewarded with abundant quantities of rum. The next morning the poll opened early. There was only one voter. Tracey was declared the winner. Bagg lodged an official protest against the result.[71]

Over the following days newspapers across the colony reported on the event. In Montreal the coroner's inquest began immediately, and there were calls on all sides for further investigations. On May 24, the funerals of the three Canadiens attracted some 5,000 people in this city of 27,000. They were given a first-class service and then accompanied to the graveyard in a convoy with Papineau and other Patriot politicians at the head, behind the coffins. Whether any women were part of the crowd is impossible to tell from the press's reporting of the event, although the suggestion that those present all wore black crepe on their hats dressed the crowd in masculine mourning attire.[72] Nor are women visible in most of the records generated by the events of May 21. None were asked to testify at the coroner's inquest, which after many adjournments resolved in September that there was no basis for a charge of murder against the colonel and the captain of the troops.[73] Women may have attended the assemblies that met in parishes across the colony after church to discuss the "horrors of the 21st of June," to deplore the actions of Canadiens like Austin Cuvillier for having "ignominiously abandoned the mass of the Canadiens to serve in a party that is not worthy of their support," to proclaim faithfulness to the king and disgust for the actions of the soldiers, magistrates, and Bureaucratic Party, and to announce special church services to pray for the souls of the three victims.[74] Yet no female names appear among the lists of local notables reported in attendance at the meetings in La Minerve. Such public assemblies, such meetings of citizens to discuss the affairs of their country and to engage in rational discourse, were the very essence of the new kind of "bourgeois public" that the German scholar Jürgen Habermas has identified as typifying the politics of eighteenth- and nineteenth-century Western states. They were resolutely male spaces.[75]

It is only in the evidence taken by the committee of the House of Assembly investigating the election that there is any mention of women as electors or as members of the crowds at the hustings. And of the witnesses called, only Jacques Viger seemed interested in alerting the politicians to the question of women voting. He did so again and again, at first soliciting few reactions. Early in January 1833, he reported seeing a great many women voting on both sides. The next day he used the data he had so carefully collected to place women's voting in the public record. In authoritative, statistical detail he reported that "225 women came to the Hustings, 26 of whom did not vote. There were 199 that voted; of whom 95 voted for Mr. Tracey and 104 for Mr Bagg; that is to say 49 spinsters, 20 of whom voted for Mr. Tracey, and 29 for Mr. Bagg; 131 widows, 68 of whom voted for Mr. Tracey, and 63 for Mr. Bagg; and 19 married women, 7 of whom voted for Mr. Tracey, and 12 for Mr. Bagg." Then he gave committee members his listing showing the numbers of women voting on each day of the election. He informed them that "six married women voted . . . jointly with their husbands." There was no immediate reaction to this information. The questioning turned to how the magistrates and members of the House of Assembly had voted. Viger could use his careful records to tell all.[76]

Once other issues had been investigated in depth, these minute details and statistical tables about voting women finally provoked some interest among committee members, and particularly from Mr. Leslie, the main questioner. Early on, Viger informed him that he had refused to let married women vote during the Montreal East election.[77] Four weeks later, Leslie wanted to know which women "were brought to vote toward the end of the hour, so as to feed the poll?" At this point widows, wives, and spinsters no longer appear as statistical categories. Giving evidence that can only have been read from his transcription of the poll book in which the women were so visibly identified in red ink, he started naming individual female voters.[78]

Yet Viger mentioned only women who had voted just after the returning officer proclaimed that the election would be over if no one voted in the next sixty minutes. This was easy for him to do, for he had identified such moments in his document with little stars. Thus Viger carefully painted a picture that ignored all the women who had voted at other times. He failed to mention the many men who also voted at similar critical moments in the election process. Twenty-three women were mentioned by name—less than 5 percent of the female voters. Fifteen of them were supporters of Bagg. This in itself lent some credence to the accusation of Patriots that Bagg's supporters were pulling women in to the hustings to increase his chances.[79] James Leslie also wished to know which "married women have voted as well as their husbands?" Again, Viger was able to be specific. He named six couples, including "Marie-Claire Perrault who voted on the 18th May for Mr. Bagg; wife of Austin Cuvillier, Esquire, who had voted on the 18th for the same candidate."[80] Viger mentioned Mme Cuvillier twice—as a woman voting to prevent the poll closing and as a wife voting the same way as her husband. He did so without casting any obvious judgment. Yet this publicity must have added to the broader discourse in newspapers and the assemblies throughout the province that castigated those Canadiens in general who had supported the Bureaucratic Party and that named Austin Cuvillier in particular as the most prominent of the Canadiens "wishing to crush their compatriots."[81]

Viger, with his careful lists, numbers, and tracking of citizens' votes thus placed information about women's voting squarely on the floor of the Legislative Assembly, in the public record, and on the agenda of electoral reform in the colony. In late January 1834, a year after the committee's lengthy investigation was over, the Patriot politician John Nielson picked up the issue, identifying a range of doubtful practices revealed at recent elections that should be dealt with. These included whether women had the right to vote, how oaths should be sworn, and how tension and struggles at the poll could be reduced. Not once was the possibility of a secret ballot raised, a choice that would have avoided many of the electoral problems and that was already practiced in most states south of the border.[82]

> It was then that Louis-Joseph Papineau rose in the Assembly pronouncing: As to women voting, that is something it is right to destroy. It is ridiculous, nay odious to see wives dragged to the hustings by their husbands, girls by their fathers, often even against their wishes. The public interest, decency, the modesty of the sex demand that these scandals should not be repeated any more. A simple resolution of the Chamber would exclude such people from the right to vote.[83]

This widely quoted statement has been read by historians as a general expression of the new understandings of gender and citizenship that the Patriots were articulating. Greer rightly notes how little sense it made, given that most female voters were widows. He also shows how well it fitted with Rousseauian ideas about gender in which "sexual disorder on the part of women, as evidenced by political self assertion, was considered deplorable."[84] Yet Papineau's words were more than a succinct representation of the gender ideals of his times. They also continued the very personalized Patriot attacks on Austin Cuvillier as a traitor to the Canadien cause and the critique of his wife's vote during the election as a signifier of both domestic and political instability. Papineau was explicitly impugning the honor of Cuvillier and his wife in his reference to wives dragged to the hustings. Cuvillier, who was present in the Assembly at the time, was well aware of it. So no doubt were the other politicians. Cuvillier shot back expressing surprise that Papineau would "accuse the women who vote of immodesty" when he had seen him "receive their votes with pleasure." The debate was brief. The only exchange in the Assembly on this subject was between these two men. Under attack from Cuvillier, Papineau wriggled between his language of gendered citizenship and individual critique, finally asserting unconvincingly that his were "general and not individual reflections . . . I was not accusing anyone." The debate went no further. The motion to insert such a clause into the wider electoral reform bill was passed without amendment.[85]

It was only because other parts of the bill were subsequently found unconstitutional that the question of women's right to vote remained unresolved.[86] It was not until after the discontent so evident in the 1832 election had mushroomed into rebellion, repression, rule by an appointed Special Council, and the amalgamation of the largely British province of Upper Canada with the mixed but largely French-speaking province of Lower Canada that the question was again addressed. In 1849, a year after U.S. feminists had come together at Seneca Falls, New York, seeking greater rights for women, including the right to vote, Canadien politicians put the last nail in the possibility of widows and other women voting, by passing another omnibus electoral reform bill. I have yet to find evidence that the clause excluding women was even debated.[87]

Conclusion

A total of 200 women attempting to vote in this colonial city of some 27,000 inhabitants may not seem like many. Yet the widows and other women who stepped up to the poll over the twenty-three days of voting between April and May 1832 made up 14 percent of the voters. On some days, women represented over a third of those voicing their choices at the hustings. A significant proportion of widows with the required property qualifications clearly embraced the possibility of exercising the right to vote. What motivated these women to take part in this highly contentious election? Historians writing about other jurisdictions have suggested that candidates desperate to win were "willing to ignore convention to secure as many supporters as they could."[88] Such arguments support the representations of the time, which downplayed women's initiative and interest by suggesting that women at the hustings had been dragged there. The women who braved the hustings in 1832 were taking advantage of a right that growing numbers of Canadien and immigrant women had embraced since the creation of an elected assembly in 1791. They followed the legacy of Patriot leader Louis-Joseph Papineau's grandmother, who, in an earlier bitterly contested 1809 Montreal election, voted for Papineau's father. When asked for whom she wished to vote she is reported to have stated, "For my son M. Joseph Papineau, for I believe that he is a good and faithful subject."[89]

The numbers of women involved, the patterns of their voting, and the courage they exhibited in exposing their bodies and reputations at the hustings all suggest that politics mattered to them. They were willing to openly pronounce their commitment to the Patriot and Tory politics that were causing such virulent divisions in this colonial town by appearing at the poll. And the heatedness of political, ethnic, and religious divisions made it more likely that they wished to express their choice in the future of the colony. The women voters were diverse in their class origins—they voted as the widows, daughters, and occasionally the wives of laborers and craftsmen as well as of wealthy merchants. They were Jews, devout Catholics, and committed Protestants. Outside the city they included First Nations women. Some came from families resident in Canada for centuries; others were relative newcomers, mostly from Scotland, the United States, England, and Ireland. Although many owned close to the minimum property required to be eligible to vote, this amount still marked them as among the privileged in this city, where renters were rapidly outnumbering landowners.

That so many eligible women chose to vote in 1832 is powerful evidence that the understanding that male and female spheres should be separate and that politics and citizenship required capacities found only in males were contested notions at this time in Lower Canada. Furthermore, women continued to vote between the time of the 1834 attempt to exclude them and the successful law in 1849. In 1844 Agathe Perrault—the widow Nolan, Emilie Tavernier's cousin—voted again in a Montreal election, as she had done in 1827 and in 1832, although Emilie did not. Once again the widow Nolan chose the reform candidate—and once again she was joined by another woman from her family—this time her widowed sister-in-law.

Women challenged new understandings of citizenship, politics, and the public by choosing to vote. Yet their presence at the poll in such large numbers, especially during the 1832 election, also helped seal their fate. Louis-Joseph Papineau was no doubt influenced by ideas about gender deriving from Rousseau and more broadly from the growing hold of the idea of separate spheres in the Anglo-American world, as Alan Greer and Nathalie Picard have argued. There is ample evidence of these understandings in newspapers and other print media during the 1820s and 1830s. A commentary in an issue of the *Quebec Mercury* in 1827 caricatured the idea of women voting by suggesting that they would also seek to enter the Assembly, where their presence would distract men from "the affairs of State." Worse, this English newspaper suggested, alluding to the particularly high birth rates among Canadien women, "in this prolific country," pregnancies could mean that many women would be unable to attend, "and the natural consequence would be that the business of the state must be neglected whilst these family concerns were going forward.[90] This evocative image of a political institution both peopled and rendered empty by pregnant women promotes the desirability of the separation of home and politics and of men and women. It ignores the reality that single women and especially widows were the usual voters, conflating all women with married women, as became so common in the nineteenth century.[91]

The diffusion of new understandings of citizenship is not sufficient to explain the timing of politicians' decision or to interpret the minimal debate in the House of Assembly in 1834, when the first attempt was made to exclude women. Critical, I have argued here, were two local personalities. Jacques Viger played a key role as the modern producer of knowledge who gendered the record, made the numbers known, pinned them down in statistical tables, and entered them into the public record, contributing more information about women voting in his testimony before the Select Committee investigating the election than did any elected politician.[92] Important too, especially in interpreting the brief debate in 1834, was the reaction of the Patriots to Canadiens like Austin Cuvillier, who chose to support their enemies—the Bureaucrats, Tories, "the English Party," represented in this election by the merchant Stanley Bagg. As Patriots struggled to articulate a new vision of nation and citizenship, the disloyal challenged their claim to speak for the conquered nation, exposing the fragility and constructed character of ethnicity. The line between the public embarrassment of Mme Cuvillier in the newspapers during the 1832 by-election and the attempt by the Patriot-controlled assembly to remove women's right to vote in 1834 was a direct one. Only constitutional errors in other sections of the bill prevented it from becoming law.

In 1849, when the new bill to remove women's right to vote passed so quietly, the political and cultural context had changed. Owning property, or renting at a specified value, ceased to bestow citizenship rights on widows, even when that property was secured through a legitimate contract. In the wake of the rebellions of 1837 and 1838, the Catholic Church gained a new hegemony over institutions and Catholic citizens. Patriots became reformers and liberals. The divisions between Canadiens and others hardened into a less ethnically inclusive strand of nationalism that idealized francophone Catholic women's contribution to the nation as mothers of large families. The numbers of Catholic women taking vows and working as teachers, nuns, and charity workers within religious orders increased dramatically. Protestant Montreal women became heavily involved as lay charity workers. Emilie Gamelin transformed her work with the elderly into a religious order that was rigidly overseen by male religious authorities, and she herself took vows. At her death from cholera in 1851, she was the mother superior of the Sisters of Providence. Her order had housed over a hundred elderly and sick widows since its consecration in 1843 and was one of the two major orders in the city that provided for the elderly and visited the poor in their homes.[93] Later it would establish institutions throughout much of the Canadian and American West.

Emilie Monjean, the painter's widow, and Sarah Harrison, widow of a tinsmith, both remarried not long after the election. So did Marguerite Paris. Marguerite Gagnon, the mason's widow, continued to live in the Saint Lawrence suburb, where her one-room wooden house secured her shelter until her death in 1866. The last of the voting widows whose lives I have been following, Sarah Campbell, whose merchant husband had died shortly after going bankrupt in 1831, died in Montreal in 1884 at the age of eighty-three. By that time, a new generation of Montreal women, Protestant and Catholic, English and French speaking, were organizing to change women's rights. A year later the Canadian prime minister raised the issue of enfranchising widows and spinsters in federal elections.[94] In the pages and pages of *Hansard* recording the debates, women's involvement in earlier elections was not mentioned. The battle to regain suffrage in Quebec was long and difficult. Whereas early nineteenth-century observers had commented on Quebec as a place where wives and widows had too much power, a century later Québecoises were generally viewed as being behind the rest of the country. Finally, in 1940, Quebec became the last Canadian province to allow women to vote in provincial elections.

Acknowledgments

This research was supported by Social Sciences and Humanities Research Council of Canada grants as well as a grant accorded the Montreal History Group by Le Fonds québécois de la recherche sur la société et la culture. I am grateful to these funding bodies, and especially to Nathalie Picard and Dr. Robert Sweeny, who allowed me to use their databases.

Notes

1. Nathalie Picard's master's thesis as well as her database on the widows who voted have been invaluable to me in writing this section of the chapter. Nathalie Picard, "Les femmes et le vote au Bas-Canada de 1792 à 1849" (master's thesis, University of Montreal, 1992); Nathalie Picard, "Database of Women Voters." So has Robert Sweeny's computerized version of a different transcription of the poll book by Jacques Viger and Sweeny's database derived from Jacques Viger's enumeration of six of the city's eight wards. Robert Sweeny, "By-Election of 1832" (database); Robert Sweeny, "A Partial Tax Roll for the City and Suburbs of Montréal, 1832" (St. John's, Newfoundland: Memorial University of Newfoundland, 2002).

2. The three poll locations are indicated on the map included in John MacGregor, *British America* (Edinburgh: William Blackwood, 1833; London: T. Cadell, 1833), 2:192–193.

3. *Montreal Gazette,* 30 April 1832; Elinor Kyte Senior, *Redcoats and Patriots: The Rebellions in Lower Canada, 1837–38* (Ottawa: National Museums of Canada, 1985), 7.

4. *La Minerve,* 30 April 1832.

5. Robert Rumilly, *Histoire de Montréal* (Montreal: Fides, 1970), 2:83–84.

6. Alan Greer, *The Patriots and the People: The Rebellion of 1837 in Rural Lower Canada* (Toronto: University of Toronto Press, 1993); Jane Rendall, "Women and the Public Sphere," *Gender and History* 11, no. 3 (November 1999): 475–488; Joan Landes, ed., *Feminism, the Public and the Private* (New York: Oxford University Press, 1998); Mary Ryan, *Women in Public: Between Banners and Ballots, 1825–1880* (Baltimore: Johns Hopkins University Press, 1990); Leonore Davidoff, *Worlds Between: Historical Perspectives on Gender and Class* (Oxford: Blackwell Publishers, 1995), 227–276; Leonore Davidoff and Catherine Hall, *Family Fortunes: Men and Women of the English Middle Class, 1780–1850* (Chicago: University of Chicago Press, 1987).

7. It is in this light that most historians have presented the election, even when their analyses vary dramatically. France Galarneau, "L'élection partielle du quartier-ouest de Montréal en 1832: Analyse politico-sociale," *Revue d'Histoire de l'Amérique Française* 32, no. 4 (March 1979): 565–584; France Galarneau, "L'élection pour le quartier Ouest de Montréal en 1832: Analyse politico-sociale" (master's thesis, University of Montréal, 1975), 33; Fernand Ouellet, *Lower Canada, 1791–1840: Social Change and Nationalism* (Toronto: McClelland and Stewart, 1980), 226–229; Elinor Senior, *British Regulars in Montreal: An Imperial Garrison, 1832–1854* (Montreal: McGill–Queen's University Press, 1981); John Dickinson and Brian Young, *A Short History of Quebec,* 2nd ed. (Toronto: Copp Clark Pitman, 1993); Denis Monière, *Ludger Duvernay et la révolution intellectuelle au Bas Canada* (Montreal: Québec Amérique, 1987).

8. I use the term Canadien to designate the French-Catholic population, most of whose ancestors had settled in the colony during the century or so before the British Conquest of 1760. This was the self-designation chosen by the precursors of the Patriots—the Parti Canadien.

9. Joan B. Landes, *Women and the Public Sphere in the Age of French Revolution* (Ithaca, NY: Cornell University Press, 1988); Olwen Hufton, *Women and the Limits of Citizenship in the French Revolution* (Toronto: University of Toronto Press, 1991); Ryan, *Women in Public;* Joan Wallach Scott, *Only Paradoxes to Offer: French Feminist and the Rights of Man* (Cambridge, MA: Harvard University Press, 1996); Anna Clarke, *The Struggle for the Breeches: Gender and the Making of the British Working Class* (Berkeley and Los Angeles: University of California Press, 1997); Eleanor Gordon and Gwyneth Nair, *Public Lives: Women, Family and Society in Victorian Britain* (New Haven, CT: Yale University Press, 2003); Judith Apter Klinghoffer and Lois Elkis, "'The Petticoat Electors': Women's Suffrage in New Jersey, 1776–1807," *Journal of the Early Republic* 12, no. 2 (1992): 159–193; Rendall, "Women and the Public Sphere," 484–485; Kim Klein, "A 'Petticoat Polity?' Women Voters in New Brunswick before Confederation," *Acadiensis* 26, no. 1 (1996): 71–75.

10. Greer, *Patriots;* Picard, "Les femmes and le vote" (1992). Picard's database, which is derived only from the poll books that have survived, shows that 14 women voted

in Montreal elections in the late eighteenth century. In elections in Montreal East, 102 women voted in 1820, 6 in 1824, 2 in 1827, 72 in 1832, and 2 in 1844, while in Montreal West 111 voted in 1827 and 224 in the 1832 election. The surviving polls show that overall, between the years 1800 and 1844, a minimum of 950 women voted throughout the province. Well over half voted in the city of Montreal.

11. *New Brunswick Royal Gazette,* 20 June 1820, citing the *Montreal Gazette,* 25 April 1820, as quoted in Klein, "Petticoat Polity," 71.

12. Ouellet, *Lower Canada,* 226; Collectif Clio, *Quebec Women: A History* (Toronto: Women's Press, 1987), 122–123.

13. Of course voting was not a "traditional" right. An Assembly was fought for by British merchants and loyalist immigrants in the decades following the conquest.

14. Greer, *Patriots,* 202; Picard, "Les femmes et le vote" (1992); Nathalie Picard, "Les femmes et le vote au Bas-Canada," in *Les bâtisseuses de la cité,* ed. Évelyne Tardy, Francine Descarries, Lorraine Archambault, Lyne Kurtzman, and Lucie Piché (Montreal: Actes du Colloque, ACFAS, 1993), 57–64; Françoise Noel, *Family Life and Sociability in Upper and Lower Canada, 1760–1870* (Montreal and Kingston: McGill–Queen's University Press, 2003), 109–110, 127–128.

15. I draw here on my research for "Wife to Widow: Lives, Laws and Politics in Nineteenth-Century Montreal" (forthcoming), in which I followed cohorts of women who married during the years 1823–26 or 1842–45, from the time of their marriages through to the death of their husbands and then to their own deaths. For this information I examined parish registers, marriage contracts, wills, inventories of their goods, censuses, and other documents. Here I make use of the collective biographies created through this process to focus on a few of the widows who voted.

16. On the importance of Viger, see Robert Sweeny, "La fabrication d'une capitale bourgeoise, 1800–1850," in *L'histoire du Vieux-Montréal à travers son patrimoine,* ed. Gilles Lauzon and Madeleine Forget (Ste. Foy: Publications du Québec, 2004); and Jean-Claude Robert, s.v. "Jacques Viger," *Dictionary of Canadian Biography* (*DCB*), http://www.biographi.ca (accessed 14 April 2007).

17. Picard, "Les femmes et le vote" (1992), 72–73.

18. Lower Canada Statutes, 1825, chap. 33: "An Act to repeal certain Acts therein mentioned, and to consolidate the Laws relating to the Election of Members to serve in the Assembly of this Province, and to the duty of Returning Officers, and for other purposes" (assented to 22 March 1825). In the English version the pronoun "he" is used in some sections, whereas the French wording implies no gender. One pound in Quebec currency was worth about four dollars.

19. Klein, "Petticoat Polity," finds evidence of a few women voting in New Brunswick elections prior to 1843. Most were widows, but the numbers are much lower than in Montreal, and the requirement that voters own £25 of real estate was much higher.

20. Constitutional Act, 1791; John Garner, *The Franchise and Politics in British North America, 1755–1867* (Toronto: University of Toronto Press, 1969), 74–75; William Renwick Riddell, "Woman Franchise in Quebec a Century Ago," Royal Society of Canada, *Proceedings and Transactions* 22 (1928): 85–99, as cited in Picard, "Les femmes et le vote" (1992), 14; David DeBrou, "Widows and Tenants on the Hustings: Estimating Voter Turnout in Early Nineteenth-Century Quebec City" (paper presented to the annual meeting of the Canadian Historical Association Queen's University, June 1991), 6; Ouellet, *Lower Canada,* 25.

21. Hugh Gray, *Letters from Canada Written during a Residence There in the Years 1806, 1807 and 1808* (London, 1809; repr., Toronto: Coles Publishing Co., 1971), 141–143.

22. Bettina Bradbury, *Wife to Widow: Class, Culture, Family, and the Law in Nineteenth-Century Quebec,* Grandes Conférences Desjardins, pamphlet 1 (Montreal: Programme d'études sur le Québec de l'Université McGill, 1997), 1–45; Bettina Bradbury, Alan Stewart, Evelyn Kolish, and Peter Gossage, "Property and Marriage: The Law and Practice in Early Nineteenth Century Montreal," *Histoire Sociale/Social History* 26 (May 1993): 9–39.

23. Picard, "Les femmes et le vote" (1992). Making a marriage contract was common practice among French Canadians and increasingly used by English-speaking migrants to avoid community property.

24. *Journals of the House of Assembly of Lower Canada (JHALC),* 28 January 1833. The poll book for that election indicates that some 72 women voted. Of these, 53 were clearly identified as widows. Picard, "Database."

25. *Montreal Gazette* and *La Minerve,* 25 April–25 May 1832; Galarneau, "L'élection pour le quartier Ouest," 33; Senior, *Redcoats and Patriots,* 7, states that the poll could be closed after thirty minutes, but the Electoral Law states one hour. Lower Canada Statutes, 40 George III (1800), chap. 1, art. 9, as cited in Picard, "Les femmes et le vote" (1992), 42. L. E. Fredman describes open voting in England in *The Australian Ballot: The Story of an American Reform* (East Lansing: Michigan State Press, 1968), 2–3.

26. The electoral law as revised in 5 George IV, chap. 33 (1825), forbad the carrying of any "flag, ribbon, or cockade or other badge or mark whatsoever, to distinguish him or them as supporting any particular candidate" (sec. 28) and continued the penalties set out by earlier laws for attempting to buy votes. This revision does not seem to have hindered these behaviors by persons in this or many other elections.

27. This name continues to be evoked in history texts and popular histories, in printed form and on the Web, as a reminder of British brutality during this election. See Gilles Boileau, *Le 21 mai 1832 sur la rue du Sang* (Montreal: Editions de Meridien, 1999).

28. Bibliothèque et Archives Nationales du Québec–Montréal (BANQM), poll book, Montreal West by-election, 1832. This version is the official one.

29. Montreal *Gazette,* 25 April 1820, as cited in Klein, "Petticoat Polity," 71; *Montreal Gazette,* 31 December 1833, as cited in E. A. Heaman, "Taking the World by Show: Canadian Women Exhibitors to 1900," *Canadian Historical Review* 78, no. 4 (December 1997): 604; petition of Pierre Faucher, Romain Robitaille et al., electors in the City of Quebec, 3 December 1828, reprinted in *La Minerve,* 22 December 1828, as cited in Picard, "Les femmes et le vote" (1992), 48.

30. *La Minerve,* 13 August 1827, as cited in Picard, "Les femmes et le vote" (1992), 54–55.

31. H. St. George Dupré to Benjamin Delisle, 15 May 1832, as cited in *JHALC,* 20 December 1832, 36.

32. The law stated that any candidate or their representative could demand the swearing of an oath by voters and set out specific oaths depending on whether the person lived in a town or city, or was an owner or renter. Lower Canada Statutes, 5 George IV (1825), chap. 33.

33. The statistics that Montreal city surveyor and future mayor Jacques Viger and "pioneer sociologist" would later produce for the House of Assembly indicate that 1,378 people voted and that some 82, or about 5.6 percent, were deemed not qualified. His reporting suggests that 225 women presented and 26, or 11.5 percent, were disqualified. These figures would mean that 1,153 men presented and 56 were disqualified, or 4.8 percent. Picard, "Database," also shows that 12 percent of women were disqualified. Les archives du Séminaire de Québec (ASQ), P32 Fonds Viger-Verreau, "Statistique

de l'élédtion de 1832, au Quartier-Ouest de la Cité de Montréal," *JHALC,* Appendix 1832–1833: Evidence of Jacques Viger, 26 January 1833.

34. *JHALC,* Appendix, 9 January 1833.

35. BANQM, Notary Doucet, marriage contract of Emilie Tavernier and Jean-Baptiste Gamelin, 4 June 1823.

36. Denise Robillard, *Emilie Tavernier-Gamelin* (Montreal: Éditions du Méridien, 1988), 101–104.

37. Ibid., 101–104.

38. Gordon and Nair, *Public Lives,* 3, 4.

39. Jean-Claude Marsan, *Montreal in Evolution* (Montreal: McGill–Queen's University Press, 1981), 144.

40. Kathleen Jenkins, *Montreal, Island City of the St. Lawrence* (New York: Doubleday, 1966), 285. In his map reproducing the history of the election and its aftermath, John MacGregor refers to the location as the Number 1 Pump Eng. (MacGregor, *British America,* 2:192–193).

41. Robillard, *Emilie,* 90.

42. Picard, "Les femmes et le vote" (1992), 94–101. For an English Protestant visitor's view of the city's peoples, see Isabella Lucy Bird, *The Englishwoman in America,* with foreword and notes by Andrew Hill Clark (London: John Murray, 1856; repr., Toronto: University of Toronto Press, 1966), 251–252. On the 1827 election and Robert Nelson, see Richard Chabot, Jacques Monet, and Yves Roby, s.v. "Robert Nelson," *DCB,* http:// www.biographi.ca (accessed 14 April 2007).

43. Ouellet, *Lower Canada,* 25, 226.

44. France Galarneau, s.v. "Daniel Tracey," *DCB,* http://www.biographi.ca (accessed 14 April 2007).

45. Legislation in 1825 set a fine of ten pounds for anyone attempting to influence votes. Lower Canada Statues, chap. 33: "An Act to repeal certain Acts" (assented to 22 March 1825) ; Jean Hamelin and Marcel Hamelin, *Les moeurs électorales dans le Québec de 1791 à nos jours* (Montreal: ditions du Jour, 1962), 44.

46. Jacques Monet and Gerald J. J. Tulchinsky, s.v. "Austin Cuvillier," *DCB,* http://www. biographi.ca (accessed 14 April 2007).

47. *La Minerve,* 16 April 1832. Tracey had publicly criticized Cuvillier and recently been released from prison along with Ludger Duvernay, editor of *La Minerve.* Both were charged with treason and greeted by a huge crowd on their release. Galarneau, s.v. "Tracey."

48. *La Minerve,* 24 May 1832; Ouellet, *Lower Canada,* 226–229.

49. *La Minerve,* 21 May 1832.

50. Picard, "Les femmes et le vote" (1992), 73.

51. These estimates were made on the following bases. First, among the women whose lives I have been tracing who married in Montreal between 1823 and 1826, at least 35 were definitely still living in Montreal in 1832 and were widowed. Of these, 8 had already remarried. Nine of the remaining 27 (33 percent) widows definitely voted in these by-elections. Second, Viger's evaluation roll, computerized by Robert Sweeny, which covered most of the city's wards, identified 115 widows as owning property worth more than £100. He did not enumerate the properties in the two most westerly wards of Saint Antoine and Saint Joseph, otherwise known as the Recollet suburb, where a considerable number of widows, including Emilie Tavernier, lived. Allowing that twice the number of widows lived in these two wards as in the other parts of the city and that widows were equally spread throughout the rest of city, I estimate that would add about

70 more widows than are present on Viger's roll, making roughly 185 eligible widows in the whole city. In the two by-elections of 1832, some 171 widows with property presented themselves at the poll. This measure suggests that pretty well all the eligible widows with property voted. Third, in the census of 1831, the only women who can be identified as widows were household heads, of which there were about 371. One year later, 171 widows, or about 46 percent of the 1831 total, sought to vote. On the politics and pitfalls of this census, see Bruce Curtis, *The Politics of Population: State Formation, Statistics, and the Census of Canada, 1840–1875* (Toronto: University of Toronto Press, 2001).

52. Of the 198 women who voted in the Montreal West by-election, 128, or 65 percent, were recorded as owning property. Picard, "Database." When Viger calculated similar proportions for all the electors, in contrast, he found that only 53 percent were proprietors. Jacques Viger, Statistique de l'éléction, ASQ, fonds Viger-Verreau, reproduced in Galarneau, "L'élection pour le quartier Ouest," table 8, 75.

53. Diane Lamoureux, *Citoyennes? Femmes, droit de vote et democratie* (Montreal: Remue-menage, 1989), 41.

54. BANQM, Notary Labadie, inventory of the goods of Marguerite Paris and Joseph Guilbault, 3 March 1830; Bettina Bradbury, "Itineraries of Marriage and Widowhood in 19th Century Montreal," in *Mapping the Margins: Families and Social Discipline in Canada, 1700–1980,* ed. Michael Gauvreau and Nancy Christie (Montreal and Kingston: McGill–Queen's University Press, 2004), 108–115; Sweeny, "Partial Tax Roll, 1832."

55. BANQM, Notary Cadieux, 6 November 1824; Mount Royal Cemetery records.

56. Sweeny, "Partial Tax Roll, 1832"; BANQM, Notary Ritchot, marriage contract of Emilie Moujeon and Antoine Laurent, 22 November 1824. The contract retained community property and promised a dower of £2,400, and a preciput—a sum she could take out of the community as hers of £1,200 ancien cours, which translates into £100 and £50, respectively, in the new currency of the times, or roughly $400 and $200.

57. *Gazette,* 16 April 1832; Cecilia Morgan, *Public Men and Virtuous Women: The Gendered Languages of Religion and Politics in Upper Canada, 1791–1850* (Toronto: University of Toronto Press, 1996), 5, 6.

58. *Gazette,* 16 April 1832, 30 April 1832, 5 May 1832, and 17 May 1832.

59. *La Minerve,* 3 May 1832, 3.

60. For example, *La Minerve,* 16 April 1832, 30 April 1832, 26 April 1832, and for an earlier formulation, 23 April 1827. "French Canadiens don't tend to exclusive power, they don't hold a national hatred against the English, and as soon as an inhabitant of this country shows they are really a citizen, there is no longer any difference"; as cited in Monière, *Ludger Duvernay,* 64.

61. Carole Pateman, *The Sexual Contract* (Stanford, CA: Stanford University Press, 1988); Carole Patemen, *The Disorder of Women: Democracy, Feminist and Political Theory* (London: Polity Press, 1989); Davidoff, *Worlds Between;* Joan Scott, "The Uses of Imagination: Olympe de Gouges in the French Revolution," in Scott, *Only Paradoxes;* Linda Kerber, "'I Have Don . . . Much to Carrey on the Warr': Women and the Shaping of Republican Ideology after the American Revolution," in *Women and Politics in the Age of the Democratic Revolution,* ed. Harriet B. Applewhite and Darline G. Levy (Ann Arbor: University of Michigan Press, 1990), 227–257.

62. Greer, *Patriots.*

63. *La Minerve,* 26 April 1832, 14 May 1832, and 21 May 1832.

64. *Gazette,* 24 May 1832, citing the *Montreal Herald.*

65. Robert, "Jacques Viger." The Act of Incorporation received royal assent in June 1832 and was put into effect a year later. Jenkins, *Montreal,* 289.

66. *JHALC,* Appendix 1832–1833: Evidence of Jacques Viger, 30 January 1833, 23 February 1833.

67. Robert, "Jacques Viger"; Curtis, *Politics of Population; JHALC,* Appendix 1832–1833: Evidence of Jacques Viger, 30 January 1833; BANQM, P148, Collection Charles Phillips, 1770–1957, Livres d'élection à Montréal, quartier Ouest.

68. Ouellet, *Lower Canada,* 376, suggests that the original poll book had disappeared. Galarneau's detailed thesis and article on the election are based entirely on Viger's statistics rather than the poll book. Galarneau, "L'élection partielle"; Galarneau, "L'élection pour le quartier Ouest." Nathalie Picard found this and many other poll books in the BANQM and the National Archives of Canada, and has been able to give a much more detailed analysis of women's role in Lower Canadian elections, in general, and this one in particular, than any other researchers have to date. Picard, "Les femmes et le vote" (1992); Picard, "Les femmes et le vote" (1993).

69. BANQM, Collection Charles Phillips, 1770–1957, Livres d'élection de 1832.

70. *Montreal Herald,* as cited in the *Montreal Gazette,* 24 May 1832.

71. *La Minerve,* 24 May 1832.

72. *La Minerve,* 28 May 1832; Pat Jalland, *Death in the Victorian Family* (New York: Oxford University Press, 1996), 300–305; Barbara Dodd Hillerman, "'Chrysalis of Gloom': Nineteenth-Century American Mourning Costume," in *A Time to Mourn: Expressions of Grief in Nineteenth-Century America,* ed. Martha V. Pike and Janice Gray Armstrong (Stony Brook, NY: Stony Brook Museum, 1980), 23–26; Lou Taylor, *Mourning Dress: A Costume and Social History* (London: George Allen and Unwin, 1983), 134–136.

73. Galarneau, "L'élection pour le quartier Ouest," 142–143.

74. *La Minerve* reports on the following assemblies: 31 May 1832 on St. Athanase; 7 June 1832 on St. Remy; 14 June 1832 on Chambly; 25 June 1832 on St. Hyacinthe; 5 July 1832 on Deux Montagnes; and 12 July 1832 on St. Benoit. Note how similar assemblies would be critical to the building of Patriot support leading up to the rebellions of 1837. Greer, *Patriots,* 146–149.

75. Nancy Duncan, ed., *Body Space: Destabilizing Geographies of Gender and Sexuality* (London: Routledge, 1996); Carole Pateman, *The Disorder of Women: Democracy, Feminism, and Political Theory* (Cambridge, MA: Polity Press, 1989); Alison Blunt and Gillian Rose, eds., *Writing Women and Space: Colonial and Postcolonial Geographies* (London: Guildford, 1994); Landes, *Feminism.* Ruth Sandwell grapples with similar issues in "The Limits of Liberalism: The Liberal Reconnaissance and the History of the Family in Canada," *Canadian Historical Review* 84, no. 3 (September 2003): 423–450; Davidoff, *Worlds Between;* Rendall, "Women and the Public Sphere"; Geoffrey Eley, "Nations, Publics, and Political Cultures: Placing Habermas in the Nineteenth Century," in *Habermas and the Public Sphere,* ed. Craig Calhoun (Cambridge, MA: MIT Press, 1992), 289–339; Dena Goodman, "Public Sphere and Private Life: Toward a Synthesis of Current Historiographical Approaches to the Old Regime," *History and Theory* 31, no. 1 (1992): 1–20.

76. *JHALC,* Appendix 1832–1833: Evidence of Jacques Viger, 25 and 26 January 1833.

77. Ibid., 28 January 1833, 23 February 1833. Viger reported that he had acted in this capacity in the East Ward elections of 1820 twice, in 1825 and 1830 as well as 1832, and that three of these elections had been "warmly contested."

78. BANQM, P148, Collection Charles Phillips, 1770–1957, Livres d'élection de 1832.

79. *La Minerve,* 3 May 1832.

80. *JHALC,* Appendix 1821–1833: Evidence of Jacques Viger, 23 February 1833 (my translation).

81. *La Minerve,* 14 May 1832, 16 April 1832, and 21 April 1832. In one of the parishes that he represented, St. Remy, the assembly resolved, "as part of the county that Austin Cuvillier represents," to "thank him for the good he has done until last year, and refuse in the future" to give him the honor of representing them "because he has ignominiously abandoned the mass of the Canadiens to serve in a party that is not worthy of their support" (*La Minerve,* 7 June 1832; my translation).

82. *La Minerve,* 3 February 1834, citing debate of 27 January 1834; Fredman, *Australian Ballot,* 20–21.

83. *La Minerve,* citing debate of 3 February 1834.

84. Greer, *Patriots,* 206, 202.

85. *La Minerve,* 3 February 1834.

86. Debates, House of Assembly, Lower Canada, as reported in *La Minerve,* 3 February 1834; "L'Acte pour régler la manière de procéder sur les contestations relatives aux lections des Membres pour servir dans la Chambre d'Assemblée et pour révoquer certains Actes y mentionnés," 4 William IV, chap. 28, 1834; Picard, "Les femmes et le vote" (1992), 58; Greer (*Patriots,* 205) wrongly claims that women were no longer admitted to the hustings after the passage of this act.

87. Picard, "Les femmes et le vote" (1992), 59; Catherine L. Cleverdon, *The Woman Suffrage Movement in Canada,* with an introduction by Ramsay Cook (1950; repr., Toronto: University of Toronto Press, 1974), 158, 216; Collective Clio, *Quebec Women,* 122; Lower Canada Statutes, 12 Victoria (1849), chap. 27: "Acte pour abroger certains Actes y mentionnés, et pour amender, refondre et résumer en un seul Acte les diverses dispositions des statuts maintenant en vigueur pour regler les éléctions des membres qui représentent le peuple de cette province a l'Assemblée Legislative," 30 May 1849, art. 56; Elizabeth Gibbs, ed., *Debates of the Legislative Assembly of United Canada* (1849), 6, 13, and 16 March; 17, 18 April.

88. Klein, "Petticoat Polity," 74.

89. "Les femmes électeurs," *Bulletin de Recherches Historiques* (1947–1958): 222.

90. *Quebec Mercury,* 14 August 1827.

91. Karin Wulf, *Not All Wives: Women of Colonial Philadelphia* (Ithaca, NY: Cornell University Press, 2000), 1.

92. Denise Robillard, "Marguerite Lacorne, conseillère de Jacques Viger," in Tardy et al., *Les bâtisseuses de la Cité,* 57–64.

93. Bettina Bradbury, "Elderly Inmates and Caregiving Sisters: Catholic Institutions for the Elderly in Nineteenth-Century Montreal," in *On the Case: Explorations in Social History,* ed. Franca Iacovetta and Wendy Mitchinson (Toronto: University of Toronto Press, 1998): Huguette Lapointe-Roy, *Charité bien ordonnée: Le premier réseau de lutte contre la pauvrété à Montréal au 19e siècle* (Montreal: Boréal, 1987).

94. On these debates see Veronica Strong-Boag, "'The Citizenship Debates': The 1885 Franchise Act," in *Contesting Canadian Citizenship: Historical Readings,* ed. Robert Adamoski, Dorothy E. Chunn, and Robert Menzies (Peterborough, Ontario: Broadview Press, 2002), 69–94.

CHAPTER 5

Business Widows in Nineteenth-Century Albany, New York, 1813–1885

SUSAN INGALLS LEWIS

*T*he figure of the woebegone widow struggling to survive—like that of the starving spinster—dominates our picture of women who lived without male support in nineteenth-century America. Indeed, this image was popularized by charity workers and reformers during the Victorian period. Journalist Helen Campbell provided a typical, if florid, description in 1887: "Through burning, scorching days of summer; through marrow-piercing cold of winter, in hunger and rags, with white faced children at their knees, crying for more bread, or, silent from long weakness, looking with blank eyes at the flying needle, these women toil on, twelve, fourteen, sixteen hours even, before the fixed task is done."[1]

Yet far from the wretched figures of Victorian fiction and reform literature, Albany's mid-nineteenth-century business widows were self-sufficient, competent, and among the most prominent female entrepreneurs in the city. Albany's widowed proprietresses included Julia Ridgway, licensed plumber to the Albany waterworks; Doretha Kirchner, owner of a thriving brewery; Grace Anderson, an enterprising ornamental confectioner; Catherine Blake, the African American proprietress of a fashionable hotel; and Hannah Pohly, owner of a dry-goods company valued at $150,000. Yet these exceptional women represent only a tiny proportion of the numerous widowed dressmakers, milliners, fancy goods dealers, boardinghouse keepers, and saloon operators who competed for position and profits in the urban marketplace of nineteenth-century Albany.[2] Indeed, widowed women plied their trades across a wide range of endeavors—many respectable, others marginal, some illicit—in order to support themselves and their families through their business acumen.

Research on Albany, the capital of New York State and a prominent American city during the mid-nineteenth century, has identified more than 2,500 individual women who owned, operated, or managed business enterprises between 1813 and 1885. (I am defining business as any venture that generated cash profits in contrast to wage work, piecework, outwork, or unpaid household labor.) In

Albany, female proprietors ranged from peddlers to manufacturers, and forms of female proprietorship varied from self-employment to formal incorporation. Linking evidence from city directories, the R. G. Dun & Co. credit records, and the manuscript census makes it possible to present an overview of the business pursuits in which widows engaged, explore the scope of their endeavors, and offer a demographic profile of widowed female proprietors based on a statistical analysis of the federal census of 1880.[3] In addition to examining the range of widows' business activities, this essay portrays widowed businesswomen in a variety of typical trades and highlights the entrepreneurial activities of a few exceptional business widows. Exploring the ways in which widows entered the business world, I argue that most were not suddenly forced to take over their husband's concerns but had instead been active in the family enterprise long before his demise. Finally, I end with a discussion of how the seemingly fixed category of widow proved more fluid than anticipated and propose that the state of widowhood might be reconceptualized.

Although the Victorian stereotype of the distressed widow lives on in popular imagination and in major works of nineteenth-century U.S. women's history, several enterprising nineteenth-century American widows have become fairly well known to women's historians and even the public.[4] For instance, Pennsylvania iron manufacturer Rebecca Lukens appeared in Caroline Bird's *Enterprising Women* (1976), reappeared twenty years later in Angel Kwolek-Folland's *Incorporating Women* (1998), and recently attained a starring role in the first national traveling exhibit on women and business in the United States (2001–2004), also titled "Enterprising Women" and organized by the Radcliffe Institute for Advanced Study's Schlesinger Library.[5] Other nineteenth-century widows whose business exploits have been featured by Bird, Kwolek-Folland, or the "Enterprising Women" project (which includes a museum exhibit, Web site, and book of the same title) include Sarah Josepha Hale, editor of *Godey's Ladies Book;* Martha Coston, who produced pyrotechnic flares for the navy; Margaret Haugherty, a cracker manufacturer who became known as the "Bread Woman of New Orleans"; Eliza Poitevent Holbrook (later Nicholson), who took over the *New Orleans Picayune* in 1875; and Miriam Follin Squier Leslie, who legally changed her name to Frank Leslie when her husband died in order to carry on their publishing empire.[6] Once identified on the national stage, these "exceptional" figures have become staples in those popular compendia of female achievements marketed to teenage girls and school libraries.

Little is known of the population of less remarkable female proprietors from which business widows like Lukens, Hale, and others emerged.[7] Despite intriguing studies in the 1980s and early 1990s demonstrating that some women were able to prosper in business, there have been no monographs focused on women's business participation in any U.S. community for any period of the nineteenth century.[8] Scholarly studies of individual female entrepreneurs (like Lydia Pinkham), important areas of female proprietorship (like millinery and dressmaking), and immigrant women active in business (like the Irish) are vital to the study of nineteenth-century businesswomen but do not precisely fill this gap.[9] And although such investigations discuss marital status, they rarely focus on widows as a category of analysis.

Without community studies of female proprietors, the most prominent historians of businesswomen have been reduced to tentative, undocumented statements about the mid-nineteenth century such as that of Kwolek-Folland: "Most women business owners were probably older married women or widows."[10] Even experts in the field lack published statistical surveys to rely on. However, research on nineteenth-century Albany demonstrates that it is not difficult to investigate the marital status of businesswomen, as well as their race, nativity, family structure, trades, and the longevity of their concerns. In fact, thousands of businesswomen can easily be identified in the most obvious sources: city directories, the federal and state censuses, and the R. G. Dun & Co. credit records.

Although today, with a population of less than 100,000, Albany is far from being a major metropolitan area, at the turn of the nineteenth century Albany was the largest inland city in the new nation, and by 1810 it was the tenth largest city in population overall. After 1825, as the eastern terminus of the Erie Canal, Albany became a vital commercial hub and transshipment point for goods traded between the Great Lakes, western New York State, New York City, and the rest of the world. The censuses of 1830 and 1840 ranked Albany as the ninth largest city in population, slightly smaller than Cincinnati but larger than Washington, D.C. Although it never rivaled the port city of New York in size or importance, Albany was linked to Manhattan through regular steamship service on the Hudson River, to Canada in the north and New England in the east through regular stages, and soon it would be linked through railroad lines in all directions as well. Although its sister city across the Hudson, Troy, became a center of manufacturing, Albany engaged primarily in commerce and politics. As in other American cities of this era, residents were self-consciously proud of Albany's prominence. Politically, it housed the government of the most populous and richest state in the union. In the realm of culture, Albany regularly hosted national lecturers such as Ralph Waldo Emerson and performers like Jenny Lind. Famous travelers, including Alexis de Tocqueville, Harriet Martineau, and Frances Trollope visited Albany on their American tours. On the eve of the Civil War, the city ranked thirteenth in population (after Louisville, but still larger than Washington, D.C.) and twenty-first in manufactures among all American cities, placing it "roughly on a par with Chicago and Pittsburgh."[11] By 1880, however, Albany had slipped to twenty-first in population (between Providence and Rochester); despite continued dramatic growth, New York State's capital never became a major industrial center, and its relative population and importance as a major urban center continued to decline through the twentieth century. Because of its size and importance during the period under study, in contrast to its minor importance today, Albany offers the nineteenth-century historian an ideal venue for examining businesswomen in the urban context—well documented at the time but investigated by few previous scholars.[12] And although other towns and cities along the route of the Erie Canal (Utica and Rochester, for example) or along the Hudson (such as Troy and Poughkeepsie) have been the subjects of community studies that focus on or at least include a discussion of women, a major study concerned with Albany during the 1800s, Brian Greenberg's *Worker and Community,* presents Albany's workforce as exclusively male.[13]

Worthy Widows

Who were Albany's business widows and under what circumstances did they enter the competitive, cutthroat world of the nineteenth-century market-place—the very sphere that Victorian ideology classified as a male province, in contrast with the protected, dependent feminine sphere of home and hearth? Albany's mid-nineteenth-century widowed proprietresses can be divided into three categories. In the first are women who started their business career after they were left widowed, often with a family to support; these individuals usually selected a trade within the "traditional" female sphere, such as dressmaking or millinery. In the second are widows who continued to work at their own preexisting business after the death of their spouse, and most of these concerns were in the female sphere as well. Finally, in the third are a significant number of women who continued to operate a family business after their husband's death. Although these enterprises were usually located in trades associated with both male and female proprietors, such as baking, confectionery, hotel and saloon keeping, or dry and fancy goods sales, some widows took over family businesses far removed from the female sphere. For instance, Albany's business widows included dealers in cigars and retail liquor, two undertakers, a blacksmith, and the owners of a livery stable. One characteristic of widows in all three groups, however, was that they were almost universally judged, by R. G. Dun & Co. credit examiners, to be respectable and "worthy" in terms of character, although often not worthy of credit.

Let us consider a widow from the first category, one who was left to make her way alone after the death of her husband. A good example of such a propri-etress is Mrs. Julia Donn, who in 1858 was widowed at the age of twenty-eight, with no estate and a boy of four. Beginning her millinery business in a "sm[all] estab[lishment] in an out of the way place," she had by 1860 joined forces with Isabella Crew, a single woman and corset maker, sharing both her home and her shop with Crew and her sister Sarah (who presumably kept house for the rest). Ac-cording to credit reports, the "very worthy and prudent" Donn and the "hon[est] & industrious" Crew never made "m[u]ch above a living," despite more than twenty years in business; at the time their credit records end, in 1881, they each appear to have been "worth" less than a thousand dollars.[14] Still, Donn had supported herself, arranged an informal partnership, provided commodities and services, and raised her son to a productive adulthood as a bookbinder; Crew had done the same while supporting her sister, and both women continued to be listed in city directories until the late 1890s. Businesswomen like Julia Donn and Isabella Crew failed to amass handsome profits or to build up their businesses significantly. Yet in light of the difficulties facing these women and others like them—limited capi-tal and credit, for instance, as well as lively competition—it is remarkable how many (more than 40 percent of all widows active in their trades between 1875 and 1885) managed to survive in business for ten years or more.

An example of the second type of business widow, one who was active in business while married and remained in the trade after her husband's death, would be Irish-born grocer Margaret Clear. According to the credit entry of 1873, Clear was doing a "very small business" running a grocery and saloon, while her husband William worked as a moulder. No matter how small her enterprise (in 1878 her stock was estimated at $100), with a son Patrick born in 1872, a second son William in 1874, and a daughter Mary in 1876, Clear must have had her hands full. At some point after 1878, William died, and Margaret was left a widow in her late twenties with three young children. The census enumerators of 1880 recorded a household consisting of Clear herself, her children, her mother (aged sixty), two uncles, and one male boarder. In 1882, her last city directory listing identifies Mrs. Margaret Clear as the proprietor of a "Refreshment Saloon"; her final credit entry of the same year states: "Good for 00/C.O.D," after which she is lost to history. Previous credit reports such as "D[oin]g small bus[iness] & cr[edit] limited" (1874), "sell for cash" (1876), "Not m[a]k[in]g anything over a living. Cash only here" (1878), and "there are sev[era]l judg[men]ts vs her & there is a suit now pending in which she is the def[e]n[dan]t . . . she is not regarded as wor[thy] of cr[edit] & is sold COD" give a sense of how marginal Clear's venture remained through its decade-long existence. The reports also echo the flavor of entries concerning numerous other widows with small businesses as they struggled before and after their husbands' deaths to make ends meet.[15]

A third type of widow entered business by taking over a preexisting family venture. Instead of conceptualizing widows as "stepping into" a husband's shoes, let us view of them as "stepping up" into the light of the historical record. Unlike Rebecca Lukens, the Pennsylvania iron manufacturer, most such widows were not newcomers to the business world, bravely shouldering new burdens. Research in credit records reveals that numerous women in Albany were active in family-run businesses before their husbands' deaths.[16] The death of male spouses, by removing the official, male name under which a company had been operating, simply exposes to the light of history the contributions their wives had been making all along. Indeed, I propose that the very fact that a wife continued in "her husband's" business suggests that she was familiar with that business already. For example, Rosa Orthelier was a "smart" entrepreneur who had been a forewoman at a large fancy goods store before her marriage to peddler Daniel Orthelier in the late 1860s. During his lifetime she was described as the manager of their dry goods and millinery shop, and at the time of his death in 1874, credit examiners reported: "wife manages the bus[iness] well. She is intelligent &c. Think the bus[iness] will prosper in her hands."[17] Numerous other widows in Albany (including confectioners, bakers, grocers, dry goods dealers, and cigar makers) were said by the credit reports be "continuing" the business after their husbands' deaths.

These stories provide a glimpse into the careers of three representative business widows, but what can be said about the group as a whole? In fact, early city directories and the 1880 federal manuscript census for Albany confirm previous assumptions—like that of Kwolek-Folland quoted earlier—that the majority of female proprietors were middle-aged women, particularly widows.[18] At the beginning of the period covered by this study, Albany's first city directory, of 1813, listed 39 women engaged in occupations that fit my definition of businesses, 56 percent of whom (22) were clearly identified as widows.[19] At the end of the period, the 1880 federal manuscript census reveals that the largest portion—40 percent—of Albany's female proprietors were widowed, whereas about one-third were married and approximately one-quarter were single.[20] The prevalence of widows (and married women) in this population reflects the way that a tiny, home-based enterprise could mesh with a woman's responsibilities at home, as a housekeeper and mother. Single women, who could go out to work, had more choices of employment in nineteenth-century cities like Albany. Although a few of the city's most prominent business widows maintained separate living and commercial establishments, the vast majority lived and worked in the same dwelling.

A statistical analysis of female proprietors identified in the census of 1880 shows that widowed proprietresses were older than other businesswomen and significantly more mature than most other nineteenth-century working women. The average widowed proprietress entered business around age forty-five (about seven years older than the average age for all of Albany's female proprietors) and left business at age fifty-one (about three years younger than average).[21] Again, these findings confirm previous suppositions, such as Kwolek-Folland's educated guess that female proprietors were "probably older married women or widows," and suggest that entering business was related to marital status and life cycle in much the same way that going out to work was associated with an earlier stage in working women's lives.

As with female-run enterprises as a whole, businesses run by widows clustered in relatively few trades, those associated with the housewifely skills of homemaking, sewing, and providing food or liquid refreshment. Typically, widows in nineteenth-century Albany operated boardinghouses and hotels, dressmaking and millinery establishments, as well as saloons, bakeries, breweries, confectioneries, and small groceries that usually sold liquor. According to the city directory of 1813, the business widows of 1813 were primarily grocers (40 percent) or boardinghouse or innkeepers (40 percent).[22] In 1880, the most common business for a widowed proprietress in Albany was a small grocery store (almost 25 percent ran groceries), followed by boardinghouses (about 20 percent of widowed business owners took in boarders), then saloons (about 12 percent), and finally dressmaking establishments (approximately 10 percent). Grouping business occupations into the broad categories of needlework and clothing trades, boardinghouses and hotels, the provision of food and drink (in groceries, saloons, and restaurants), and storekeeping (as in fancy and dry goods stores) demonstrates dramatic differences between the trades of female proprietors based on marital status. For example, more than 70 percent of single businesswomen were in the clothing and needlework trades, as compared with less than 15 percent of widows, whereas about 46 percent of widows were providers of food and drink, as compared with only 10 percent of single women.

It is impossible to determine place of birth for business widows from the city directory of 1813, but one might assume that most were native born or immigrants from the British Isles. Names such as Lydia Anderson, Martha Brown, Penelope Denny, Catharine Field, Elizabeth Hawley, and Anna Wood suggest British extraction; only one business widow of 1813—Rebecca Van Yorx—had a Dutch name. By 1880, however, the majority of widowed businesswomen in Albany, more than 65 percent, were foreign-born.[23] Approximately 40 percent of all widowed proprietresses had been born in Ireland, 19 percent in German states, and about 5 percent in the British Isles, with other countries representing only 2 percent of the total. Under 35 percent had been born in the United States, with the vast majority of those—more than 85 percent—born in New York State. Few of the widows in business had been born in North America outside of New York, and in fact it was far more likely for a business widow to have been born in Bavaria or Prussia than in New England or Canada.[24] Widows were far more likely than single businesswomen to be foreign-born; almost 68 percent of single proprietresses had been born in the United States, as compared with the less than 35 percent of widows who were native born. Almost twice as many business widows as single businesswomen had been born in Ireland (almost 40 percent versus 22 percent, respectively), whereas widowed proprietresses were more than nine times as likely to have been born in Germany as single businesswomen (19 percent versus 2 percent, respectively).

How might one explain the dramatic differences between single and widowed businesswomen in terms of trade and nativity? The evidence for 1880 suggests that it was far more acceptable for immigrant widows to enter business than it was for the native born. And considering that these businesses were often home based and either served or sold liquor, it seems that immigrant widows had fewer scruples about violating the domestic sphere with a mixed-gender clientele or by selling alcohol. One might go further and suggest that immigrant widows did not subscribe to the ideology of separate spheres or the American middle-class morality based on temperance.[25] Immigrant families headed by widows clearly used female-run businesses both to sustain women and children without adult male economic support and to supplement wages earned by sons as they became employable.

When native-born widows did enter business, they were far more likely to become dressmakers or boardinghouse keepers than were Irish and German women. Twenty-seven percent of native-born widowed proprietresses were in the needlework and clothing trades, while 38 percent operated boardinghouses or hotels. In comparison, only 3 percent of Irish business widows opened needlework or clothing establishments, and a mere 2 percent of German widows offered room or board to their customers. Meanwhile, 65 percent of Irish widows, 49 percent of German widows, and 42 percent of British sold food and drink, in contrast to 26 percent of native-born widows who went into business. German widows were most likely to be storekeepers (about 30 percent), whereas only 7 percent of native-born widows opened shops.

Scholars of nineteenth-century businesswomen and of small business overall have generally assumed that such ventures did not last long. For example, in his survey of small business in American history, Mansel Blackford estimates that "relatively few" small endeavors lasted more than five years. Similarly, Kwolek-Folland concludes that between 1830 and 1880, "in general, women's individual businesses continued to be short-lived."[26] As I have argued elsewhere, however, even a business lasting five years or less compares favorably to the length of women's careers in many fields during the nineteenth century. For example, Thomas Dublin has measured the average length of employment for mill workers in Lowell at 2.7 years and for domestic servants in Boston as 4.8 years.[27] That business may actually have provided longer employment than other female occupations is indicated by Wendy Gamber's finding that the average millinery establishment in Boston lasted about six years.[28]

In fact, it appears that business widows in Albany enjoyed careers significantly longer than those of mill workers, domestic servants, or even milliners in Boston. As far as can be determined by records linkage, the widowed women located in the 1880 census remained in business an average of eleven years, with eight years as the median longevity of their enterprises. In comparison to single and married proprietresses in Albany, widows were less likely to be in business for a very short time: whereas 21 percent of single women operated for a year or less, as did 18 percent of married women, only 8 percent of widows closed shop within a year. These data may reflect the fact that many widows who appear to have entered business on the death of their husbands were actually continuing established family concerns, in contrast to single women who were just starting out. However, widows—probably because they entered business at a later age—were also less likely to carry on their ventures for more than twenty years: 21 percent of single women were in business for twenty years or more, as compared with 20 percent of married women but only 17 percent of widows.

Evidence from the 1880 census also allows us to consider the living situations of widows within families and households. In nineteenth-century Albany, as in other cities in the United States and industrializing Europe, working-class families depended on the labor of multiple family members.[29] This pattern is evident in most of the families of Albany's female proprietors. Whatever their marital status, the majority of businesswomen operated within working families—that is, they lived with husbands, parents, siblings, or children who were also employed. The vast majority of widowed businesswomen lived in households with other members of their own families. In 1880, only 7 percent of business widows lived alone, in single-person households, and just 13 percent boarded in households without another family member (as compared to the 24 percent of single women who boarded in households without family members, and the 6 percent of unmarried women who lived alone). The average family size for Albany's widowed proprietresses was four, and the average household size five individuals. Most lived with their children, most had one or more adult child at home, and in fact more than half lived with at least one working son. It was much less likely for daughters to be recorded as working (only 13 percent were), yet it is important to remember that adult daughters living at home would have contributed to the family economy by both working in the home-based family business and assisting their mother with housework and, if necessary, child care. Clearly, Albany's business widows were enmeshed in family networks where they supported—and in turn were supported by—their relatives. Such networks assisted in both the economic survival of the family and, one assumes, the emotional support of the widowed mother.

If we transform these average statistics into individual female proprietors, what do we find? As we have seen, operating a grocery was the most common trade for Albany's business widows. A typical female grocer can be represented by Julia Shields, an Irish-born widow whose business was evaluated by credit examiners as "small" and not paying "anything over a living" in 1882, when her stock was estimated to be worth less than $200. Shields operated her grocery from 1878 to 1882, according to credit records, although she was not listed in city directories. In the 1880 census she was recorded, at age fifty, as living with four children: one fourteen-year-old son who worked in a brickyard and three younger children, aged nine to eleven, who were still in school. Shields was typical in that she was Irish born, was running a very small concern, was living with four children, including one employed son, and was considered a bad credit risk by the R. G. Dun & Co. examiners, who suggested that she should pay COD.[30]

In addition to considering the average or typical characteristics of Albany's nineteenth-century business widows, let us consider variations among widowed female proprietors in mid-nineteenth-century Albany. Statistics show that their total years in business ranged from less than one to forty-eight years. The youngest had entered business at age twenty-one; the oldest was still in business at age eighty-seven. Although most were clustered in traditionally female trades, as previously discussed, a few widows also ran drugstores, news depots, or bookstores. One widow became a coal dealer, another the operator of a cooperage, a third the proprietor of a fleet of express wagons, and a fourth the principal owner of a company that manufactured saws.

Widows ranged from the wealthiest and most successful of Albany's businesswomen to the poorest and most marginalized. It is difficult to determine the correspondence between monetary values of nineteenth-century dollars and those of today. Using the value of women's labor as one's standard results in a multiple close to one hundred. In Albany, the average wage for a working woman in 1860 appears to have been between $3.00 and $3.50 per week.[31] Virginia Penny—who investigated women's wages and working conditions in the mid-nineteenth century—reported in 1863 that average wages for "a girl, at most mechanical employments" was $3 for sixty hours of work per week, the equivalent of five cents an hour.[32] Indeed, according to Penny, "one clothier in Albany, New York, pays $3 a week to his hands working eleven hours a day."[33] Whatever factor one selects, it is important to conceive of the worth of mid-nineteenth-century businesswomen's endeavors as the equivalent of many times more than the amounts reported below.

Peddlers who plied their trade on the street without benefit of a store, or even a stand, were obviously the most humble of Albany's self-employed businesswomen. With minimal stock, tiny capital outlay, and no rent to pay, these women were recorded in the census but not in city directories or the credit ledgers.

Similarly, women who ran small candy shops were far more likely to be identified by the census than the directories and were never evaluated for credit. Widows predominated in both of these areas—69 percent of hucksters and 85 percent of women who ran small candy shops were listed as widows in the census.[34] Some widowed proprietresses of small groceries also had small reserves, as with illiterate Irish-born grocer Alice Cassidy, who supported herself and three children aged six, three, and one in 1860; their total family worth was estimated at $250. At the low end of the scale, dozens of widowed grocers, saloon keepers, fancy goods dealers, variety store owners, dressmakers, and milliners struggled to make a living for themselves and their families. One specific example was Mrs. Philip Stein, a widow who was said to offer "a few vegetables and fruits" in the same room as "a bar" in 1870.[35]

Although many widowed businesswomen like Cassidy and Stein were left without substantial "means," few were entirely destitute. Indeed, most female proprietors had to have some capital at their disposal in order to enter a business enterprise at all, and in many cases widows inherited their husbands' "entire" estates. Such estates might amount to $1,000 (or less) in real estate and personal property, but they could range far higher.[36] At the lower end of the scale, Mary Conroy inherited "by will the entire estate" of her husband Charles in 1878, including his saloon: "the prem[ise]s worth $3[000]—ho[use] & lot $3[000]—m[or]tg[ag]e $8[00]."[37] Receiving substantially more was Magdalene Hoffman, who inherited "all" that her husband Philip, a grocer, had left in 1878, estimated to be worth in the $10,000 range.[38] Four years later, the brewing business of Jacob Kirchner and Co., "est[imate]d worth $40[000] or $50[000] independent of the Real Estate," was left entirely to his widow Doretha.[39] Kirchner carried on and improved her business with the assistance of her sons. Although in this case the sons Jacob and Augustus, described as "practical experienced men," took responsibility for managing the brewery, it was under her authority that brewing facilities were "improved" and production increased. The fact that her husband chose to leave this considerable estate to his wife rather than grown sons suggests that he himself trusted her entrepreneurial abilities.[40] What is notable in all three of these cases is that the widows did not unload the property or merely transfer ownership to male relatives (although Kirchner was assisted by her sons, and Hoffman lived with a son—a bookkeeper—old enough to run the business). Instead, all three women—two of whom could clearly have afforded to step out of the marketplace—continued to do business in their own names for years. Indeed, both Hoffman and Kirchner carried on their enterprises for more than a decade, demonstrating that some widows made a deliberate choice to remain active in the marketplace.

The Mighty Widows

A series of remarkable "mighty widows" stand out as most noteworthy among the larger population of unexceptional businesswomen in Albany. In chronological order, we look at the life stories and business careers of widows who were unusually successful and entrepreneurial, proving that such women

could attain both status and wealth. Interestingly, none of these women operated in the typical trades discussed previously: none were grocers, boardinghouse keepers, or dressmakers; none ran saloons or fancy goods stores. These
exceptionally successful widows took over trades associated with the male rather
than female sphere, or at least trades in which men as well as women were often
proprietors, such as confectionery shops. This fact suggests that one could make
considerably more money in a male-associated business than in an enterprise associated with the female sphere—not surprising, since nineteenth-century wages
followed the same pattern.

My first example, confectioner Grace Anderson, took great care to promote
her wares and skills. The widow of confectioner Charles Anderson, who appears
to have died after 1841, Grace described herself in the Albany city directory of
1844–45 as an "Ornamental Confectioner" whose creations included "Pastry, Jel-
lies, Charlotte Russe, Creams, &c., served up daily," as well as "Wedding Cakes,
Ornamental And Plain, Ornamental Pyramids, &c., & every requisite for par-
ties."[41] Ten years later, in 1854, Anderson's advertisement described her "EATING
ROOMS, Cake Bakery, &c. &c." as being located "within one minute's walk of the
different Rail Road Depots" and offering "a large assortment of Cakes and Pastry. Oysters in every style. Together with a large assortment of Confectionery, Ice
Creams & Soda Water, manufactured daily on the premises."[42] Evidence provided
by these advertisements also reveals that Grace Anderson changed her business
with the times and responded to market demand in that she added oysters to her
bakery and ice cream saloon. That Anderson's attitude was unusually entrepreneurial is confirmed by credit reports from 1849 to 1857, which describe her as
"enterprising," "v[er]y smart," "act[ive]," and "making money."[43]

The widowed proprietress involved in the most unlikely trade in nineteenth-
century Albany was Julia Ridgway, plumbing entrepreneur. Ridgway's career illustrates how a business widow of exceptional drive and vision could move to the top,
even in a trade one might have assumed to be closed to women. When her husband
Frederick died in 1851, the twenty-six-year-old English-born Ridgway assumed
control of the plumbing concern. She regularly advertised her business—the New
York State Plumbing Establishment, later Ridgway and Company, later Ridgway
and Russ—in Albany's city directories, describing herself as "Proprietress" and
"Licensed Plumber to the Albany Water Works."[44] Ridgway's early ads featured
her own name in bold print plus a line drawing of plumbing fixtures, including a
bathtub and toilet (confounding our notions about Victorian propriety). According
to credit records, Ridgway provided most of the capital for the company and kept
the books, while she took on two partners who provided "the practical part of the
concern." That is, unlike the most successful milliner or dressmaker, Ridgway
was not an artisan carrying out her trade—she was clearly the owner-manager
of a large enterprise. She was also the mother of a four-year-old daughter at the
time she commenced business in her own name. By 1865, Ridgway was "doing
the best bus[iness] of any firm or man in the line in Albany undoubtedly making
money," with a business worth estimated at $10,000—about three times the worth
of the business her husband had left at his death. The "well managed" business

NEW YORK STATE
PLUMBING ESTABLISHMENT,
Nos. 115 & 117 State street, Albany.

The Subscriber, Proprietress and Licensed Plumber to the Albany Water Works, would respectfully inform her patrons and the public, that she still continues to carry on the Plumbing business in all its branches, as heretofore, by F. W. Ridgway, deceased.

This Establishment is one of the largest in the State, and is well known throughout the country as one of the leading establishments in the Plumbing business.

The following articles manufactured and constantly for sale at this Establishment: Hatters' Kettles, Iron, Copper and Brass Pumps, Bathing Apparatus, Water Closets, Kitchen Ranges, Copper Boilers, Stationary Fire Engines for Factories, Deep Well Pumps, Hydraulic Rams, Lead, Copper and Iron Pipes, Sheet Lead, Brass Cocks, Valves, Couplings, Leather Hose, and all other articles appertaining to the business.

The trade supplied with all or any of the above named articles at New York prices. Orders executed in any part of the United States by competent workmen.

Persons desiring the insertion of Water Pipes into their dwellings, will find it to their advantage to call and ascertain our prices, and examine the method of inserting the pipes, &c.

JULIA RIDGWAY.

Agent for Pierce's Kitchen Ranges, Chilson and Richardson's Metropolitan Hot Air and Cooking Range; also Stebbins' patent Compression Cocks, which will be supplied to the trade at the manufacturer's prices.

38

FIGURE 5.1 Advertisement for Julia Ridgway's plumbing business in the Albany city directory of 1853–1854. Courtesy of the M. E. Grenander Department of Special Collections and Archives, University at Albany, SUNY.

continued to make money, providing Ridgway with funds to invest in real estate as well. Although one partner retired in 1871—surely providing a natural opportunity for her own retirement after twenty years in business—Ridgway chose instead to reorganize her partnership, continuing to oversee and "attend closely" to the business. By then the estimated worth of the firm had grown to $20,000.[45] An advertisement of the late 1870s reads (in part):

> Ridgway & Russ, Plumbers and Hydraulic Engineers, Wholesale Dealers in Plumbers' Materials, Agents for Mott's St. George Elevated Oven Range ... Hydraulic Rams and Deep Well Pumps for Farmers.... Plumbing done in any part of the country and warranted.[46]

Clearly, twenty-five successful years in business had not diminished Julia Ridgway's ambition, self-promotion, appetite for expansion, or willingness to become involved in new ventures. About ten years later, in 1889, Ridgway and

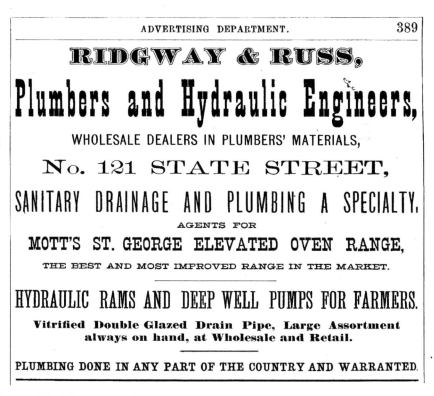

FIGURE 5.2 Advertisement for Ridgway and Russ in the Albany city directory of 1878. Courtesy of the M. E. Grenander Department of Special Collections and Archives, University at Albany, SUNY.

Russ had added a telephone number to their advertisement, as well as a line announcing

> TELEPHONE COMMUNICATIONS to all parts of the city; and we are prepared to furnish a Plumber at any time during the Day or Night, or on Sunday.[47]

The most powerful business widow in Albany, measured in terms of capital, was German-born Hannah Pohly, the widow of Nathan Pohly, a Jewish dry goods dealer who had been described by credit examiners as "a close cautious man" with an estate worth $75,000 to $100,000. On her husband's death in 1872, Hannah was thirty-four years old with five children ranging in age from two to fourteen. The credit records noted that "the probabilities are that the widow will take a partner who underst[an]ds the trade & continue." Forming Pohly and Co., Hannah took her husband's former bookkeeper Joseph Friedman as a partner, lending him most of the capital for his share and offering "1/3 of the profits." Although the credit examiners feared that "there is not the same energy & keen judgm[en]t ab[ou]t the present conc[ern] as there was when 'P' was at its head," they were satisfied that the firm—with stock worth $40,000 to $50,000—was creditworthy. According to the credit ledgers, Pohly, unlike Ridgway, did not "interfere much with the bus[iness]," but by 1875 Pohly and Co.—now described as jobbers in cloth (and described in city directories as dealers in "cloths and cassimeres")—maintained an "excellent standing." Two years later the credit records note that "Mrs. P." had $30,000 in investments outside the business plus a residence that she owned "free and clear." By 1879, the business of Pohly and Co., now described as wholesale clothiers, was estimated to be worth $125,000 "safely"; by 1881, Joseph Friedman was identified as Pohly's son-in-law, and the business—with a working capital of $85,000—was doing a trade of about $225,000 a year. In 1883, credit records note that the firm stood well "with the manufacturers & Jobbers of Cloths both in the home & foreign markets"; in the final entry of 1884, credit examiners added that "their capital has been increased from accumulations of profits," "that they are buying largely for cash," and that "they appear to be in easy circumstances." Easy indeed! Hannah Pohly's shrewd decision to invest in a junior partner and stay in trade after her husband's death had been a wise business move, as well as a wise move for her family. Not only had Friedman become a son-in-law, but Pohly's own growing sons were left with a business to inherit.

A final example of an exceptionally mighty widowed entrepreneur is Catharine Blake. Unlike Julia Ridgway, Mrs. Blake was widowed relatively late in her marriage. Thus, her name does not appear in the business records until 1881, although her husband had been operating a hotel (presumably with, at the very least, her assistance) since 1868. In that year Adam Blake, described by R. G. Dun & Co. credit reports as "a gentleman of color," was set up in business by "subscription of citizens." Congress Hall, his hotel, was largely patronized by members of the New York State legislature. The hotel appears to have experienced a shaky beginning, with start-up debts to be paid and a slack summer season when the legislature was out of session. Blake's stock speculations also had a negative impact on the business's cash flow and ability to meet its obligations. By 1878, however, the Blakes could afford to lease a newly constructed hotel, the Kenmore, at an annual rent of $6,000, and at one point they attempted to lease and run a resort at Sand Lake as well. It is hard to determine how much responsibility each party had for the running of these hotels, but Adam Blake was noted for "intemperate" habits and "indulging freely." Credit records indicate that after her husband's death, Catharine Blake originally intended to dispose of the business, as long as she could do it "to advantage." An offer of $50,000, however, did not suit her, and under her sole management the concern prospered even more than it had before. According to an R. G. Dun & Co. entry of 1882:

> She made money last year & there is every reason to believe she will have done equally well this year, provided she does not sell out. There is now being an effort made by C. E. Leland of the Delevan House [a rival hotel] to buy her out & some think he will succeed. She has been offered $50,000 for the bus[iness] & furn[iture] in the Hotel, but asks $75(000) and will prob[ably] get that or 00.[48]

Presumably Catharine Blake was not satisfied with the offer she received, since she was listed as the proprietress of the Kenmore Hotel in city directories until 1887, some six years after her husband's death.

Reconceptualizing Widows

In conclusion, I propose that we reconsider, reconceptualize, and complicate the seemingly fixed category of "widow." The very definition of widow can be questioned, since it is unclear whether all women identified as such in the census or city directory were actually widowed or perhaps simply deserted by their spouses or actually unmarried mothers who called themselves widows. For example, the census of 1880 recorded sixteen businesswomen as married but living without a spouse present in their households. We cannot know whether their husbands were away briefly or had deserted them permanently, but women such as boardinghouse keeper Elizabeth Bronk and grocer Jane Collins may have been widows in all but name. The 1880 census also identifies seven female proprietors, with children aged a year old or younger, as widows. Although it is possible that their husbands had died recently, it is also possible that some unmarried mothers may have called themselves widows. In particular, it seems likely that dressmaker Rosa Stoliker—living with her mother, sister, and children aged four and less than a year old—had been widowed shortly before or after the birth of her youngest child; it is equally possible that candy dealer Kate McGowen—boarding with nonrelatives and herself the mother of a year-old baby—might never have been married at all.[49]

An interesting example of how the categories of married and widowed are more difficult to determine than one might expect arises in the R. G. Dun & Co. credit records for "a notorious woman named Elizabeth Dayton," who owned a hotel at the time of her remarriage to William Burnett in 1857. According to reports, "the old widow 'Dayton'" had a reputation "bad eno[ugh]h to sink" her new husband, adding that her "first husband is s[ai]d still to exist." This intriguing aside reminds us that just because a businesswoman described herself or was known as a widow does not necessarily prove that she had actually been married or that her husband was really dead. Such doubts undercut the absolute validity of statistical analysis and remind us that it is difficult to force real people into neat, fixed categories.

On its face, the term "widow" simply refers to a woman whose husband has died; once she has remarried, a woman is no longer a widow. But in some cases in Albany, it appears that widows remarried yet held onto the business identities they had established as widows—as in the case of Elizabeth Dayton Burnett. For example, Dayton was a "notorious" widow (according to the credit records) before remarrying Burnett, and her previous character carried through into the business she ran with her new husband—described as "a low crib" housing "the worst kind of depraved women" in 1865.[50] Or consider Rebecca Rhino, listed as a merchant in the first city directory of 1813. According to Joel Munsell, one of Albany's first amateur historians, the prosperous widow Rhino remarried an irresponsible and eccentric Englishman, Samuel T. Penny. When her second husband began to "squander" her resources, Rhino went to Vermont to establish residency specifically to obtain a divorce. Returning to Albany as an independent individual, she resumed her previous name, opened "quite a large dry goods store," and "transacted an extensive business, while Penny kept a store a few doors above in the same street." In 1858, Munsell commented that "many of our oldest citizens will remember Mrs. Rhino's Cheap Store, and the crowds of customers she attracted thither," whereas Penny became an impoverished and slightly insane umbrella repairman.[51] This business widow clung to her identity as "Mrs. Rhino," the successful merchant, valuing that role so far above her second marriage that she was willing to move to another state to obtain a divorce.

Another interesting case of the 1870s is that of the widowed baker Elizabeth Herzog, who, even after she married dry goods dealer Joseph Belser, carried on the bakery business "in her own name & independent of that of her husband," according to credit reports.[52] Herzog even lived separately from Belser and his children while, with her own children, she operated the business she had inherited from her first husband.

Finally, let me stitch together the story of the widowed-but-remarried Elizabeth McDuffie. Credit records make clear that as the widow Leddy, Elizabeth had established herself as the operator of a dyeing and scouring establishment before her second marriage in the late 1850s. Born in Scotland, McDuffie carried on the business of her first husband (P. Leddy) while married to her second, a former police captain turned stove and hardware dealer; indeed, they ran their establishments separately. She herself was praised by credit examiners as "d[oin]g a g[oo]d bus[iness] making money" and was said to have "furnished" her second husband with the money to go into business for himself. Meanwhile, John McDuffie was criticized for knowing "nothing of the bus[iness]" he had entered and not giving it proper attention. By 1863, in fact, he was said to be "of no a[ccount]," although she was estimated to be worth some $20,000 when she sold out the following year.[53]

More than a decade later Elizabeth McDuffie returned to Albany, having (according to the credit examiners) lost money in the lumber business in Sullivan County. Her advertisement in the city directory of 1880 presented her background, experience, and skills in impressive detail:

ALWAYS DYEING & YET LIVING!
MRS. JOHN MCDUFFIE
NEW DYEING AND SCOURING ESTABLISHMENT,
37 BEAVER STREET, Formerly of Norton Street.

Mrs. McDuffie would respectfully inform her old and new patrons, that she has resumed her old business of Dyeing and Scouring in all its various branches. And she was the first one in 1855 in this city that applied STEAM to DYEING and FINISHING, therefore has made that business a SPECIALTY. Ladies' Silk Dresses Cleaned Entire without Ripping, also Lace Curtains, Shawls, Blankets, &c., cleaned in first-class style.

PRINCIPAL OFFICE, 37 Beaver Street
BRANCH OFFICE, No. 5 CLINTON AVENUE[54]

It appears that such advertising did not overstate her expertise, since McDuffie remained in business until 1895, when she would have been sixty-nine years old. Thus, although she had been widowed before the age of twenty-nine, Elizabeth Leddy McDuffie retained her commercial identity as a business widow through her second marriage and approximately forty years in trade.[55]

Was it widowhood that gave these women their autonomy and commitment to business careers? Or was it their original marriage–business partnerships that carried them from marriage through widowhood and into remarriage in the same trades? Were widows an exceptionally successful portion of Albany's population of nineteenth-century businesswomen? The answer is yes, but with several caveats. As we have seen, widows—ranging from plumbers to peddlers, from cloth merchants to candy shop owners—made up both the wealthiest and poorest, the most and least prominent, the most independent and the most marginal of female proprietors. Second, it is difficult to determine how "mighty" these widows may have been within their marriages, before the death of their husbands. In arguing that business widows were not woebegone, I believe it is important to keep in mind that these women might well have been equally effective as business wives. That is, although some remarkable entrepreneurs like Julia Ridgway clearly built up the businesses left to them beyond what was expected of them by the business community, it is impossible to know what role others, like Catherine Blake, played while their husbands were still alive. That is, was Blake the widow really more "mighty" than Blake the wife? Similarly, how can we judge whether—say, in the case of Hannah Pohly, dealer in cloth and cassimere—their spouses might have been even more successful in increasing their business empires?

Evidence for this assumption can be found in the story of Clara and Frank Martineau, successful dealers in gloves, hosiery, fancy goods, and trimmings from the 1860s through the 1880s. According to the credit ledgers, Frank was a barber who sold out to enter retail trade with his wife, although it was unclear (even to the credit examiners) whether the business was in her name or his. In either case, Clara—then in her twenties—appears to have been the active member of the family venture.[56] An entry for 1867 read, "Frank C. Martineau owns the conc[ern] but is most of the time in NY & his wife manages the bus[iness] in his absence." In 1868, the examiners noted, "she is the bus[iness] man smart first rate saleswoman & understands the bus[iness]." By 1873, Martineau was "doing splendid trade"; in 1874, Frank was said "to do the best bus[iness] in the city in his line"; in 1875 the business was said to be worth at least $20,000; in 1876 he introduced a "Patent Glove Powder"; in 1877 he "enlarged his store"; while in 1878 he was said to be "running two stores." From 1874 to 1879, in fact, the credit records make no mention of Clara, and one might assume that she had retired from business. However, an entry of 1880 makes it clear that this had not been the case. In answer to the query Was "anything wrong?" the entry explains that "his wife who has attended to his financial affairs for some time, has for several months past been unable to assist him owing to illness & it may be in consequence some bills have not rec'd proper attention." By 1882, Frank's affairs appeared to be on somewhat shakier footing, since "the bus[iness] suffers from the loss of his late wife's attention." His reputation in the trade began to suffer, he was accused of bad habits, and he eventually moved to reduce his overhead. Because Clara died before Frank and never became a widow, we never see what she could have done with the business on her own—yet the records reveal that their business suffered without her attention.[57]

Women's historians have sometimes assumed that married women had only a limited ability to engage in business.[58] If this were true, then widows would have enjoyed a unique legal opportunity to become proprietors. In Albany, however, married women did pursue business careers as demonstrated by listings in the city directories or census, and by entries in credit records that reveal wives running family enterprises alongside or in the place of otherwise employed husbands. Although, on the basis of the historical record, the legal independence and autonomy of widows are far clearer than those of wives, it is perfectly possible that business wives operated successfully within the confines of marriage and either enjoyed what was in effect a partnership with their husbands, or in fact were operating businesses independently without assistance or interference from their spouses. In that case, the loss of a husband may not in fact have added to the widows "might" but may have left her with burdens that presented obstacles to be overcome rather than new opportunities to be enjoyed. Unlike marriage, divorce, or remarriage, widowhood was an accident, not a conscious choice. The fact that hundreds of widows were able to survive, and dozens even triumph in business despite the death of their spouses should not blind us to the fact that at least some of these might have gladly traded their new autonomy for their old interdependence. The remarriage of ambitious widows like Rebecca

Rhino, Elizabeth Herzog, and Elizabeth McDuffie—despite successful business careers—suggests such a possibility. Without further research, we cannot be sure to what extent business widows represent a true contrast to business wives, and to what extent they represent more of a continuous career story.

Luckily, the history of nineteenth-century businesswomen, including widows, is so understudied that literally tens of thousands of cases across the United States remain to be identified, linked, and analyzed.[59] Although this rich vein of material will provide only part of the story of mighty widows across the centuries, their individual stories will both complete and complicate the narrative of business widows from medieval times to the present, across continents and cultures. Around the world today, we see micro-entrepreneurship and micro-credit promoted as ways for widows to achieve self-sufficiency and independence for themselves and their families.[60] I believe that the evidence from industrializing cities like Albany will illuminate the importance of very small business in transforming many widows from woebegone to worthy, and a few from mournful to mighty.

Notes

1. Helen Campbell, *Prisoners of Poverty: Women Wage Workers, Their Trades and Their Lives* (New York: Garret Press, 1970), 31.
2. This essay represents a new approach to the research undertaken for my dissertation, "Women in the Marketplace: Female Entrepreneurship, Business Patterns, and Working Families in Albany, New York, 1830–1885" (PhD diss., Binghamton University, NY, 2002), which did not include a thorough analysis of differences based on marital status. My published articles include Susan Ingalls Lewis, "Female Entrepreneurs in Albany: 1840–1885," *Business and Economic History* 21, 2nd ser. (1992); "Beyond Horatia Alger: Breaking through Gendered Assumptions about Business 'Success' in Mid-Nineteenth-Century America," *Business and Economic History* 24, no. 1 (Fall 1995); "Businesswomen in the Land of Opportunity: Immigrant Proprietresses in Albany, New York, 1880," *Hudson Valley Regional Review* (Fall 1997); and "Business or Labor? Blurred Boundaries in the Careers of Self-Employed Needleworkers in Mid-Nineteenth-Century Albany," in *Famine and Fashion, Needlewomen in the Nineteenth Century,* ed. Beth Harris (Burlington, VT: Ashgate, 2006).
3. The number 2,500 is a conservative estimate; linking evidence from city directories, the federal census of 1880, and the R. G. Dun & Co. credit records, I have identified 1,500 women who operated businesses in Albany during the decade 1875–1885 alone. According to city directories, 32 women operated businesses in Albany in 1813, 60 in 1830–1831, 132 in 1841, 84 in 1850, 201 in 1860, 260 in 1870, 351 in 1875, 409 in 1880, and 495 in 1885. In addition, I located 774 entries for individual women in the credit ledgers for the city of Albany, housed in the R. G. Dun & Company Collection at the Baker Library of the Harvard Business School, covering the years 1840–1885. I identified 623 individual women who were active in business at any time between 1875 and 1885, 505 of whom were actually in business in that year, the rest of whom either left business before 1880 (36) or entered after 1880 (82). These women were identified through the census alone, while the rest were listed in at least one other source. This population of 623 women formed the cases for an SPSS analysis based on more than a hundred variables. Of these 623 businesswomen, 250 were widows in 1880.

4. Nineteenth-century reformers' reports provided sources for important works on nineteenth-century women. For example, Christine Stansell's *City of Women* states that "widowhood was virtually synonymous with impoverishment" and includes the stories of destitute widows attempting to support themselves on outwork, particularly sewing. According to Stansell, "any woman, whether the wife of a prosperous artisan or a day laborer's daughter, was vulnerable to extreme poverty if, for some reason, she lost the support of a man . . . but married women with children experienced the loss of men's wages, either through death or desertion, as devastating." Christine Stansell, *City of Women: Sex and Class in New York, 1789–1860* (Urbana: University of Illinois Press, 1987), 12, 16–17, 45, 110–111.

5. Caroline Bird, *Enterprising Women* (New York: W. W. Norton, 1976); Angel Kwolek-Folland, *Incorporating Women: A History of Women and Business in the United States* (New York: Twayne, 1998). The exhibit "Enterprising Women," funded by the Ford Motor Company and AT&T, traveled from the National Heritage Museum in Lexington, Massachusetts, to the New-York Historical Society, the Atlanta History Center, the National Museum of Women in the Arts, the Women's Museum in Dallas, the Los Angeles Public Library, and the Detroit Historical Museum. Accompanied by appropriate publicity, "Enterprising Women" debunked the myth that women did not—indeed could not—enter business before the mid-twentieth century. Virginia G. Drachman, *Enterprising Women: 250 Years of American Business* (Chapel Hill: University of North Carolina Press, 2002).

6. Interestingly, only Lukens and Hale appear in all three sources: Bird, *Enterprising Women;* Kwolek-Folland, *Incorporating Women;* and Drachman, *Enterprising Women.* Leslie is mentioned by Bird and Drachman; Haugherty and Holbrook-Nicholson are included only by Bird; and Coston is described only in Drachman.

7. Although Drachman's *Enterprising Women*—the companion volume to the exhibition—includes some background on nineteenth-century business and the economy of the United States, that background is sweeping in scope and lacking any detail or statistics on businesswomen as a group. Indeed, the format of the museum exhibit, Web site, and monograph—focusing on forty exceptional female entrepreneurs over the course of 250 years of American history—conveys the impression that as a group, female proprietors were few, unremarkable, or both, despite statements in the text to the contrary.

8. Studies include those by Mary Ryan and Suzanne Lebsock on Utica, New York, and Petersburg, Virginia, respectively, and Jane Pease and William Pease's comparison of women in Boston and Charleston: Mary P. Ryan, *Cradle of the Middle Class: The Family in Oneida County, New York, 1790–1865* (Cambridge: Cambridge University Press, 1981), 205; Suzanne Lebsock, *The Free Women of Petersburg: Status and Culture in a Southern Town, 1784–1860* (New York: W. W. Norton, 1985), 185; and Jane H. Pease and William H. Pease, *Ladies, Women, and Wenches, Choice and Constraint in Antebellum Charleston and Boston* (Chapel Hill: University of North Carolina Press, 1990). Two dissertations have appeared specifically on businesswomen: my own and that of Edith Eleanor Sparks, "Capital Instincts: The Economics of Female Proprietorship in San Francisco, 1850–1920" (PhD diss., University of California, Los Angeles, 1999). And see Edith Sparks, *Capital Intentions: Female Proprietors in San Francisco, 1850–1920* (Chapel Hill: University of North Carolina Press, 2006).

9. See Sarah Stage, *Female Complaints: Lydia Pinkham and the Business of Women's Medicine* (New York: W. W. Norton, 1979); Wendy Gamber, *The Female Economy: The Millinery and Dressmaking Trades, 1860–1930* (Urbana: University of Illinois

Press, 1997); Hasia R. Diner, *Erin's Daughters in America: Irish Immigrant Women in the Nineteenth Century* (Baltimore: Johns Hopkins University Press, 1983).

10. Kwolek-Folland, *Incorporating Women,* 57.

11. Albany's population grew from less than 11,000 in 1810 to about 98,000 in 1884. The comparative size for Albany appears in Brian Greenberg, *Worker and Community: Response to Industrialization in a Nineteenth-Century American City, Albany, New York (1850–1884)* (Albany: State University of New York Press, 1985), 12.

12. The relative size of the largest cities in the United States over time (1790–1990) is presented on the Web site of the U.S. Census Bureau. Albany's population/rank ranged from 3,498/19 in 1790 to 94,923/29 in 1890; Albany remained among the top hundred cities until the census count of 1970. See http://www.census.gov/population/documentation.

13. I am thinking here of Ryan, *Cradle of the Middle Class;* Nancy Hewitt, *Women's Activism and Social Change: Rochester, New York, 1822–1872* (Ithaca, NY: Cornell University Press, 1984); Carole Turbin, *Working Women of Collar City: Gender, Class, and Community in Troy, New York, 1864–86* (Urbana: University of Illinois Press, 1992); and Clyde Griffen and Sally Griffen, *Natives and Newcomers: The Ordering of Opportunity in Mid-Nineteenth-Century Poughkeepsie* (Cambridge, MA: Harvard University Press, 1978).

14. R. G. Dun & Co., New York, 7:205, 9:185 (Donn, Don, or Dunn [these were the different spellings of Julia Donn's last name in various sources]; Crew), R. G. Dun & Co. Collection, Baker Library, Harvard Business School.

15. Ibid., 10:50.

16. Space does not permit examination of this phenomenon here, but the R. G. Dun & Co. credit ledgers record many cases in which the nominal male proprietor of a business worked "by the day," while his wife, or wife and daughters, "ran the shop."

17. R. G. Dun & Co., New York, 8:378, 11:129.

18. It is not possible to produce reliable statistics on widowhood on the basis of evidence from city directories and credit records. Although directories sometimes identify a proprietress as "Widow" plus last name, they may also use the title Mrs. or even simply list her first name without marital status indicated. The R. G. Dun & Co. credit entries usually identify a woman's marital status, but not always, and at times the entries contradict themselves. Thus, the only fairly reliable source of marital status for businesswomen is the census; these figures are based on an SPSS analysis of the 1880 manuscript census for the city of Albany, in which I located 632 businesswomen.

19. The directory of 1813 lists only forty-four women with trades, but 88 percent of these trades were business occupations. Joseph Fry, *The Albany Directory* (Albany, NY: Websters and Skinners, 1813).

20. These figures are based on my statistical analysis (using SPSS) of all female proprietors located in the 1880 census; about two-thirds of these were identified as businesswomen in the census occupational category, and a third of these can be identified as proprietors from city directories or credit records, although they are not listed as such in the census itself. Of the 632 businesswomen located in the 1880 census, 22 percent were single, 33 percent were married, and 40 percent were widowed. Of the remainder, 2 percent were listed as married but had no mate living with them, 1 percent can be identified as widowed and remarried, and only one-half of 1 percent were divorced.

21. These figures were calculated from businesswomen located in the 1880 census (thus providing a birth date), who could be linked to city directories and/or credit records to find beginning/ending dates for business careers.

22. Specifically, the directory of 1813 listed the following female proprietors: nine grocers, six boardinghouse keepers, three innkeepers, two school mistresses—listed as "school" not "teacher"—one leather dresser, and one merchant.

23. Widowed businesswomen were even more likely to have foreign-born parents—less than 25 percent had fathers and mothers born in the United States.

24. In 1880, only 2 percent of Albany's business widows had been born in Vermont or Connecticut, versus 9 percent in Bavaria or Prussia; 5 percent were from unspecified German states, compared with less than 1 percent from Canada.

25. I argue that middle-class values in an urban center like Albany, with a large Irish and German immigrant population, would not have been identical to the middle-class values of a small town during the same period. As Roy Rosenzweig points out in his study of Worcester, Massachusetts: "Whereas Worcester officials viewed these female liquor dealers as disreputable and criminal, the Irish community apparently looked at them quite differently. In Ireland, the keeping of a shebeen (a home-based liquor shop) was a 'recognized resource of widows,' and they had a 'privileged' status in the liquor trade. . . . Almost invariably, a woman arrested for illegal liquor selling would plead . . . that 'she was compelled to sell a little beer and whiskey in order to make a living.'" Roy Rosenzweig, *Eight Hours for What We Will: Workers and Leisure in an Industrial City, 1870–1920* (Cambridge: Cambridge University Press, 1983), 43.

26. Mansel Blackford, *A History of Small Business in America,* 2nd ed. (Chapel Hill: University of North Carolina Press, 2003), 201; Kwolek-Folland, *Incorporating Women,* 84. I propose here reasons why my method of calculation could have overselected for longevity, why other methods probably underselected for longevity, and why the businesses I discuss here are not identical to "small business" as defined by business historians. First, by determining the length of a business enterprise through records linkage of the census with city directories or the credit records, I was using two sources that tend to overrepresent more established businesswomen. Had I compared businesswomen in the censuses of 1860 and 1870, or 1870 and 1880, I might have come up with a lower rate of longevity. However, a comparison of businesswomen identified in city directory listings and the R. G. Dun & Co. credit entries with the federal census of 1880 demonstrates that the census by itself underidentified businesswomen active between 1875 and 1885 by 33 percent, and widows in particular by 24 percent, and so does not represent an accurate measurement for women's business activity in this period. Indeed, each of the sources used overrepresents and underrepresents a different segment of the female business community: the census identifies the most marginal businesswomen, like peddlers, while not identifying respectable, native-born married women as having occupations; the credit records overrepresent businesses that required credit, like millinery shops, and underrepresent those that needed less capital, like dressmakers; and the city directories—although the most inclusive source—list businesses run by women under the names of their male relatives. (See my dissertation for a full discussion of the limitations of each source.) The average longevity of "small" business, as defined by Mansel Blackford and other historians, includes far larger businesses than any of those operated by Albany's mid-nineteenth-century female proprietors. Although Blackford includes family farms, retail shops, and artisanal ventures in his definition, he also discusses mid-nineteenth-century industrial firms employing up to one hundred men. It is possible that larger enterprises that required more capital actually failed more often than the tiny, home-based ventures through which women employed themselves and a few assistants, often relatives.

27. Thomas Dublin, *Transforming Women's Work: New England Lives in the Industrial Revolution* (Ithaca, NY: Cornell University Press, 1994), 134.

28. Wendy Gamber, "Gendered Concerns: Thoughts on the History of Business and the History of Women," *Business and Economic History* 23 (Fall 1994): 137.

29. The classic description of this family wage economy appears in Louise A. Tilly and Joan W. Scott, *Women, Work, and Family* (New York: Routledge, 1987), 15, 20, 63, 104–106, 112–113, 123–136, 226.

30. R. G. Dun & Co., New York, 12:348.

31. The Federal Census of Manufactures for Albany in 1860 reported millinery and trimmings businesses employing female hands whose earnings averaged from $2.50 to $5.00 per week. For example, the millinery business of Hannah Singer employed five female hands at $60 a month, milliner Mary E. Wood employed two female hands at $20 a month, and the trimmings business of John and Sarah Denmead employed five female hands at $50 a month.

32. To roughly translate this amount into current values, one might compare the five cents an hour of 1863 to five dollars an hour today—approximately minimum wage. This comparison means that dollar values from the mid-nineteenth century would have to be multiplied by a factor of one hundred—that a woman investing only $100 in her business would have been risking the equivalent of $10,000 in today's dollars. Using the same ratio, a business worth $5,000 in the 1860s would compare to an enterprise worth $500,000 today; those exceptional female-run enterprises worth from $20,000 to $100,000 would compare to businesses worth $2,000,000 to $10,000,000. An alternate, and somewhat less dramatic, computation would be based on the late nineteenth-century "living wage" of $9 a week, compared to the late twentieth-century's $9 an hour—or, a factor of forty. Using this ratio, an investment of $50 in the nineteenth century would equal about $2,000 in today's dollars, while $100 would equal $4,000, $1,000 would equal $40,000, $5,000 would equal $200,000, and $100,000 would equal $4,000,000.

33. Virginia Penny, *How Women Can Make Money, Married or Single, in All Branches of the Arts and Sciences, Professions, Trades, Agricultural and Mechanical Pursuits* (1863, 1870; repr., New York: Arno Press, 1971).

34. That these trades were among the least prestigious and profitable of women's business options is reflected by the fact that such women were almost never listed in city directories or evaluated for credit and can only be located through the census.

35. Mrs. Stein's first name has been lost to history; she is listed as Mrs. Philip in both the city directories and credit ledgers, and has not been located in the census. R. G. Dun & Co., New York, 9:210.

36. Estimating the value of money for this period is tricky. In the past, I have compared the income of female workers of the time with the minimum wage of today to come up with a rough evaluation. In the mid-nineteenth century, many female workers in Albany made as little as $3 per week (according to the Census of Manufactures). Thus, a woman who had capital on hand of $300 would have saved roughly one hundred times a woman's weekly wage.

37. The R. G. Dun credit records employ a shorthand, where *c* stands for hundreds and *m* for thousands; thus this entry is actually written as "3m$—ho & lot 3m$—mtge 8c$"; R. G. Dun & Co., New York, 19:206 (Conroy).

38. Ibid., 13:95.

39. Ibid., 10:92.

40. Ibid.

41. *Hoffman's Albany Directory and City Register, for the Years 1844–5* (Albany: L. G. Hoffman, 1844), 9.

42. *Munsell's Albany Directory and City Register for 1854* (Albany: J. Munsell, 1854), 441.

43. R. G. Dun & Co., New York, 7:90.

44. *Munsell's Albany Directory and City Register for 1852–53 with Map and Index* (Albany: J. Munsell, 1852), 433.

45. R. G. Dun & Co., New York, 7:221, 9:73–442.

46. *The Albany Directory for the Year 1877, containing a General Directory of the Citizens, a Business Directory, Record of the City Government, Its Institutions, &c., &c.* (Albany, NY: Sampson, Davenport, 1877), 376.

47. The Albany Directory for the Year 1889, including Bath, East Albany and Greenbush, also a Business Directory and Records of the City and Village Governments, Their Institutions, &c, &c. (Albany, NY: Sampson, Murdock, 1889), 491.

48. R. G. Dun & Co., New York, 9:83, 90; 12:257.

49. This speculation is based on trade and household situation, not ethnicity or prejudice; Kate McGowen was a native New Yorker born of New York parents, and Irish women had a low rate of unmarried pregnancy, as discussed by Hasia Diner. Dressmaking was a relatively high-status trade that depended on middle-class customers and a respectable reputation, and Rosa Stoliker was listed in the city directory for two years, whereas candy dealers like Kate McGowen were engaged in a more marginal trade, as evidenced by the fact that they were not listed in the city directories or evaluated for credit by R. G. Dun & Co. examiners.

50. R. G. Dun & Co., New York, 7:85 (William Burnett).

51. This note appears to have been written in 1858 as a commentary on Penny's demise in 1833; it appears in Joel Munsell, "Notes from the Newspapers," *Annals of Albany* (Albany: Munsell and Rowland, 1858), 9:264.

52. R. G. Dun & Co., New York, 10:463.

53. Federal Manuscript Census of Population, 1880, Albany, NY, ward 5, p. 23, line 36; R. G. Dun & Co., New York, 8:297, 377, 582.

54. *The Albany Directory for the Year 1880, containing a General Directory of the Citizens, a Business Directory, Record of the Government, Its Institutions, &c., &c.* (Albany, NY: Sampson, Davenport, 1880), 421.

55. Although the census lists her second husband John as a dyer, credit records make it clear that dyeing had been her business even before she married him, and that Elizabeth, not John, was the responsible party and head of the concern. Federal Manuscript Census of Population, 1880, Albany, NY, 1880, T9, reel 805, ED 11, p. 23, line 36; R. G. Dun & Co. Collection, New York, 8:297 (McDuffie). .

56. The federal manuscript census of 1870 lists Clara as twenty-seven, which means that she would have been approximately twenty-one when entries under her name appear in the credit records in 1864; the census of 1880 lists her as thirty years old, but that would have been impossible because her eldest son was nine in 1870 and nineteen in 1880.

57. R. G. Dun & Co., New York, 8:385, 437; 11:263, 397; 14:36.

58. According to classic studies of the 1970s, including Nancy Cott, *The Bonds of Womanhood* (New Haven, CT: Yale University Press, 1977), 21, "marriage placed legal obstacles in the way of women's entrepreneurship. ."

59. Interestingly, a recent project titled "Women, Enterprise and Society" for the Harvard Business School Library significantly underestimates the number of female-owned businesses described in the R. G. Dun & Co. ledgers. Although the authors claim that

"hundreds" of female-owned businesses are listed, I have identified approximately 750 for the city of Albany alone, and Pamela Nickless (professor of economics at the University of North Carolina at Asheville) has found 250 for the state of North Carolina—adding up to 1,000 for a single northern city plus a single southern state. Laura Cochrane, "From the Archives: Women's History in the Baker Library's Business Manuscripts Collection," *Business History Review* 74 (Autumn 2000): 465–476 (http://www.library.hbs.edu/hc/wes/intro/phase_one_summary).

60. Examples of such programs are Women for Women and similar charitable groups that provide widows with the means for investing in self-supporting, micro-entrepreneurial activities.

CHAPTER 6

"His Absent Presence"

THE WIDOWHOOD OF MRS. RUSSELL SAGE

————⊰●⊱————

RUTH CROCKER

*W*hen New York financier and railroad baron Russell Sage died in 1906, a few weeks short of his ninetieth birthday, it should have been a severe blow to his widow, Olivia Sage. (Her full name was Margaret Olivia Slocum Sage but she preferred Olivia.) Her social and legal standing during the previous thirty-seven years had derived entirely from her status as wife; she was customarily known as Mrs. Russell Sage, and indeed she had been an affectionate and loyal wife. She was now elderly, and her education at the famous Troy Female Seminary (since 1895 the Emma Willard School) was no more than a distant if fond memory. The roles of intellectual, social scientist, professional woman, and mother—all these were unavailable to her; she had been nothing but a wife, and now she would be nothing but a widow.[1]

But she would be an enormously wealthy widow. For her financier husband, the partner of Jay Gould, had left almost everything to her, and there were no children of the marriage. At seventy-eight, Olivia Sage came into possession of a fortune worth over $75 million, more than $1 billion in 2006 currency.[2]

Obituaries for Russell Sage were respectful, leaving a lot unsaid. "Like many another American, he knew how to accumulate money but not how to distribute it," wrote one tactfully.[3] While he was alive the press portrayed him frankly as a miser and a skinflint. The author of "Russell Sage—A Man of Dollars. The Story of a Life Devoted Solely to the Chill Satisfaction of Making Money for Its Own Sake" (1905) described an old man, "broken in body under the overreaching task set by his cold, grim hunger for innumerable dollars."[4] To Olivia, Russell Sage's death came both as the tragic loss of her companion of almost forty years and as a longed-for release. It would have been difficult for her to disentangle these two, and it is impossible for us. The public performance of grief was conventional: at the funeral she wept quietly while the coffin was being lowered, then directed that a cluster of lilies of the valley from the garden at the couple's summer home be placed on the casket. She "walked to the head of the grave and stood in deep meditation and wept." Her brother then led her away, and they left by the evening train for New York City, where she was reported to have taken to her room in a state of collapse.[5]

A brief look at the Sage marriage is necessary to understand Olivia's transition of widowhood. Olivia and Russell exemplified what Catherine Kelly calls the nineteenth century's "gendered dichotomies of making and spending." Russell Sage was the "robber baron" or financial wizard (depending on your point of view) who helped modernize and consolidate the nation's transportation systems and its capital markets; Olivia Sage models the nineteenth-century woman involved in the traditional charity work of the wealthy matron, the work of benevolence.[6]

As Mrs. Russell Sage, a socially prominent New York matron in Gilded Age New York, Olivia mobilized the image of the benevolent Christian woman whose generous impulses were restrained only by her tight-fisted husband. Married to one of the nation's wealthiest men, she went without the travel and the discretionary income customary for women of her class.[7] She represented herself as a philanthropist, in the sense of someone who wishes to do good for others, though because she had few funds at her disposal, "philanthropist" was more a subject-position than a description of activity, and the three significant donations she persuaded her husband to make were all attributed to him.[8] Her modest donations to favorite causes (such as the New York Women's League for Animals) gestured toward the role she would play after widowhood, when she would give enormous sums to these same causes.

Although she was fond of her husband, Olivia also felt keenly what historian Drew Gilpin Faust calls "the paradox of being both privileged and subordinate."[9] She compensated by constructing an identity of benevolence and moral authority, and this propelled her into public life as it did thousands of other white middle- and upper-class nineteenth-century women. She concerned herself with voluntary and reform associations: she was a supporter of "Indian reform" at the Carlisle Indian School, a lady manager at the New-York Woman's Hospital, and a member of missionary societies and patriotic organizations.[10]

All of these associations reflected, of course, the blinkered perspectives of her class and race position. And so did her support of suffrage. By the 1890s, Olivia had become an advocate for political and economic rights for women of her class, including the vote. She opened her New York home to parlor suffrage meetings and participated in the campaign for woman suffrage in New York in 1894. Yet her role was limited to a kind of performative philanthropy that left the suffrage cause dependent on the funds of others, such as Alva Belmont.

A different kind of associational activism was the Emma Willard Association, founded in 1891 as an alumnae association for Troy Female Seminary. Here Sage found a voice, presiding over a community of educated women and funding the compilation and publication of a significant volume, a directory of 3,500 graduates of the school, titled *Emma Willard and Her Pupils, or Fifty Years of Troy Female Seminary, 1822–1872.*[11] Speaking as an alumna and disciple of the educator Emma Willard, she held up Willard as the archetype of republican womanhood, "the illustrious woman who three quarters of a century ago saw into the possibilities of womanhood, as her Creator had planned her, the moulder of a race."[12]

By 1900, however, with her husband the subject of at least one paternity suit, she went public with her complaints about the institution of marriage, particularly the economic dependence of wives. The press duly reported on her as the long-suffering wife, bearing up under her husband's eccentricities and his affairs, thwarted in her philanthropic ambitions by the stingy old miser whose good health in his eighties drew astonished comments.[13] As Russell Sage approached ninety, college presidents began to get excited at the prospect of receiving Sage money. The chancellor of New York University even arranged for Olivia to get an honorary degree in 1905 in the hope that this deed would prompt her to donate to his university (it did).

When Russell Sage died in 1906, Olivia came into her own. In the remaining eleven years of her life until her death in November 1918, she spent over $45 million (around $700 million in today's money). Ten million went to endow the Russell Sage Foundation. The remaining $35 million ($500 million in today's money) she spent in a great outpouring of philanthropy, working from her own home with the assistance of secretaries E. Lilian Todd and Catharine Hunter. She would leave over $23 million more to colleges and universities in her will, and millions more to charitable, religious, cultural, and benevolent causes.

By January 1907 she had made a decision that suggests her feelings toward her late husband were deeply contradictory: she gave instructions that she was to be buried next to her mother and father at Oakwood Cemetery in Syracuse, not in Troy with Russell Sage and his first wife, Maria Winne Sage.[14]

Now that she was widowed, public expectations ran high. A writer in the *Outlook* praised Russell Sage's decision to leave his fortune to his wife, "who has the reputation, among those who know her, of being at once charitable in her sympathies and wise in her judgements." Another described her as "a woman of strong charitable instincts."[15] Now the nation held its breath. Dr. Schmuck, a family friend, commented that "in leaving his fortune to Mrs. Sage, Mr. Sage has left it to charity."[16]

The busiest years of Olivia's life now began. At the age of seventy-eight and a multimillionaire, she turned her hand to philanthropy. As a widow, Olivia would mobilize her relationship to her absent husband in order to achieve some goals that were her own. I have described elsewhere how Sage was deluged with letters of appeal and how she turned for help to Robert de Forest, her late husband's attorney, a reformer and philanthropist in his own right. Her largest gift, made only months after the death of her husband and with de Forest's advice, was for $10 million to set up the Russell Sage Foundation (RSF) "for social betterment," one of the first general-purpose foundations in the United States. The foundation became the institutional home of the social sciences in America in the first decades of the twentieth century and a significant funder of social work professionalization and of reform of industrial conditions, health and welfare, housing, and urban planning.[17]

The role of philanthropist was of course congruent with the Victorian gender system, which defined women by their willingness to give (of themselves, of their time). It is an irony that when this ideology was at its height in the nineteenth century, women had little to give: they owned only a tiny fraction of the nation's property. Historically, women's powerlessness has stemmed in part from their poverty relative to men. In the nineteenth century as today, women owned far less real and personal property than men did. Lee Soltow calculated that in 1860, women and children together constituted only about 5.6 percent of wealth holders and owned only 7.2 percent of all wealth.[18] Married women's property rights were established only after 1848, and then only gradually, state by state. Women's relation to property (and thus to capitalism and the market) was peculiar. But if they had little to give, women could give that little—"the widow's mite."[19] Or they could give of themselves, donating hours of volunteer labor.[20]

Widowhood seemed to offer Olivia Sage new opportunities and responsibilities (in her own words): more access to public places and a chance to have a voice in the many issues of her time about which she felt strongly.[21] She joined the Equal Franchise Society, formed in December 1908, whose members dubbed themselves "suffragists" in distinction to the "suffragettes," who were adopting the daring methods of the English feminists. They would win the vote, but in ladylike ways. "Certain wealthy, and fashionable and intelligent ladies," members of the Four Hundred, "have undertaken to play Royalty to the Equal Suffrage cause," the *New York Evening Journal* commented. They had decided that taxation without representation is "tyranny now, just as it was in the days before '76."[22] She attended suffrage bazaars in New York, where wealthy women came to spend money ostentatiously to help the cause; some came to survey the scene from boxes, as spectators of this political fundraising activity that used the traditional language of women's fundraising and voluntarism.[23] When Olivia Sage attended a suffrage bazaar held at the Martha Washington Hotel in New York City, the papers accorded her the status of celebrity suffrage patroness.[24]

Sage experienced bursts of freedom. During an illness in January 1912 that had fund-raisers worried it might be her last, de Forest fired off a letter to Harvard's president A. Lawrence Lowell. If you are hoping for a donation from Sage for the university, he wrote, "frankly I would move as quickly as possible." But a few months later de Forest reported that she now went out every day for "pleasure trips." The car and chauffeur gave her a mobility unimaginable in her younger days.[25]

There were also new constraints. Press coverage of Sage the widow reveals some anxiety that one woman should have so much money. Stereotypes of the elderly widow as pitiable, dependent, and passive competed with an image of her as powerful and independent—even out of control. The impatience that often characterizes the very old reinforced this impression and seemed to offer a golden opportunity for fund-raisers, as the following episode shows. In a letter to Harvard president Lowell, Harvard trustee Henry Lee Higginson told just how easy it was to get money out of the elderly widow. Princeton fund-raiser John Cadwalader "had gone to Mrs. Sage, not knowing her, and asked her if she would put up a building for the students of Princeton."[26] To his surprise, she immediately agreed to donate $250,000 for a building that was then (after additional gifts totaling over $165,000) named Holder Hall after Christopher Holder, a seventeenth-century ancestor.[27] Higginson recounted how Princeton had secured the additional amount for the building, which was larger than initially planned. Cadwalader "returned to her and showed her what part of the building she had built, being one side of a quadrangle. She asked: 'Why not the whole?,' and he said, 'Because the whole cost more money than you furnished,' whereupon, after consideration, she gave the rest." She had had no previous connection to Princeton.[28]

To fund-raisers such irrational bursts of generosity reinforced the impression that Sage's behavior was volatile and idiosyncratic, and encouraged them to redouble their efforts. The popular press portrayed her as both powerful and vulnerable—powerful because of wealth but vulnerable because of age, with its associations of failing health and mental impairment. Her enormous wealth seemed an anomaly—an embarrassing intrusion into what was conventionally a period of dignified, personal grieving, according to the author of "Mrs. Sage's Burden." He pointed out that for a widow to have such large responsibilities meant she would have to relinquish "the ease, leisure, and mental repose and contentment that are the cherished privileges of old age." In their place, she would be besieged by advisers "just jam full of panaceas": "From now on these professionals will unmercifully pelt and bombard Mrs. Sage with schemes and suggestions as to the best and most adequate way of getting rid of her surplus millions. . . . Professional Christians, professional patriots and professionally charitable people will ransack the vocabulary . . . in their hunt for persuadable and alluring sentences with which to picture to Mrs. Sage the monuments which will be erected to her memory if she follows their advice."[29] There was some truth in all of this. After 1906 came a frenzy of check writing, the agony of choice between competing worthy causes, and the ruthless pressure of fund-raisers and false friends. During summers at Lawrence, Long Island, she could still take her daily stroll, but once she returned to New York City she felt like a prisoner in her own home, and at least once threatening crowds gathered at her front door.[30] Now, maintaining some privacy became the task of the close circle around her. Breaching it became the goal of hundreds of fortune seekers, letter writers, and self-described long-lost relatives. In a letter to an old friend, also recently widowed, Olivia complained that she could not visit in "this sad and sorrowful time of both our lives." She was pestered by "Job's comforters"—"would-be friends," coming "from the ends of the earth" with their "needless applications for help."[31] The pressure from petitioners became overwhelming. A family story tells how her brother's grandson, a student at Rensselaer Polytechnic Institute, came complaining to his great-aunt that because of his family connection he had received a grade of B when he deserved to fail. "I am nothing but the great nephew of Mrs. Russell Sage." She replied, "Jermain, I am nothing but the widow of Russell Sage."[32]

The disabilities of age, as well as her diminutive stature, belied her enormous power as a multimillionaire. The press tried to sort out the contradictions. For example, she was the nation's largest taxpayer, and yet she could not vote. A reporter covering the suffrage parade of 330,000 marchers down Fifth Avenue in October 1915 described Olivia Sage, "enjoying wonderful health for a woman of her years, . . . [and] keenly alive to subjects that are occupying public attention," as "a tiny, white-haired figure" who was watching at her favorite spot—a round, second-floor window that gave her a commanding view of the street below.[33] At about the same time a news item on land sales in Queens jarringly referred to how "Mrs. Russell Sage and other capitalists" were contemplating a large purchase (the land would subsequently become the site for the RSF-funded Forest Hills Gardens).[34]

Progressive Era ambivalence about accumulations of wealth and power complicated the reception of her philanthropy. The year that Olivia Sage inherited her wealth was marked by controversy over whether people of conscience should accept donations from those named by President Theodore Roosevelt as the "malefactors of great wealth."[35] But her status as an elderly widow sheltered Olivia from this antitrust rhetoric. No one saw Sage money as a threat to republican institutions as they did Rockefeller money. Contemporaries found nothing jarring about women's philanthropy because they understood the benevolent impulse to be feminine, just as the acquisitive instinct necessary for business was masculine. "The very process of accumulation unfits a man, as a rule, for its expenditure," Abram Hewitt had declared in 1892 to a group of donors. "Every faculty of his mind and body is absorbed in adding to his wealth, so that he has no time or even inclination left to distribute it according to the demands of society or the judgment of his fellows."[36] At a time when debate raged over "tainted money," writers depicted Russell Sage's money in the hands of his benevolent widow as somehow purified and rededicated, "a link in the chain of gold which is lifting the world up to God," as one correspondent put it. By spending Russell Sage's money, one journalist wrote, his widow would be "wiping her husband's name clear."[37]

Thus, the press that excoriated Carnegie and Rockefeller gave female philanthropists like Olivia Sage a free pass. It accorded them celebrity status and recorded their activities—dedicating a library here, a college building there, giving scholarships, saving struggling charities. Widows such as Nettie McCormick, widow of Cyrus McCormick, and Alva Belmont, divorced from a Vanderbilt and widow of August Belmont, helped shape the political culture of Gilded Age and Progressive America by their donations to suffrage, to colleges and universities, to cultural institutions, and to professional institutions such as nursing and social-work schools. Working not as professionals or from law or corporate offices but from their own homes, they founded some major social and educational institutions.[38]

At the same time, the question of philanthropy had been complicated by the rise of a social science discourse that challenged the traditional practice of charity by elites and scorned the stock figure of Lady Bountiful. Progressive Era charity experts, including her own adviser de Forest, defined the problem of charity as a supply-side problem: how to curb the donor. At the same time, old-fashioned benevolence was discursively feminized as sentimental and untrustworthy, in contrast to the cool rationality of expert, fact-based philanthropy.[39]

In this discursive landscape, how could the widow be allowed to invest her money in reform schemes or institutions of any kind? The changed valence of charity undercut claims of benevolence and limited Olivia Sage's "old-age freedom." How much more effective for her to speak and act in the name of a deceased husband than to be a benevolent agent seeking investment opportunities for her philanthropic dollars on her own and guided by her own ideals and preferences?[40] And this is what Olivia Sage did. It made little difference to the recipients: actions spoke louder than words, and the objects of philanthropy were her own choice—who knew what Russell Sage would have spent his money on, since while he was alive he hardly spent it at all (racehorses, his sole indulgence, being the exception). This rhetorical strategy, complex and evasive, was effective. When she gave in the name of a deceased husband, everyone understood this gesture as one of commemoration for a departed spouse. When she tried to give away all her wealth and keep nothing back, they understood that too, for it enacted the essential womanly ideal of self-sacrifice and self-abnegation (even though some of her gifts were in fact self-serving or were designed to enhance the reputation of her ancestors.)

As long as she continued to give in her husband's name, it was the scale of her giving that provoked comment among contemporaries, not the giving itself. In a gender system in which women could still represent themselves as naturally benevolent, charitable good works appeared as no more than a timeless attribute of womanhood, and female philanthropists were good women, only more so. To give money away, to sacrifice self or substance, was the essence of Christian womanliness: in giving, as in serving others, the woman was most herself.[41] "The turning of the great estate over to Mrs. Sage was most natural," one writer editorialized. "For years she has been her husband's advisor in gifts to charities, and has shown herself familiar with the responsibilities and obligations of large wealth."[42]

Even Robert de Forest, Olivia Sage's adviser, wrote a press release when she died in 1918 that played down her agency: "the will of her husband, who had left her virtually all his great fortune, enabled her to gratify in a very large way her lifelong desire to help others," de Forest wrote. She did no more than a generous woman should, he implied; thus he both naturalized and dismissed Sage's philanthropy.[43] De Forest perpetuated the idea that Olivia played little active role by stating in a memorial after her death that "having established the Foundation and turned over its management to trustees of her choice, [Olivia Sage] never thought to direct their action, except in a single instance, and that was in urging that a permanent home be built for the Foundation."[44]

The context for such dismissive treatment of the widow is provided by larger transformations of scale and organization. We should bear in mind that a major goal of the Progressives was a rewriting of history that emphasized the rupture between their modernist project and the past, and that for men like de Forest, John Glenn (RSF director), and Edward Devine (charity expert and RSF trustee), foundation funding meant independence not only from corrupt politicians but also from the traditional purveyors of charity, the "ladies bountiful" whose giving was too often prompted only by sentiment, not guided by science.[45] When Progressives like de Forest gendered charity as female (disorderly, sentimental, and labile) and condemned modes of giving that were traditionally women's, they consigned the Lady Bountiful figure to the past. When Paul U. Kellogg had to choose a name for a new journal of social work in 1906, he rejected the title *Charities* as appealing primarily to "spinsters and society ladies" and chose *Survey* instead.[46]

These ideas informed the public reception of Sage's philanthropy. As the authority of social science increased, the contribution of Olivia Sage faded. When she gave $10 million for the foundation, some press reports ascribed the donation to her husband although he had been dead for several months. The gendered body of the philanthropist actually disappears altogether in a cartoon commenting on the establishment of the foundation in 1907, which pictures the institution as John Glenn, an old man seated on a kind of throne labeled "Sage." It graphically illustrates Olivia's near disappearance from the foundation's official history. Even in her own time, the stereotype of Lady Bountiful was jostled by the sharply competing images of the reforming professional and the emerging New Woman. Olivia virtually disappears, too, from the history of American charitable institutions. Until recently scholars found it difficult to assess, or even to see, the Russell Sage Foundation and its associated centers of reform activism. Business and organizational historians who focus on technological rationalization and the growth of corporations and state capacities viewed this foundation as somehow less than authentic and found its association with social work troubling.[47]

If Olivia Sage mobilized the Victorian ideology of the modest, submissive widow, her philanthropy nevertheless enacted a recovery of personhood. It was investment, it was reform, and it fulfilled her own wishes (some of them admirable, others not, but her own nonetheless). She was not a stranger to business or businesslike values—after all, her responsibility at the Woman's Hospital had been that of treasurer and fund-raiser—her philanthropy was investment, not largess, and her evangelical ideals suggested stewardship and careful financial accounting.[48] Moreover, she managed her own investments. In the fall of 1906, she was making large investments in New York real estate. In December, she loaned $1.2 million at 4.5 percent on the New York Hippodrome. A week later she made another huge loan, $1.5 million on Wall Street property, and ten days later another $500,000 loan on real estate. Her investments in Manhattan real estate in the six months after Russell Sage's death totaled about $10 million, and a few years later, when she refused to give a donation to the New York Exchange for Woman's Work, it was with the explanation that she was "no longer familiar with property values."[49] And when it came to the Russell Sage Foundation, Olivia followed its activities even in her very old age. Evidence is fragmentary, but she seems to have considered its work an extension of her own.

Tracking her gifts yields another perspective on the widowhood of Mrs. Russell Sage. It supports the idea of widowhood as a time of fulfillment, when small gifts made early in her career blossomed into huge legacies. A few examples suffice. Her donation of $25 to the New York Zoological Society in January 1906 was followed by a $1,000 gift in 1912 and an $800,000 legacy in her will. Another example was her purchase of 79,300-acre Marsh Island, Louisiana. A bird lover all her life, Olivia now was able to found Audubon clubs across the nation and to buy an entire island as a sanctuary for migrating birds. A third example is the Woman's Hospital, which earlier she had supported with volunteer hours as a lady manager; now she was able to leave it a bequest of $1.6 million.[50]

In this way, $35 million got spent in just over eleven years. She continued a frenetic pace of spending every day. She also became more and more isolated. Her brother John Jermain Slocum, the de Forest brothers, and E. Lilian Todd comprised the circle around her that tried to keep away visitors who might abuse the intimacy of a friendly visit by launching without warning into an appeal for money. Even close friends were not to be trusted. In May 1914, Lilian alerted Olivia about a social visit that threatened to turn into an appeal on behalf of the American Society for the Control of Cancer. Lilian warned that the visitors "may spring it on you over a game of backgammon. They want $5,000 now and failing to get that, they want the amount you gave last year doubled." Olivia was forewarned, and the visit was canceled.[51]

Increasing age also limited her public appearances. Olivia was under constant pressure from her protectors, who had their own ideas about how she should spend her money. De Forest, a reformer whose Progressive agenda sometimes differed from her own, steered large amounts to his own favorite causes. He secured an enormous gift for Yale, his alma mater. Olivia's brother Joseph Slocum netted $7 million in her will.

The charge of madness has historically been used to control and contain the feminine. In 1916, a Rutgers fund-raiser trekked to Olivia's summer home at Lawrence, Long Island, only to be met at the door by her physician, Dr. Carl Schmuck. "No one sees her," Schmuck warned. The fund-raiser reported back to the president that Schmuck "told me some things which prove to me that all further effort along such lines is hopeless."[52] But correspondence from this period shows that Olivia, though elderly, was as mentally alert as ever. Clearly this was simply a way to keep fund-raisers away.

Who then could speak for Sage? Widowhood complicated the question. In the Russell Sage Foundation Papers at the Rockefeller Archive Center are approximately 5,000 letters of Olivia Sage.[53] Many of these are begging letters to Sage. On incoming letters, Sage often wrote a reply indicating the amount she wanted to give or comments such as "Neglect" and "Fool thing." On an appeal from the Babies' Hospital for $250 for a bed, her secretary had written, "Shall I send check?" Olivia wrote a note, "Yes. I know the good work the Babies Hospital does."[54] Others in the collection are letters from Sage but are signed by her secretary, E. Lilian Todd.[55] Apart from the few personal and business letters from Sage that have survived, much of what we have is fragmentary. Her voice is deflected or indirect.

Carolyn Heilbrun writes that "biographers often find little overtly triumphant in the late years of a subject's life, once she has moved beyond the categories our available narratives have provided for women."[56] I have suggested some ways in which the category "widow," cultural constructions of aging, and an essentialist view of gender worked together to enable the unprecedented philanthropic activism of Sage's last decade. Silently, and from the privacy of her New York home, she spent the money her husband had accumulated in his career as financier and railroad speculator to reward many of the institutions of the Victorian women's world. The category "widow" allowed her to spend in his name (her twelve fur coats drew little comment—old age should have its comforts).

Sociologist Helena Lopata refers to widowhood as the last stage in the role of wife.[57] As a wife, Olivia Sage was typical of a class of elite women who carried on an activism not adequately described by the terms "philanthropy" or "benevolence." As a widow, she invoked her relationship to her absent husband in order to achieve some goals that were her own. Widowhood offered a moment for recovery of personhood, even though his identity still eclipsed her own and even though she clung to the identity of wife, keeping up the fiction that in spending his money she was enacting his wishes. At times Olivia Sage's disappearance was complete. Announcing a gift of $15,000 from Mrs. Russell Sage to found Audubon clubs, a press release ascribed it to "the wife of the noted philanthropist."[58] Her self-representation was often misleading or deliberately self-effacing so that, for scholars, looking for Mrs. Sage has been made difficult by her determined efforts to cover her traces. In a gesture that some have seen as ironic, she named many institutions for her husband even though his miserliness was legendary. At eighty-eight, encouraged by her secretary E. Lilian Todd and by Eliza Kellas (principal of the Emma Willard School in Troy), she gave $500,000 to found a brand-new college for women in Troy, where students could obtain education in professional fields other than the underpaid and oversubscribed field of teaching. She called it Russell Sage College.

When Olivia Sage refused the name Sage Foundation for the new foundation in 1907, insisting instead on Russell Sage Foundation, RSF trustee Louisa Lee Schuyler commented, "You cannot but admire her loyalty to her husband and her desire to suppress herself."[59] She was not able completely to suppress herself, however. Spending $45 million inevitably left traces in many (too many) archives. It enabled me to piece together her life from letters, speeches, and scattered papers. And if she modestly declined to give in her own name, she nevertheless harnessed her husband's money to her own purposes. That, at least, was her intention: the outcomes were often not of her making. The record reveals a subtle form of resistance and self-activity, different qualitatively from the more familiar struggles of middle-class suffragists and labor activists. Like their middle-class sisters in the settlement houses, elite women such as Sage were at work on the reconstruction of identities. How else can we interpret her exclamation, overheard as the trustees dispersed after the first meeting of the Russell Sage Foundation: "I am almost eighty years old but I feel I have just begun to live"?[60]

Notes

1. I trace the career of Olivia Sage from governess to philanthropist in Ruth Crocker, *Mrs. Russell Sage: Women's Activism and Philanthropy in Gilded Age and Progressive Era America* (Bloomington: Indiana University Press, 2006).
2. There were payments of $25,000 each to his nephews and nieces. Russell Sage had set aside another $10,000 for his sister, Fanny Chapin of Oneida, but she had died two years earlier. "Sage Will a Surprise; Mrs. Sage to Get All?" *Troy Record,* 26 July 1906; "The Will of Russell Sage," *Troy Record,* 28 July 1906.

    Estimates of Sage's wealth varied. One report stated that attorneys for Mrs. Sage estimated it at $70–$80 million, with $30 million in outstanding loans. "Sage Fortune

All for Wife," newspaper clipping, Onondaga County Public Library, Syracuse, New York (hereafter OCPL). But "Sage's Estate at Least $150,000,000," *Troy Record,* 4 August 1906, 8, announced: "In the Sage strong boxes have been found millions of dollars' worth of securities bearing high interest and guaranteed as to principal and income which have been for years unknown to the manipulators of Wall Street." See also "Thrifty Old Man of Wall Street Has a Peaceful End," clipping file, OCPL.

For conversion of 1906 dollars, see John J. McCusker, "How Much Is That in Real Money? A Historical Price Index for Use as a Deflator of Money Values in the Economy of the United States," *Proceedings of the American Antiquarian Society* 101 (1992), part 2.

3. "Russell Sage's Estate," *Outlook* (New York), 4 August 1906, 779. The only published study is the entertaining but untrustworthy biography by Paul Sarnoff, *Russell Sage: The Money King* (New York: Ivan Obolensky, 1965).

4. Lindsay Denison, "Russell Sage—A Man of Dollars. The Story of a Life Devoted Solely to the Chill Satisfaction of Making Money for Its Own Sake," *World's Work* 10 (May 1905–October 1905): 6301.

5. Accounts of Olivia Sage's behavior at Russell Sage's funeral are in the *New York Daily Tribune,* 25 July 1906, 1; "Funeral of Russell Sage Yesterday Afternoon," *Troy Record,* 26 July 1906, 5.

6. Catherine Kelly, "Gender and Class Formations in the Antebellum North," in *A Companion to American Women's History,* ed. Nancy A. Hewitt (Malden, MA: Blackwell Publishing, 2002), 101; Lori D. Ginzberg, *Women and the Work of Benevolence: Morality, Politics, and Class in the Nineteenth-Century United States* (New Haven, CT: Yale University Press, 1990).

7. "Mrs. Russell Sage on Marriage," *Syracuse Sunday Herald,* 21 June 1903, 29.

8. These three donations were $120,000 to Troy Female Seminary (1899), $50,000 to the New York Woman's Hospital (1899), and $150,000 to the American Seamen's Friend Society (1904).

9. Drew Gilpin Faust, *Mothers of Invention: Women of the Slaveholding South in the American Civil War* (New York: Vintage Books, 1996), xiii.

10. "Mrs. Russell Sage on Marriage." For an example of where Sage's class background was called into question, see the gossipy account in Alice Northrop Snow, with Henry Nicholas Snow, *The Story of Helen Gould, Daughter of Jay Gould, Great American* (New York: Fleming H. Revell Co., 1943), 224–225.

11. These women were chosen out of a total of 12,000 who were estimated to have attended the Troy Female Seminary during those years. Mary J. Mason Fairbanks, comp., *Emma Willard and Her Pupils; or, Fifty Years of Troy Female Seminary, 1822–1872* (New York: published by Mrs. Russell Sage, 1898).

12. Margaret Olivia Sage, "Response to Welcome, by Mrs. Russell Sage, delivered to the Trustees of the Troy Female Seminary, Mr. Gurley, and Members of the Emma Willard Association," [1896], typescript, folder, "Mrs. Russell Sage, Addresses," Emma Willard School Archives. John Lord, *The Life of Emma Willard* (New York: n.p., 1873), 41; Frederick Rudolph, "Emma Hart Willard," in *Notable American Women, 1607–1950: A Biographical Dictionary,* ed. Edward T. James, Janet Wilson James, and Paul S. Boyer (Cambridge, MA: Harvard University Press, 1971), 3:610–613.

Willard had died in 1870, but in the Emma Willard Association, as scholar Mary Poovey remarks of Florence Nightingale, another major and enigmatic nineteenth-century figure, Willard was "displaced by her own image." "It hardly mattered." Poovey writes. "Because her image displaced her own antifeminist sentiments, the name of Florence Nightingale could be enlisted in the feminist cause the woman herself refused to support." Mary Poovey, *Uneven Developments: The Ideological Work of Gender in Mid-Victorian England* (Chicago: University of Chicago Press, 1988), 198.

13. "Mrs. Russell Sage on Marriage."
14. James D. Phelps to Margaret Olivia Sage (MOS), 29 January 1907, 15 February 1907, and 16 February 1907, Russell Sage Foundation Records (hereafter RSFR), box 94, folder 938, Rockefeller Archive Center, N. Tarrytown, NY.
15. "Russell Sage's Estate," *Outlook,* 4 August 1906, 779; C. B. Carlisle, "Mrs. Sage's Burden," 31 July 1906, unidentified newspaper clipping, OCPL.
16. "Sage Will a Surprise," *Troy Record,* 28 July 1906.
17. Robert de Forest (RdeF) to MOS, 7 February 1907, RSFR, box 2, folder 11. *The Last Will of Margaret Olivia Sage, dated October 25th, 1906; First Codicil, Dated February 17, 1908; Second Codicil, dated July 19, 1911,* 22. "Mrs. Sage Leaves Millions to Charity," *New York Times,* 14 November 1918; "Mrs. Sage's Estate Worth $49,051,045," *New York Times,* [November 1919].

   Between 20 May 1920 and April 1929, the foundation would receive a total from Sage's residuary estate of $5,712,854, or 7/52 of the residuary estate. John Glenn, Lilian Brandt, and F. Emerson Andrews, *Russell Sage Foundation, 1907–1949,* 2 vols. (New York: Russell Sage Foundation, 1947), 1:269, 271–272.

   On the origins of the Russell Sage Foundation, see Crocker, *Mrs. Russell Sage,* 216–226. See also David C. Hammack and Stanton Wheeler, *Social Science in the Making: Essays on the Russell Sage Foundation* (New York: Russell Sage Foundation, 1994), 1–34. The foundations are beginning to attract interest from scholars. See Judith Sealander, *Private Wealth and Public Life: Foundation Philanthropy and the Reshaping of American Social Policy from the Progressive Era to the New Deal* (Baltimore: Johns Hopkins University Press, 1997); Ellen Lagemann, ed., *Philanthropic Foundations: New Scholarship, New Possibilities* (Bloomington: Indiana University Press, 1999), 101–118. Highly critical but still useful is John F. McClymer, *War and Welfare: Social Engineering in America* (Westport, CT: Greenwood Press, 1980). M. Glenn, Brandt, and Andrews, *Russell Sage Foundation,* is the official history.
18. Lee Soltow, *Men and Wealth in the United States, 1850–1870,* as cited in Carole Shammas, "Reassessing the Married Women's Property Acts," *Journal of Women's History* 6 (Spring 1994): 20.
19. Ruth Crocker, "From Widow's Mite to Widow's Might: The Philanthropy of Margaret Olivia Sage," *American Presbyterians* 74 (Winter 1996): 253–264.
20. The literature on nineteenth-century women's voluntary associations is large and growing. In addition to Ginzberg, *Women and the Work of Benevolence,* the following have been influential for this study: Kathleen Sander, *The Business of Charity: The Woman's Exchange Movement, 1832–1900* (Urbana: University of Illinois Press, 1998); Anne Firor Scott, *Natural Allies: Women's Associations in American History* (Urbana: University of Illinois Press, 1991); Kathleen D. McCarthy, "Parallel Power Structures," in *Lady Bountiful Revisited: Women, Philanthropy, and Power,* ed. Kathleen D. McCarthy (New Brunswick, NJ: Rutgers University Press, 1990); Mary Ryan, "Gender and Public Access: Women's Politics in Nineteenth-Century America," in *Habermas and the Public Sphere,* ed. Craig Calhoun (Cambridge, MA: MIT Press, 1992), 259–288; Elisabeth S. Clemens, "Organizational Repertoires and Institutional Change: Women's Groups and the Transformation of U.S. Politics, 1890–1920," *American Journal of Sociology* 98 (January 1993): 755–798. On the representation of the public sphere as space into which nineteenth-century women moved, see Carmen

Nielson Varty, "Proxemics, Politics, and the Patriarchal Public Sphere: A Critique of Habermasian Counternarratives," *Journal of Canadian Studies* (forthcoming). See also Eileen Yeo, ed., *Radical Femininity: Women's Self-Representation in the Public Sphere* (Manchester: Manchester University Press, 1998).

21. M. Olivia Sage, "Opportunities and Responsibilities of Leisured Women," *North American Review* 181 (1905): 712–721.

22. "Woman Suffrage Made Fashionable By the Four Hundred. May Its Tribe Increase," *New York Evening Journal,* [1909], Mrs. Robert Abbe, Scrapbooks of Newspaper Clippings and Other Material Relating to Woman Suffrage (hereafter Abbe Scrapbooks) (microfilm), 1894–1921, vol. 5, New York Public Library.

Wealthy suffragist Gertrude Foster Brown later recalled that "suffrage had taken on a new tone." Gertrude Foster Brown, "On Account of Sex," Sophia Smith Collection, Smith College, Northampton, MA, chap. 4, 4. Pagination is inconsistent. See also Margaret Finnegan, *Selling Suffrage: Consumer Culture and Votes for Women* (New York: Columbia University Press, 1999).

23. Beverly Gordon, *Bazaars and Fair Ladies: The History of the American Fundraising Fair* (Knoxville: University of Tennessee Press, 1998); Nancy Hewitt, *Women's Activism and Social Change: Rochester, New York, 1822–1872* (Ithaca, NY: Cornell University Press, 1984), 249–251.

24. "Women Suffragists Plan Hot Campaign," *New York Times,* 25 October 1908, 7. Carrie Chapman Catt to MOS, 15 October 1908, thanking Mrs. Sage for letting the Interurban Woman Suffrage Council use her name as patroness for the woman suffrage bazaar, RSFR, box 98, folder 995.

25. RdeF to President Lowell, 21 January 1911, Harvard University Archives. "Pleasure Trips," see unidentified clipping, *New York World,* 9 May 1912, in "The Sage and Slocum Book," John Jermain Memorial Library, Sag Harbor, New York; "Deny Report That Mrs. Sage Is Ill," *New York Herald,* 5 June 1914.

26. Henry Lee Higginson to President A. Lawrence Lowell, 16 December 1910, Harvard University Archives.

27. MOS to Trustees of Princeton University, 7 April 1908, 19 June 1911; W. Wilson to MOS, 2 November 1908; MOS to Mr. John L. Cadwalader, 3 June 1910; RdeF to MOS, 2 January 1912. Mrs. Sage requested a copy of her ancestor's signature, RSFR, box 99, folder 1001.

28. Henry L. Higginson to President A. Lawrence Lowell, 16 December 1910, Harvard University Archives; John Cadwalader to MOS, 3 June 1910, RSFR, box 91, folder 892.

29. Carlisle, "Mrs. Sage's Burden."

30. "I will close this hurried note and go for my morning stroll as the day is beautiful," MOS [from Lawrence, Long Island] to Mrs. Nelson Aldrich, 16 October 1907, RSFR, box 92, folder 902. "Like a prisoner in her own home": "Death of MOS in the Ninetieth Year of her Age," unidentified clipping, Troy Scrapbook, Troy, NY, Public Library.

31. MOS to Mrs. Morris Jesup, 12 March 1908, RSFR, box 97, folder 980.

32. "Speech of John Jermain Slocum at the Pierson Re-Dedication," *Sag Harbor Express,* 1982, incomplete newspaper clipping, Florence Slocum Wilson Collection.

33. "Mrs. Sage, Now 87, Calls for Vote," *New York Sun,* 31 October 1915.

34. "Mrs. Russell Sage and Other Capitalists," as quoted in Susan L. Klaus, *A Modern Arcadia: Frederick Law Olmstead, Jr. and the Plan for Forest Hills Gardens* (Amherst: University of Massachusetts Press, 2002).

35. Controversy over Rockefeller's activities would increase again after 1910, when Congress rejected a bill to incorporate the Rockefeller Foundation, which then sought and

gained incorporation under the laws of the state of New York. Robert H. Bremner, *American Philanthropy* (Chicago: University of Chicago Press, 1960), 118–119; Ron Chernow, *Titan: The Life of John D. Rockefeller, Sr.* (New York: Random House, 1998), 550–551.

36. "Address of the Hon. Abram S. Hewitt at the Thirty-Seventh Anniversary of the Woman's Hospital, held 1 December 1892," in Woman's Hospital in the State of New York, *Thirty-seventh Annual Report of the Woman's Hospital* (New York, 1892), 37. Russell and Olivia Sage were in the audience for this speech and were probably the target of his remarks.

37. "Wiping Her Husband's Name Clear," in Arthur Huntington Gleason, "Mrs. Russell Sage and Her Interests," *World's Work* 13 (November 1905): 81–82. "Your Chain of Gold," Caroline Borden to MOS, 10 February 1908, RSFR, box 66, folder 590. This letter acknowledged Sage's gift of $10,000 for the College for Girls in Constantinople.

I explore the meanings of gifts and charity at the turn of the twentieth century in Ruth Crocker, "'I Only Ask You Kindly to Divide Your Fortune with Me': Begging Letters and the Transformation of Charity in Late Nineteenth-Century America," *Social Politics: International Studies in Gender, State, and Society* 6 (Summer 1999): 131–160.

38. For example, see the study of women patrons of art and art museums, in Kathleen D. McCarthy, *Women's Culture: American Philanthropy and Art* (Chicago: University of Chicago Press, 1991).

39. Dawn Greeley, "Beyond Benevolence: Gender, Class, and the Development of Scientific Charity in New York City, 1882–1935" (PhD diss., SUNY Stony Brook, 1995); Crocker, "I Only Ask You Kindly to Divide Your Fortune with Me."

Several scholars have explored the gendered consequences for reform of the triumph of social science. See Helene Silverberg, ed., *Gender and American Social Science: The Formative Years* (Princeton: Princeton University Press, 1998); Kathryn Kish Sklar, "Hull-House Maps and Papers: Social Science as Women's Work in the 1890s," in Silverberg, *Gender and American Social Science,* 127–155; Guy Alchon, "Mary van Kleeck of the Russell Sage Foundation: Religion, Social Science, and the Ironies of Parasitic Modernity," in Lagemann, *Philanthropic Foundations,* 151–168.

40. Younger women could and did embrace social science–based reform, for example, Florence Kelley, Mary Richmond, Mary Van Kleeck, and Crystal Eastman. Significantly, the latter three all found institutional homes at the Russell Sage Foundation; Richmond and Van Kleeck based lifelong careers there.

41. Lori Ginzberg elegantly characterizes this inherited nineteenth-century gender system as one in which the dominant ideology "conflated ideas about femininity with ideas about morality itself"; Ginzberg, *Women and the Work of Benevolence,* 1. Important studies are McCarthy, *Lady Bountiful Revisited;* McCarthy, *Women's Culture;* and Kathleen D. McCarthy, *Noblesse Oblige: Charity and Cultural Philanthropy in Chicago* (Chicago: University of Chicago Press, 1982).

42. "The Will of Russell Sage," *Troy Record,* July 28, 1906. In our time such "benevolent stereotyping" still operates to make people expect women to be more compassionate and more caring than men. The conviction for insider trading of businesswoman and style maven Martha Stewart in March 2004 is only the latest reminder that the public is uncomfortable with successful and wealthy women.

A recent dissent is Laura Flanders, *Bushwomen: Tales of a Cynical Species* (London: Verso, 2004). What has been called "the altruism gap" drew support from the earlier work of Carol Gilligan. See Gilligan, *In a Different Voice: Psychological Theory and Women's Development* (Cambridge, MA: Harvard University Press, 1982); Carol Gilligan, Nona P. Lyons, and Trudy J. Hanmer, *Making Connections: The Relational Worlds of Adolescent Girls at Emma Willard School* (Cambridge, MA: Harvard University Press, 1990). The debate over Gilligan's findings is ably discussed in Seyla Benhabib, *Situating the Self: Gender, Community, and Postmodernism in Contemporary Ethics* (New York: Routledge, 1992), 142ff. It is a nice coincidence for this present work that Carol Gilligan's research on young women's values was based on research carried out at the Emma Willard School—the former Troy Female Seminary in Troy, New York, which Olivia Sage attended in the 1840s and to which she gave $1 million in 1907.

A useful earlier discussion of women and altruism by four feminist philosophers is Larry Blum, Marcia Homiak, Judy Housman, and Naomi Scheman, "Altruism and Women's Oppression," in *Women and Philosophy: Toward a Theory of Liberation,* ed. Carol C. Gould and Marx W. Wartofsky (New York: G. P. Putnam's Sons, 1976), 222–247. The authors analyze the tension between altruistic qualities, "which can be seen as universal values which are good for men as well as for women to possess," and altruism linked to self-sacrifice and "stemming from guilt, fear, and low self-esteem, rather than from freedom or self-love" (222). See also Margaret Adams, "The Compassion Trap," in *Women in Sexist Society,* ed. Vivian Gornick and Barbara K. Moran (New York: New American Library, 1972).

43. Robert W. de Forest, "Memorial Minute, 1918," reprinted in Glenn, Brandt, and Andrews, *Russell Sage Foundation,* 1:269; "Margaret Olivia Sage, Philanthropist," *Survey* 41 (1918): 151. It continues: "This she did from that time on, up to the close of her long life, not impulsively, but with due regard to helping wisely and permanently; and this she is continuing to do after her death through the provisions of her will."

James A. Hijaya, "Four Ways of Looking at a Philanthropist: A Study of Robert Weeks de Forest," *Proceedings of the American Philosophical Society* 124 (December 1980): 418.

44. De Forest, "Memorial Minute," 269.

45. Dorothy Ross writes: "Progressive era social scientists filled their writings with a sense of discontinuity and turned away from the outmoded past. . . . No sooner did these theorists enter history, as it were, than they turned against the past." Ross, "Modernist Social Science in the Land of the New/Old," in *Modernist Impulses in the Human Social Sciences, 1870–1930,* ed. Dorothy Ross (Baltimore: Johns Hopkins University Press, 1994), 183.

46. "Spinsters and Society Ladies," as quoted in Clark A. Chambers, *Paul U. Kellogg and the Survey: Voices for Social Welfare and Social Justice* (Minneapolis: University of Minnesota Press, 1971), 42. "Social scientists repeatedly cast their scientific enterprise and its goal of rational control in masculine terms." Ross, "Modernist Social Science in the Land of the New/Old," 183 (quote), 179; Nancy Cohen, *The Reconstruction of American Liberalism, 1865–1914* (Chapel Hill: University of North Carolina Press, 2002), 13, 259–260n21. But see also Sklar, "Hull-House Maps and Papers."

47. "[It] employed the form and rhetoric of the foundation with a general purpose but in fact it represented a continuation and modernization of the tradition of social work"; Barry Karl and Stanley Katz, "The American Private Philanthropic Foundation and the Private Sphere," *Minerva* 19 (Summer 1981): 247. Recent studies are correcting this omission. See Sealander, *Private Wealth and Public Life;* Meg Jacobs, "Constructing a New Political Economy: Philanthropy, Institution-Building, and Consumer Capitalism in the Early Twentieth Century," in Lagemann, *Philanthropic Foundations,* 101–118.

One obvious reason for the neglect of the RSF was size. Other foundations were far larger than Sage. By the time John D. Rockefeller Sr. died in 1937, he and his son John D. Rockefeller Jr. had given an estimated $600 million to seven interconnected foundations. Andrew Carnegie's various philanthropies—the Carnegie Corporation, the Carnegie Fund for the Advancement of Teaching, the Carnegie Institution of Washington, and the Carnegie Hero Fund—received about $350 million.

48. Crocker, "Widow's Mite to Widow's Might," 253–264; Ginzberg, *Women and the Work of Benevolence;* Susan Yohn, "'Let Christian Women Set the Examples in Their Own Gifts': The 'Business' of Protestant Women's Organizations," in *Women and Twentieth-Century Protestantism,* ed. Margaret Bendroth and Virginia Brereton (Urbana: University of Illinois Press, 2002), 213–235.

49. "No longer familiar with property values," [MOS] handwritten note on envelope, RSFR, box 1, folder 7, n.d.

    Real estate transactions can be followed in the *New York Daily Tribune.* See "Mrs. Sage Lends Again: $1,200,000 on the Hippodrome and $1,650,000 on the Breslin," *New York Daily Tribune,* 12 December 1906, 1; "Another Big Sage Loan: Financier's Widow Lends $1,500,000 on Wall Street Property," *New York Daily Tribune,* 19 December 1906, 1; and "Mrs. Sage Lends Half a Million," *New York Daily Tribune,* 28 December 1906, 7.

50. J. J. Slocum to Miss Todd, 6 December 1912, RSFR, box 88, folder 854. The bequests are listed in "Mrs. Sage Leaves Millions to Charity," *New York Times,* 14 November 1918, 13.

51. When the charity appealed to her, she scrawled a note to Lilian: "Had the courage to refuse to see Dr. Cleveland, suspecting his errand." Lilian to MOS, May 15, 1914, RSFR, box 68, folder 606.

52. Rev. Andrew Hagemann to President Demarest, 15 September 1916, Papers of President Demarest, Special Collections and University Archives, Rutgers University Archives, New Brunswick, NJ.

53. Olivia Sage's letters are in series 1, Mrs. Russell Sage; series 3, Early Office Files; and series 10, Personal Giving. All are in RSFR.

54. MOS handwritten in pencil on envelope, 9 March 1915, RSFR, box 70, folder 622. Her earliest recorded donation to this cause had been ten dollars in 1891. Other collections have yielded letters written by Sage. For example, at the Beinecke Rare Book and Manuscript Library at Yale, about a dozen letters from her to Richard H. Pratt, director of the Carlisle School, express her pleasure in the "Americanization" of Native American children at Carlisle.

55. For more about Todd, a remarkable woman, an inventor and engineer who ended up as Sage's secretary, see Crocker, *Mrs. Russell Sage.*

56. Carolyn G. Heilbrun, *Writing a Woman's Life* (New York : W. W. Norton, 1988), 31.

57. Helena Znaniecki Lopata, *Widowhood in an American City* (Cambridge, MA: Schenkman Publishing, 1973). See also Yeo, *Radical Femininity.*

58. The passage reads in full: "A gift from Mrs. Russell Sage launched the Audubon Junior Clubs in 1910. The wife of the noted philanthropist was shocked by the widespread slaughter of robins which she observed during a trip through the Southern states." "Nine Millionth Member Enrolled in Audubon Junior Club," press release, typed, n.p., RSFR, box 1, folder 4 ("National Association of Audubon Societies. 1910–1915").

59. Louisa Lee Schuyler to RdeF, 23 March 1907, Columbia Rare Book and Manuscript Library, Columbia University Library, New York, NY. Sage's philanthropy is an example

of what literary scholar Paula Backscheider calls "deliberate erasure." Paula R. Backscheider, *Reflections on Biography* (New York: Oxford University Press, 1999).

60. Provocative and contrasting interpretations of these turn-of-the-century economic transformations that integrate gender, consumerism, and reconstruction of selves are James Livingston, *Pragmatism and the Political Economy of Cultural Revolution, 1850–1940* (Chapel Hill: University of North Carolina Press, 1994); and Nan Enstad, *Ladies of Labor, Girls of Adventure* (Ithaca, NY: Cornell University Press, 1999).

CHAPTER 7

"Great Was the Benefit of His Death"

THE POLITICAL USES OF MARIA WESTON CHAPMAN'S WIDOWHOOD

LEE V. CHAMBERS

On October 15, 1855, Maria Weston Chapman celebrated the silver anniversary of her marriage to the antislavery cause. As she wrote on the occasion, "the dates about this time are interesting ones to me. The 6th is the date of my marriage & of my husband's funeral. The 14th the beginning of the mob of '35. 'The past is sealed.'"[1] Thus Maria linked key personal and public events: her 1830 marriage to abolitionist Henry Grafton Chapman in which her formal antislavery activity was incubated and nurtured; the 1835 mobbing of the Boston Female Anti-Slavery Society, which catapulted her to international fame; and her 1842 widowing, which inaugurated a period of extraordinary productivity in abolitionist fundraising, publishing, and international advocacy.[2] In defining herself as a widow married to her cause, Chapman returned to a narrative she had begun to construct over a decade earlier as a means of discursively recouping her gender rebellion as a female abolitionist.[3] Chapman closely guarded her public image, using the publicity attendant upon her celebrity to authorize her stand on slavery and legitimate the strategies with which she sought to move it politically. She devised a narrative about her husband's death that gave a specific meaning and purpose to her widowhood: one that enhanced her reputation, asserted women's right to political subjectivity and agency, and countered the retreat of antislavery women to a deferential form of politics.[4]

The narrative went as follows. On October 3, 1842, surrounded by his family, Boston abolitionist Henry Grafton Chapman, a good and just man, died.[5] During his last illness, his self-sacrificing and loving wife devoted herself to his care, never leaving his side.[6] At the moment of transfiguration, Henry pronounced a benediction upon her. "His last thoughts & directions were about the cause[,] leaving me to its service, with the charge to lose no opportunity of promoting its interests," wrote his widow. "Great was the benefit of his death, as well as the sorrow."[7]

The public account of Henry's last moments bore little resemblance to the experience described in Chapman and Weston family letters. For years Henry had suffered the listlessness, fatigue, wracking cough, chest pain, fever, labored breathing, phlegm production, joint swelling and pain, throat ulcers, night sweats, diarrhea, and lung hemorrhages characteristic of tuberculosis.[8] His symptoms had turned sharply worse in the spring of 1840, "[settling] a dark cloud down in the distance over every thing."[9] Henry's obituary pictured a man who faced his debilitation with untroubled mien: "during this protracted period, and under all his sufferings, he was sustained by a cheerful and resigned spirit, and unshaken fortitude." However, family documents tell of his irritability, mood swings, and panic, all of which made it difficult to distract, placate, and nurse him. Maria's sisters worried that she was "almost beat out being with him day & night, & he is so variable that it is difficult to amuse him."[10]

Henry's alternating impatience, fear, denial, and restlessness undermined all attempts to assist him. He refused to submit to medical regimens or technologies that might ease his suffering or extend his life.[11] Scrambling for a new treatment, Maria sent for an apparatus designed by Dr. Rumadge of London consisting "of a tube 4 feet in length—which forces as you breathe backward and forward through it—more air into the chest than it would naturally obtain & obliges it to be retained longer." Henry lacked the perseverance to use it. As Henry's breathing became "toilsome," his nights poor, and "his appetite variable & delicate," he became "more & more discouraged daily."[12] Tuberculosis was hard on families as well as patients. The unpredictable course of the disease raised hopes in times of apparent remission. During one such period, Maria complained that Henry only "thinks he is in a consumption, but why he must of necessity be in one I cannot see[.] [T]here seems no reason why he shouldn't get well, & if it were a hopeful person I should think he would. As it is, I have only to endeavour not to despair."[13]

Dramatic weight loss evoked the frightening appearance of a living yet barely breathing corpse. The use of opium enhanced this effect. Maria was filled with horror when Dr. Ware, a specialist in lung complaints, began to administer opium to Henry in August 1842. "It is awful to me, to see any one under its effect," she wrote. "It ought to be called 'death-in-life.' It alleviated every bad symptom[,] reduced the pulse from 125 to 90[,] lengthened the breathing, helped the cough, lessened the expectoration, stayed the perspiration. Yet I cant abide it."[14] Death often arrived suddenly and horrifically with an outpouring of arterial blood from the mouth and nose that choked and suffocated the patient in a crimson flood.

For public consumption, Maria mitigated the seriousness and impact of Henry's illness on her activism. When, in the winter of 1840, the couple sought warm air in the hopes of easing his cough and improving his lungs, they decided on Haiti, an ideologically loaded choice. For slaveholders, the Haitian revolution offered the lesson that emancipation resulted in race war. The Haitian republic merely reinforced the view that slaves were an ignorant and uncivilized people incapable of self-governance. For abolitionists, on the other hand, the first black republic symbolized the potential for emancipated slaves to rule themselves. They blamed the violence that racked the island of Santo Domingo at the turn of the century on Napoleon's effort to reimpose slavery and drew the moral from this history that slave revolt and race war would result if U.S. slave owners did not free their slaves.[15] Maria addressed abolitionists' concerns about her withdrawal from public activism into private nursing by defining the trip as a political mission:

> My husband's health was the cause of [the trip] primarily. We left home for his sake, & came here rather than anywhere else, for the sake of the cause. If we should find a republic of men of colour, all going on harmoniously in the push to civilization, it would we thought, subserve the cause of the slave in our own republic. We have been greatly gratified since our arrival here, by much that we have observed, & find nothing which candor would not compel us to account for without supposing the blacks to be an inferior race to others.[16]

Both Chapmans kept journals, from which Maria crafted ten "Haitien Sketches," published in the *National Anti-Slavery Standard* between June and November of 1845.[17]

When Henry's condition did not greatly improve, Maria recognized that a retreat to Haiti might prove an annual necessity. She began preparations in August 1841 for the December Boston Anti-Slavery Bazaar, the antislavery fundraiser under her management, "so that the burden may not be left on any one, in case the cold weather should prove too much for Henry." When they sailed again in February 1842, the couple settled into a boardinghouse in Gonaives and ventured to Port au Prince to interview, for the abolitionist press, individuals active in the revolution and interested in human rights.[18] But yellow fever rampaged through the population, and Henry panicked when he contracted diarrhea. Maria arranged a fast passage home.[19] Their abrupt departure frustrated Haitian colleagues, who had expected the Chapmans to provide them access to the American media.[20] Defensively, Maria instructed her sister Deborah about what should be said publicly about their swift turnabout. "I'm sure (since you wonder what good reason can be put forward for coming home so soon,) that the real [reason] is creditable to our patriotism, family affection, selves & friends alike—namely, that we were so homesick we could not stay away longer. Henry was, at least," she acknowledged, suggesting some frustration with his trepidation.[21]

Upon their return, the Chapmans first visited a water-cure treatment center and then retreated to a rented house in Boston. From June 1842, Maria rarely left the house as Henry's breathing had become so "toilsome" that he had "no good nights."[22] Maria apologized to her siblings for the dullness of her letters saying, "I suppose I should pick up something [about the cause] if I were out much."[23] Focused on nursing, Maria reported her retirement from active abolitionism. "The care of him occupies me all the time," she wrote, "so I have no adventures to tell you of. I can only give you cogitations & speculations & observations—few enough of the latter, as the [peep]hole through which I look is extremely small."[24] By mid-September, Henry no longer spoke and barely moved. He died two weeks later.

Immediately, Maria considered the public face of his death. Long attuned to the advantages and disadvantages of publicity for the abolitionist cause, she knew from experience that it was an unstable and fickle resource not easily controlled, particularly by women.[25] Yet the nature of the antislavery enterprise and the interests of the press had brought Maria Weston Chapman to the public's attention in 1835, and thereafter her political calculus took into account both her celebrity and infamy.[26] Abolitionist women carried on a highly public battle for the American soul and their particular vision of American society. Their manner of doing so, and the nature of their ideological attack on the social and political order, attracted attention, often of the most salacious and pernicious kind. Called monstrous, unsexed, overly sexed, manly, and irreligious, they drew public insult.[27] Maria was "gazetted." "The papers keep firing away," Maria's sister Caroline Weston explained. "You know that Maria has been posted—and her name is bandied about in the papers like household words—or *office* words."[28]

Public curiosity and abolitionist notoriety created a cult of personality around Maria.[29] She proved an attraction on both sides of the Atlantic. "Your name is one of our household words," wrote Richard D. Webb from Dublin. Edinburgh abolitionist Jane Smeal acknowledged, "I feel quite well acquainted with the *Chapmans* [and] the *Westons.* . . . I hear them so often spoken of." Mary Carpenter of Bristol queried, "Why do you not come over my dear Mrs Chapman, to stimulate the ladies in England; & that we may know & love you better?"[30] When a subscription agent called at the home of Dr. Fifield, physician to the Weston family, while Maria was making a call, an introduction produced excessive delight: "he acted as if she was the queen of England." Maria served as the celebrity guest for abolitionists. "The Alcotts have invited M[aria] to go there Saturday night as they think that she may do Mrs M[orrison] great good . . . so I suppose Maria is considered quite a shew [*sic*]," Caroline reported.[31] Conventions and fairs across New England solicited her participation and advertised her presence.

Fans developed an urge to know detailed information about the subject of their interest. Antislavery agent Henry C. Wright remarked on the curiosity of his Irish hostess. "I'm now in Ann Allen's parlor," he wrote. "She asks 'what sort of a woman is Mrs Chapman?' 'No *sort* of woman' I say 'but simply a woman, who thinks it a greater glory to be a woman than an American[,] Englishman or Sectarian—or Queen or nobleman.'" Allen asked several more questions. "So we *gossip* about you," Wright admitted.[32] While traveling on an antislavery mission in Britain, James N. Buffum found "many, many people, in this Country who are Curious to know all about the peculiar characteristics of each of our prominent Anti-Slavery friends." He acknowledged having "drawn quite a number of Portraits, for their gratification in private."[33]

Chapman recognized the value of the public's curiosity. She praised *The Antislavery Advocate,* a British newspaper that presented "the abolitionists as personalities to the circle that read it. How large a number of that circle . . . would forget the abolitionists & the slaves—their clients, if the Advocate should stop?" she asked.[34]

Thus she quickly acquiesced to Mary Ireland's request for a letter of instruction on fair work: "even your *name* will do much. . . . every heart is filled with admiration of Mrs Chapman. There is a feminine pride associated with the accounts we hear of your untiring efforts which made any one here feel gratified in following any suggestion that may come from your pen." And she used her acclaim to raise financial support for *The Anti-Slavery Standard.* "If you meet, as you may, any of my clientele," she advised Wendell Phillips, "you may make my opinion useful."[35]

Beginning with the elections of the 1820s, politicians in America solicited women's attention and support by distributing sewing boxes and commemorative dishware decorated with candidates' portraits and mottoes of their campaigns.[36] Chapman devised similar materials for the same purpose, soliciting poems, stories, and essays by well-known abolitionists for publication in the *Liberty Bell,* a magazine sold in concert with the annual Boston bazaar. In a manner calculated to draw women to the cause, she signed and sent complimentary copies to various individuals in recognition of their contributions to the fair or as an inducement to future participation. A. J. Winslow responded appreciatively to a copy "addressed to me by Mrs Chapman[,] a Lady whom I have not the honour of knowing personally, but whose devotedness to the cause of *Abolition* renders her name dear to all who have hearts to feel for the sufferings of the oppressed slave; allow me madame to express to you my thanks for your *souvenir.*"[37]

In their desire for a connection with the famous Maria Weston Chapman, fans harbored the belief that these "favors" were "personal" in nature, extended to them out of friendship rather than political calculation. Eliza McIntyre thanked Chapman for her copy of the *Liberty Bell,* sure that its arrival signified a new and intimate stage in her relationship with Maria: "Why I should be favoured with such a mark of friendship from you I know not, for I am but an inexperienced and inefficient worker in the great cause for the promotion of which your energies have been so nobly devoted. Be that as it may however I thank you most sincerely and gratefully for your kindness which shall be for me an encouragement and incentive to increased exertion." Like McIntyre, Susanna Fisher conflated political association with personal friendship, confiding that "the true value & use of love gifts [was] that they make us 'try harder to be good.'"[38] To reach and inspire an audience for her cause, Chapman made use of all available tools.[39]

Recognizing the thrall of gossip in the new, nineteenth-century celebrity culture, Chapman practiced elusiveness. At midcentury, an aura of withdrawal enhanced the appeal of a public personality and might be accomplished in various ways, such as by use of pseudonyms, gender masquerades, or even complete (and thus dramatically enticing) retirement. Chapman's practice involved retreating periodically into the exclusive arms of a small family circle so as to maximize gossip while managing information. Even close friends and colleagues characterized Maria as "notoriously *secretive,*" and charged her and her sisters with concealing "all matters relating to themselves, and [being] profoundly mysterious towards all the outer barbarians respecting their own affairs no matter how trivial or uninteresting to the public at large."[40] Such criticism missed the point of celebrity culture, which valued the trivial for the sense of intimacy it represented to fans and the emulation it inspired.

As part of this practice of eye-catching mystery making, Chapman periodically staged her retirement from or reemergence into the public eye.[41] Henry's death offered such a moment. Chapman packaged for public consumption and bent to political purpose the usually well-guarded details of an intensely personal and private moment. She, her family, and her fans circulated her story about Henry's death. It achieved an official seal in newspaper accounts and was reified in the resolutions of abolitionist societies.[42] In constructing the narrative, Maria incorporated crucial aspects of mid-nineteenth-century consolation literature and mourning ritual so as to emphasize her womanliness and make her ideological case for women's political activism.[43]

Utilizing religious and gender tropes familiar to a Christian audience, Maria first emphasized the tranquility of Henry's death. "My Darling Henry departed this morning & a good man & a just, & died in sweet peace," Maria wrote. Mary Gray Chapman, Henry's sister, told a similar story of his "lying just raised on the bed, in their back-chamber, the window open, the sun shining cheerfully in, flowers on the table, altogether the peace & the beauty that reigned there struck me very forcibly. It was death deserted of its tensions—Henry told me of his wishes when He should be no more with perfect tranquility." A death deserted of "its tensions" was vacated of horror and anxiety, a death "not strange." In Henry's obituary, the *Liberator* emphasized that death came eventually to all. "No strange thing has happened to him, or to those who are so deeply affected by his death; but this common event of mortality almost always takes the living by surprise, come when it may." A good and just man, Henry was seen as having lived a full and worthy life, and thus had no reason to fear death, this natural part of life's cycle. He could rest in peace, free from pain, sorrow, or regret.[44]

A resolution to honor Henry and sympathize with Maria by the Boston Female Anti-Slavery Society (to which Maria, her sisters, sister-in-law, and mother-in-law belonged and no doubt influenced by them) put it this way: "His sincerity was perfect,—his conscience, his guide,—his sympathy, with those who suffer wrong,—his sacrifice, for those who do wrong,—his life, one act of duty—his death, saintly peace." The *Liberator,* too, emphasized the calm resignation with which Henry faced his illness and demise: "For two or three years past, his health had been seriously affected . . . but, during this protracted period, and under all his sufferings, he was sustained by a cheerful and resigned spirit, and unshaken fortitude." Both the "sweet peace" his wife recalled and the "saintly peace" of the resolution suggested transparent states that could not be faked and thus evidenced Henry's sincere acceptance of what was to come. He had "lived honestly and died like a Saint," and his well-lived life begat a death without fear.[45]

Yet descriptions of Henry's death testified not only to his calm but also to Maria's. Mary Gray Chapman insisted that "there never could have been two people that watched the approach of death with more perfect calmness & philosophy than they did." Intimate family friend Edmund Quincy reported that "the serenity of Mrs. Chapman was as perfect as I had ever seen it & she told all the little incidents of the last few hours with the utmost tranquility. Her sisters were not all as calm as she, but they all felt the power of her peace upon them."[46]

Maria said that her serenity emerged from her sense of consolation. Utilizing the tropes of Christian resignation, she explained that "while *life* holds out, I am afflicted. When it ceases, I am consoled." She spoke of Henry's death not as a terminus or partition but rather as a transition toward greater and lasting marital unity.

> His life & death have both shed a radiance over the spot where he dwelt chasing away all the customary shadows of death. I do not feel divided from him because he is called to another life a little before me but on the contrary I seem to find that his departure was the completion of our union. Twelve years from the date of our marriage, his remains were removed to the grave. I was able to be with him day & night as long as he lived so that we reached together the very boundary of the bitter land.[47]

"She said she had no feeling of separation, that she had gone down with him to the brink of the River, & that he had gone over & she returned."[48] In the nineteenth century, death had come to be seen as a sweet deliverance from life's pain and struggle, bringing with it the promise of salvation. Those left behind, although encouraged to mourn, were also instructed not to grieve excessively. Great lamentation revealed a lack of religious conviction. The centrality of Henry's calm and Maria's tranquility in this death narrative confirmed their faith in God and confidence in their own salvation. Their union was complete because it extended beyond the grave to their reunion in Heaven.[49]

The key words and symbols embedded in Henry's death narrative served to counter contemporary doubt as to the Chapmans' Christian orthodoxy. Not only did both Chapmans support William L. Garrison, whose supposed heresy undermined his leadership of the antislavery movement, but also Maria signed calls for public conventions addressing the sanctity of the Sabbath and the divine authority of the Bible.[50] The Chapmans abhorred what they saw as the dogmatism, narrowmindedness, moral cowardice, and hypocrisy of the church and many of its clergy in the face of the monumental sin of slaveholding. As Maria wrote from Haiti, the lack of established religion there proved "one obstacle the less to the promulgation of true religion."

> There is here immorality but not hypocrisy: with professedly Christian nations of the north, there is both immorality & hypocrisy. For the same reason that Christ & the disciples went first to the cities of Israel rather than to the gentiles, would I have the gospel preached in Cape Haitien— they need it more in their state of phariseeism than do these in their state of comparative simplicity.

A Unitarian, Maria had gradually distanced herself from the church. In January 1842, Rev. William Ellery Channing visited her "in [his] pastoral capacity," urging a return to worship. She seized upon the opportunity to testify to her antislavery faith and "excommunicated" the church before formally withdrawing her membership.[51]

Orthodox clergy responded to the news of Henry's death by questioning his faith and therefore his "translation." Maria's sister reported meeting the Reverend Hawley in the street.

> After we had shaken hands he said "Well, Mr Chapman is dead!" I assented, for what could I say, though I felt so aggravated by his heartlessness & ignorance that I hardly knew *what* to say. "What was the state of his mind?" Had I answered just as I felt, I thought he would misconstrue it. I therefore said as gently as I could "Very happy indeed." A few words more passed & I broke away as quick as I could hoping I should never set my eyes on him again.

Henry refused to have clergy attend his bedside, unwilling to submit in death any more than in life to what he saw as cant. He wanted no formal religious ceremony or funeral oration. In deference to his parents' sensibilities, Henry asked that the abolitionist and Unitarian minister Samuel J. May speak a few words "not as a priest but as a friend."[52]

Maria's views coincided with Henry's. She did not believe "in a future state of rewards and punishments & in the Christian revelation generally," she wrote. "Eternity & infinity come in like a flood of consolation for *any* thing, whenever I open the gates, although *God and immortality* never were much to me—or rather I don[']t discriminate, not having really, selfishness enough to enable me to draw my lines distinctly on *those* regions."[53] What Maria valued was not life hereafter but the accomplishments of the well-lived life.[54] Henry had led a moral life, she believed, devoted to godly deeds in seeking to free the enslaved, and to his credit he had done so "without the intermixture of any mean idea of being rewarded for it in this life or the next."[55]

Maria's faithful nursing in Henry's death narrative evoked the trope of Christian and female devotion. She emphasized that she alone had cared for him, relying on no outsiders: "I am most grateful that my health and strength were entirely sufficient for the occasion—no nurse or hired watcher disturbed the quiet of our chamber—no professional person was called in to array his remains for the grave—but those nearest & dearest to him performed the services." Stories of her "constant & unremitting devotion" circulated widely among abolitionists, fueled by her reports that she had "not one minute to herself" and left him only to do the marketing. Wrote Henrietta Sargent, a member of the Boston Female Anti-Slavery Society, to her nephew in the Far East, Henry's "noble minded wife never left him day or night, no wonder he could not bear to have her out of the room a moment, so kindly did she minister to him." Edmund Quincy told Irish gossip Richard D. Webb that Maria's "devotion to [Henry] during his last illness was truly beautiful. She gave up all to him & scarcely left him for a moment." The *Liberator* extolled the "estimable wife" whose attentions to her spouse "were unremitted."[56]

What purpose did such details serve? To the growing public legend surrounding Maria Weston Chapman, these brought tenderness, self-sacrificing fidelity, and wifely subordination, thus emphasizing her womanliness. In a culture that conflated femininity with morality, the story of Henry's tender nurse enhanced Maria's claim to private faithfulness and honor, and thus to public virtue.[57] She felt it necessary to enhance her womanly reputation in this way because her public behavior had opened her character, indeed her very nature, to question. Anti-Garrisonian and antiabolitionist partisans spread rumors during the late 1830s that, in pursuing the cause, Chapman had neglected her children and her husband.

For example, in May 1838, Maria attended the second National Women's Anti-Slavery Convention in Philadelphia. There she spoke before a large, mixed-sex audience in the newly built Pennsylvania Hall. Antiabolitionist riots, the burning of the hall, and attacks on the city's black population led the delegates to flee Philadelphia. A fellow traveler described Maria's demeanor and her impact on the "flying abolitionists":

> the other abolitionists were drooping, tired, despondent, while she stood glorified like a prophetess, triumphant in nominal defeat—
>
> "Calm and resolute and still.
> And strong and self possessed."[58]

Yet when the abolitionists detrained at Stonington, Connecticut, to catch the boat to Boston, her sisters took Maria to a boardinghouse, her body racked with fever and her mind hallucinating. Doctors diagnosed phrenitis.

Phrenitis was an inflammation of the brain or its surrounding membranes with potentially devastating effects—convulsions, insanity, coma, and death. Physicians believed it to be caused by the "frequent and violent indulgence of passion . . . fostering particular trains of thought and emotion, whether pleasant or painful, [that] irritate and inflame the organ of thought."[59] "Strong passions" such as sorrow, pride, or "mortified" (unfulfilled) ambition could do it.[60] So too, physicians attributed phrenitis to the suppression of bodily discharges such as occurred in weaning, with the increased blood circulation to the brain causing its inflammation. Prognosis was "always unfavourable, often fatal from the third to the seventh day. If prolonged . . . it is apt to terminate in mania or idiotism."[61]

Too many people had seen Chapman on the train, and she was too well known for her condition to go unremarked. Rumors circulated rapidly. With a kind of ghastly fascination, William Garrison followed her reported symptoms and treatment, attributing her illness to the excitement of the convention. "How awful, how sudden this transition from active life to inanimate clay! Mrs. C. took a very active part in the Anti-Slavery Convention of Women in Philadelphia, and was consequently in a high state of mental excitement, which has resulted in a brain fever. She got as far as Stonington, Connecticut on her return home, where she now lies—a raving maniac. There is no hope for her recovery." Sarah T. Smith, herself a delegate to the convention, an evangelical abolitionist, and no fan of Chapman's, spread the story that "Mrs. Chapman was in the Insane Hospital, because at the convention a majority opposed certain views of hers, and she could not carry her point." Another, lamenting Chapman's enthusiastic devotion to the cause of the slave as "a piece of amiable fanaticism," recalled that "she had left her young child to attend the meeting, at great risk of her health, and this, with the excitement of the preceding night, had nearly thrown her into a fever. She only just escaped with her life from this exposure." One Bostonian, not an abolitionist although friendly to many, wrote that "the amazonian abolitionist" had "made herself quite conspicuous" in Philadelphia by "walking up Chestnut street with two blackies, one on each hand, and with arms endearingly entwined with hers." She had spoken "at the public meeting before some thousands," he said, "and I believe was in the thickest of some part of the melee" which followed. It was not, therefore, surprising to him that "on her return, her behavior in the boat was very peculiar, & she became in fact raving crazy, . . . has had a brain fever & is not now expected to live many hours."[62]

Maria's family and friends attributed her illness to the stress associated with the riot or the too rapid weaning of her daughter Ann in order to attend the convention. To her enemies, the latter choice evidenced an unwomanly nature. Her abandonment of proper female decorum in public advocacy also suggested unfeminine ambition and undisciplined passion. Any of these were sufficient to have driven her mad. In illness Maria's companions saw a martyr for the cause, her enemies a woman overreaching her sphere and appropriately punished. Madness, having raised questions about her womanly nature and character, undermined Maria's honor and reputation. One Bostonian drew the moral from her illness that women's sphere "is not in public life" and prayed: "God grant that our [female] relations may be restrained from stepping out of their proper sphere. May he guard our dear country from the dangers, thick & dark, into which it seems as if she were drifting fast."[63]

Throughout the crisis, Maria's sisters nursed her and sought to control the flow of information about her condition. From Connecticut, Caroline Weston instructed their younger sister Lucia to keep track of rumors and inquiries that circulated in Massachusetts: "remember who inquires for us—& who is afflicted by our troubles for I shall wish to know." She instructed Lucia on what to say in public, even putting out a false story about her absence from school teaching while nursing Maria. Caroline asked Lydia Maria Child to be alert to slander and counter it, and when misapprehensions arose, they moved quickly to squelch them. To an inquiry about Maria's condition made by a "Philadelphia gentleman," her sister Anne wrote reassuringly: "I trust it will not be long before her health will be perfectly restored; her mind became so when the fever left her." At the time, Maria was still feverish and delusional, and her sisters had no clear idea when or if she would recover. When well enough to travel, Maria chose to recuperate in her parents' Weymouth home, where few would see or hear of her shorn hair and pale features. She delayed her return to Boston for two months.[64]

Personal difficulties continued to dog Maria's steps when her fourth child, an infant daughter, died shortly after she left for Haiti.[65] Anne Weston sent word to the abolitionist community reassuring them that Maria would not remove herself from the cause as a result of this personal tragedy. "This is the first child Maria has lost and I know how much she will grieve over it; but it will not lead her to inaction. She will only labour the more devotedly for those who mourn over children took from them not by the providence of God but the cruelty of man."[66] Chapman and her family translated their grief for baby Gertrude into feelings of identification with slave mothers whose children were sold away from them or died in bondage of abuse or neglect. However, and despite the high rate of infant mortality in Boston at the time, Maria's response to Gertrude's death offered her enemies yet another example of her unnatural behavior and twisted passions.

These two years, 1839–1841, also saw the Boston Female Anti-Slavery Society riven over the role of women in the movement. Members were divided into women's rights and evangelical groups, with the former pursuing their right to advocate as citizens for the slave and the latter falling back upon a model of deferential politics in which the political access of women depended upon their connections to powerful men.[67] Drawing for their authority on a gender ideology of bourgeois feminine respectability, evangelicals in the Boston Female Anti-Slavery Society rejected Chapman's radical vision of women's independent citizenship.[68] Under attack by the clergy for insubordination, Maria's faction opposed the reelection of Mary Parker, a conservative evangelical who had long served as president and whose conduct of the election raised charges of procedural manipulation.[69] Illegally in Chapman's view, the evangelicals disbanded the association and formed the Massachusetts Female Emancipation Society, which was affiliated with conservative clergy. Eight months' pregnant, Maria refused to accept the dissolution. She and her allies retained the name of the Boston Female Anti-Slavery Society, and the organization limped along thereafter, focusing primarily on an annual fund-raising bazaar.

Maria's celebrity had arisen from her position as the chief ideologue of the Boston Female Anti-Slavery Society. As corresponding secretary she maintained the relationship of the society with others in both the United States and Great Britain. She also wrote the annual reports of association activities, transforming them into histories of the antislavery movement that addressed ideological and tactical matters shaping the course of antislavery politics in Massachusetts. One example of Chapman's writing was the 1836 "Address of the Boston Female Anti-Slavery Society to the Women of Massachusetts," a letter introducing a petition drive to end slavery in the District of Columbia.[70] Chapman argued that women had a right to petition their government not only as inhabitants of the United States and members of families—as *"wives and mothers,* as *sisters* and *daughters"* represented in that government by husbands, fathers, brothers, and sons—but also as individuals in their own right. The language of the petition called for women to do their duty as citizens.

> Let us petition:—petition, till, even for our importunity, we cannot be denied. Let us know no rest till we have done our utmost to convince the mind, and to obtain the testimony of every woman, in every town, in every county of our Commonwealth, against the horrible Slave-traffic, which makes the District of Columbia a disgrace to the earth.

Chapman cast doubt upon men's adequate representation of women in politics and called on them to take women's views seriously.

> By a *resolution* of the *Last* Congress, that no petition respecting slavery,
> shall be printed for the information of the members, and that no vote
> shall be taken on it, by which we may know whether the men we call our
> representatives are truly such, the whole nation is made to feel the slave-
> holder's scourge. The best and noblest of our countrymen, thus seeing,
> and thus feeling these things, have spoken and acted like freemen—Oh,
> let us aid them to rouse the slumbering manhood of the rest!

Thus Chapman endorsed petitioning as a means by which women might encourage "men to cease to do evil, and learn to do well." As historian Anne Boylan has
argued, abolitionist women turned petitioning into an instrument of mass can-
vassing and mobilization rather than using it as an instrument of special pleading. "For them, petitioning became a means to demand, not simply a request, and
to do so as a collection of political subjects, equals to each other and, in this one
arena, male voters."[71]

Maria utilized Henry's death narrative to reduce the distance or, more accurately, paper over the contrast between evangelical and radical visions of a
woman's duty by reinforcing Maria's spousal status after she had made a name
for herself as an individual. The 1836 address was signed "M. W. Chapman," not
Mrs. Henry G. Chapman. The transformation from Mrs. Henry G. Chapman to
Maria W. Chapman to M. W. Chapman and eventually to MWC was performed
in and through the *Liberator* over the years 1835–1837, as Maria's annual reports,
songbooks, letters, hymns, and poetry were published and reviewed.[72] By June
1837, for example, when the front page of the *Liberator* prominently displayed "A
Prophecy" by "M. W. C.," the initials were sufficiently recognizable to identify
Maria as the poet to the reading public.[73] Evangeline A. S. Smith concluded that
Maria's contributions made the antislavery newspaper "very interesting. M. W. C.
is a signature that I care not how often I see."[74]

Maria's representation of herself as an individual political subject and her
insistence upon female political agency contrasted with the evangelical women's
view of themselves as subject to and adjuncts of men. With her narrative of Henry's death, Maria sought to counter this evangelical critique of her independence
by emphasizing her spousal devotion. She used it to counter charges that she was
an unnatural mother and a public woman, a term that in the nineteenth century
carried connotations of unrestrained and dangerous sexuality, by reinserting her
back into the family identity and containing her domestically. It did so not only
by detailing her abandonment of abolitionist activity for devoted nursing but also
by emphasizing Henry's death en famille. Henry's death at home, surrounded by
his wife and family, "shed a radiance over the spot where he dwelt" and all who
lived there.[75]

This fourth trope of a death en famille was represented in visual terms.
Describing "the most striking scene" he ever beheld, for example, a visitor to
the Chapman home shortly after Henry's demise reported that "the body was
surrounded by the surviving family, Maria standing with all the composure &
peace of a guardian angel at its head & his venerable father seated in resignation

at his feet."[76] Consolation literature offered many scenes of bereaved relatives gathered around the deathbed. These domestic pictures served to demonstrate the enduring strength of family ties, the belief that far from severing the bonds of domestic love, death reinforced among surviving family members a devotional practice of attachment that prefigured the perfect domesticity that would reunite them in Heaven.

Nevertheless, the image of Maria standing at the head of the bed and Henry Chapman Sr. seated despairingly at the foot somewhat complicated the usual order by reversing the symbolic hierarchy of men over women in the family. Maria demonstrated both emotional strength and authority by standing tall in circumstances that prostrated her father-in-law.[77] Positioned at the head of bed and family, she offered both a sense of family unity and a disruption of the gender order. The rupture broke the smooth surface of her narrative, revealing its manufacturing and representing Maria's refusal to submit entirely to patriarchy's assumption of female dependence and subordination despite her use of the trope of family unity to recoup some of her gender rebellion.

The last trope at work in the Chapman death narrative had to do with the social benefits accomplished through proper mourning of the dead. As the *Liberator* predicted, "a large circle of friends will participate in the sorrow which this event must create in the bosom of the widow of the deceased, and among all the relatives of both."[78] Those who had mourned loved ones were expected to find themselves moved again by newly grieving family and friends. God's healing consolation worked upon the hearts of all who had lost loved ones, enabling them to empathize with the suffering of acquaintances and even strangers. The death of an individual benefited an entire social circle by transforming family love into Christian benevolence. Mourning taught men and women to love one another and thus worked to establish God's peace and social harmony on earth.[79] As Maria's sister Anne ruminated poetically,

> while in fervent grief we weep above each lowly grave,
> May we like them the weak protect, from wrong the helpless save;
> Their pure devotion, earnest faith, and love of human kind,
> Within our inmost souls let these an answering echo find.[80]

Henry Chapman left no doubt as to the benevolent work his death must serve. He charged his wife, and through her his friends and associates, "to lose no opportunity" of promoting abolition.

Maria responded to Henry's bidding and "turned her strength upon the world." She asked Garrison to speak at Henry's funeral. According to those present, he "made a very excellent address, to the no small astonishment of certain of the relatives, who had not looked for an anti-slavery lecture at such a time." Shortly thereafter, Maria announced a donation in Henry's name to support the *Liberator,* whose finances had deteriorated with the schism of 1839–1840. "I hasten to fulfill one of the last wishes of my husband," she wrote the editor, "by enclosing fifty dollars for *The Liberator,* of which he always entertained the highest opinion, as an effectual instrumentality in the anti-slavery cause."[81] Chapman turned the trope of death's beneficence into the radical paths of racial and gender equality, goals many of her peers believed to be more disruptive of the social order than constructive of social harmony.

Here too Maria complicated the symbolism of the consolation trope. At midcentury, proper mourning was enacted through elaborate codes regulating dress and behavior. As historian Karen Halttunen has written of sentimental middle-class culture, "To mourn was to grieve inwardly over a lost loved one; but to be 'in mourning' was to wear black, to assume a demeanor of bereavement, to limit one's social activities for the appropriate period following the death." Fashion stipulated the proper style and color of dress and accessories according to the mourner's relationship to the deceased and the amount of time elapsed since the death. So too, because mourning was deemed to be a private emotion, it was best expressed at home. Guidelines for mourners detailed when family members might properly leave the home after a death according to the purpose of the excursion and the relationship of the family member to the deceased.[82] To the shock of proper Bostonians, Maria abjured mourning dress and the domestic seclusion of the bereaved.

Despite Maria's sorrow, she refused to provide a show of lamentation, displaying her grief to the curious bystander or avid fan. Friends reported that "the household fell naturally back into its usual liveliness & helpfulness without any effort or affectation." Henry's injunction to Maria authorized an unorthodox mourning ritual with a distinctive claim to sincerity.[83] In dedicating her life to the cause, Maria served her husband's memory. Although never as isolated from anti-slavery politics as the narrative of her total immersion in nursing suggested, Maria returned to her usual activities upon her husband's demise. Using the narrative of Henry's death to stage her reentry into the public arena, Maria financed, wrote, edited, and distributed the *Latimer Journal,* a short-run newspaper reporting the legal case of George Latimer, a fugitive slave captured in Boston and held for extradition back to his master.[84] She attended Latimer's November trial, instigating considerable public commentary on the appropriateness of women in the courtroom, although there was nothing new in their attending criminal trials, those of murderers being particularly popular.

The defiance with which Maria rejected proper mourning "in a community where the claims of custom & public opinion are like links of iron" reminds us that she was a fierce woman dedicated to a cause in which she willingly used up herself and everyone else, and whose motto was *La carriere ouverte aux talens*—the tools to whosoever can use them.[85] Both adored and despised, Chapman was never a woman around whom one might get too comfortable.[86] Her grandson, with equal parts awe and horror, saw in her a fanatic.

> A Cause like this solves all questions whether they be matters of metaphysical doubt or of practical life. One's business is ruined, of course. A child dies; alas, it is severe, but let the Cause consume our grief. All social ties were snapped long ago; it is a trifle. The old standard-bearers are

dropping out from time to time through death; peace be unto them, we have others. The discipline of such a life—so unusual, so singular—wore down men and women into athletes; the stress made them strong.[87]

When Henry's death accorded his radical wife a political moment, she seized it.

Maria had challenged the gender ideology of separate spheres, the subordination of women to men, and women's political dependency. She moved to recoup her gender rebellion discursively by constructing a narrative that resonated with the religious and gender ideals of her class. She sought not only to enhance her reputation and extend her influence but also to counter women's retreat from equal rights activism and their evangelically inspired return to deferential politics. Chapman crafted a sanctified rationale for female activism in her husband's change and heavenly ascent. In this way she seized the moral high ground from those clergy and their followers who had repudiated her morality, attacked her femininity, and led her "weak" abolitionist sisters into their fold. The narrative she devised offered a mixture of the familiar and comforting language of consolation with the unconventional renunciation of proper mourning ritual, which paradoxically enhanced the potency of her symbolic return to abolition from his deathbed. It provided legitimacy for her actions and brilliant publicity for the widow who had long asserted that "the sword of the spirit is the word."[88]

Acknowledgments

I thank the Massachusetts Historical Society and the Graduate Committee on Arts and Sciences of the University of Colorado for financial support of this project.

Notes

1. Maria Weston Chapman to Mary A. Estlin, Leeds, 15 October 1855, Estlin Papers, Boston Public Library.
2. When Henry Grafton Chapman married Maria Ann Weston, his parents, Henry and Sarah Greene Chapman, were ardent abolitionists. They joined the Boston Female Anti-Slavery Society and Massachusetts Anti-Slavery Society shortly after their founding in 1833. Henry served as treasurer for the Massachusetts Anti-Slavery Society from 1836 until his death. The family held annual family meetings to decide how they might support emancipation during the year to come. As ship chandlers and shippers, father and son made a powerful symbolic contribution to the cause by discontinuing, "from conscientious scruples on the subject," their lucrative business transporting agricultural products that would have embroiled them in the slave economy. Caroline Weston to Samuel J. May, Weymouth, 21 October 1871, May Collection, Boston Public Library. *Liberator* 12 (7 October 1842): 39, 159; Lydia Maria Child to Francis and Sarah Shaw, Northampton, 17 August 1838, in Milton Meltzer and Patricia G. Holland, eds., *Lydia Maria Child: Selected Letters, 1817–1880* (Amherst: University of Massachusetts Press, 1982), 85–86.

   In her extraordinary productivity during her widowhood, Chapman was not unique. Anne Boylan has described a linkage between antebellum women's activism and life course such that women stepped on and off the leadership track as their family responsibilities and domestic duties required. See Anne Boylan, *The Origins of Women's Activism: New York and Boston, 1797–1840* (Chapel Hill: University of North Carolina Press, 2000), 63–90.

3. My analysis owes much to Kristina Straub, "The Guilty Pleasure of Female Theatrical Cross-Dressing and the Autobiography of Charlotte Clarke," in *Body Guards: The Cultural Politics of Gender Ambiguity,* ed. Julian Epstein and Kristina Straub (New York: Routledge, 1991), 142–166.

4. Cornel Reinhart, Margaret Tacardon, and Philip Hardy argue that widowhood created a symbolic rebirth into sexual purity, carrying with it the moral authority of wife and motherhood that endowed widows such as Josephine Shaw Lowell and Luella Robinson North with the respectability and independence they required to undertake a public role in benevolence. See Reinhart, Tacardon, and Hardy, "The Sexual Politics of Widowhood: The Virgin Rebirth in the Social Construction of Nineteenth-and Early-Twentieth Century Feminine Reality," *Journal of Family History* 23 (January 1998): 28–47.

5. Maria Weston Chapman to Ann and Wendell Phillips, 3 October 1842, Blagden Collection, Houghton Library, Harvard University; Anne Warren Weston to Deborah Weston, New Bedford, 22 October 1842, Weston Papers, Boston Public Library.

6. "I do not leave him for an hour," wrote Maria. See Maria Weston Chapman to Ann Phillips, 6 September [1841], Boston; and Maria Weston Chapman to Friends [Wendell and Ann Phillips], n.p., 6 August 1842, Blagden Collection. Edmund Quincy repeated her words: "She gave up all to him & scarcely left him for a moment." Edmund Quincy to Richard D. Webb, Dedham, 29 January 1843, Quincy/Webb Correspondence, Boston Public Library.

7. Maria Weston Chapman to Lucretia Mott, as quoted in Sarah Pugh to Richard and Hannah Webb, Philadelphia, 24 March 1843, Weston Papers.

8. Clare Taylor has suggested that the drains in the Chapman's Chauncy Place house may have harbored the germ, given that his cousin Ann Terry Greene Phillips, his sister Ann Gray Chapman, and Maria's sister Lucia Weston all developed "consumption" after living there.

9. Anne W. Weston to Deborah Weston, Groton, 13 July 1842, Weston Papers.

10. Caroline Weston to Deborah Weston, Roxbury, [June 1842]; Anne W. Weston to Deborah Weston, New York, 11 May 1842; Anne W. Weston to Lucia Weston, Boston, 21 September 1840, 28 September 1840; Anne W. Weston to Deborah Weston, Northampton, MA, 4 May 1842; Hervey E. Weston to Deborah Weston, Boston, [1841], Weston Papers.

11. Anne W. Weston to Lucia Weston, Boston, 28 September 1840; Caroline Weston to Deborah Weston, Roxbury, [1841], Weston Papers.

12. Caroline Weston to Deborah Weston, Roxbury, [June 1842]; Anne W. Weston to Deborah, Boston, 3 June 1842; Caroline Weston to Deborah Weston, Roxbury, 17 June 1842, Weston Papers.

13. Maria Weston Chapman to Deborah Weston, Boston, [28 June 1842], Weston Papers.

14. Maria Weston Chapman to Deborah Weston, Boston, 1 August 1842, Weston Papers.

15. Alfred Hunt, *Haiti's Influence on Antebellum America: Slumbering Volcano in the Caribbean* (Baton Rouge: Louisiana State University Press, 1988), 2–4.

16. Maria Weston Chapman to Elizabeth Pease, Haiti, 22 February 1841, Garrison Papers, Massachusetts Historical Society, Boston. See also Robert F. Walcott, "Haiti and the British West Indies," letter to the editor, *Liberator* 8 (24 August 1838): 133.

17. Both Edmund Quincy and Wendell Phillips drew on these journals for antislavery articles and speeches. See Edmund Quincy to Maria Weston Chapman, Dedham, 15

November 1842, Weston Papers; Edmund Quincy to Caroline Weston, Dedham, 13 November 1844, Francis Jackson Papers, Massachusetts Historical Society. Maria Weston Chapman to Wendell Phillips, n.p., n.d., Blagden Collection. The Chapmans made contacts with local benevolent association leaders, among whom they passed petitions seeking the abrogation of color laws in the United States and favoring America's official recognition of Haitian independence. They established connections so as to open an official abolitionist correspondence with the Haitian government, that Haiti might "become a powerful coadjutor with the Antislavery Society of the United States." Maria arranged for the Boston Female Anti-Slavery Society to pay for a French-language edition of the *Liberator* for distribution in Haiti. Maria Weston Chapman to William L. Garrison, Cape Haitien, 19 January 1841, Garrison Papers. The United States did not officially recognize Haiti until 1864.

18. The Massachusetts Anti-Slavery Society officially authorized the Chapmans to represent them in Haiti "and to obtain such information as may be in their power, especially from official sources, respecting the true condition of that republic, in order that the friends of liberty and equality in this country may be the better enabled to repel the calumnies of the enemies of Haitien independence, and of negro emancipation; and thus to hasten the day when that emancipation shall be gloriously realized in the United States." William L. Garrison to Henry G. Chapman, Boston, 19 February 1842, in *The Letters of William Lloyd Garrison: No Union with the Slaveholders, 1841–1849,* ed. Walter M. Merrill (Cambridge, MA: Harvard University Press, 1974), 3:48–49.

19. Anne W. Weston to Deborah Weston, Boston, 11 April 1842; Deborah Weston to Anne W. Weston, New Bedford, 14 April 1842, Weston Papers.

20. See letter from Joseph Baltazar Inginac to William L. Garrison, Port au Prince, 1 April 1842, *Liberator* 12 (29 April 1842): 67.

21. Maria Weston Chapman to Deborah Weston, Boston, 22 April [1841], Weston Papers.

22. Caroline Weston to Deborah Weston, Roxbury, 17 June 1842, Weston Papers.

23. Maria Weston Chapman to Deborah Weston, Boston, [28 June 1842], Weston Papers.

24. Maria Weston Chapman to Friends [Wendell and Ann Phillips], n.p., 6 August 1842, Blagden Collection. Ann Terry Greene was Sarah Greene's niece, the daughter of her brother Benjamin. Thus the Phillips were related by marriage to the Westons.

25. Anne Boylan says this was one reason why reform women produced their own newspapers. Boylan, *Origins of Women's Activism,* 144. On notions of publicity see Nancy Isenberg, *Sex and Citizenship in Antebellum America* (Chapel Hill: University of North Carolina Press, 1998). Maria, however, served as interim or co-editor of several reform papers, including the *Liberator,* the *Non-Resistant,* and the *National Anti-Slavery Standard.*

26. Chapman's fame was international. Harriet Martineau introduced her to the British by means of "The Martyr Age of the United States," an article published in the *Westminster Review,* which gave glowing tribute to Chapman's beauty, charisma, and intelligence while extolling her courage.

27. She received hate mail, was spied and beset upon by neighborhood ruffians, and snubbed on the streets by those who despised her politics. Anne W. Weston to Mary Weston, Boston, 1 September 1835; Caroline Weston to Anne W. Weston, Boston, 13 August 1835, Weston Papers.

28. Caroline Weston to Anne W. Weston, 1836, Weston Papers. The *Oxford English Dictionary* gives the origins of the term "gazetted" as the listing in official gazettes of the names of men who have achieved a new position, honor, or rank. Commonly used from the late 1670s through the 1890s, the term connoted a positive change of public status

and signified some degree of renown. Not so for women, for whom such notice had been limited to private matters such as her marriage, the birth of a child, or her death. To be gazetted for any other reason was deemed inappropriate for a woman and to be avoided. According to the *OED* the term "household word" first appeared in 1833, evidence of an era of celebrity.

29. For use of the term, see Edmund Quincy to Henry and Maria Weston Chapman, Dedham, 18 May 1841; Edmund Quincy to Maria Weston Chapman, Dedham, 4 November 1844; Edmund Quincy to Caroline Weston, Dedham, 2 July 1847, Weston Papers.

30. Richard D. Webb to Maria W. Chapman, Dublin, n.d.; Lucia Weston to Debora Weston, Boston, 18 December 1836; Mary Carpenter to Maria Weston Chapman, Bristol, 17 October 1846, Weston Papers.

31. Mary Weston to Deborah Weston, Weymouth, 11 September 1836; [Caroline Weston] to Anne W. Weston, Boston, [1839], Weston Papers.

32. Henry C Wright to Maria Weston Chapman, Dublin, 28 November 1843, Weston Papers.

33. Mary Carpenter to Maria Weston Chapman, Bristol, 17 October 1846; James N. Buffum to Caroline Weston, Perth, Scotland, 25 June 1846, Weston Papers.

34. Maria Weston Chapman to Mary Anne Estlin, Weymouth, 8 March 1858, Weston Papers. Richard D. Webb, its publisher, reflected Chapman's philosophy when he bought the newspaper: "I think it a good way of maintaining an Antislavery interest in peoples minds is by enlisting their sympathy on behalf of its most distinguished advocates." Richard D. Webb to Maria Weston Chapman, Dublin, 1 September 1846, Weston Papers.

35. Mary Ireland to Maria Weston Chapman, Royal Academical Institution, Belfast, 24 January 1846; Caroline Weston to Wendell Phillips, Paris, 25 April 1849, Blagden Collection.

36. See Ann Douglas, *The Feminization of American Culture* (New York: Avon Books, 1977); Elizabeth Varon, *"We Mean to Be Counted": White Women and Politics in Antebellum Virginia* (Chapel Hill: University of North Carolina Press, 1998).

37. J. Winslow to Maria Weston Chapman, Havre, France, 10 January 1846, Weston Papers.

38. Eliza McIntyre to Maria Weston Chapman, Belfast, 1 April 1847; Susanna Fisher, Lifford, Ireland, 27 March 1843, Weston Papers.

39. Leo Braudy, *The Frenzy of Renown: Fame and Its History* (New York: Oxford University Press, 1986), 476. On the print revolution, see Cathy Davidson, *Revolution and the Word: The Rise of the Novel in America* (New York: Oxford University Press, 1986); Richard Brown, *Knowledge Is Power: The Diffusion of Information in Early America, 1700–1865* (New York: Oxford University Press, 1989); Michael Schudson, *Discovering the News: A Social History of American Newspapers* (New York: Basic Books, 1978); and David M. Henkin, *City Reading: Written Words and Public Spaces in Antebellum New York* (New York: Columbia University Press, 1998).

40. Samuel J. May, n. p., n. d. [penciled note, July 1, 1859], May Collection; Richard D. Webb to Edmund Quincy, Dublin, 11 June 1852, Quincy/Webb Correspondence, Boston Public Library.

41. For example, Maria and her sisters removed to Paris in 1848. Harriet Beecher Stowe visited and prominently featured them in her travel memoir. She used only initials, not names, in referring to "Mrs. C.," "the two Misses C.," and "Miss W." The author of *Uncle Tom's Cabin* and an even greater public celebrity than Chapman, Stowe was read avidly on both sides of the Atlantic. It did not take long for the reading public to identify Chapman and her family. See Harriet Beecher Stowe, *Sunny Memories of Foreign Lands* (Boston: Phillips, Sampson, and Co., 1854), 2, 145–190. The book reintroduced

Chapman just before her 1855 return to Boston, reviving public interest in her antislavery politics.

42. For example, Mary G. Chapman to Ann Phillips, Boston, 25 September 1842; Maria Weston Chapman to Ann and Wendell Phillips, 3 October 1842, Blagden Collection; Sarah Pugh to Richard and Hannah Webb, Philadelphia, 24 [March] 1843, Weston Papers; Edmund Quincy to Richard D. Webb, Dedham, 29 January 1843, Quincy/Webb Correspondence.

43. On consolation literature and mourning ritual, see Karen Halttunen, *Confidence Men and Painted Women: A Study of Middle-Class Culture in America, 1830–1870* (New Haven, CT: Yale University Press, 1982), chap. 5; Ann Douglas, "Heaven Our Home: Consolation Literature in the Northern United States, 1830–1880," in *Death in America*, ed. David E. Stannard (Philadelphia: University of Pennsylvania Press, 1975), 48–59.

44. Maria Weston Chapman to Ann and Wendell Phillips, 3 October 1842, Blagden Collection; Mary G. Chapman to Ann Phillips, Boston, 25 September 1842, Blagden Collection; *Liberator* 12 (October 7, 1842): 159; *Liberator* 12 (October 21, 1842): 167.

45. "Report of the Ninth Annual Meeting of the Boston Female Anti-Slavery Society," *Liberator* 12 (October 7, 1842): 159; *Liberator* 12 (October 21, 1842): 167; Henrietta Sargent to George B. Dixwell, Boston, 6 October 1842, Wigglesworth Collection, Massachusetts Historical Society.

46. Mary G. Chapman to Ann Phillips, Boston, 25 September 1842, Blagden Collection; Edmund Quincy to Richard D. Webb, Dedham, 29 January 1843, Quincy/Webb Correspondence.

47. Maria Weston Chapman to Anne W. Weston, n.p., n.d. [after the 10 June 1855 death of John B. Estlin], Weston Papers.

48. Edmund Quincy to Richard D. Webb, Dedham, 29 January 1843, Quincy/Webb Correspondence; Sarah Pugh to Richard and Hannah Webb, Philadelphia, 24 March 1843, Weston Papers.

49. These descriptions evoked the popular memoirs of evangelical women who increasingly held forth on religious subjects from their own deathbeds in defiance of conventions that gave to men the role of religious commentary. See Mary Ryan, *Cradle of the Middle Class: The Family in Oneida County, New York, 1790–1865* (Cambridge: Cambridge University Press, 1981), 88.

50. Maria signed the call for the convention, along with transcendentalists Bronson Alcott and Ralph Waldo Emerson, and abolitionists Edmund Quincy and William Lloyd Garrison.

51. Maria Weston Chapman to William L. Garrison, Cape Haitien, 19 January 1841, Garrison Papers; Anne W. Weston to Deborah Weston, Chauncey Place, Boston, 15 January 1842, Weston Papers.

52. Anne W. Weston to Deborah Weston, New Bedford 22 October 1842, Weston Papers; Edmund Quincy to Richard D. Webb, Dedham, 29 January 1843, Quincy/Webb Correspondence.

53. Maria Weston Chapman to Anne W. Weston, n.p., n.d. [after 10 June 1855], Weston Papers.

54. Her grandson said of Maria, "Her religion was totality as to conduct, but was fragmentary in statement. It was made up of proverbs, poems, and anecdotes from all ages,— wisdom-scraps of an encouraging and militant nature." John Jay Chapman, *Memories and Milestones* (New York: Moffat, Yard, and Co., 1915), 217.

55. Maria Weston Chapman to Anne W. Weston, n.p., n.d. [after 10 June 1855]; Sarah Pugh to Richard and Hannah Webb, Philadelphia, 24 March 1843, Weston Papers.

56. Sarah Pugh to Richard and Hannah Webb, Philadelphia, 24 March 1843; Caroline Weston to Deborah Weston, Boston, 24 June 1842; Maria Weston Chapman to Deborah Weston, Boston, 28 June 1842, Weston Papers; "Another Serious Bereavement," *Liberator* 12 (7 October 1842): 39, 159; Mary G. Chapman to Ann Phillips, 25 September 1842, Boston, Blagden Collection; Henrietta Sargent to George B. Dixwell, Boston, 6 October 1842, Wigglesworth Collection; Edmund Quincy to Richard D. Webb, Dedham, 29 January 1843, Quincy/Webb Correspondence.

57. For discussion of this conflation, see Lori D. Ginzburg, *Women and the Work of Benevolence: Morality, Class, and Politics in the Nineteenth-Century United States* (New Haven, CT: Yale University Press, 1990).

58. "Some Reminiscences of Mrs. Maria W. Chapman," newspaper clipping, Bigelow Collection, Essex Institute, Salem, MA.

59. S. Henry Dickson, M.D., *Manual of Pathology and Practice, Being the Outline of the Course of Lectures Delivered* (Charleston, SC: published by the author, 1842), 178–179, 180–181; J. S. Bartlett, M.D., *The Physician's Pocket Synopsis: Affording a Concise View of the Symptoms and Treatment of the Medical and Surgical Diseases Incident to the Human Frame. Compiled from the Best Authorities, with References to the Most Approved Modern Authors. Together with the Properties and Doses of the Simples and Compounds of the National Pharmacopoeia of the United States. Alphabetically Arranged* (Boston: Munroe and Francis, 1822), 223–224.

60. William Willis Mosely, "Predisposing and Exciting Causes of Insanity," in *Eleven Chapters on Nervous and Mental Complaints* (London: Simpkin, Marshall and Co., 1838), 123–140, as quoted in Vieda Skultans, *Madness and Morals: Ideas on Insanity in the Nineteenth Century* (Boston: Routledge and Kegan Paul, 1975), 41–50.

61. George Man Burrows, "Brain, Heart and Will," in *Commentaries on Insanity* (London: Underwood, 1828), 112–113, as quoted in Skultans, *Madness and Morals*, 35–36.

62. William L. Garrison to George W. Benson, Boston, 25 May 1838, in *The Letters of William Lloyd Garrison: A House Dividing against Itself, 1836–1840,* ed. Louis Ruchames (Cambridge, MA: Harvard University Press, 1971), 2:366; Lydia Maria Child to Caroline Weston, Northampton, 13 August 1838, Garrison Papers; "Some Reminiscences of Mrs. Maria W. Chapman," unlabeled newspaper obituary, Bigelow Collection; Epes Sargent Dixwell to John James Dixwell, Boston, May 28, 1838, Wigglesworth Collection.

63. Charges of madness shadowed Chapman. A Mrs. Marshall of Exeter, England, for example, insisted to friends that "Mrs Chapman left Boston for Europe because she was mad. . . . all Boston know it was so quite well." British colleagues defended her from such charges: "You know Mrs M it cannot be true . . . Mrs C. *could never have found time for it.*" Mrs. Mitchell to Maria Weston Chapman, Bristol, 13 January 1853, Estlin Papers.

64. Caroline Weston to Mary G. Chapman, Stonington, CT, [1838]; Caroline Weston to Lucia Weston, Stonington, CT, [1838]; Caroline Weston to Lucia Weston, Stonington, CT, [1838] Weston Papers; Lydia Maria Child to Caroline Weston, Northampton, 27 July 1838, Garrison Papers; Lydia Maria Child to Lydia B. Child, 7 August 1838, Child Collection, Schlesinger Library, Radcliffe College.

65. Maria gave birth for the fourth time late in May 1840, and the baby died on 6 April 1841. Gertrude's illness came on suddenly and lasted only two days. The family believed that she died of a fever produced by teething, although Caroline Greene Chapman was quite ill with a fever at the same time. Caroline to Maria Weston Chapman and Henry G. Chapman, Boston, 5 April 1841; Anne W. Weston to Maria Weston

Chapman, Boston, 15 April 1841; Mary G. Chapman to Deborah Weston, Boston, 16 April 1841, Weston Papers.

66. Anne W. Weston to Elizabeth Pease, Boston, 31 May 1841, Antislavery Papers, Boston Public Library.

67. In addition to the discussion in Ryan, *Cradle of the Middle Class,* and Boylan, *Origins of Women's Activism,* of deferential politics in benevolent reform, see, for a discussion of such a politics in a different context, Catherine Allgor, *Parlor Politics: In Which the Ladies of Washington Help Build a City and a Government* (Charlottesville: University Press of Virginia, 2000).

68. For the critical role of the Pastoral Letter of 1837 and Chapman's response, see Maria Weston Chapman, *Right and Wrong in Boston: Annual Report of the Boston Female Anti-Slavery Society, with a Sketch of the Obstacles Thrown in the Way of Emancipation by Certain Clerical Abolitionists and Advocates for the Subjection of Women in 1837* (Boston: Isaac Knapp, 1837); and Boylan, *Origins of Women's Activism,* chap. 4.

69. For discussion of the election, see Debra Gold Hansen, *Strained Sisterhood: Gender and Class in the Boston Female Anti-Slavery Society* (Amherst: University of Massachusetts Press, 1993); and Shirley J. Yee, *Black Women Abolitionists: A Study in Activism, 1828–1860* (Knoxville: University of Tennessee Press, 1992).

70. *Liberator* 6, no. 33 (13 August 1836): 130. Cosigner was Maria's close childhood friend and Boston Female Anti-Slavery Society colleague Melania Ammidon.

71. Boylan, *Origins of Women's Activism,* 159. See also Julie Roy Jeffrey, *The Great Silent Army of Abolitionism: Ordinary Women in the Antislavery Movement* (Chapel Hill: University of North Carolina Press, 1998); Richard S. Newman, *The Transformation of American Abolitionism: Fighting Slavery in the Early Republic* (Chapel Hill: University of North Carolina Press, 2002); and Susan Zaeske, *Signatures of Citizenship: Petitioning, Antislavery, and Women's Political Identity* (Chapel Hill: University of North Carolina Press, 2003).

72. *Liberator* 6, no. 8 (20 February 1836): 30; *Liberator* 6, no. 14 (2 April 1836): 54; *Liberator* 6, no. 42 (15 October 1836): 168; *Liberator,* 6, no. 14 (2 April 1836): 54; *Liberator* 6, no. 24 (11 June 1836): 99; *Liberator* 6, no. 35 (27 August 1836): 140; "To the Seventy Abolitionists Who Are about to Become Public Advocates of the Cause of Human Rights," *Liberator* 6, no. 45 (5 November 1836): 178; *Liberator* 6, no. 42 (24 December 1836): 207; *Liberator* 7, no. 1 (2 January 1837): 4; *Liberator* 7, no. 2 (7 January 1837): 8. Anne M. Boylan argues that unlike benevolent or moral reform organizations, distinctions based on marital status were deemed irrelevant to Boston's antislavery activists. They had a far larger proportion of unmarried officers, and after 1836 they generally adopted the Quaker practice of refusing to indicate their marital status by the use of titles. In contrast, however, the more evangelically oriented New York Female Anti-Slavery Society did use theirs in public documents. Boylan, *Origins of Women's Activism,* 72–73. For discussion of the use of marital titles among female associationalists and the rituals of female deference in the 1850s South, see Suzanne Lebsock, *Free Women of Petersburg: Status and Culture in a Southern Town, 1784–1860* (New York: W. W. Norton, 1985), 230.

73. *Liberator* 6 (30 June, 1837): 27; reprinted in *Liberator* 7, no. 29 (14 July 1837): 116. By 1839, Maria's initials alone appeared on her published work. See a poetic advertisement for the Boston fair, "St. Nicholas in the Cause," *Liberator* 9, no. 45 (8 November 1839): 180; and sonnets by "M.W. C." republished from the *Liberty Bell,* in *Liberator* 9, no. 47 (22 November 1839): 188; *Liberator* 9, no. 58 (13 December 1839): 200.

74. E. A. S. Smith to Caroline Weston, Hingham, [December 1842], Weston Papers.

75. Edmund Quincy to Richard D. Webb, Dedham, 29 January 1843, Quincy/Webb Correspondence. Her nursing of Henry was not altogether successful in shifting public attention away from her public advocacy. One Bostonian, indifferent to slavery and abolition, reduced the news of Henry's funeral to a comment on his wife's notoriety: "Mrs Maria W Chapman is even more looked up to than her husband ever was." Esther Dixwell to George B. Dixwell, Boston, 2 October 1842, Wigglesworth Family Collection.

76. Edmund Quincy to Richard D. Webb, Dedham, 29 January 1843, Quincy/Webb Correspondence. Indeed, Chapman's obituary in the *Liberator* recalled the earlier death of Henry's sister Ann Gray Chapman and the family's devastation. "Another Serious Bereavement," 159.

77. One historian of fatherhood suggests that once a child's illness had been professionally diagnosed as beyond the scope of woman's nursing, a father might intervene in the child's care as Henry Sr. did in a moment of panic as he seized his son and ran with him to the wharf in an effort to put Henry Jr. on the regular packet to Haiti in search of a warmer clime to stem his dangerous deterioration. The care of a sick child provided fathers an opportunity to explore the softer side of manliness. A child's death, then, might legitimately prostrate him while other setbacks and woes could not without undermining his masculinity and paternal authority. Although such an expectation might help explain Henry Sr.'s position in this verbal description of the deathbed, it does not vitiate Maria's stance or the power it attributed to her. Stephen M. Frank, *Life with Father: Parenthood and Masculinity in the Nineteenth-Century American North* (Baltimore: Johns Hopkins University Press, 1998), 76–80. Anne W. Weston to Deborah Weston, Boston, 11 February 1842, Weston Papers.

78. "Another Serious Bereavement," 159.

79. Francis Parkman, *An Offering of Sympathy to the Afflicted, Especially to Parents Bereaved of Their Children* (Boston: Lilly, Wait, Colman and Holden, 1833), 134; Halttunen, *Confidence Men,* 130–131.

80. Anne W. Weston, "Lines Written on Hearing the Remark of a Friend, That a Large Number of Abolitionists Had Died during the Preceding Year," *Liberty Bell* 1, no. 48 (29 November 1839): 192. Weston's insistence that the deaths of so many abolitionists should inspire those who remained to recommit themselves to the cause partook to some degree of what Jeffrey Steele has identified as a new rhetoric of mourning in antebellum America. Nineteenth-century writers constructed themselves as both object and agent of a politicized mourning through which they generated sympathy for the oppression that they and others suffered as individuals and groups exiled from the benefits and promises of republican citizenship. According to Steele, in mourning their representative losses (women's exclusion from the body politic, slaves' exclusion from liberty), such writers positioned themselves as objects of their readers' sympathy so as to move themselves and their readers to challenge oppression. Jeffrey Steele, "The Gender and Racial Politics of Mourning in Ante-bellum America," in *An Emotional History of the United States,* ed. Peter N. Stearns and Jan Lewis (New York: New York University Press, 1998), 91–106.

81. Maria Weston Chapman to Lucretia Mott, as copied by Sarah Pugh in a letter to Richard and Hannah Webb, Philadelphia, 24 March 1843, Weston Papers; Edmund Quincy to Richard D. Webb, Dedham, 29 January 1843, Quincy/Webb Correspondence; *Liberator* 12, no. 45 (11 November 1842): 179.

82. Halttunen, *Confidence Men,* 36–38.

83. Edmund Quincy to Richard D. Webb, Dedham, 29 January 1843, Quincy/Webb Correspondence. Interestingly, and by contrast, Deborah and Anne Weston went into deep

mourning and seclusion after their father's death in 1855, much to the annoyance of those who disapproved of such demonstrations, including Maria. See Edmund Quincy to Richard D. Webb, Dedham, 12 February 1856, Quincy/Webb Correspondence.

84. Samuel May Jr. to Maria Weston Chapman, n.p., 5 November [1842]; Edmund Quincy to Maria Weston Chapman, Dedham, 15 November 1842; Susan Cabot to Maria Weston Chapman, West Roxbury, 17 November 1842; Fred S. Cabot M.S.C. to Anne W. Weston, Boston, 30 November 1842, Weston Papers.

85. Edmund Quincy to Richard D. Webb, Dedham, 29 January 1843, Quincy/Webb Correspondence; Maria Weston Chapman, *Right and Wrong in the Anti-Slavery Societies: Seventh Annual Report of the Boston Female Anti-Slavery* (Boston: Anti-Slavery Office, 1840), 28.

86. The Weston papers show multiple examples. For example, Sydney Gay, editor of the *National Anti-Slavery Standard,* urged Richard D. Webb to meet the Westons on their arrival in Europe. "You will deserve never to see anybody worth seeing again if you do not. I should like to know how they impress you. Caroline I know will, as a delightful, well-bred, cultivated woman. But y[e] Capt. tho' highly cultivated, of high breeding, & fine conversational powers, is not a *personal* favorite. People are not at ease in her presence." Sydney H. Gay to R. D. Webb, New York, 19 July 1848, Anti-Slavery Papers.

87. Chapman, *Memories and Milestones,* 218.

88. Maria Weston Chapman to Mary Anne Estlin, 24 January 1852, Weston Papers.

CHAPTER 8

The United Daughters of the Confederacy, Confederate Widows, and the Lost Cause

"WE MUST NOT FORGET OR NEGLECT THE WIDOWS"

JENNIFER L. GROSS

On January 24, 1898, after a full week of attending speeches given in celebration of Virginia Day by the presidents of the Association for the Preservation of Virginia Antiquities, the United Daughters of the Confederacy (UDC), the Preservation Association of Mount Vernon, and the Confederate Memorial Literary Society, Lucy Bagby, a Confederate widow from Richmond, Virginia, remarked, "Enough, Enough of Woman[']s Work! I am sick of it all."[1] Despite this outburst, Bagby had been and would continue to be an active participant in woman's work, especially when it came to Confederate-oriented groups. For Bagby and other Confederate widows, participation in the UDC along with other Confederate memorial work allowed them to take part in an ongoing dialogue about the Confederacy, the men who had fought and perhaps given their lives for it, and the widows these men had left behind.

The commemorative and benevolent activities of women in memorial associations and the UDC contributed in several ways to the creation of an acceptable place for Confederate widows within the reassertion of traditional gender roles in the postbellum South.[2] First, by venerating Confederate soldiers who gave their lives, memorial activities reassured still-living Southern men of their masculinity by reinforcing the masculinity involved in fighting for the Cause—despite loss of the war to the North. As LeeAnn Whites observes in her study of the war's effects on gender relationships in Augusta, Georgia:

> Memorial activity was designed to address the erosion of the power of white men to "protect" their women as they had in the past. . . . By understanding Confederate men's participation in the war as grounded in the first instance in their commitment to the defense of their homes and their women and children, the memorial movement served to validate the role that those men still living . . . had played in the conflict,

despite their military defeat to the North and the loss of the right to slave ownership.[3]

Additionally, by contributing to the women's memorial activities, either financially or rhetorically, still-living men could become symbolic providers and protectors of their dead comrades' widows. As an editorialist in Augusta, Georgia, avowed, "the knowledge of sympathy is to an afflicted soul, what curatives are to the sick, and it was never more so than with this great class. . . . To know that their husbands or sons live in the hearts of the people, is to wives and mothers almost a sufficiency in life."[4] In the mind of this editorialist, as well as in those of many Southerners, support for memorialization activities could take the place of actual provision among Confederate survivors if necessary, at least while the region recovered from the effects of the war. In other words, even if Southerners could not afford to give regular monetary assistance to widows after the war, they could support memorial activities that recognized such women's ultimate sacrifice. Of course, for many of the widows themselves, financial assistance might have meant a lot more.

Second, the commemoration of Confederate soldiers' valor and sacrifice also implicitly drew attention to the valor and sacrifice of the widows and families whom the dead soldiers had left behind. As Margaret Davis, the historian of the Confederated Southern Memorial Association, gushed:

> Nothing need be said of the trials that beset and perplexed the women of the Confederacy in their efforts to rescue from oblivion the memories of men who stand recorded as the world's greatest heroes, but through trials and persecutions these women persevered and to-day their noble deeds are told in history and song, and side by side with the Veterans they gather each year in reunion, recognized North and South, their devotion rewarded by the recognition and appreciation of the world, who loves a faithful woman; faithful aye, even more so, than the usual acceptance of the word, have the women of the Confederacy been to their heroes, traditions, and the Cause for which they struggled four long eventful years.[5]

For memorial associations, Confederate widows, with their gracious abnegation and glorious martyrdom, came to symbolize the ideal in Southern womanhood— just as Confederate soldiers represented the ideal Southern man. Within the Lost Cause, dead Confederates, living veterans, and Confederate widows were the ultimate icons, deserving of honor, respect, and, in the case of those still alive, benevolence when available and deemed necessary.

Third, during the war, women and widows across the South had contributed to the Confederate effort by taking over jobs left open in schools, hospitals, government offices, and factories by the men's departure for the war. More importantly for the postwar period, women had also banded together to form volunteer aid societies. These volunteer societies had focused on supplying soldiers with clothing and other sundries needed in the field or on doling out aid to their families at home, left without the benefit of a male provider and protector. By contributing to the war effort in this way, women extended their traditional role as wives into the public sphere. As Whites argues, "from the perspective of these women [who volunteered in aid societies], patriotism took on a peculiarly domestic cast. While their men may have enlisted to defend their position as 'free men,' their women entered the war to protect their position as dependents, as mothers, wives, and daughters."[6] Moreover, aid to soldiers' families reaffirmed wives' dependence on their husbands in that the assistance they received was offered because the soldiers were fulfilling their masculine duty by going to war to protect their homes. This assistance, then, reassured Southern men of their position as patriarchs, despite their absence from home. After the war, Confederate groups continued to provide assistance to the widows and orphans of soldiers, but the main focus of their work turned to memorialization of those who fought, those who died, and those who were left behind.

Beginning immediately after the war, groups of white Southerners throughout the South, primarily the same women who had volunteered their services in aid societies during the war, began memorializing the valor and heroics of Confederate soldiers, both those who lived through the war and, more importantly, those who did not. These women—many of them widows, like Lucy Bagby—banded together into memorial associations and began commemorating the Confederacy. Accordingly, their first order of business was to tend to the graves of the Confederate dead. This task was particularly difficult if soldiers had been buried in mass graves on far-off battlefields. Not to be deterred, women like Nancy Branch, the widow of General Lawrence O'Brien Branch who died at Antietam in 1863, began the process of locating, collecting, and reinterring the Confederate dead. Leading the Ladies' Memorial Association (LMA) of Raleigh, North Carolina, in its efforts to establish a Confederate cemetery in the city of Raleigh, Branch oversaw the establishment of Oakwood Cemetery upon a plot of land donated by Henry Mordecai. After reinterring the bodies of Confederate soldiers who had been buried on land earmarked by the federal military to become a Union cemetery, the women turned their attention to those North Carolina soldiers not buried within the state. Eventually, the LMA of Raleigh oversaw the reburial of 137 men from the Gettysburg battlefield and another 107 who had been laid to rest in Arlington. Each grave boasted a granite headstone with the soldier's name and the state from which he came.[7] Across the South, women—"true to their nature, cling[ing] to their loved and lost, and with a devotion that is undying"—were involved in similar "labors of love" regarding the Confederate dead.[8]

In Richmond, Virginia, the Hollywood Memorial Association (HMA) and the Hollywood Confederate Cemetery itself took on an effort of great significance within the postwar Confederate identity. Organized on May 3, 1866, the HMA raised over $26,000 to care for the graves of 12,000 Confederate soldiers from across the South who were laid to rest on the sixteen acres of the cemetery known as the Confederate Section. Additionally, the HMA oversaw the reinterment of 3,000 men from Gettysburg and 1,000 men from the various battlefields around Richmond.[9] Holding the graves of well-known Confederates and Virginians as well as unknown soldiers who died in or around Richmond, Hollywood Cemetery became a shrine to the Confederacy, welcoming within its somber walls many seeking the Confederate past as well as locals looking for a quiet place for a picnic with a view of the James River.

Women's work in the reburial of the Confederate dead in Raleigh, Richmond, and elsewhere represents not only an allegiance to the Cause but also a fulfillment of women's traditional role as mourner. During the war, many women had been unable to oversee the death and burial of their spouses. By "bringing the boys home," memorial associations acted en masse in place of these individual mourners, simultaneously drawing attention to survivors' bereavement and reassuring Southern men that Southern women were behaving according to traditional gender prescriptions in mourning the loss of their loved ones.

Having commenced and in some cases completed the work of reinterment, memorial associations across the South began celebrating Confederate Memorial Day as an occasion to pay homage to the Confederate dead by decorating their newly laid graves. Immediately upon the completion of Oakwood Cemetery, Nancy Branch and the LMA of Raleigh chose the day that Stonewall Jackson died, May 10, to commemorate all the dead of the Confederacy. At their first celebration in 1867, the *Raleigh Sentinel* reported that almost all the stores in Raleigh were closed in honor of the event, and nearly six hundred "deeply moved" spectators gathered to watch as the ladies decorated the graves, paying homage both to the common soldier who gave his life as well as to the "other numerous and distinguished gallant dead," among them Nancy Branch's husband.[10]

Although Confederate Memorial Day celebrations sprang up independently throughout the South during the first few years after the war, Southern legend appropriately assigns its origins to a Confederate widow. In 1866, the widow of Charles J. Williams of Georgia published "an appeal to southerners to set apart a day 'to be handed down through time as a religious custom of the South to wreathe the graves of our martyred dead with flowers.'" At first the day varied by locale, but eventually Jefferson Davis's birthday, June 3, became the official Confederate Memorial Day throughout much of the South.[11] Because of the impetus put upon women by Victorian mourning rituals to grieve—and grieve well—at the death of a husband else they risk public censure, it is significant that a Confederate widow is honored for issuing the first call for a Confederate Memorial Day. What better way to ensure "grieving well" than to make your bereavement an annual public event? Moreover, the institutionalization of a specific day to honor the dead would remind Southerners of those who had sacrificed their men for the Cause. In arguing for the establishment of a Confederate Memorial Day in Georgia, the Georgia Ladies' Memorial Association asserted that "not only would this recognition of the Confederate Dead serve to preserve the 'lost cause' of their men's economic and political position. . . . It would also serve to console the widow and orphan, who could look to few other comforts in this world."[12] Year after year, throughout the South, Southerners, especially Southern women, celebrated Confederate Memorial Day by attending ceremonies in graveyards and decorating the graves of the Cause's deceased.

After they returned the Confederate dead to their Southland if not their homelands, began the tradition of decorating their graves, and initiated a Confederate Memorial Day, Confederate memorial groups turned their attention to the construction of larger, all-inclusive monuments to the Confederate soldiers who died. "Confederate men would indeed rise again" in all their patriarchal glory if the women in the memorial (now monument) associations had anything to say about it.[13] The monuments that sprang up across the South did two things. First, they honored the men who had died as "true Southern men," because they died protecting their homes. "The role of monuments and memorials, as elements of the present landscape," David Lowenthal, a historical geographer asserts, "is to direct attention toward the remembered or imagined past."[14] Within this remembered past, Confederate soldiers, regardless of their class, took on the mantle of glorious martyrs for the Cause who died living up to their roles as men by going to war to protect their homes. Second, Confederate monuments implicitly drew attention to the wives and children left behind as "true Southern women," who deserved the respect and protection of Southern society in the absence of their husbands. The widows of those soldiers who did not survive the war took on an exalted status as true Southern women, regardless of their class, because they had made the greatest sacrifice possible—their husbands—and there were massive pillars and statues dotting the Southern landscape to that effect in case anyone happened to forget.

As graves were decorated, Confederate Memorial Day celebrated, and monuments raised to the Confederate dead, the widows became increasingly defined by their status as survivors. Commemoration, in effect, made a widow's loss of her husband meaningful for the rest of society. Orators consistently remembered widows when they pontificated over a monument or at a Confederate Memorial Day celebration. Typically, monument dedications began with prayers invoking "the blessings of the Almighty on the widows and orphans of veterans." Moreover, orators almost always asked the audience when they looked upon the monument to remember not only those who died for the Cause but also the wives and families they had left behind.[15]

As the nineteenth century progressed and the activities of monument associations became more grandiose, many began applying to their various local and state governments for monetary support for their projects. In almost every case, their wishes were granted. The LMA of Raleigh, for example, had begun discussing the construction of a monument to the Confederate dead almost immediately after the end of the war, but the region's economic devastation had made it impossible to raise the necessary funds. By the late 1880s, the LMA had raised a good portion of the money and applied to the North Carolina state legislature for the rest. A cartoon in the *Raleigh News and Observer* makes clear the LMA's reasons for wanting to commemorate the dead. The women are pictured huddled around an unfinished monument, pleading with the North Carolina General Assembly to give them the money necessary to complete the project. The quote underneath reads, "Let us teach posterity that patriots die not in vain. A land without monuments is a land without memories. Lend us of your means to commemorate the virtues of our fallen dead." The other half of the cartoon shows North Carolina's legislators gathered around the coffin of Frederick Douglass. The caption below reads, "It is not your dead, but our Fred over whom we weep. Bear with us; our hearts are in the coffin there with Caesar, and we must pause till they come back to us."[16] The legislators' refusal to fund the monument translated into a lack of Southernness, for the cartoon clearly implies that they were the allies of the "Black Republicans" as a result of their initial resistance to grant the women's funding request. Not surprisingly, shortly after the cartoon appeared a barrage of letters critical of the legislature flooded the paper, and editorials appeared proclaiming "SHAME, SHAME, SHAME! This is the indignant refrain of the public press of the country [as to the] General Assembly's Infamy."[17] Soon thereafter, the women received $10,000 from the General Assembly to complete the monument. Other Southern states took similar action. The Virginia General Assembly, at the behest of the HMA, authorized an annual appropriation beginning in the late 1890s for the care and preservation of Confederate graves and cemeteries throughout the state; Georgia also appropriated government funds for memorial work, including the reinterment of the Confederate dead and the construction of monuments throughout the state.[18] By contributing money to memorialization projects, legislators—some more willingly than others—involved themselves in the reassurance of proper Southern gender roles. They provided the financial needs of memorialization, while the women mourned.

In response to women's efforts to memorialize Confederate soldiers, male Confederate groups began to contribute to the place of Confederate widows in the postwar South by constructing monuments to honor the "Women of the Confederacy." Because one of the primary stimuli for monument building was the "perceived need to promote social stability among white Southerners," the "expressions of southern women's devotion to Confederate veterans served to reassure these men of the value of their wartime sacrifices" and the Cause for which they fought and their comrades had died.[19] In an age in which black men and women were trying to assert their rights and the Populists were trying to unite poor Southerners, black and white, against the elite establishment, Southern men needed to know that Confederate widows lived up to the standards of "true Southern womanhood," just as they needed to believe the same about their own wives and daughters. Evidence lies in the language used to commemorate Confederate women in monuments and memorials. Calling for donations for a monument to honor North Carolina's women of the Confederacy, Commander H. C. Bourne beseeched the members of the Lewis, Dowd, Myatt Camp of the Tarboro, North Carolina, United Confederate Veterans Association to do their duty in honoring the "self-sacrificing deeds of the women of the Confederacy during the death-struggle for Southern independence."[20]

Although the bravery, courage, and valor of Southern women in the face of the Northern enemy had become commonplace in Confederate mythology by that time, Southern men most often chose to eulogize women as nurturers and supporters of their men, that is, as fulfillers of traditional roles. As Elise Smith has persuasively argued, "the major purpose in perpetuating these images was to sustain the traditions of the 'glorious old South,' a patriarchal system based on 'frail, tender' women and their chivalric knights."[21] In his speech accepting the North Carolina Monument to the Women of the Confederacy, Governor Craig Locke invoked the memory of those women who had said good-bye to their husbands for the last time when they left for war, intoning: "Lovers say good-bye with tokens of plighted troth; the young mother and the father in uniform, kneel together, weeping over the cradle of the new born babe; there are tears and everlasting fare-wells; the cavalcade is filing off." He continued emotionally: "At home alone, the wives and mothers, these Women of the Confederacy, in patience and suffering, are listening for the coming of those who will never return—will never return. . . . We dedicate this monument as a symbol of our veneration."[22] Calling on God in a prayer at the same dedication, the Rev. E. A. Osborne continued Locke's themes: "And especially do we now desire to thank Thee, O Lord, that thou didst endue the hearts and souls of the women our land with such wonderful courage, fortitude and zeal to bear the hardships, sufferings and afflictions of the dreadful period of bloody and deadly conflict enable them to comfort and encourage their loved ones, while they offered and sacrificed their lives upon their country's altar. . . . May this monument now being dedicated to their memory stand for all ages as a faith-ful and enduring witness of their loyalty and devotion to their country's cause, and of their love and sympathy for those who suffered for their homes."[23] For Locke, Osborne, and other Southerners, it was important that Confederate widows be seen as honorable, noble, and indeed worthy of veneration so that Southerners could imagine Confederate widows to be "true Southern ladies" rather than chal-lenges to the security of patriarchy as legally independent women.[24]

More important than the incantations memorializing Confederate widows as noble heroines who sacrificed for the Cause is the idea that they did so readily and without complaining. In her 1926 volume *North Carolina Women of the Con-federacy,* Lucy Huske attempted to tell what she referred to as the "REAL HISTORY of the part the women of North Carolina took in the Confederacy."[25] Not surpris-ingly, she opened her first chapter with a poem celebrating how Southern women willingly became widows for the Cause:

> The loving mothers, sisters, sweethearts, wives,
> Who, when the war drum's fatal summons came,
> Gave up the dearest treasures of their lives
> And bore the Martyr's cross in Freedom's name.[26]

Similarly, in his oration at the unveiling of the Monument to the North Carolina Women of the Confederacy, Daniel Harvey Hill of the North Carolina Historical Commission intoned, "The silent woman of the memorial will typify the uncom-plaining women of the South."[27] Yet many women of the South were not silent about their woes during the war and did not actively encourage their menfolk to fight, so it became necessary to remake these "dissenters" into "typical" Southern women during the postwar period in order to properly venerate the Cause.[28] As H. E. Gulley contends, "Southern men relied on women to restore their honor after the Confederate military defeat and expected women to revert to their previous inferior status" both in reality and symbolically.[29] Continuing in his speech to celebrate the character of Southern women, Hill boasted, "When war came, and came in her [Southern women's] case with unusual horrors, she met it, not with mere passive fortitude, but with aggressive spirit. To the husband promptly volunteering she meted out encouragement and help; to the husband who faltered, she said, 'I know how to live as the widow of a brave man, but I do not know how to live as the wife of a coward.'"[30] Hill went on throughout the speech to laud Southern women's behavior during the war as self-sacrificing, inventive, and courageous but made sure to close with a reminder that Southern women were, above all, "womanly": "She never thought of doubting that her sphere of action was the home, and she centered her effort on making that home a place of refinement and comfort."[31] For those women whose homes were destroyed by the loss of a husband, it was doubly important to imagine them as supremely womanly, despite their anomalous position in Southern society as manless women.

Confederate celebrations glorified Confederate widows and women in general, but the widows of Confederate heroes received special veneration. While the heroes were alive, they had symbolized the Cause both during the war and after. When those luminaries died, their widows took their places, becoming cult heroes because of their ties to their deceased husbands—ties that were rarely broken by remarriage. Among the hundreds of Confederate war heroes memorialized in the postwar Confederate celebrations that raged throughout the South in the second half of the nineteenth century, few if any of their wives remarried, giving birth to what amounted to a Cult of Dead Generals.[32]

That many of the widows of prominent men did not remarry is perhaps not surprising given the cachet attached to their names. Rarely were widows referred to by their own names. Although it was not unusual during this era for married women to be addressed as Mrs. John Doe, it is significant that widows of war heroes were addressed not only by their husband's name but also by his rank. For example, Mary Anna Jackson was not just Mrs. Thomas Jackson but Mrs. General Stonewall Jackson. Similarly, Flora Stuart was not Mrs. J.E.B. Stuart but Mrs. General J.E.B. Stuart. The failure, or more likely refusal, of such women to remarry lent credence to the idea that "in woman's nature there is a God-given sentimentality that makes her cling to her loved and lost with a devotion that is undying."[33] Such must have been especially true of a woman who had been married to a Confederate hero. After all, what can shore up a man's masculinity more thoroughly than a widow who will seemingly mourn for him forever when he dies? Just as these widows' perpetual mourning embellished their deceased husbands' memories, so too did all Confederate widows, who would not or, in most cases, could not remarry, become perpetual mourners in Southerners' minds.

Members of the Cult of Dead Generals, like other Confederate widows, attended veterans' reunions, monument unveilings, and Confederate Memorial Day celebrations, actively participated in memorial and monument associations including the UDC, and wrote and published their dead husbands' memoirs for an eager reading public.[34] In La Salle Pickett's obituary, which lauded her commitment to the Confederate cause, special mention was made of her attendance at the unveiling of the Lee monument in Richmond, Virginia, where she "was the recipient of marked attention as the widow of one of the great generals of the Confederate army."[35] And it was not just the wives of the most famous generals who found themselves the recipients of such attention within the Cult of Dead Generals. Individual communities also regarded the wives of their local heroes as special for their continued association with their deceased husbands. In a letter of invitation, a United Confederate Veterans camp wrote to Eliza Cook, the widow of Brigadier General Edmond C. Cook of North Carolina, a relatively minor hero in the grand scheme of the Cause: "It is most proper that the widow of the brave, gallant, chivalrous, Col. Ed. Cook should grace our reunion with her presence on the 18th inst, and we therefore beg you to come. . . . The gallant dead of our state, are, our pride and we delight to do them honor. Among the many from Williamson who sacrificed themselves in the 'Lost Cause' none achieved more undying fame, and certainly no one would be more welcome than his dearly loved wife."[36] Similarly, at the 1913 Great Reunion at Gettysburg—an event that reunited veterans of both the Grand Army of the Republic and the Confederate States Army—Cassie Moncure Lyne, the widow of Confederate Major William H. Lyne, another relatively minor war hero, was asked to compose and read the "Ode of Welcome."[37]

A widow's continued association with her husband made her all the more appealing as a spokeswoman for the Cause. Widows of renowned generals joined widows of unknown foot soldiers as members, and often as leaders, of Confederate groups such as the UDC and other women's memorial organizations. Nancy Branch, the widow of Lawrence O'Bryan Branch, regarded by Jefferson Davis as a "distinguished Citizen, Statesman, and Soldier," served as the president of the Ladies' Memorial Association of Raleigh, North Carolina, for years.[38] Similarly, Helen Plane was a founding member of the Georgia UDC and honorary president of the division beginning in 1896. She often referred to her own widowhood in her speeches to give some oomph to her points. In an 1896 speech calling on the Daughters to stay the course in accomplishing their goals, she alluded to the "noble part that Southern women had taken in the late war, and of the sudden fall of her brave, distinguished husband, who was captain of a Macon company." The official record reports that while she spoke, "many eyes filled with tears, and wept with her over the brilliant hopes of her young life that went down in to the darkness of the grave with him."[39] Mary Anna Jackson and Flora Stuart were perhaps the most noteworthy Confederate widows to serve in postwar Confederate groups. Jackson was the president of the Stonewall Jackson chapter of the UDC in Charlotte, North Carolina, for eleven years, while Stuart was an active member and held various offices in the Virginia UDC. At the end of her active service, the UDC made Jackson an honorary president for life.[40] Even if a famous widow was relatively inactive in the UDC, many were made honorary presidents. Such was the case for the widows of Confederate president Jefferson Davis, Confederate postmaster general John H. Reagan, legendary generals Braxton Bragg, Robert E. Lee, Fitzhugh Lee, and George E. Pickett, and even the not-so-legendary generals John S. Williams and William Humes.[41]

When a member of the Cult of Dead Generals died, Southerners reacted in much the same way that they had upon the death of the hero-husband. When Mary

Anna Jackson died, the South mourned almost as intensely as they had when her husband fell in battle. She was even interred under the statue of her husband at Lexington, Virginia.[42] Forever linked to him in life—Mary Anna Jackson, after Stonewall Jackson's death, had become for Southerners the Widow of the Confederacy—she was symbolically buried with him at death. When the widow of General Pickett died, Southern newspapers eulogized her extensively. Moreover, her death notices were not for La Salle Pickett alone but for "La Salle Corbell Pickett, 86, Widow of General George E. Pickett, Leader of the Last Confederate Charge at Gettysburg," or "Gen. Pickett's Widow Is Dead: Mate of Noted Confederate Leader Succumbs in 83rd Year."[43] Similarly, Flora Stuart's identity was lost in that of her deceased husband at her death. The *Richmond Times Dispatch* memorialized her simply as the "widow of Stuart" and linked her with her "romantic past" as the "child-bride of the Confederacy." Although many attended her funeral, including an ex-governor, special mention was made of the twenty or more Confederate veterans from the soldiers' home in Richmond who attended her burial beside their general in a vault in Hollywood Cemetery.[44]

Even the wives of not-so-famous Confederates garnered attention when they passed because of their links to local heroes. When Nancy Branch, often known as Mrs. General Branch, died, the Raleigh papers memorialized her thus:

> The widow of the distinguished solider, Larry O'Brien [*sic*] Branch, whose life went out upon the field of battle while leading his brigade, she has passed her life among his and her people with only a desire to serve faithfully her God, to do good deeds and by precept, to cherish the memory of her heroic husband and to manifest at all times a sympathetic pride in the members of the old Brigade which won imperishable glory under his command.[45]

If Branch (or for that matter, Jackson, Pickett, or Stuart) had remarried, she could hardly have "cherished the memory of her husband" quite as well in the minds of Southerners. Similarly, Mrs. Junius Daniel, "the Oldest Widow of [a] Confederate Veteran in N.C.," also became venerated because "while leading a gallant charge near Spottsylvania [*sic*] Court House, Va., her husband [a brigadier general] gave his life for the Confederate cause." That she never remarried allowed her to remain the "oldest widow of a Confederate Veteran." If she had remarried, her death would likely not have been as noteworthy.[46] The death of the widow of Edmond Cook registered similarly in North Carolina newspapers. She was the "wife of the late Col. Ed. C. Cook," who fell in the battles around Atlanta on June 23, 1864.[47] For the widows of famous or locally noteworthy Confederates, the following poem certainly holds true:

> To die for Dixie! Oh how blessed!
> Are they who early went to rest,
> And deemed the cause they fought for true
>   As Heaven itself.
> To live for Dixie! Harder part!

To knit one's broken threads again,
And keep her memory free from stain,
                This is to *live* for Dixie.[48]

Although memorial associations continued to pay homage to dead Confederate men and confer honor and respect on the widows left behind, they simultaneously opened their coffers to widows in financial need, be they the former wives of common soldiers or of great generals. Benevolence to the widows and orphans of Confederate soldiers continued in the years after the war in much the same way that it had during the war. And as it had during the war, charity reassured proper gender roles. In calls for aid to Confederate widows, orators routinely described them as noble and worthy. No matter how poor or debased they had become, widows became for Southern society heroines in their own right. Moreover, the manner of their husbands' deaths was unimportant. Whether the men had died in camp of disease before ever seeing battle or fell in the thick of the fight, they all became martyrs and their widows heroines. Confederate widows were not the poor, pitiful, old widows of the antebellum period but young war widows who deserved respect always and assistance when necessary.

Although memorial associations provided some assistance—for example, the ladies of the Augusta, Georgia, Ladies' Memorial Association banded together in 1868 to create a widows' home—the majority of their funds still were dedicated to monuments rather than survivors.[49] For the UDC, however, benevolence was another story.[50]

Although most well known for its memorial work, the UDC believed "charity" to needy Confederate widows had "always been one with its memorial work."[51] Indeed, although the national organization placed historical work ahead of philanthropy, most chapters and state divisions listed benevolence to veterans and widows as their first object.[52] The minutes from the 1894 organizational meeting of the Grand Division of Virginia, for example, stated that the "object of this society [is] to co-operate with the Camp in the noble work of charity & relief which it has undertaken & to give cordial aid & sympathy in caring for the families of all worthy Confederates in our midst who are in need." They went on to specify that the annual dues collected, one dollar per member, would go to "worthy Confederate families in need of help."[53] The James B. Gordon chapter in North Carolina also cited benevolence as their first objective. Article 2 of their Constitution read: "The object of this association shall be Benevolent, Educational, Memorial, Historical and Social. To accomplish these purposes it will seek: 1—To give assistance, when needed to survivors of the War, and those dependent upon them." They accomplished this task by both contributing to the Home for Needy Confederate widows in Fayetteville, North Carolina, and administering a benevolent fund that distributed outside relief to Confederate widows in the state.[54] The benevolent work of Confederate groups, which prevented needy widows from being consigned to the poor house, contributed to their collective martyrdom and the establishment of them as icons of the Cause. Poverty had always been something scorned in the South. Certainly, champions of the Lost Cause could not stand by and see the heroines of that same Cause wallow in poverty. As Charles Kent, a prominent Southerner avowed, "No charity . . . seems to me to be sweeter and saner than that which concerns itself with ameliorating the condition of those whom the exigencies of war deprived of their natural supporters."[55]

In the UDC's efforts to help needy widows, calls often reverberated with challenges to the populace, especially its male segment, to aid the women left manless by the war, thus directly implicating the public in providing for Confederate widows. Florence Barlow, the associate editor and manager of the *Lost Cause,* a Louisville periodical "owned, controlled, and edited by women," wrote vitriolic editorials chastising the region's populace for failing to provide for Confederate women. At times her language openly questioned elite men's manhood for not caring for women who had sacrificed all for the Cause.[56] Indeed, UDC women often chastised male Confederate groups for not doing enough for the widows of their comrades. In her *History of the Richmond Home for Needy Confederate Women,* Mildred Rutherford of Athens, Georgia, wrote: "It is a sacred duty of the UDC to care for these women; it should be an honor for the Sons of the Confederate Veterans to do their manly part in this glorious work, & I feel assured that there is not one camp in our state which is unwilling to contribute money or provisions." Implicating more than just Confederate groups, she continued, "Yes, I may go further & predict that every true Virginian or Southern heart will vibrate when the chord is touched asking for help to those left desolate by their brave fallen comrades. . . . any needy woman . . . widow . . . 'You need only to plead your honorable privilege.'"[57] If the South, in particular Southern men, did not care for its women, especially its Confederate widows who had sacrificed so mightily for the Cause, how could they consider themselves proper Southern men? Many men agreed. Famous champion of the Lost Cause, Fitzhugh Lee, in a letter to the president of the Richmond home, asserted, "But we must not forget that when brave men fell on the battle-field brave women, in many instances, became necessitous because the provider had given his life for his cause."[58] James Smith, the commander of the Confederate Veterans Camp in Richmond, concurred, lamenting, "When the war ended many of these noble women had lost their breadwinners and were without home or inheritance." For Rabbi Calisch of Richmond, the claims of Confederate widows on public assistance were "strong and true, and, above all, just."[59]

After the turn of the century, the national UDC began an earnest campaign to find the best way to provide relief for Confederate widows. In their fund-raising efforts in individual states, the Daughters elicited great public support for their cause, often forcing state governments, inherently male groups, to address the situation of Confederate widows. Much of the UDC's efforts to garner state support for poverty relief among Confederate widows coincided with the nationwide Progressive movement to ameliorate the conditions of poverty among the general populace.[60] In the South, where they regarded Confederate widows as martyrs for the Cause, what more worthy segment of the population was there to assist?

One of the more grandiose ways that Confederate groups assisted Confederate widows was through the construction of homes for the needy among them.[61]

Indeed, the UDC more than other groups led the charge for such homes and lobbied for state assistance to the wives and widows of Confederate veterans. They argued that the widows of soldiers were just as deserving, if not more so, than surviving veterans because they no longer had men in a "man's world." As Karen Cox maintains, "the UDC assumed responsibility for the welfare of these southerners as an outward sign of the gratitude members held for their Confederate ancestors . . . women highly regarded for self-sacrifice."[62] Accordingly, it was unacceptable to consign them to almshouses or poor farms, the primary agencies of public welfare in the South during this period. One way to prevent this circumstance was to construct Confederate widows' homes.

Many states that made up the former Confederacy had homes for Confederate soldiers, but few had homes for Confederate women until the UDC began their campaign.[63] During the 1880s a South Carolina Women's Memorial Group had established a Home for the Mothers, Widows, and Daughters of Confederate Soldiers in Charleston. In addition to providing these women with a place to live, the home also ran a school for children, most often the female children, of Confederate soldiers. In response to an 1887 call to change the form and name of the Charleston Home because it "had already accomplished its purpose," the organizers of the home responded passionately that not only was the home still attending the needs of Confederate widows and daughters but that "no one familiar with the history of our State for the last few years, needs be told that the destitution has been greater, and, especially the lack of facilities in sparse populations, of a serviceable education, than during the period immediately following the war. Moreover, the constitution of the Home makes its benevolent work cover, as far as possible, the impoverishment by the war, as well as bereavement." In regard to changing the name, the organizers of the home pointed out the importance of keeping the name because it "embodied and expressed the tender concern and care of our people, for our sufferers by the war. . . . The name which is distinctive of our organization is not only historic in its relation to the past, but monumental in its functions to the future, and any modification of its plans and purposes should still recall the sacred uses to which it was at first dedicated."[64]

Like South Carolina, Virginia also had a Home for Needy Confederate Women. Opening its doors in 1900, it closed them only in the second half of the twentieth century. Although not originated by the UDC, local UDC members took it over not long after its establishment.[65] There were also homes for Confederate widows in Texas and North Carolina, which opened in 1908 and 1915, respectively.[66] In North Carolina, individual Daughters as well as the various chapters, the state's Children of the Confederacy (CoC) auxiliaries, and the state division all contributed to the upkeep and maintenance of the home.[67] Although all of these homes were originally established by the UDC or other earlier Confederate women's groups, they eventually received their primary funding from individual state governments.

Only a few state homes existed, and the UDC lamented the lack of more facilities in other states. One proposal put forward to address the issue of needy Confederate women was to build a regional home sponsored solely by the UDC.

In a 1905 speech, Helen Plane, honorary state president of the Georgia UDC, disputed the objection that there were "so few to occupy it," lamenting:

> Where are the women who represented the six hundred thousand valiant soldiers who constituted the grandest army the world has yet known? Where are those who with unflinching courage sent forth husbands, sons, fathers, brothers and lovers to swell that immortal host which marched and suffered beneath the "Stars and Bars"? . . . Hundreds of these women . . . are still with us, but many of them in poverty and obscurity, suffering in silence. . . . Think you that such as these are not deserving the help of those of us who have been more fortunate? In the language of Mrs. Vincent, of Texas, a native Georgian, "because they have stifled their cries, and in silent self-reliance labored all these years for subsistence, are we Daughters to close our ears to their appeals, now that the patient hands and feeble footsteps hesitate in the oncoming darkness?"[68]

Despite good intentions, her idea met with much criticism and was voted down. Plane had envisioned the UDC home as one for women of formerly elite status whose circumstances had been reduced. Cornelia Branch Stone put it best when she argued, "the wives and daughters of the humblest soldiers were as much entitled to such homes as the wives and daughters of officers of the army."[69] Ironically, in this instance the UDC, an elitist organization, perceived the enforcement of class distinctions among Confederate widows as insidious.[70] If Confederate widowhood were the result of gracious, self-sacrificing, true Southern womanhood, then how could some widows be worthy of benevolence and others not? As Mrs. N. V. Randolph, president of the Richmond chapter, avowed, "the daughters [and wives] of the poorest soldiers that marched with Lee have equal rights with the daughters [and wives] of the generals who rode at his side."[71] Either all Confederate widows were worthy of assistance or Southern society could not imagine Confederate widows as a whole to be "true Southern women." Upon the demise of discussions for a regional home, the UDC resolved to establish a national relief committee whose purpose it would be to investigate and administer appropriate aid for needy Confederate women.

Such relief committees had already been operating within individual chapters and state divisions for years. Members of the Savannah chapter, for example, could boast in 1900 that they distributed annually $250 in monthly stipends to Confederate veterans and widows along with other "sums . . . as the needs of these old soldiers and their widows are brought to [their] attention."[72] Similarly, the Virginia Division, in addition to contributing to the Home for Needy Confederate Women in Richmond, also founded the Mrs. Norman V. Randolph Relief Fund, reasoning that they could help more widows outside of the home than could be admitted as residents to the home.[73] The Albemarle, Virginia, chapter also proudly reported that they contributed a "generous proportion of the[ir] funds" to "monthly pensions to needy Confederate women in the city or county."[74] And throughout Georgia, various chapters had "the pleasure of relieving the necessities of afflicted families of the old veterans."[75]

Although men participated in Confederate memorialization and benevolent activities either directly or indirectly, it was Southern women who thrived as the keepers of Confederate memory. For women, commemoration activities after the war were an extension of the work they had performed during the war. Instead of assisting the soldiers and their families while they fought, they turned their work to paying homage to those soldiers who had not returned. The Confederate soldier had been "reincarnated as the Confederate Dead." As Fitzhugh Brundage has asserted and other scholars have concurred, "white women created an infrastructure for the dissemination of a collective historical memory at a time when no other groups were able to do so. And they did so 'at a time of heightened concern about the perpetuation of social and political hierarchies.'"[76] It is no coincidence that Confederate celebrations began to thrive after the end of Reconstruction, although they had begun immediately after the close of the war. In his study of the monument movement in America, John Bodnar asserts that "monument dedications are . . . cultural expressions of public memory, those beliefs about the past that help a society comprehend its past as well as its present. . . . Such commemorative activities may be viewed as expressions of official culture, since they encourage maintenance of social order and existing institutions, discourage disorder and radical change, and stress the duties of citizens rather than their rights."[77] Accordingly, around the 1890s, there was a shift in Confederate monument building and celebrations that removed the focus from cemeteries to town squares, where the message could reach more people.[78] Combined with the establishment of Jim Crow laws and the race-baiting that destroyed the Populist Party in the South, the memorialization of the Cause and of the men and women who had fought for it and were now fast passing away worked together to unite Southern whites under a racist vision of the New South in which they could enjoy the same elevated position they had held before the war. But if whites were to enjoy this position, Southern society had to address the presence of Confederate widows, account for how they fit into the definition of true Southern womanhood, and identify what that definition meant for Southern manhood. The ways in which Lost Cause celebrations, most of them managed by the UDC, included and often focused on Confederate widows contributed to the construction of a place for Confederate widows in the postbellum South within traditional patriarchal definitions. Although they were heroic and deserving of respect and honor, Confederate widows were still in need of the protection and provision of Southern men.

Notes

The quotation in the subtitle is from a letter by John Lamb to Mrs. A. J. Montague, 18 October 1904, in Mildred Lewis Rutherford, *The History of the Home for Needy Confederate Women with Reports of the Officers from October 15, 1900 to October 15, 1904* (Richmond, VA: J. L. Hill Printing Co., n.d.), 49.

1. Bagby Diary, 24 January 1898, Chamberlayne Family Papers, Virginia Historical Society. Virginia Day was replaced by [George] Washington and [Robert E.] Lee Day, which was subsequently replaced by Washington, Lee, and [Martin Luther] King Day.

2. Before the UDC, some earlier women's groups strived to "maintain the conventional forms of public gender subordination," LeeAnn Whites argues, by resigning typically male jobs such as public speaking, managing finances, and negotiating to prominent local men. The UDC, by contrast, subscribed to traditional gender roles and engaged male speakers on occasion, but the members managed the organization. LeeAnn Whites, *The Civil War as a Crisis in Gender, Augusta, Georgia, 1860–1890* (Athens: University of Georgia Press, 1995), 189.

3. Ibid., 183.

4. Editorial, as quoted ibid.

5. Margaret Cary Green Davis, "The Confederated Southern Memorial Association," in *History of the Confederated Memorial Associations of the South* (New Orleans: Graham Press for the Confederated Southern Memorial Association, 1904), 30.

6. Whites, *Civil War as a Crisis in Gender,* 53. For a discussion of ladies' aid societies, see *ibid.,* 47–63, 69–79.

7. In addition to reburying the North Carolina soldiers, the LMA reburied 46 South Carolinians, 44 Georgians, 8 Alabamians, 8 Mississippians, 4 Virginians, 2 Floridians, 2 Tennesseans, 1 Texan, 1 Louisianan, 1 Arkansan, 3 Confederate States Marines of unknown origin, and 106 unknown dead. Apparently, the LMA believed that if they could not get soldiers to their home states, at least they could get them back in the South. Margaret Arthur Call, "North Carolina," in *History of the Confederated Memorial Associations,* 227–231.

8. Ibid., 238. There were memorial associations throughout North Carolina, Virginia, and Georgia that established cemeteries, collecting and reinterring the remains of known and unknown Confederate servicemen. Ibid., 227–240; n.a., "Virginia" and "Georgia," in *History of the Confederated Memorial Associations,* 275–318 and 80–164, respectively

9. "Virginia,"299–302.

10. "First Memorial Day Exercised in Raleigh," *Raleigh Sentinel,* 14 May 1867, clipping in Ladies Memorial Association file, North Carolina State Archives. See also Letters, Branch Family Papers, North Carolina State Archives.

11. Lizzie Rutherford Chapter, UDC, *A History of the Origin of Memorial Day* (Columbus, GA, 1898), 24, as quoted in Charles Reagan Wilson, "The Religion of the Lost Cause: Ritual and Organization of the Southern Civil Religion, 1865–1920," *Journal of Southern History* 46 (May 1980): 226.

12. Whites, *Civil War as a Crisis in Gender,* 184.

13. Ibid., 183.

14. David Lowenthal, "Age and Artifact: Dilemmas of Appreciation," in H. E. Gulley, "Women and the Lost Cause: Preserving a Confederate Identity in the American Deep South," *Journal of Historical Geography* 19 (April 1993): 126.

15. Stephen Davis, "Empty Eyes, Marble Hand: The Confederate Monument and the South," *Journal of Popular Culture* 3 (Winter 1982): 12.

16. Newspaper clippings, Branch Family Papers, North Carolina State Archives. The General Assembly did indeed cave in to the women's pleas, appropriating $10,000 for the monument. It was completed in 1895 and stands on the grounds of the state capitol.

17. Newspaper clippings, Branch Family Papers, North Carolina State Archives.

18. Mary Crenshaw, "Hollywood Memorial Association. Richmond, Virginia," in *History of the Confederated Memorial Associations,* 301. Georgia gave money to various memorial associations throughout the state to complete or conduct their work. For information on all of those activities, see "Georgia," 83–164.

19. Gulley, "Women of the Lost Cause," 130–131.

20. H. C. Bourne, "Monument to the Women," 4 October 1905, Clark Papers, box 235.2, North Carolina State Archives.

21. Elise L. Smith, "Belle Kinney and the Confederate Woman's Monument," *Southern Quarterly* 32 (Spring 1979): 27.

22. Locke Craig, "Address of Acceptance," in *Addresses at the Unveiling of the Memorial to the North Carolina Woman of the Confederacy,* compiled by R. D. W. Connor (Raleigh, NC: Edward and Broughton, State Printers, 1914), 24–25.

23. Rev. E. A. Osborne, "Invocation," in *Addresses at the Unveiling of the Memorial,* 8.

24. As Victoria Bynum has argued, white Southern men had used every means at their disposal—social, economic, and political—to restrict Southern women who were not behaving like "true Southern ladies" in the Old South. Most such women were single or widowed and existed in a perpetual state of need. Confederate widows, because of their similarly tenuous economic and social positions in society, could easily have fallen into the same "unladylike" behaviors. See Victoria Bynum, *Unruly Women: The Politics of Social and Sexual Control in the Old South* (Chapel Hill: University of North Carolina Press, 1992).

25. Lucy London Anderson Huske, *North Carolina Women of the Confederacy* (Fayetteville, NC: published by author, 1926), foreword.

26. Ibid., 9.

27. Daniel Harvey Hill, "The Women of the Confederacy," in *Addresses at the Unveiling of the Memorial,* 10.

28. Southern women's extensive dissension during the war has been often debated by historians. For a discussion of women not abiding by the rules of Southern womanhood during the war, see particularly George Rable, *Civil Wars: Women and the Crisis of Southern Nationalism* (Urbana: University of Illinois Press, 1989); Whites, *Civil War as a Crisis in Gender;* Drew Gilpin Faust, *Mothers of Invention: Women of the Slaveholding South in the American Civil War* (New York: Random House, 1996); Gulley, "Women and the Lost Cause."

29. Gulley, "Women and the Lost Cause," 128.

30. Hill, "Women of the Confederacy," 11.

31. Ibid., 20.

32. None of the wives of the most prominent Confederate heroes remarried, although it is possible that some of the wives of local heroes did.

33. Mrs. W. C. Sibley, "Address," *Augusta Chronicle,* 6 February 1896, reprinted in Tommie Phillips LaCavera, *History of the United Daughters of the Confederacy, Georgia Division, 1895–1995* (Atlanta: Georgia Division, 1995), 28.

34. Widows of Confederate heroes such as Mary Anna Jackson were especially successful going this route, as various Northern publishers were willing to pay highly for the words of famous men. Jackson published her husband's memoirs in 1895, writing in the preface: "For many years after the death of my husband the shadow over my life was so deep, and all that concerned him was so sacred, that I could not consent to lift the veil to the public gaze. But time softens, if it does not heal, the bitterest sorrow; . . . as I went on, the grand lessons or submission and fortitude of my husband's life gave me strength and courage to persevere to the end." Mary Anna Jackson, *Memoirs of "Stonewall Jackson" by His Widow Mary Anna Jackson* (Louisville, KY: Prentice Press Courier—Journal Job Printing Co., 1895), v–vi. La Salle Corbell Pickett not only published her husband's letters but also enjoyed success at penning "intimate stories" of Mrs. Jefferson Davis and Mrs. Robert E. Lee as well as a stirring description of the battle of Gettysburg. "Gen.

Pickett's Widow Is Dead," *Richmond Times Dispatch,* 2 April 1922. See also Gary W. Gallagher, "A Widow and Her Soldier: LaSalle Corbell Pickett as the Author of George E. Pickett's Civil War Letters," in *Lee and His Generals in Civil War Memory* (Baton Rouge: Louisiana State University Press, 1998), 227–242.

35. "Gen. Pickett's Widow Is Dead."

36. Committee of Invitation to Mrs. Cook, n.d., Murfree Family Papers, box 2066, Southern Historical Collection, University of North Carolina.

37. "Ode of Welcome at the Great Reunion of the G.A.R. [Grand Army of the Republic] and C.S.A. [Confederate States Army]," Broadside 1913, Lyne Papers, Virginia Historical Society.

38. Jefferson Davis to Mrs. L. O'B. Branch, 4 August 1864, Branch Family Papers, North Carolina State Archives; Ladies Memorial Association file, Branch Family Papers, North Carolina State Archives.

39. Lula Kendall Rogers, recording secretary, "Fourth Session Report," in *Minutes of the Second Annual Convention of the Georgia Division of the United Daughters of the Confederacy* (Atlanta, 1896), 5.

40. Mrs. J. A. Fore, "The Stonewall Jackson Chapter," October 1919, Lowry Shuford Collection, North Carolina State Archives. Flora Stuart, in her role as principal of the Virginia Female Institute, encouraged support for the institute as a worthy charity. In an 1896 article, the *Confederate Veteran* cheered that "this institution, besides being of high merit, has sentimental claims upon the Southern people, and to this pride is taken in calling attention." The author then sympathetically points to Stuart's widowhood: "Twenty-one years ago Mrs. Stuart undertook this laudable work to provide means for educating her children. She was left a widow at an early age, and has made a diligent struggle for independence and the proper rearing of her family." Closing with a tug on the heart strings, he implored, "she ever looks hopefully for patronage to those who knew and loved her noble husband, and it seems opportune at this time, when there is such vivid interest in the great events in which he was so conspicuous, that those give attention to what is of so much consequence to her." The *Confederate Veteran* obviously thought that Flora Stuart's position as the widow of the famous J.E.B. Stuart made her a worthy person to be sympathized with and her causes assisted. Indeed, upon her death the school was renamed in "her" honor: "in grateful memory of the services of Mrs. J.E.B. Stuart, so long the honored and beloved principal of this institution, the name of the corporation and the school which it conducts shall be changed from the Virginia Female Institute to Stuart Hall, Incorporated"—not Flora Stuart Hall, but Stuart Hall. Stuart article, UDC Scrapbook, Boydon, Virginia, 1921, Mss5:7Un33:1, Virginia Historical Society.

41. "List of Honorary Presidents and President Generals," Jessica Randolph Smith Papers, North Carolina State Archives.

42. Susan Youhn, "The Lives of the Generals' Wives" (paper presented at the annual meeting of the Conference on Women and the Civil War, Shenandoah, VA, June 1999).

43. "Widow of General Pickett Dies in Maryland Hospital," newspaper clipping, Holman Collection, North Carolina State Archives; "Gen. Pickett's Widow Is Dead."

44. "Widow of Stuart Dies from Fall," *Richmond Times Dispatch,* 12 May n.y., clipping in UDC file, Virginia Historical Society.

45. "Mrs. General Branch Dead," newspaper clipping, n.d., Branch Family Papers, North Carolina State Archives.

46. "Mrs. Junius Daniel Dies at Henderson, Oldest Widow of Confederate Veteran in N.C. Passes after Long Illness," newspaper clipping, Holman Collection, North Carolina State Archives.

47. "Wife of the Late Col. Ed. C. Cook," newspaper clipping, n.d., Cook Papers, Southern Historical Collection/University of North Carolina. Interestingly, the obituary also mentions that his battle flag, made by Eliza Cook from her wedding dress, still exists and "is in the possession of the McEwen bivouac."
48. Untitled poem, Holman Collection, North Carolina State Archives (italics in the original).
49. For a discussion of the widows' home, see Whites, *Civil War as a Crisis in Gender,* 191–192.
50. The United Daughters of the Confederacy was founded in 1894. Only five years later, they were flourishing in every Southern state, eclipsing other Confederate organizations, including male groups such as the United Confederate Veterans (UCV) and the Sons of Confederate Veterans (SCV). By World War I, the UDC claimed almost 100,000 members in chapters across the nation. Mary B. Poppenheim, Maude Blake Merchant, May M. Faris McKinney, Rassie Hoskins White, Eloise Welch Wright, Anne Bachman Hyde, Susie Stuart Campbell, Charlotte Osborne Woodbury, and Ruth Jennings Lawton, *The History of the United Daughters of the Confederacy* (Richmond, VA, 1938), 221. For a discussion of the UDC, see Charles Reagan Wilson, *Baptized in Blood· The Religion of the Lost Cause, 1865–1920* (Athens: University of Georgia Press, 1980), 25–26, 51, 105, 140–149, 156, 162, 169; Wilson, "Religion of the 'Lost Cause,'" 219–238; Gaines M. Foster, *Ghosts of the Confederacy: Defeat, the Lost Cause, and the Emergence of the New South, 1865 to 1913* (New York: Oxford University Press, 1987), 7, 107–135, 157–158, 172–179, 186–190; Karen Lynn Cox, "Women, the Lost Cause, and the New South: The United Daughters of the Confederacy and the Transmission of Confederate Culture, 1894–1919" (PhD diss., University of Southern Mississippi, 1997).
51. Poppenheim et al., *History of the United Daughters of the Confederacy,* 221.
52. United Daughters of the Confederacy home page, http://www.hqudc.org/objectives/index.html (accessed 10 June 2001).
53. "Minutes of Meetings, Daughters of the Confederacy," 15 October 1894, UDC Grand Division of Virginia Scrapbook, Mss4:UN3008b, Virginia Historical Society.
54. Janet Blum Seippel, "History James B. Gordon Chapter United Daughters of the Confederacy March 30, 1898–1973," UDC Collection, box 8, North Carolina State Archives.
55. James Power Smith to Mrs. A. J. Montague, n.d; Charles Kent to Mrs. A. J. Montague, n.d.; both in Mildred Lewis Rutherford, *History of the Home for Needy Confederate Women with Reports of the Officers from October 15, 1900 to October 15, 1904* (Richmond, VA: J. L. Hill Printing Co., n.d.), 55, 60.
56. Cox, "Women, the Lost Cause, and the New South," 117–120.
57. Rutherford, *History of the Home,* 11, 41.
58. Fitzhugh Lee to Mrs. A. J. Montague, 4 November 1904, *ibid.,* 46.
59. Rabbi Edward N. Calisch to Mrs. A. J. Montague, n.d., *ibid.,* 53.
60. The UDC's efforts can be placed within the larger context of Progressive reform. Much has been written on Southern Progressivism since historian Arthur Link identified the presence and indeed proliferation of Progressivism in the South; Arthur S. Link, "The Progressive Movement in the South, 1906–1913," *North Carolina Historical Review* 23 (April 1946): 172–195. Some of the best works on Progressivism in the South include Anne Firor Scott, "A Progressive Wind from the South, 1906–1913," *Journal of Southern History* 29 (February 1963): 53–70; William Link, *The Paradox of Southern Progressivism, 1880–1930* (Chapel Hill: University of North Carolina Press, 1992); Dewey Grantham, *The South in Modern America: A Region at Odds*

(New York: Oxford University Press, 1994); and J. Morgan Kousser, "Progressivism for Middle Class Whites Only: North Carolina Education, 1880–1910," *Journal of Southern History* 46 (May 1980): 169–194. For Southern women's participation in Progressivism, see Anastasia Sims, *The Power of Femininity in the New South* (Columbia: University of South Carolina Press, 1997); Jacquelyn Dowd Hall, "O. Delight Smith's Progressive Era: Labor, Feminism, and Reform in the Urban South—Atlanta Georgia, 1907–1915," in *Visible Women: New Essays on American Activism,* ed. Nancy Hewitt and Suzanne Lebsock (Urbana: University of Illinois Press, 1993): 166–98; Anne Firor Scott, "The 'New Woman' in the New South," *South Atlantic Quarterly* 61 (August 1962): 473–483; Elizabeth Hayes Turner, *Women, Culture, and Community: Religions and Reform in Galveston, 1880–1920* (New York: Oxford University Press, 1997).

61. See "The Constitution of Georgia Division United Daughters of the Confederacy," in LaCavera, *History of the United Daughters of the Confederacy, Georgia Division,* 59.

62. Cox, "Women, the Lost Cause, and the New South," 111.

63. Almost every state in the former Confederacy had a home for Confederate soldiers. For a detailed discussion of soldiers' homes, see R. B. Rosenberg, *Living Monuments: Confederate Soldier Homes in the New South* (Chapel Hill: University of North Carolina Press, 1993). Only the soldiers' homes in Mississippi and Missouri allowed veterans to bring their wives with them when they became residents. This practice, however, did nothing to ameliorate the situation of Confederate widows.

64. "Home for the Mothers, Widows and Daughters of Confederate Soldiers," in *Twentieth Annual Report and the Constitution of the Association* (Charleston, SC: Lucas, Richardson and Co., 1888), 5–6, in Rare Books, Southern Pamphlet Collection, Wilson Library, University of North Carolina.

65. The Home for Needy Confederate Women in Richmond, Virginia, accepted as residents needy maiden or widowed daughters and sisters of Confederate soldiers as well as Confederate widows. After 1956, they expanded to include needy granddaughters. Both outside and resident funds supported the home. Upon entering the home, women relinquished control of all their assets to the home. This practice is similar to the way that many nursing homes operate today. Although not the only cause that the Virginia UDC supported with respect to aid to Confederate widows, it was a major charity of the organization, and they were active in pressuring the state to contribute to its maintenance as well.

66. Cox, "Women, the Lost Cause, and the New South," 120.

67. It became accepted practice, for those chapters that could afford to do so, to furnish a widow's bedroom or common room of the house. The North Carolina Confederate Woman's Home accepted residents in the order their applications were filed, except for those women already residing in county-sponsored homes. They were given special consideration for admittance. *Minutes of the Nineteenth Annual Convention of the United Daughters of the Confederacy, North Carolina Division Held at Charlotte, North Carolina, October 6, 7, 8, 1915* (Wilmington, NC: Wilmington Stamp and Printing Co., n.d.), in the North Carolina State Archives.

68. Address of Mrs. C. Helen Plane, in *Minutes of the Seventeenth Annual Convention, 1905, Georgia Division, United Daughters of the Confederacy* (Atlanta, 1905), 60–63.

69. Ibid., 57.

70. The majority of the UDC's members were affluent, although membership was not limited officially to the upper class. Wealthy women had far more time for club activities than lower-class women did because their days were not as constrained by household

chores. As Fred Bailey has suggested, they were "unfettered by domestic duties"; Fred Bailey, "Mildred Lewis Rutherford and the Patrician Cult of the Old South," *Georgia Historical Quarterly* 77 (Fall 1994): 516. For similar behavior among elite women in Barcelona, Spain, see Temma Kaplan, "Female Consciousness and Collective Action: The Case of Barcelona, 1910–1918," *Feminist Theory* (Spring 1982): 545–66. The racist attitudes of the UDC are rife throughout their literature and records; one particularly poignant example lies in an 1899 suggestion by Mrs. M. A. Lipscomb that in the interest of justice, the Daughters demand compensation from the U.S. government for slaves freed by Abraham Lincoln; *Minutes of the Fifth Annual Convention of the Georgia Division, United Daughters of the Confederacy* (Atlanta, 1899), 30.

71. Mrs. N. V. Randolph, "Address of Welcome," *1899 Minutes,* UDC Grand Division of Virginia Scrapbooks, Mss4:UN3008b, Virginia Historical Society, 2.

72. "Synopsis of the Work of the Savannah [GA] Chapter," *Directory of the Savannah Chapter No. 2 United Daughters of the Confederacy, Founded May 19, 1894*, 17, Hargrett Library, University of Georgia.

73. The Mrs. N. V. Randolph Relief Fund even garnered an appropriation from the General Assembly. Mrs. Cabell Smith, "Forty Years with the Virginia Division, United Daughters of the Confederacy," UDC Grand Division of Virginia scrapbooks, Virginia Historical Society, 12.

74. Isabelle H. Goss, "History of Albemarle Chapter, United Daughters of the Confederacy," in *Papers of the Albemarle County Historical Society, Volume 4, 1943–44* (Charlottesville, VA: Albemarle County Historical Society, 1944), 37.

75. *Minutes 1897, Georgia Division, United Daughters of the Confederacy* (Atlanta, 1897); *Minutes 1898, Georgia Division, United Daughters of the Confederacy* (Atlanta, 1898).

76. W. Fitzhugh Brundage, "White Women and the Politics of Historical Memory in the New South, 1880–1920," manuscript, 1–2. See also W. Fitzhugh Brundage, ed., *Where These Memories Grow: History, Memory, and Southern Identity* (Chapel Hill: University of North Carolina Press, 2000).

77. John Bodnar, *Remaking America: Public Memory, Commemoration, and Patriotism in the Twentieth Century,* as cited in Gulley, "Women and the Lost Cause," 125.

78. For an appraisal of this shift, see John J. Winberry, "'Lest We Forget': The Confederate Monument and the Southern Townscape," *Southeastern Geographer* 23 (November 1983): 107–121.

CHAPTER 9

Modernity's Miss-Fits

BLIND GIRLS AND MARRIAGE IN
FRANCE AND AMERICA, 1820–1920

CATHERINE KUDLICK

We women, whose gender makes us naturally sweet and compassionate, being deprived of sight we can, even must, not associate our lot with that of men, for what pleasure could marriage possibly offer us? If we were to marry a blind man, . . . one of us could not offer great help to the other, and if heaven were to send us children, we would be obliged to entrust them to strangers. . . . If this portrait is horrifying, that of a young, unmarried blind woman marrying a sighted man is even worse.—Thérèse-Adèle Husson, 1824

I feel less inclined than ever to embark upon the great adventure. I have fully made up my mind that a man and a woman must be equally equipped to weather successfully the vicissitudes of life. It would be a severe handicap to any man to saddle upon him the dead weight of my infirmities. I know I have nothing to give a man that would make up for such an unnatural burden.—Helen Keller, 1929

Since Western culture cringes at drawing links between disability and sexuality, and since marriage has long been the one positively acknowledged place where women are expected to be sexual, the views of Thérèse-Adèle Husson and Helen Keller should come as no surprise. Some people today might even share them. Yet the similarities between these two women—the first an unknown blind daughter of French provincial artisans writing in the 1820s, and the second the world's most famous disabled person, a blind-deaf woman writing over a hundred years later—should give us cause for thought. The two led vastly different lives separated not just by an ocean but by a century that witnessed some of human history's most dramatic changes in demography, economic structure, and social relations. Between the year in which Husson declared a blind girl should never marry and the one in which Keller echoed her views, Europe and North America had embraced industrialization, grappled with women's rights, and struggled with the implications of increasing secularization. Moreover, phenomena such as urbanization, the rise of mass culture, the changing role of the family, and professionalization had become an integral part of Keller's world, no doubt offering her access to many new ideas about women and marriage. And even when individual examples contradict assertions such as Husson's and Keller's, documents from France and America show how blind women and professionals who wrote about them perpetuated these attitudes by using justifications that changed over time. In other words, the taboo against blind women marrying remained constant, but the reasons supporting it enjoyed unusual fluidity.

What are we to make of the persistence of the blind spinster as a staple of nineteenth- and twentieth-century autobiography and literature in the face of these changes? And what can she teach us about mainstream ideas of marriage and womanhood?

Disability studies, an interdisciplinary field that looks upon disability as a social category of equal importance to race, class, sexual orientation, and gender, offers valuable insight.[1] Some in fact argue that disability often trumps these others as the "master trope of human disqualification" because it underpins all discussions of inequality and therefore all conceptions of hierarchy and social order.[2] In an article titled "Disability as Justification for Inequality in American History," for example, Douglas Baynton shows how opponents of suffrage discredited women's claims to political participation by hurling the insult of disability at them ("women are *unfit* to vote"), while those demanding women's rights claimed that not having such rights unfairly *disabled* women, making them lesser citizens.[3] Meanwhile, a growing subfield of disability gender studies seeks to unpack the complex relationship between the two, showing how ideas of gender and disability can simultaneously contradict and reinforce one another.[4]

Husson's and Keller's writings serve as chronological bookends on either side of a particular historical epoch—modernity—a period when disability came to play an unprecedented role in establishing gender order in the bourgeois West. Following in the path of Michel Foucault, historians have looked to the nineteenth and early twentieth century as a period when the concomitant rise of capitalism and the medical profession enlisted the family as a key ally in the struggle to tame a population seemingly out of control.[5] Accordingly, private matters such as sexuality, marriage, and childrearing became subjected to public scrutiny and regulation, along with education and work environments. At the same time, individual bodies needed—often literally—to fit within increasingly specific understandings of health and "normality." Disability slips neatly into this now-familiar interpretation of nineteenth- and twentieth-century history.[6] Scholars are just beginning to grapple with its central place in discussions of eugenics, evolving ideas of physical and civic fitness, as well as its impact on the creation of normality itself. But more important, the discussions that linked blindness and the single life of women have revolutionary implications for how historians have thought about the complex relationship between gender and modernity for everyone. After all, if "crippled girls" could marry, what incentive would women have for maintaining a household that met ever narrowly defined ideals of respectability and social fitness?

Until disability rights (not to mention disability pride) came of age in late twentieth-century America, nearly everyone shared the belief that those with disabilities should not marry.[7] Laws in France and the United States included physical and mental disabilities among the reasons for prohibiting a marriage, although the nature of the disabilities and the reasons would change over time. As early as 1801, a French specialist in legal medicine declared it to be "a strict duty for those who head societies to forbid any citizen stricken with a contagious or hereditary disease to communicate or transmit them through the instrument of marriage."[8] As the century progressed, more and more French doctors singled out "handicapped beings [*très infirmes*], the deformed [*contrefaits*], or those who carry within them the seeds of a grave hereditary disease." Even at midcentury such statements grew out of fears that the resulting "sickly, puny children . . . would in turn perpetuate a bastardized race."[9] By the 1870s and 1880s, in the aftermath of France's humiliating defeat at the hands of Prussia and a brush with civil war, the discussions of who should not marry added specific diseases linked more to sociocultural values: alcoholism, syphilis, tuberculosis, rickets, and epilepsy. Dr. Charles Richet, who won the Nobel Prize in 1913, went so far as to call for excluding "those lacking sufficient size or muscular strength, and those not in a state of being able to read, write, or count."[10] Although this view was an extreme one and in reality regulations were never strictly implemented, social anxieties that linked disability with the decline of the French race permeated public discourse about marriage.

Although Americans took a few decades longer to arrive at a clear formulation of how disabilities might affect the racial stock, marriage prohibitions grew in number and severity, particularly in the second half of the nineteenth century.[11] Early on, "age, sexual integrity, kinship ties, and mental health" became the criteria that would determine who should marry. Initial discussions of mental health made it clear that authorities sought to protect an individual from victimization rather than the nation from impurities, this despite the fact that even in the early decades of the century both lay and professional opinion held that mental disabilities were inherited. But growing racial anxieties in the wake of the Civil War and increased immigration prompted spokespersons from across the spectrum to call for regulating marriage to prevent the country from being overrun by "imbeciles and defectives." Taking up Elizabeth Cady Stanton's cry that only those "who can give the world children with splendid physique, strong intellect, and high moral sentiment may conscientiously take upon themselves the responsibility of marriage and maternity," the feminist clergywoman Anna Garlin Spencer warned against the marriage of people "who are not physically, morally, or economically able to make marriage a social advantage."[12] With the advent of medical and scientific breakthroughs, French and Americans began to turn increasingly to "experts" to regulate the most intimate details of their lives, not the least of which included deciding whom to marry.

Even though the rhetoric appeared to be gender neutral, disabled women would bear the brunt of the responsibility and stigma for remaining single, as the writings of Husson and Keller make clear. More than a simple acknowledgment of women's childbearing functions, the taboo can be traced back to a long-standing association between femininity and disability that had existed at least from the time of Aristotle. Sustained by modern medical professionals, politicians, and social commentators in France and America, these classical ideas held that *all* women's bodies were imperfect, mutilated, even monstrous, replicas of men's.[13] Not surprisingly then, prevailing ideas about health, youth, bodily perfection—and their opposites—shaped how nineteenth- and twentieth-century women viewed their own marriageability. At the same time, modern views held the single woman to be an aberration, a freak, a pathological challenge to the social order. The relationship between womanhood and disability, then, was both intricate and intimate for all women, with disability implicitly helping define every woman's marital status.

An early expression of this view emerged in a remarkable manuscript written around 1824 or 1825 titled "Reflections on the Physical and Moral Condition of the Blind."[14] Thérèse-Adèle Husson, the twenty-two-year-old blind daughter of artisans in the provincial city of Nancy, hoped to curry favor with the director of the Quinze-Vingts Hospital, the premier institution that aided blind people in Paris. "Reflections" offered Husson's thoughts on everyday life and objects, and culminated in an "Educational Plan" for blind children and young adults. Thus after chapters about flowers, table manners, the heavens, cloth, and animals, Husson held forth on topics such as proper reading for young girls, ways to handle issues of vanity, and finally an involved discussion of courtship and marriage prospects. Raised by nuns and having benefited from the aid of the Catholic Church, Husson wrote in a manner that celebrated the conservative religious values of her day; her language drips with piety and condescension as she urges blind girls to be meek and good. At the same time, her ambition and determination came through on virtually every page.

In a discussion that contains her most passionate prose, Husson presented her thoughts on marriage largely within a moralistic framework, pleading with her imaginary coterie of "female comrades in misfortune" to remain single. After describing why blind men should do everything possible to marry sighted women in order to be fully supported in life, she announced, "I beseech women deprived of sight but with some money to live and die keeping hold of their precious freedom, and to make worthy use of their possessions. They need not doubt that God will bless and protect them if they never stray from the path of honor and virtue." Lest inattentive readers miss her main point, the next chapter in the eighty-eight-page pamphlet used shameless melodrama to claim that many sighted women would envy their single blind sisters. "How many unfortunate mothers are pressured into seeing a despicable son, a young man with an empty head filled with hideous crimes, a being that they have carried in their breast, nourished with their milk, deposited on the scaffold!" she exclaimed.[15]

Significantly, Husson condemned marriage at a time when French society celebrated it and childbearing with renewed vigor. In the aftermath of what many believed to be revolutionary excesses, everyone from the writers of sermons to those entrusted with girls' education to the architects of government policies celebrated marriage as every woman's destiny, believing that a stable family unit

would mean a stable empire. Viewing marriage and womanhood as virtually synonymous, perpetuators of custom had long attacked old maids and spinsters as
anomalies.[16] By the second half of the eighteenth century, medical discourse was
offering new reasons for daughters to marry by pathologizing the single woman,
and this campaign gained momentum over the course of the following century.[17] A
woman of her times, Husson would have internalized these values.

In some respects, Husson's calls for female independence fit within the status quo. European societies always had acceptable places for those who did not
marry, from convents to domestic service.[18] Husson herself had thrived in communities of single women, receiving her education from nuns and other benefactors
who took her in. Her blindness no doubt also played a role in making her message
less threatening. As disability and single womanhood each became increasingly
understood as pathologies rather than as forms of difference that made up the social fabric, it became easier to conflate the two phenomena. Thus, a blind woman
calling for blind women to remain single posed far less of a danger than a sighted
one would making the same case for her sighted sisters. In fact, many may interpret Husson's plea as a deliberate rhetorical ploy aimed at showing just how well
she understood the rules as she attempted to win over possible benefactors at the
Quinze-Vingts Hospital.

Throughout the century, French writers unknowingly followed Husson's
lead. In particular, they framed their concerns about blind women and marriage
in terms of men's welfare, be they blind or sighted. Dr. Henri Truc, the often-cited
nineteenth-century sighted French authority on blindness, put it this way, his word
choice underscoring a common disparity: "Among the blind, girls marrying is much
less frequent than is the case with men, [a fact that] accords with the psychology
of the two sexes, and I think, in general [this is] a rule that works well."[19] Despite
certain disadvantages, such as a blind man "not being able to carry out his duties
as husband and father as well as he might like," Truc believed marriage was still a
good idea for a blind man if the circumstances were favorable. "Not only is feminine aid virtually indispensable to him," a correspondent wrote, agreeing with Truc,
"but more than other men he needs to live in the midst of beings whom he can call
his own, whom he can trust, and who will surround him with effect."[20]

Blind people themselves continued to espouse such views in the decades
after Husson. Maurice de la Sizeranne, one of the most articulate forward-looking
spokesmen of the French blind community at the end of the nineteenth century,
noted: "Love affairs for young blind girls almost always end sadly, after a few
struggles, a few hesitations, a few promises of faithfulness in memory, the sighted
man withdraws in a melancholy fashion. Then time passes . . . soon he meets other
more alluring young girls, and forgetting soon follows. Nothing comes to distract
the blind girl . . . she lives with her embalmed memory in sadness."[21] For Sizeranne, the big problem was housework and motherhood, a highly charged issue
because France faced a marked population decline in late century.[22] "In effect
when a competent, well-prepared blind woman can take care of lots of chores and
even household chores at her father's house (as a girl) or her spinster's residence
(later in life), it is one thing," he explained, "but quite another is for her to take

care of an entire household on her own . . . to be the mother of a family with children."[23] He believed that even a competent blind girl would never fully grow into real womanhood. For an aware person like Sizeranne, the issue had less to do with blindness than with social assumptions exacerbated by it; the blind girl stood a greater danger of being a victim because men would take even more advantage of her feminine vulnerability.

Across the Atlantic, Helen Keller was coming of age in a climate similarly wary of blind women's prospects. Approximately a century after Husson wrote "Reflections on the Physical and Moral Condition of the Blind," Doubleday published Keller's *Midstream: My Later Life,* a work that introduced the American public to the "miracle child" who was now an active, accomplished, sought-after woman in middle age.[24] She presented her thoughts on marriage with unusual candor by relating a conversation she had had with Alexander Graham Bell. The respected inventor was especially well known for his interests in deaf education, ideas shaped by the fact that the two most important women in his life—his mother and his wife—were deaf.[25] Bell met Keller when she was a young girl, and despite their thirty-three-year age difference, the two enjoyed a sometimes flirtatious friendship until Bell's death in 1922. This remarkable exchange touches on many features that link disability to the single life, while modernizing the picture in interesting ways compared to Husson's account:

> After a long pause [Bell] said, "It seems to me, Helen, a day must come when love, which is more than friendship, will knock at the door of your heart and demand to be let in."
>
> "What made you think of that?" I asked.
>
> "Oh, I often think of your future. To me you are a sweet, desirable young girl, and it is natural to think about love and happiness when we are young."
>
> "I do think of love sometimes," I admitted; "but it is like a beautiful flower which I may not touch, but whose fragrance makes the garden a place of delight just the same."
>
> He sat silent for a minute or two, thought-troubled, I fancied. Then his dear fingers touched my hand again like a tender breath, and he said, "Do not think that because you cannot see or hear, you are debarred from the supreme happiness of woman. Heredity is not involved in your case, as it is in so many others."
>
> "Oh, but I am happy, very happy!" I told him. "I have my teacher and my mother and you, and all kinds of interesting things to do. I really don't care a bit about being married."
>
> "I know," he answered, "but life does strange things to us. You may not always have your mother, and in the nature of things Miss Sullivan will marry, and there may be a barren stretch in your life when you will be very lonely."
>
> "I can't imagine a man wanting to marry me," I said. "I should think it would seem like marrying a statue."[26]

Clearly, Bell and Keller disagreed about her marriage prospects. Married to a deaf woman, Bell had already bent the rules, although he justified it by reminding Keller that heredity did not play a part in her deafness. (Like Keller, his wife Mabel Hubbard had suffered from scarlet fever at a young age.) Bell, who fancied himself a crusader for the rights of deaf people, was also an avid proponent of eugenics, arguing that inbreeding among deaf people was threatening to bring about "the deterioration of the nation."[27] To put an end to this unhealthy drift in American society, he urged professionals to "1. *Determine the causes that promote intermarriages among the deaf and dumb*; and 2. *remove them*" (Bell's emphasis).[28] This outlook explains his crusade against the use of sign language in residential schools for deaf students and his ultimate goal to eliminate the schools altogether, believing that they fostered inbreeding among the deaf. Bell held such views to the end of his life, as indicated by an article in *National Geographic,* in which he described relations between deaf men and deaf women as "the marriage of inferiors."[29]

Other respected Americans expressed similar views about intermarriage "between defectives" or even between "defectives" and "healthy" Americans. Dr. Lucien Howe, chair of the Committee of Hereditary Blindness of the Section of Ophthalmology of the American Medical Association (AMA), became obsessed with the question of reducing the number of the "most pitiable of human beings," noting that the cost of institutional care for blind people was probably as much as $25 million a year, a large sum in 1880.[30] Taking his case to the AMA and the American Ophthalmological Association, Howe urged his colleagues to help him determine the cost of these "defectives" to society and began considering laws that called for sequestering or sterilizing adults who might pass on hereditary blindness. By the 1920s, when his campaign reached its height, such laws regarding "the feeble-minded" had already been put into effect in numerous states and, as models, were studied with keen interest by the Nazi Party in Germany.[31]

For unknown reasons, Howe backed away from extreme views like sterilization, instead attempting to nip potential relationships in the bud through the reform of state marriage laws. Claiming to be acting "in justice to innocent taxpayers," Howe and his colleagues supported a law proposed in 1921 that would require those with hereditary blindness to post a hefty bond of $10,000 in order to receive a marriage license. Medical experts were to interview the prospective spouses, and if professionals determined them to be capable of producing "children likely to become public charges," the court would require the bond. In another version, any member of the community could ask such a couple to pay. The prospective law received mixed responses in the medical community, running the gamut from those who found it tyrannical to those who believed it did not go nearly far enough. Such varying opinions indicated that the legislation remained problematic, while the dilemma of marriage for "defectives" continued to cause anxiety.

Although ultimately no state passed the laws Bell and Howe allegedly advocated, the men's professional stature and the serious discussions they inspired suggest that Americans were drawing links between marriage customs and a healthy population.[32] During the heady days of the Progressive Era, the American public embraced scientifically respectable eugenics as one possible way of achieving "human betterment."[33] The growth of the professions, dramatic advances in medicine and science, and renewed faith in the state all contributed to an overwhelming sense of optimism in western Europe and the United States; humans seemed poised to control their destiny both at the macro- and the microlevel. What better way to measure progress than to point to fewer imperfections such as blindness, deafness, and other disabilities? To ensure that the plan would be carried out rested on making the dream of universal fitness the responsibility of the healthy family, beginning with a healthy man and wife. Thus, all discussions of marriage and disability such as Bell's and Howe's would involve shifting cultural assumptions about who should *not* marry and why. Such ideas would filter into the work of blindness professionals and would come to influence blind people themselves.

American educators of the blind cast their ambivalence about the marriage of blind girls in terms of eugenics and practicality. A Dr. Sibley put the matter bluntly in a paper titled "Our Girls" and delivered at the Biennial Meeting of the American Association of Instructors for the Blind held in Jacksonville, Illinois, in June 1890.[34] "Blind girls should not be permitted the society of blind boys for fear of an attachment being formed and marriage resulting," Sibley explained. "I have known of a number of instances, some in Missouri, and some elsewhere, where blind men and women have married and the result has generally been disastrous. It is a noticeable fact that, although the increase of blindness is not in proportion to the increase of population, there is a steady increase nevertheless."[35] Responding to the paper, one Mr. Battles said, "It has been in my mind for some years that if we make [blind girls] useful in their own households great good will result. Of course I mean the home of their parents, for I cordially agree with Dr. Sibley that the marriage of a totally blind girl is a most unwise thing."[36]

More often, the message that blind girls should remain single came through conspicuous omission.[37] The leading professional journal in the blindness field, *Outlook for the Blind,* for example, devoted many pages to highlighting discussions of a "domestic science" curriculum. Taught by sighted women with names such as Miss Corey and Miss Hoyt, the young blind girls learned cooking, cleaning, and other household tasks. But unlike the pages of popular women's magazines or even curricula for "normal" girls, *Outlook* made no mention of learning these skills to lure a man. In fact, the articles on domestic science seemed to go out of their way to desexualize blind women by placing them in distinctly unflattering situations. In one photograph from 1911, for example, a young lady in Victorian dress stands in the middle of a chicken coop with the fetching caption, "Station B of the Poultry Class at the Missouri School for the Blind." Even the scenes depicting more traditional domestic images such as meals around the dining room table imply that these young women were being prepared to serve relatives rather than to be wives and mothers themselves. Reflecting the most advanced professional ideas, a journal such as *Outlook* transmitted attitudes regarding marriageability to teacher-trainers, who in turn brought them to the classroom, where they found their way into the hearts and minds of their students.

STATION B OF THE POULTRY CLASS AT THE MISSOURI SCHOOL FOR THE BLIND

FIGURE 9.1 "Station B of the Poultry Class at the Missouri School for the Blind," *Outlook for the Blind* (Winter 1911). Courtesy American Foundation for the Blind Library, New York.

DINING ROOM FOR DOMESTIC SCIENCE PUPILS AT MISSOURI SCHOOL FOR THE BLIND

FIGURE 9.2 "Dining Room for Domestic Science Pupils at the Missouri School for the Blind," *Outlook for the Blind* (Winter 1911). Courtesy American Foundation for the Blind Library, New York.

Yet just because a prevailing set of beliefs suggested that blind girls should remain single did not mean that they should go through life alone. On the contrary, blind women and sighted professionals in both France and America constantly referred to alternative support networks that implicitly protected the blind woman from the cold, cruel world. In addition to families of origin and charity families that took in "unfortunates," these writers described institutions such as schools and residential work environments that created respectable alternatives to the home.[38] Most striking of all were discussions of female friendships that served as stand-ins not just for the companionship of marriage but sometimes for its erotic content as well. Begun between young girls, such friendships helped set the stage for later relationships.

Husson's "Reflections on the Physical and Moral Condition of the Blind" opens with a celebration of her friendship with Charlotte, "a girlfriend who was very dear to me, and whom an untimely death carried away from me as well as from her adoring parents." The two shared so much that they took a dramatic vow of blind sisterhood. "We kept not a single secret from one another," she reported, noting that people often mistook one of them for the other. "Always united in heart and mind, the intimate union that made us each so happy charmed our parents." Husson then took the friendship to a depth that many would find extreme:

> We were so accustomed to our lot that when one day I asked my friend what she desired most in the world, she responded, putting her arms around me: "the happiness of everyone I love." When I continued, "But Charlotte, you could wish first for your own happiness," she answered in a tender tone, "it's your affection that I always want to have. . . . I would fear that the return of my sight would destroy our friendship because we would have less in common." "Oh, good Charlotte," I cried with enthusiasm, "If God willed me to see again, I would beg him to leave me in physical darkness, which I cherish so much because I share it with you."[39]

Clearly this intimacy pushed the boundaries of "normal" behavior. Yet the social values expressed by parents and professionals went beyond simple toleration to encourage and indulge it, as if everyone understood such connections as a form of atonement or recompense for the single life they assumed for these poor little blind girls.

Such friendships captured the imagination of the numerous professionals and laypersons who wrote about blindness throughout the nineteenth and early twentieth centuries. In an odd book from the early twentieth century, E. de Werbrouck doled out an especially large helping of pity for the plight of the blind—one stripped of all politeness and nuance. Promising a study of "the unfortunates whose bodies are plunged into opaque obscurity" that would help those with "unlimited horizons" fulfill their charitable destiny, Werbrouck gave the same advice to men and women:

> Marriage, if it is the constant dream of the blind of both sexes, is also almost invariably a pure pipedream caressed by their ever-delirious

imaginations. For the most part, these pariahs will always remain single. Better that someone be self-sacrificing and refrain from following the natural passions common to all who exist than to unite oneself with a being who one will never see, [a being] who one can neither direct nor help.

To avoid such misery, Werbrouck advised, "restrict your ambitions, young girls and young men, to the culture of friendship, this pale sentiment, pale like the pale moon, sweet as sweet can be in its light."[40] Writers such as Werbrouck believed that friendship would be compensation for both love and sight.

Discussions that viewed these friendships as stand-ins for marriage often elided distinctions between childhood and adulthood. At the turn of the century, for example, *La Revue pour les Jeunes Filles* published an article titled "The Young Blind Girls" that explored intimacies between Germaine and Marie, two students at a school for the blind in Saint Mandé outside of Paris.[41] "The friendship between these two young blind girls had something closer, more intimate, and infinitely more precious about it than any other friendship between young girls," the author, Augusta Latouche, explained, later noting that "friendships between blind girls achieve the ideal of friendship." Pointing out that blindness required more touching, she quickly added: "But above all it is for moral reasons that they need a companion friend [*compagne amie*]," because given "all the feelings, fervor, and enthusiasm that come with being an age where aspirations are so great, [these girls] put into their feelings for their friends."[42] Latouche mentioned in passing that Marie would be twenty the following year.

If writers needed to infantilize blind women in order to preserve a sense of sexual propriety, they could also hint more directly at the erotic content of friendship when discussing young girls. In her 1886 story "The Blind Lark," Louisa May Alcott recounts a meeting between the main character, Lizzie, a sweet blind girl, and her new friend from "the happy school" (an allusion to the Perkins School for the Blind, which had commissioned the story):

> "This is Minna, the little girl I told you of. She wanted to see you very much, so we paddled away like a pair of ducks, and here we are," said Miss Grace gayly; and as she spoke Lizzie felt soft fingers glide over her face, and a pair of childish lips find and kiss her own. The groping touch, the hearty kiss, made the blind children friends at once, and, dropping her flowers, Lizzie hugged the new-comer, trembling with excitement and delight.[43]

Those who express this sort of homoeroticism may sometimes feel discomfort about the relationship, as seen, for example, in the story of Helen Keller and Anne Sullivan, herself visually impaired. Interestingly, the material on other disabilities doesn't enlist homoeroticism in this way, perhaps largely because touch enters so centrally into stories about blindness.[44] Unthinkable between nineteenth-century boys or men, these sorts of relationships invoke historian Carroll Smith-Rosenberg's "The Female World of Love and Ritual," in which deep friendships between women in nineteenth-century America walked the fine line between the platonic and the homoerotic.[45] Because Alcott's characters are children, however, disability, helplessness, and sentimentality add something both more acceptable and more disturbing to Smith-Rosenberg's analysis of Victorian culture. Because of the implications of needing to see through touch, blindness challenged the Victorian imperative that the female body remain a guarded fortress. Thus, it was acceptable for blind girls to touch each other freely in ways and in places that otherwise might raise eyebrows in polite company. At the same time, such touching invited hungry Victorians to think more consciously about female sexuality, and especially about childhood pornography or other forms of unacceptable sexual practices that historians have documented as flourishing in such a repressive society.[46]

The fluid boundaries among childhood, adulthood, and sexuality in discussions of blind women must be understood within the complex relationship between modernity and capitalism.[47] Modernity introduced definitions of "normalcy," rendering them scientifically measurable and seeing deviations from the norm as a form of pathology. As science and medicine came to have greater political, cultural, and economic sway, western Europeans and Americans would learn to understand health more broadly in such a way that both disability and a woman's marital status came under new kinds of scrutiny. The professionals who pathologized the single woman and saw the regulation of sex and sexuality as key to maintaining the social order happened upon the blind adult-juvenile as a respectable alternative for beings who would otherwise have no legitimate place on the social grid. As adults, such miss-fits could be seen as challenging Victorian propriety in that they failed to marry or bear children while still invoking unmistakable hints of sexuality; as juveniles they were not expected to adhere to these demands, which allowed them to still live by the rules and even to help perpetuate them.

Capitalism, meanwhile, brought values of productivity and exchange to the domain of human interactions. Generally speaking, in the evolving socioeconomic structures of the nineteenth and early twentieth centuries, an able-bodied woman from the lower classes was supposed to find employment, while one from the wealthier classes would marry and run a household. As labor became a commodity, individuals of any social class unable to meet the newly defined demands of strength, reliability, and fitness found themselves stigmatized or even discarded. Believed to be living in a state of heightened and prolonged dependence, blind women threatened to expose flaws in a system that celebrated values of independence and utility while providing little or no place for those who had legitimate reasons for not fitting in. Approaching blind miss-fits as adult-juveniles helped maintain the system's overall integrity because an adult blind woman's close links to childhood offered a reasonable explanation for why she would be exempted from both work and marriage.

Despite these cultural exemptions, both Husson and Keller understood that work and marriage had a complicated relationship in the lives of blind women. Not content to accept the status of the adult-juvenile, each woman fought to achieve respectability through work *and* marriage. To be sure, both displayed a profound ambivalence about their convictions to remain single. On the one hand, both expressed the idea that women with disabilities were unworthy of marriage, with both of them strongly suggesting that a woman with a disability would be incapable of holding up her end of the bargain. At the same time, each saw themselves as challenging their own notions about the incapacity of disabled women. Both women presented their competence *despite* their marriage prospects, and—perhaps not coincidentally—both chose the path of becoming writers. Husson published nearly a dozen novels of edifying fiction for young adults before she died in a fire at twenty-nine.[48] Meanwhile, after graduating from Radcliffe cum laude, Keller went on to a distinguished career as the author of numerous books and articles, in addition to playing on the vaudeville circuit, starring in a Hollywood film, serving as a spokesperson and fund-raiser for the American Foundation for the Blind, and living to the impressive age of eighty-eight.[49] In some senses, the two women displayed unusual gumption: thwarting low expectations to tell their stories, secure publishing contracts, and enjoy careers that did not depend on marriage. Yet although both writers clearly advised other blind women to remain single, and both demonstrated that they could get by without needing to be married, Husson and Keller each suggested that marriage might be desirable after all. And both would pay a terrible price for making choices that reflected this ambivalence.

Husson's story was especially tragic. If the young French provincial knew how to play by the rules, she also flagrantly disregarded them by marrying a blind man in Paris on February 1, 1826, less than two years after she had dictated and sent off her "Reflections on the Physical and Moral Condition of the Blind." In fact, her marriage to an educated blind musician, Pierre-François-Victor Foucault, may have resulted in her subsequent falling out with the director of the Quinze-Vingts Hospital and her failure to receive the support she so desperately sought by writing to him. After marriage and the birth of the first of their two children, the young family found its economic circumstances deteriorating so substantially that they entered the city's poverty rolls, causing Husson to try yet again to gain support from the Quinze-Vingts. Unfortunately, she had alienated her benefactors because not only was her plea for help refused but the director scrawled in the margin of her petition that a number of people "had expressed serious complaints regarding the moral values of this couple," noting that "the woman is a schemer who has taken advantage of several individuals."[50] Although it cannot be proven that Husson died for her "transgression," the family's impossible circumstances surely hastened her demise. In a bitter irony that fulfilled Husson's dire warnings in the "Reflections," Foucault went on to live another forty years, enjoying a modestly successful career as an inventor, having married a sighted woman shortly after Husson's death.

Keller also suffered devastating consequences by flirting with marriage. Several chapters after reporting her exchange with Alexander Graham Bell, she elaborates on her failed elopement in 1916 with Peter Fagan, an assistant to John Macy, Anne Sullivan's husband. In this chapter Keller covers her anger and frustration only imperfectly, a quality of *Midstream* as a whole.[51] In vague terms she narrates how, when she was thirty-six, Fagan (whom she describes only as "the young man who was acting as my secretary" while Sullivan was away) took a romantic interest in her. "For a brief space I danced in and out of the gates of Heaven, wrapped up in a web of bright imaginings," she exclaimed. Sensing that no one in Keller's immediate circle would approve of the courtship and her marriage, Fagan urged Keller to keep their relationship secret. But Fagan had been spotted applying for a license to marry Miss Keller, and word had gotten out to the press. Thwarted, the couple continued to communicate in secret, but when Keller's mother learned of this, she banished Fagan from the premises, a demand backed up on several occasions by male relatives chasing him away with a shotgun. Keller's closest chance at marriage ended rather poignantly: one night she packed her bags, sneaked downstairs, and waited for Fagan to come for her, but he never arrived.

Why would anyone care so much about whether women like Husson and Keller married or wished to marry at all? Clearly both came from a modernizing culture struggling to define not just marriage but also how women's roles and abilities should be understood. The same historical epoch also grappled with disability and normality, as massive social and economic changes increased the desire among governments and individuals alike for certainty and minimizing difference. Such anxieties produced rules and an eagerness to enforce them. Husson had thwarted traditional expectations of someone who was blind, female, and from the provincial artisan class. She had broken the rules by entering into a relationship that broadened the definitions of marriageability not just for her but for every woman who might contemplate it. Keller also challenged these assumptions. But more important, many people around her, not the least her mother and teacher, had livelihoods that depended on her single status, for Keller's public appeal was much greater when she came off as an adult-juvenile, a virginal tabula rasa who parroted back uncontroversial attitudes of the day.

People also cared about whether women such as Husson and Keller married because establishing identity categories came to have increasing importance in a rapidly changing world. The two miss-fits—and surely many others like them—occupied the awkward middle place where modern society's desire that all women should marry confronted the belief that not all of them could. By revealing the existence of such a place simultaneously created by convention yet free of actual rules, the two women posed a threat. How should such beings be classified, and what role should they play? And if women on their own already proved problematic in "normal" circumstances, these miss-fits served as reminders that following the rules could be as transgressive as breaking them.

Acknowledgments

Thanks to Susan Burch, Rosemarie Garland-Thomson (who has reinvigorated the term "misfit"),Georgina Kleege, Kim Nielsen, Martin Pernick, Elizabeth Reis, Bonnie Smith, Martha Stoddard-Holmes, Zina Weygand, the participants of the Sexualities Cluster Discussion Group at the University of California, Davis (especially Elizabeth Freeman and Gayatri Gopinath), the European Studies Seminar at the University of Wisconsin, Madison, and the attendees at the RCHA seminar where I first presented this work.

Notes

1. Simi Linton, *Claiming Disability: Knowledge and Identity* (New York: New York University Press, 1998).
2. The term "disability studies" is from David T. Mitchell and Sharon Snyder, *Narrative Prosthesis: Disability and the Dependencies of Discourse* (Ann Arbor: University of Michigan Press, 2000), 3. For other discussions of disability and theory, see Erving Goffman, *Stigma: Notes on the Management of Spoiled Identity* (New York: Simon and Schuster, 1963); Lennard J. Davis, *Bending over Backwards: Disability, Dismodernism, and Other Difficult Positions* (New York: New York University Press, 2002); "Enabling Theory" section, in *Disability Studies: Enabling the Humanities,* ed. Sharon L. Snyder, Brenda Jo Bruggemann, and Rosemarie Garland-Thomson (New York: Modern Language Association, 2002).
3. Douglas C. Baynton, "Disability as Justification for Inequality in American History," in *The New Disability History: American Perspectives,* ed. Paul K. Longmore and Lauri Umansky (New York: New York University Press, 2001), 33–57.
4. For an excellent overview of gender and disability, see Rosemarie Garland-Thomson, "Feminist Disability Studies," *Signs* 30, no. 2 (2005): 1557–1587. For this essay, I have found the following works particularly helpful: Rosemarie Garland-Thomson, *Extraordinary Bodies: Figuring Disability in American Culture and Literature* (New York: Columbia University Press, 1997); Susan Wendell, *The Rejected Body: Feminist Philosophical Reflections on Disability* (London: Routledge, 1996); and Bonnie Smith and Beth Hutchison, eds., *Gendering Disability* (New Brunswick, NJ: Rutgers University Press, 2004). Fruitful and imaginative overlaps between marginalities can be found in Robert McRuer and Abby L. Wilkerson, eds., "Desiring Disability: Queer Theory Meets Disability Studies," special double issue, *GLQ: A Journal of Lesbian and Gay Studies* 9, nos. 1/2 (December 2002).Robert McRuer, "Compulsory Able-Bodiedness and the Queer/Disabled Existence," in Snyder, Bruggemann, and Garland-Thomson, *Enabling the Humanities,* offers an especially insightful analysis.
5. The classic study was Jacques Donzelot, *The Policing of Families* (1979, repr., New York: Random House, 1997), originally published in French in 1977.
6. On Foucault and disability, see Shelley Tremain, ed., *Foucault and the Government of Disability* (Ann Arbor: University of Michigan 2005); Michel Foucault, *Les anormaux: Cours au College de France, 1974–1975* (Paris: Hautes-Etudes Gallimard, Seuil, 1999).
7. It is important to remember that not all disabilities provoked the same reactions. Thus, while I use "disability" and "blindness" somewhat interchangeably in this context, I realize that the term is a complicated shorthand influenced by historical context as well as the nature of a specific condition.
8. Paul Mahon (1801), as quoted in Anne Carol, *Histoire de l'eugénisme en France: Les médicins et la procréation, XIXe et XXe siècle* (Paris: Seuil, 1995), 209.
9. Alexandre Debay (1853), as quoted ibid.
10. Charles Richet (1919), as quoted ibid., 219.
11. The following discussion is based on Michael Grossberg, "Matrimonial Limitations: Who's Fit to Wed?" chapter 4 in *Governing the Hearth: Law and the Family in Nineteenth-Century America,* by M. Grossberg (Chapel Hill: University of North Carolina Press, 1985).
12. Elizabeth Cady Stanton (1869) and Anna Garlin Spencer (1912), as quoted ibid.,140–141.

13. Garland-Thomson, *Extraordinary Bodies,* 19–21.

14. Thérèse-Adèle Husson, *Reflections: The Life and Writings of a Young Blind Woman in Post-Revolutionary France,* translated and with commentary by Catherine J. Kudlick and Zina Weygand (New York: New York University Press, 2001).

15. Ibid., 53–54.

16. Arlette Farge and Christiane Klapisch-Zuber, eds., *Madame ou mademoiselle? Itinéraires de la solitude féminine, 18e–19e siècle* (Paris: Editions Montalba, 1984), 7–16.

17. Arlette Farge, "Les temps fragiles de la solitude des femmes à travers les discours médicale du XVIIIe siècle," in Farge and Klapisch-Zuber, *Madame ou mademoiselle,* 251–261.

18. In 1852 (too early for Husson), the Soeurs Aveugles de Saint-Paul was founded in Paris, a Catholic order devoted to serving blind women with a desire to enter religious life. See R. P. Victor Delaporte, "Les Soeurs Aveugles de Saint-Paul," in *Etudes réligieuses, historiques et littéraires* (Paris: Institution des Soeurs-Aveugles, 1890), 7–23.

19. Dr. H. Truc, *Les aveugles en France* (Paris, 1902), 140.

20. As cited ibid., 140–141.

21. Maurice de la Sizeranne, *Les soeurs aveugles* (Paris, 1901), 119.

22. Karen Offen, "Depopulation, Nationalism, and Feminism in Fin-de-Siècle France," *American Historical Review* 89 (1984): 654.

23. Sizeranne, *Soeurs aveugles,* 119.

24. Helen Keller, *Midstream: The Story of My Later Life* (New York: Doubleday, 1929).

25. On Bell and deafness, see Douglas C. Baynton, *Forbidden Signs: American Culture and the Campaign against Sign Language* (Chicago: University of Chicago Press, 1996); Jill Lepore, *"A" Is for "American": Letters and Other Characters in the Newly United States* (New York: Knopf, 2002), 163–172; John Vickrey VanCleve and Barry Crouch, eds., *A Place of Their Own: Creating the Deaf Community in America* (Washington, DC: Gallaudet University Press, 1989), 145–152; Harlan Lane, *When the Mind Hears: A History of the Deaf* (New York: Random House, 1984).

26. Keller, *Midstream,* 133–135.

27. Susan Burch, *Signs of Resistance: American Deaf Cultural History, 1900–1942* (New York: New York University Press, 2002), 139–145; Baynton, *Forbidden Signs,* 30–32.

28. As quoted in Baynton, *Forbidden Signs,* 30–31.

29. As quoted in Burch, *Signs of Resistance,* 142.

30. The following discussion is based on Paul Lombardo, "Taking Eugenics Seriously: Three Generations of ??? Are Enough?" *Florida University Law Review* 30 (2003): 191–218, quotes at 205–208.

31. On disability and eugenics, see Martin S. Pernick, *The Black Stork: Eugenics and the Death of "Defective" Babies in American Medicine and Motion Pictures since 1915* (London: Oxford University Press, 1996); David Mitchell and Sharon Snyder, "The Eugenic Atlantic: Race, Disability, and the Making of an International Eugenic Science, 1800–1945," *Disability and Society* 18, no. 5 (August 2003). Paul Lombardo offers an extensive annotated bibliography of eugenics at http://hsc.virginia.edu/medicine/interdis/bio-ethics/bibliographylombardo.htm.

32. Bell's role in these laws has been misunderstood, because he personally thought that deaf persons should not marry each other, but he felt even more strongly that marriage was a sacred right for "good citizens" and that deaf people—as good citizens—should be allow the opportunity to marry. Alexander Graham Bell, "Marriage: An Address to the Deaf" (pamphlet) (Washington, DC: Gibbon, 1891.

33. Although it grapples with popular discussions of eugenics in the American media throughout, Pernick's *Black Stork* focuses most clearly on the issue in part 2, titled "Publicity."

34. Sibley's first name and gender remain a mystery, although I suspect female because the paper refers to "counting blind girls among my closest friends," and the opening remarks indicated that Sibley had been invited to present the paper after repeatedly bringing attention to the lack of discussion about blind girls compared to blind boys. *Proceedings of the Eleventh Biennial Meeting of the American Association of Instructors for the Blind,* Jacksonville, IL, 15 July 1890 (published 1891).

35. Ibid., 76. After making this assertion, the paper ends a few sentences later with an assertion that more schools for the blind need to be built, especially schools for blind girls.

36. Ibid.

37. The following discussion is culled from Catherine J. Kudlick, "The Outlook of *The Problem* and the Problem with *The Outlook:* Two Advocacy Journals Reinvent Blindness in Turn-of-the-Century America," in Longmore and Umansky, *New Disability History,* 202–207.

38. For a discussion of the early American versions of these, see Mary Klages, *Woeful Afflictions: Disability and Sentimentality in Victorian America* (Philadelphia: University of Pennsylvania Press, 1999), 52–54.

39. Husson, *Reflections,* 17.

40. E. de Werbrouck, *Aimons les aveugles* (Paris: Flammarion, n.d.)

41. Augusta Latouche, "Les jeunes filles aveugles," *Revue des Jeunes Filles* 100, nos. 20–21 (1899): 350–361.

42. Ibid., 360–361.

43. Louisa May Alcott, "The Blind Lark," *St. Nicholas* 14, no. 1 (November 1886).

44. Keller almost never described friendships with women, let alone blind women. Anne Sullivan, of course, was a different story, and one that has captured the imagination of people both past and present. See Dorothy Herrmann, *Helen Keller: A Life* (New York: Knopf, 1998). Anne Finger, in "Helen and Frida," imagines a cross-disability relationship between Keller and the famous artist Frida Kahlo, in *The Disability Studies Reader,* ed. Lennard J. Davis, 401–407 (New York: Routledge, 1997).

45. Carroll Smith-Rosenberg, "The Female World of Love and Ritual: Relations between Women in Nineteenth-Century America," 53–76, in *Disorderly Conduct: Visions of Gender in Victorian America,* by C. Smith-Rosenberg (Oxford: Oxford University Press, 1985). Interestingly, her sample is entirely made up of Protestant women, thus begging the question of whether Catholics would form their bonds in a similar way. Michel Foucault, "Friendship as a Way of Life," in *Michel Foucault, the Essential Works,* vol. 1: *Ethics, Subjectivity and Truth,* ed. Paul Rabinow (London: Penguin, 1997), discusses how such friendships between men were deliberately snuffed out by the development of formal institutional structures such as the modern army.

46. Steven Marcus, *The Other Victorians: A Study of Sexuality and Pornography in Mid-Nineteenth-Century England* (New York: Basic Books, 1974); Walter Kendrick, *The Secret Museum: Pornography in Modern Culture* (New York: Viking, 1987); Michel Foucault, *The History of Sexuality,* vol. 1: *An Introduction* (New York: Vintage, 1990).

47. This connection is only beginning to be explored with respect to disability and badly needs empirical research. The following scholars have speculated on aspects of the relationship: Jane Campbell and Mike Oliver, *The Politics of Disability: Understanding Our*

Past, Changing Our Future (London: Routledge, 1996); Lennard J. Davis, *Enforcing Normalcy: Disability, Deafness and the Body* (New York: Verso, 1995); Victor Finkelstein, *Attitudes and Disabled People: Issues for Discussion* (New York: International Exchange of Information in Rehabilitation, 1980); and Jan Branson and Don Miller, *Damned for Their Difference: The Cultural Construction of Deaf People as Disabled* (Washington, DC: Gallaudet University Press, 2002).

48. Catherine J. Kudlick and Zina Weygand, "Reflections on a Manuscript, a Life, and a World," in Husson, *Reflections,* 75–141.

49. Joseph P. Lash, *Helen and Teacher: The Story of Helen Keller and Anne Sullivan Macy* (Reading, MA: Addison-Wesley, 1980); Herrmann, *Helen Keller;* Kim Nielsen, *The Radical Lives of Helen Keller* (New York: New York University Press, 2004).

50. Husson, *Reflections,* 129. The original French states: "La femme est une intrigante qui a trompé la bonne foi de plusieurs personnes."

51. Perhaps she is writing in deliberate contrast to her wildly popular first book, *The Story of My Life* (1903). Nearly half of *Midstream's* chapter titles are somewhat negative: "I Capitulate," "In the Whirlpool" (the chapter in which she discusses the failed marriage), "I Believe I Am an Actress," "Muted Strings," and "Thoughts That Will Not Let Me Sleep."

CHAPTER 10

The Times That Tried Only Men's Souls

WOMEN, WORK, AND PUBLIC POLICY IN THE GREAT DEPRESSION

————>>●<<————

ELAINE S. ABELSON

King Kong was a sensation when it appeared in 1933 and has since become a film classic; the interaction between the beautiful white woman and the giant black gorilla has had a persistent hold on our racial fantasies. The newest version adheres closely to the original story line but is very much a product of twenty-first-century computer graphics and film technology. What is barely remembered from the 1933 *King Kong* are the opening scenes in which a young woman, played by actress Fay Wray, attempts to steal an apple from a fruit stand. Caught in the act but saved from arrest by Carl Denham, a movie director looking for "a girl" for his next picture, Wray promptly faints in his arms. Realizing that the girl is starving, Denham takes her to a luncheonette and feeds her.

> "How'd you ever get into this fix?" [he asks her when she has revived.]
> "Bad luck I guess, but then there are a lot of girls like me."
> "No family?"
> "I'm supposed to have an uncle someplace."
> "Did you ever act?"
> "I used to do extra work now and then . . . the studio is closed now."

These two scenes, which set the stage for the voyage to Skull Island, work from a prototype that Depression-era moviegoers easily recognized: young woman adrift in the city, no place to live, no work, no money, and obviously hungry. She was the woman people passed on the street in the early years of the Great Depression, but someone who remained socially invisible. She is the woman who is the subject of this study.

Recent scholarship on women and the welfare state suggests that gender ideology and racial anxieties are embedded in social policy.[1] By examining public reaction to the sudden appearance of homeless women in U.S. cities during the early years of the Great Depression, this essay examines interpretations of need and the complexity of competing claims on the state. The link between women without work and women without shelter is key, as loss of a job was invariably the crucial first step in a downward spiral that often ended in homelessness. Although the women in this study were, in the parlance of the time, "unattached"—presumably unmarried and not part of an ongoing family dynamic—their marital status is often unclear. What is clear is that they were alone at the time they came to the attention of journalists, relief authorities, and women like themselves. The key here is not whether they were literally single, or deserted, or widowed, but the fact that these formerly independent women were without resources, without support or protection.[2] I locate these women not among the habitually dispossessed or transient but among urban women who, white and nominally middle class (as was Fay Wray's character), suddenly lost their jobs, their savings, and often their homes and were cast into a particular narrative framework, the "new poor." Constructed within a context of race and gentility, the category "new poor" left out much of the white working class and all people of color.[3]

By 1930, over ten million women were in the U.S. work force, representing almost 25 percent of the total. Other than in a limited number of gender- and class-specific job categories, work for women during the Depression became as problematic as it was for men.[4] Women lost jobs at a higher rate than men in the early years of the crisis, were often unable to find other sources of income, and were routinely discriminated against in public employment and work-relief programs.[5] Although it appears that they were never more than 10 percent of the urban homeless population—and statistical data at this time were both crude and admittedly unreliable—the situation of these women loomed as a new and an increasingly difficult social problem.[6] We have ample, if somewhat sketchy, evidence but no historical narrative for homeless women, and their virtual absence from the visual record and most printed primary sources says a great deal about the conditions under which meaning is produced.[7]

Welfare agency reports and government records of the period make passing mention of women, but the twin problems of poverty and urban homelessness during the Great Depression were engendered as male; the "Forgotten Man," the family breadwinner without a job and without a regular source of income, was the focus of gender and political anxieties and the key factor for gauging the level of social and economic distress. Rehabilitation of the Forgotten Man was seen as vital to national recovery. And because the very definition of the problem in the early years of the Depression wrote women out of the narrative, the solution wrote them out as well. Posing no threat to social order and possessing no economic or political capital of any consequence, single women and women living outside of families were all but invisible to policy makers well into Franklin D. Roosevelt's first term.

Using homelessness as both a barometer and a yardstick, this essay examines the complexity of women's relationship to the state during the early years of the Great Depression. I look at the situation of homeless urban women and the discourse surrounding gender and work, asking why certain arguments had such power and what purposes they served; why the concept of rugged individualism,

FIGURE 10.1 This image of a woman selling apples in New York City, November 30, 1930, is one of the few images of poor urban women from the early years of the Great Depression. Associated Press. Photo courtesy Pictopia.

coded as male, and the political legitimacy and dominance of the male bread-winner ideal precluded seeing women—either individually or as a group—to be independent workers or providers. The ideology of female domesticity and economic dependence, no matter whether women were married or single, was deeply embedded within social policy and cultural norms. One small example: the director of New York City's newly organized Free Employment Agency, Edward C. Rybicki, announced in January 1932 that the need for married women to work part time to provide for their families resulted in a weakening of the city's home life. Children, he said, were suffering from neglect, and he personally "considered the situation as one of the MOST SERIOUS [his emphasis] aspects of the city's unemployment problem."[8]

So tied were public officials to this vision of women that the impulse to minimize and restrict their nondomestic work during an economic crisis viewed as male was an overwhelming response. In reality, of course, many women across class and racial lines were heads of households and worked outside of the home. Despite this fact, Rybicki and others blamed wage-earning women for exacerbating the brutal fallout of the economic crisis. No matter that a desperate woman could write in August 1933 that "the living depends on me," women were rarely accorded the status or moral authority of breadwinner.[9]

Homelessness was a shifting, relative, even ambiguous category strongly linked to the notion of family. What many observers in the 1930s saw as homelessness—single women living alone in furnished rooms—would not be labeled as homeless today.[10] These "unattached" women moved in and out of homelessness: literally homeless with no permanent residence anywhere for intermittent periods—days, weeks, even months—and marginally homeless for much longer periods. The imbalance between the needs of single women and the availability of affordable housing was severe, and with repeated evictions, doubling up, or forced moves from one cheap room to an even cheaper one, some single women found homelessness was an ever-present threat in the early 1930s. With one-third of the working population of New York City out of work in 1932, loss of a job meant loss of a home for large numbers of urban residents, and for the first time, the white, the middle class, and the educated—women and men who had no experience with unemployment and were accustomed to a "stable domicile"—suddenly found themselves at risk. Or as one unmarried and unemployed college woman told a social worker in 1932, "Having an address is a luxury just now."[11]

Although this group of women remained on the margins of collective consciousness throughout the long decade of the Depression, we can begin to locate them via their written pleas for recognition and help. With the inauguration of Roosevelt and the emergence of the New Deal in 1933, people wrote personal letters to the government in the expectation that their complaints and pleas would receive a sympathetic reading. One letter addressed to President Roosevelt in the spring of 1933 described the deplorable condition of the single women of Chicago, who "are roaming the streets wondering where they are going to get the price of a meal, and how they are going to pay their room rent." A Georgia woman asked, "What can be done for the woman to whom employment means life and necessities . . . women who have no men to work for them or [are the] sole support of others." A woman from Cleveland, Ohio, desperate that she had been unemployed for over two years and had "no home and no friends," pleaded for some direction.[12]

Although there was little in the way of material help or assistance in the offing, these letters were answered personally, often in detail, by someone in a relevant government agency. The following is a response from May 15, 1933.

> My dear Mrs. Bishop: Your letter to Mrs. Roosevelt has been referred to the Dept of Labor and to me. I am glad to tell you that there is a movement on foot to do something for the unemployed unattached women . . . there is some hope of organizing now a service that will be helpful to the woman who has no family. . . . Have you made application to the US Employment Service, 80 Centre Street NY, for work. . . . Signed Mary Anderson, Director, Women's Bureau, US Dept of Labor.[13]

We cannot know (or even imagine) what the expectations of these desperate letter writers were—certainly the response in this instance was not promising—but it is important to recognize that these women made tangible demands on the state. They wanted direction, they wanted a place to live, and above all they wanted jobs, for "they must live as well," a middle-aged widow from California who had been unemployed for twenty-seven weeks explained.[14]

The mere fact that women saw themselves as economic actors in their own right was still novel. Yes, women, black and white, had been independent wage earners for decades, and as Joanne Meyerowitz has shown, the self-supporting woman symbolized emancipation and modernity in the 1920s.[15] But the cultural values of one decade conflicted with the economic realities of the next. The *Milwaukee Journal* estimated that more than 60 percent of the "nonfamily" women who came to the attention of relief authorities in that city had been self-supporting and financially independent in 1929.[16] In most instances, however, a woman's savings were too low to carry her over an extended period of unemployment, and self-supporting or not she was defined by others in terms of family membership. Women's relationship to this normative institution—the family—became a political issue that prescribed the terms in which their visibility could exist. In 1931, the Service Bureau for Women in Chicago had difficulty in even defining the homeless woman without recourse to the language of family. The homeless woman—also called at various times an unattached woman, independent woman, nonfamily woman, lone woman, and one-person family—finally came to mean not only a woman without family but also a woman separated from her family, without domicile and furniture, and who constituted a problem by herself.[17]

The difficulty in discussing such women rendered them unknown and unseen. From time to time, journalists tried to force the public to "see" what had remained in the shadows. Emily Hahn, reporting for the *New Republic* in May 1933, investigated the situation of what she accurately called the "invisible" poor—jobless, unattached, often homeless women. "So far the unattached woman has got the leavings," she wrote. Neither an "unwed mother, blind or decrepit, she has no claim on the relief usually afforded the deserving case." The result, Hahn wrote, was a desperate scramble for "Half-time jobs. Temporary jobs. Free meals in restaurants that have come to the fore and offered their left-over food. Free rooms in hotels that cannot fill themselves otherwise. Failing these makeshift devices, emptiness lies before her."[18]

Hahn was surprised (as I have been) that the breadline—the ubiquitous symbol of the Depression years in cities across the country—seemed to be male space: "A breadline hand-out is poor fare," she observed, "but it is better than none; yet the women who must certainly be in want, like their brothers, were never seen in those lines. . . . WHERE DO THEY GO?" Hahn went on to observe that "even now, when it would seem that they had reached rock-bottom, the greater number of these homeless [female] drifters have not come to public attention."[19] Hahn's question "Where do they go?" is ultimately unanswerable. Writing for *New Masses* in the early 1930s, Meridel Le Sueur echoed Hahn's bewilderment. "It's one of the great mysteries of the city where women go when they are out of work and hungry," she wrote. There are no twenty-five-cent flophouses for women, and "they obviously don't sleep in 'the jungle' or under newspapers in the park, . . . so where are they?" Le Sueur suggested that some women picked up men, trading sexual favors for a night's lodging; other women lived together in furnished rooms, pooling clothes and other meager resources, with the pretty ones finding occasional work in stores and restaurants, and generally starving so quietly that "there are no social statistics concerning her."[20]

This, then, is the tension: working women had moved from proverbial chimney corner to center stage, from dependency to independence, but in the face of overwhelming economic crisis, analyses of women's evolution and new economic role had a negligible impact on either public awareness or policy. Or as Le Sueur commented in her essay "Women on the Breadlines," "try getting in to the Y.W. without any money or looking down at the heel. Charities take care of very few and only those that are called 'deserving.' The lone girl is under suspicion by the virgin women who dispense charity."[21]

The deeply held belief in the virtues of manly self-reliance and the sanctity of local hegemony helped shape initial public responses to the Depression—at least in the Hoover years before New Deal programs were in place and funded.[22] A one-time Progressive who was either unable or unwilling to grasp the severity and breadth of the gathering disaster, Herbert Hoover appeared to be ideologically timid if not rigid.[23] He remained persuaded that the laissez-faire ideology of voluntarism was the way to deal with and overcome crises, that communities should be responsible for their own residents, that private business could arrest the downswing, that the federal economic role should be only advisory, and that government activism, especially in the area of unemployment relief, was a way station to permanent dependency—that the "opiates of government charity," as he said in one speech, "and the shifting of our national spirit of mutual self-help" were to be feared.[24] Hoover was reluctant initially to even form a committee to study unemployment relief, "fearful that such action would tend to magnify the emergency in the mind of the public."[25]

For most of the first year after the Wall Street collapse in September 1929, when the extent of the cataclysm was not immediately apparent, structures already in place defined problems and responses in quite specific ways. Local and state governments, private philanthropies, community chests, and much of the public all seemed initially to firmly support the thesis that outright public charity was shameful and something to be avoided. And until 1933, with specific exceptions (veterans, Native Americans, and children), there was a consistent denial of federal responsibility for relief measures. It was axiomatic that the best help for needy individuals was based on voluntary funding and local community efforts. Direct federal or state aid to local governments was counter to both historical precedent and orthodox economic theory and, as a result, considered well outside the boundaries of prudent fiscal policy. Rooted in common law, "self-reliance, rugged individualism (both coded as male), and the primacy of local rule were articles of faith rarely questioned" by most Americans at the beginning of the decade.[26]

In the face of what was already an economic crisis of unprecedented magnitude by mid-1930, Hoover clung to the conviction that the economic machinery of the country could and would self-regulate.[27] The precipitous rise in the number of jobless and homeless would, he felt, correct itself as the economy regained its

balance and purchasing power increased.[28] His initial acts expressed his fundamental political values: he established two voluntary committees. The first, the
President's Emergency Committee for Employment (PECE) organized in October
1930, was in effect a "feel-good" measure that reinforced the twin principles of
self-reliance and self-help. The stated aim of the committee, which like many
such committees at this time had a separate women's division, was to "organize
the country so to help the country organize itself."[29] Relying on optimistic economic forecasts and cheerful public pronouncements, PECE was little more than
a clearinghouse for information. It promoted the establishment of citizen employment committees in each state and encouraged private investment in small-scale
local initiatives, which were basically spread-the-work campaigns and "make
work" projects for unemployed men. These projects included odd jobs, home re-
pairs, community "spruce-up" programs, and construction projects. For desperate
women, there was little offered beyond traditional domestic work and "household-
helper" positions—of small relief for unemployed teachers, stenographers, librarians, and secretaries. Individual communities were left with the entire burden of
raising funds and organizing whatever work programs and relief services they
deemed necessary *and* could support.

Nearly a year later, in the fall of 1931, a new committee was formed—the
President's Organization on Unemployment Relief (POUR). The dreaded U word,
unemployment, was now publicly acknowledged, as the conspiracy of optimism
could no longer be sustained. But basic attitudes remained unchanged in Washington, and this committee too functioned mainly and ineffectively as an informa-
tion-gathering and public relations campaign to raise public awareness and money
for local community chests and emergency relief committees and to counter the
increasing pressure for federal aid. POUR's chief legacy was propaganda—advertisements on billboards and in such popular venues as the *Saturday Evening Post*
and *Outlook* magazines—showing a healthy, smiling white male worker saying,
as he pulled down his tie, rolled up his sleeves, and tightened his belt, "Of course
we can do it!" and "I'll see it through if you will."[30] Masculine self-reliance and
relentless optimism became the formula for fighting the economic crisis.

Whether or not it was true, the White House *seemed* to lack compassion.
As the Hoover administration proved unwilling or unable to move beyond doctri-
naire attitudes and provide leadership to offset the staggering economic burden
that individuals, families, and communities across the country were facing, long-
established standards of local, organized relief were breaking down. Similarly,
religious and ethnic charities were overwhelmed, and hundreds of small private
agencies simply disappeared. Joint public/private work and relief committees appeared as stopgap but wholly inadequate emergency measures.

The effectiveness of emergency responses, of course, depended on a number
of variables, including state finances and available private resources as well as
both the ability and willingness to come to grips with the new dimensions of suffering caused by unemployment. New York, Philadelphia, Chicago, Detroit, Los
Angeles, and Seattle represented entirely different political and economic situations, but the burden of dealing with increasing numbers of dependent people fell

almost entirely on whatever local resources these cities could muster—and however much was raised was never sufficient. Beginning in late 1931, for example, women's emergency relief committees in Los Angeles and Chicago set up the first free lodging homes specifically for women—until (and inevitably) funding ran out, and they had to shut down.[31]

New York City, like many other cities, was constrained by its charter in the amount it could legally appropriate in any one year and how its tax moneys could be used. Without permission of the state legislature in Albany, tax increases and bonded indebtedness were circumscribed; public moneys for relief could be spent only for institutional care of the needy; outdoor relief (also known as home relief) in New York City was limited to the Board of Child Welfare, old age pensioners, veterans and their families, and the blind.[32] Private philanthropy stood as the front line of defense against need: the Salvation Army, the YM and YWCA, the newly organized Catholic Worker Houses of Hospitality, and health and welfare agencies affiliated with the major religious denominations provided limited care for particular groups: deserted women and children, the elderly, reformed prostitutes, and unwed mothers. There were also a small number of private subsidized group houses and boarding homes for specific categories of persons, including single working girls.

Although a recognized leader in the field of social service, New York City could only respond to the devastating flood of unemployment in measured steps and in ways that focused on families, not on unattached women. Private donations and emergency funding, including "voluntary" deductions of 1 percent from the wages of teachers and municipal employees, were exacted to make up for inadequate city relief moneys.[33] In 1930 the police distributed emergency grocery orders, clothing, and even a few rent vouchers to families with dependent children that legally resided in the city. This focus on families and dependent children is critical because these two categories, which reappear again and again, eliminate single women from relief by eliminating them from view.

The first work-relief program established in New York City, the Emergency Employment Committee (Prosser Committee), began operating in September 1930, one year after the Wall Street crash.[34] Financed with funds raised privately and administered by the newly organized Emergency Work Bureau in cooperation with already established social agencies, the Emergency Employment Committee had no women at either the executive or the administrative level.[35] Work relief was envisioned as a temporary measure to deal with what everyone predicted was a short-lived unemployment crisis, meaning men out of work. The thinking here was logical given the prevailing ideology and the structure of the committee. One member of the Emergency Committee carefully explained that married men who were heads of resident families had priority. With "no history of women in industry or in the professions being seriously affected in any previous period of unemployment," the all-male board of directors never considered that women who had lost their jobs and income might constitute a problem.[36] It wasn't a question of thinking outside the box; it was an absolute inability to put the words "women" and "work" together in any meaningful sense or to relate the economic crisis to women's lives.

To the surprise and obvious consternation of the board, the Emergency Work Bureau was besieged with applications from women, particularly from those who had lost white-collar jobs, begging for something to carry them through the crisis. Deciding that a limited number of women who were the "heads of families" should be given employment, work bureau administrators operated on a triage system: single women without legal dependents were not to be considered; with no work, no savings to tide them over, distressed, and often bewildered by their situation, they were left to shift for themselves.[37]

Few women were actually helped—about four thousand in all found intermittent and temporary work under Emergency Work Bureau auspices, while funding lasted. Not until the following year, 1932, did the city hesitantly extend work relief to unmarried women or open a Central Registration Bureau for Women and attempt to determine the full extent of female homelessness and financial need.[38]

The formation of a women's division within the Emergency Relief and Employment Committee in January 1931, in New York and other large cities, signaled the first public recognition of the plight of the white-collar, "nonfamily" woman. It was funded in large part by John D. Rockefeller Jr. and directed in New York City by the activist-philanthropist Mrs. August Belmont (whom one contemporary source referred to as "the guardian angel of single women"). The Special Fund for Unemployed Girls hoped to raise close to $500,000—the numbers are never clear and never the same—with the money kept separate from other funds and used in providing work and housing for single, primarily white-collar women over twenty-one "who were without family ties and [had] no one to call upon for help."[39] "The need is very real and requires immediate and extensive relief," Mrs. Belmont wrote in one fund raising appeal. "A room in which to live is an immediate need of some of these women." The Special Fund for Unemployed Girls succeeded in raising money for a select clientele, but it was clearly a stopgap measure that admittedly "met only a small part of the need" and exposed the weakness of Hoover's voluntarism in coping with a national disaster.[40]

When economic conditions deteriorated rapidly during what welfare agencies in New York and other cities commonly referred to as the Disaster Winter of 1930–1931, the combination of private and public local relief funds could not meet even minimal social needs. Despite frantic efforts by several hundred social service agencies all over New York City, including the City Welfare Bureau, only one-quarter of the estimated 390,000 jobless heads of families received *any* rent money; predictably, the situation was twice as bad for African American families.[41]

In a bold political move (and prodded by the city), then governor Franklin D. Roosevelt called the New York State Legislature into special session and pushed through the Temporary Emergency Relief Act (TERA) in late 1931. A precursor of one of the earliest and most successful New Deal relief programs, TERA was a matching grant-in-aid program to enable cities to provide both work and home relief in cash or in kind to "eligible categories" of needy people—primarily families with dependent children who could prove two years of continuous residence in any community in New York State. Although the act conferred no *right* to public relief and recognized the primary responsibility of local governments, it broadened the concept of public financial responsibility and established work relief alongside home relief as a major method of public aid to the resident unemployed.[42] Calling the state a "positive agency of social welfare" and seeing economic support for needy citizens as a matter of "social duty," Roosevelt turned Herbert Hoover's harsh social philosophy on its head and settled, at least temporarily, the crucial issue of responsibility for relief; New York State took the lead in providing emergency aid for the unemployed, and a half dozen other states followed suit.[43]

Roosevelt's more compassionate attitude toward the unemployed did not ultimately extend to single women. Legal issues, including conflict with existing law, local policies, and "customary practices," determined how TERA was implemented across the state. In this implementation we can read racial codes, age discrimination, and gender stereotyping, all of which influenced who would receive relief. Recognizing that "there would not be enough work or funds for all the persons in need," TERA administrators themselves instituted a triage system, and once again, women and men without legal dependents were the bottom rung in the equation, meaning that "unattached" adults received no help. Economic conditions in the state were so bad that in January 1932, the *New York Times* observed that only 50 percent of the needy unemployed were receiving any aid at all.[44] Without jobs, having used up savings and networks of loans, unable to pay even minimal rents, thousands were turned out of their homes and basically left to shift for themselves. One-quarter of the women in the municipal shelter in New York City told the same story of family separation: "Our home was broken up . . . my husband lost his job . . . we couldn't pay the rent."[45] One social worker explained, "the door just isn't wide enough to let in all who come to it."[46]

The lack of an all-encompassing safety net was characteristic of welfare policy nationwide, but women were in a particularly precarious position. Organized to aid families and children, neither private charities nor city agencies were prepared for the "independent woman"—the former office worker, schoolteacher, salesclerk, social worker, or nurse—who seemed to exist outside of a family structure and had "no resources upon which they could draw." The story in Chicago mirrored that in New York. Attempting to rationalize the situation, one newspaper explained that "homeless and unemployed women and girls in large numbers are something new in Chicago's experience." Apparently, they were for Cleveland as well. The city had long provided a Wayfarers' Lodge for single men and boys, but according to a *New York Times* survey in 1932, Cleveland had *no* municipal resources for needy women; with 33,000 women thrown out of work—fully one-third of the 100,000 women normally employed—the city had no emergency plan for women. Unlike men in similar circumstances, women (in New York, Chicago, Cleveland, and most other cities) were supposed to have families to provide for them.[47]

Some writers, including a few social workers, suggested that homeless women, hoping to create instant families, look to men for deliverance. "On the whole it would appear that the single woman is never quite so desperate as she appears since there is always a last card that can be played which calls to her aid the strong right arm of some man."[48] Was the writer suggesting marriage or prostitution? Prostitution seems unlikely, but it was increasingly evident as a strategy for survival in these years and increasingly worrisome for city officials and the public alike. There was real fear that women with no male provider would be forced onto the streets.[49] Val Lewton's 1932 novel *No Bed of Her Own* highlights, as few other sources at the time did, the precarious situation of young, single, white, urban working women: the enormous obstacles to finding a way to support themselves decently after their regular jobs disappeared and the losing fight to literally keep a roof over their heads. Shameful as it was to many women, hustling for a living often seemed preferable to semi-starvation, shabby clothes, torn stockings, and cat-and-mouse games played with ushers in movie theaters or with the police in Grand Central Station. But as one prostitute warned a neophyte in Lewton's novel, things won't be easy: "there is lots of competition out there." Even selling your body was difficult, and prices could be very low.[50]

Whether or not they understood the situation of unattached women, authorities in New York and other large cities were forced by sheer numbers to respond to the basic need for shelter. In October 1932, the newly organized Emergency Unemployment Relief Committee warned that an estimated 30,000 unemployed and homeless women were expected to need help during the coming winter.[51] A look at the confidential *Report on the Municipal Lodging House of New York City* (April 1932) suggests that the city was poorly prepared.

The lengthy report documents what had become evident: the numbers of homeless men were expected to swell in periods of economic crisis; large numbers of women without work and permanent shelter were still a new and poorly understood phenomenon. Additionally, in stark contrast to past experience, most of the women who sought refuge at the Municipal Lodging House and Salvation Army facilities in the early 1930s were not the chronically destitute for whom these shelters were constructed but the emergency, short-term cases—ordinarily self-supporting, often single working women who suddenly found themselves without financial resources and were isolated in their new poverty.[52] Care of these new homeless was further complicated by class issues—by official reluctance to send "high class girls who have lost their jobs and are penniless to the same place as others."[53] With cold water showers, few facilities for washing and ironing clothes, and no provision for daytime use, the women's division of the New York City Municipal Lodging House was obviously inadequate for the demands of the new clientele, many of whom kept up a desperate search for a paying job.[54]

We see here a deadly combination of what had become all too common: rapidly deteriorating economic conditions and the exhaustion of emergency funds; priority for families with children; and widespread agreement that the unemployed male breadwinner was the real problem. Perceiving that public opinion would not support home relief for unattached individuals, city agencies and private charities failed to consider the needs of unemployed single women as legitimate. Unlike homeless men, the single woman was not a category even recognized by social work professionals before the Great Depression. She had been no one's client. To the city agencies she was simply a "nonfamily woman"; to Mary Simkovitch, director of New York's Greenwich House, she was "a discard" whose individual needs seemed inconsequential in the face of more demanding priorities."[55] The *Los Angeles Times* captured the essence of the situation in September 1932:

> Organized charity knows all about male breadlines. It understands family welfare. There are institutions and homes for children, for the aged, for the insane, . . . for the woman out on probation, for down-and-out men and wayward boys. . . . But so far we have no accepted system for taking care of the lone, unemployed, homeless female . . . who would ordinarily be a self-supporting working woman if there was any work to be had.[56]

The consequences of this type of thinking led the Home Relief Bureau in New York City to rule in November 1932 that, contrary to stated guidelines, single women outside of families were not eligible for public assistance. Not until the winter of 1933–1934, four years after the onset of the Depression, did Home Relief begin to aid "unattached women who might otherwise be in need of shelter facilities."[57] And even then, discussion of the single woman on home relief came only within a family matrix. For this group, social work student Gertrude Steel-Brooke noted, the state provides "a sort of husband substitute and that so-needed sense of security."[58]

The Socialist Party was one of the few groups to take up the cause of these women. Organized by the party in New York City in 1933, the Association of Unemployed Single Women alternately pressed for jobs, housing, food tickets, and cash relief for women rendered destitute in the crisis. Estimating that there were between 100,000 and 175,000 single unemployed women in the city in November 1933, many of them homeless, the association demonstrated, circulated petitions, and pressured the city in the name of the "Forgotten Woman" to act to forestall what it perceived as an imminent disaster.[59] Whatever its legitimacy and moral justification, the seemingly radical agenda of the Association of Unemployed Single Women never found widespread support.

Although the states and municipalities were rapidly exhausting their resources, and the Hoover administration remained committed to ideological consistency in the face of precipitously rising unemployment rates and clear signs of spreading economic desperation throughout the country, the United States Congress held hearings on unemployment in 1930, 1931–1932, and again in 1933. Two relief bills, submitted in 1931 by Republican senator Robert La Follette Jr. of Wisconsin and Democratic senator Edward Costigan of Colorado, called for large appropriations for public works and direct federal aid for unemployment relief. The hearings on these two bills, which spanned nine days in late December 1931 and January 1932, are in both format and testimony typical of all the hearings on unemployment in these years, and they give a vivid sense of the extent of a deepening Depression—destitution nationwide, massive local protests demanding federal action, and the "struggles of local agencies, public and private, to meet increased needs with inadequate funds."[60] Testifying at the hearings in 1931 and 1932 were representatives from local community chests; the major welfare organizations and charities; the Russell Sage Foundation; the mayor of Detroit; the city manager of Dayton, Ohio; labor union secretaries; the governor of Pennsylvania; and Walter Gifford, president of AT&T and the director of the President's Organization on Unemployment Relief (POUR), the major federal agency charged with gathering information. In opposing any suggestion of federal relief, Gifford nevertheless admitted that he had no information on the number of unemployed nationwide, nor did he know the extent of destitution and relief needs in the country as a whole.[61]

Homelessness and the situation of women rarely emerged in the hearings. Only in the statement of Herbert Benjamin, national secretary of the Unemployed Councils—a Communist Party organization—was women's need for relief acknowledged and explicitly addressed. Testifying about the precipitous decline in living standards of American workers and their families, Benjamin touched on a subject he felt had been neglected: the effect of mass unemployment on women. "The misery of unemployment," Benjamin said, was "far more severe for girls and women than for the men." In Chicago, for example, with a population of three million, there was only one free women's lodging house, and it accommodated one hundred women. Women were sleeping in the parks throughout the city, and the same conditions were true in Pittsburgh. With far lower wages than men and almost no other options, women increasingly turned to prostitution.[62] In connecting unemployment, homelessness, and women, Benjamin understood that economic forces had transformed the social and political landscape in ways once unimaginable.

When these combined relief bills failed to pass, Costigan and La Follette introduced a new measure the following year and held hearings with many of the same witnesses. Testimony in January and February of 1933, after Roosevelt had been elected but before he took office, pictured creeping economic paralysis and an exacerbation of tax delinquencies, hunger, evictions, homelessness, separation of families, and dependence on public funds that simply did not exist.[63] In detailing the tragic inadequacy of local relief measures in the country's richest city and the absolute need for federal intervention, William Hodson, head of the Welfare Council of New York City, bluntly acknowledged to the senators what TERA administrators had determined the preceding year: few needy people in New York City were receiving adequate support, and the situation was especially bad for single adults. Although "a single unattached person who has no family is *entitled* to relief," because of the inadequacy of funds "those persons who are heads of families are given preferred rating." "Many persons," Hodson continued, "without any responsibilities (read dependents) are not taken care of as they should be."[64]

The proposed unemployment relief bill of winter 1933 morphed into what became a major piece of social legislation early in Roosevelt's first term: the Federal Emergency Relief Act (FERA) of May 1933. Modeled after TERA and headed by Harry Hopkins, who had directed the New York experiment, FERA meant an abrupt change in the concept of government and relief. Unemployment

FIGURE 10.2 Women applying for entry to a work camp, part of the New Deal response to homeless women. Work camps were a form of relief and seen as a way to rehabilitate women outside of families. New York City, June 2, 1933. Photo © Bettmann/CORBIS.

became, officially, a social problem of national concern; grants to the states substituted for loans and advances; the role of the federal government changed "from lending to giving what the states and localities could not supply by themselves." Further, FERA, with all its weaknesses and limitations in practice, symbolized a new understanding of government responsibility for human welfare; in its willingness to expand the scope of government operations, it was, in effect, an enlarged interpretation of the welfare clause in the U.S. Constitution.[65]

This change affected unattached women in two ways. First, direct home relief, although always understood as an emergency expedient, became a possibility—no, a reality—for the first time; and second, work relief, supported now by federal funds, became a primary objective for those who were labeled the "able-bodied" unemployed. Theoretically, independent women were no longer an afterthought who needed a Mrs. Belmont to plead their case. Speaking to social workers at a national conference in June 1933, Hopkins made it clear that the New Deal understood that all classes and all groups were victims of the Depression, and speedy relief was imperative in the near-panic conditions of 1933. "It seems to me," Hopkins told the social workers, "that the intent of this act is that relief should be given to the heads of families who are out of work and whose dependency arises from the fact that they are out of work; [to] single men and women who are out of work, and to transient families, as well as the transient men and women roaming the country."[66]

The reality, again, was somewhat different. Rent, the key to homelessness, was paid only sporadically; there was never, according to Hopkins, a clear-cut decision about the rent issue, but by the early months of 1934 unattached women did become legally eligible for home relief.[67] Although the desperate situation of the white-collar homeless became subject to a clearly defined public policy, social expectations had changed very little. The early New Deal largely ignored women workers. One thoughtful analyst mused that "women workers are subordinate in the times that tried only men's souls."[68] Employed or not, men were still assumed to be heads of families, the main breadwinners, and the key to recovery; women workers were still an afterthought. The bulk of the women's work-relief program in the 1930s was built around what were assumed to be traditional female skills: sewing, cooking, nursing, and elementary school teaching.

Homelessness was rarely a clear-cut category. As I indicated at the outset, single women and girls moved in and out of homelessness, but advocates for these women seemed to agree with Mary Heaton Vorse, a journalist and reporter for the *New Republic,* who wrote in 1934 that women were "the most lamentable of all the depression victims."[69] Why was this the case? I think the answer lies in the then barely understood area of gender. Beyond the fact of the unprecedented emergency and the hard-won recognition that when men lost their jobs, many families were helpless, women remained part of a secondary, often temporary, labor market and held a corresponding role in people's interpretation of the crisis. Both their labor and their earnings were considered as supplemental to anything a man might bring in. By definition, men were the breadwinners. When hard times struck, so-called independent women were supposed to return to their families, and many of them did just that. But not all did, and these women—who had no family, whose family could not or would not take them in, who had lost connection with family—these women (often over thirty-five or forty, who were "always girls until they lost their jobs") were part of a whole invisible "city of women" in the early 1930s.[70]

Expectations were inseparable from available ideologies and a sense of the social order, from the certainty of how women and men should live and act, and from how they should be and where they should be. It was a sense of the social order that reinscribed more traditional social relations and that was resistant to change in a period of severe economic upheaval. No matter the reality of women's increasing social independence, workforce participation, and prominence in political life, the assumption that women lived or should live in families as dependents of men lingered as an unacknowledged component of public discourse and revealed, as I suggested at the outset, the gender politics embedded in social policy.[71] What condemned countless numbers of women to "survive on a cracker a day" as Le Sueur wrote, also made these women marginal figures in our understanding of the crisis wrought by the Great Depression. Had Fay Wray's character not found salvation in the arms of a man, she might have been the woman people passed on the street, but someone who remained socially invisible.

Notes

1. The recent literature on the relationship of women to the state is large and growing. Among the most helpful for this essay were Linda Gordon, *Pitied but Not Entitled: Single Mothers and the History of Welfare, 1890–1935* (New York: Free Press, 1994); Linda Gordon, ed., *Women, the State, and Welfare* (Madison: University of Wisconsin Press, 1990); Mimi Abramovitz, *Regulating the Lives of Women: Social Welfare Policy from Colonial Times to the Present* (Boston: South End Press, 1988); Paula Baker, *Gender and the Transformation of Politics: Public and Private Life in New York, 1870–1930* (Boston: Free Press, 1990); Seth Koven and Sonya Michel, eds., *Mothers of a New World: Maternalist Politics and the Origins of Welfare States* (New York: Routledge, 1993); Theda Skocpol, *Protecting Soldiers and Mothers: The Political Origins of Social Policy in the United States* (Cambridge, MA: Harvard University Press, 1992); Margaret Weir, Anna Shola Orloff, and Theda Skocpol, eds., *The Politics of Social Policy in the United States* (Princeton: Princeton University Press, 1988); Alice Kessler-Harris, *In Pursuit of Equity: Women, Men, and the Quest for Economic Citizenship in 20th Century America* (New York: Oxford, 1998); Alice Kessler-Harris, "In the Nation's Image: The Gendered Limits of Social Citizenship in the Depression Era," *Journal of American History* (December 1999): 1251–1279.

2. The literature on single women is also growing exponentially. As the divorce rate in the United States has climbed over 50 percent, as same-sex relationships become mainstream, and as more women choose to become single mothers, the attitudes and expectations toward single women and about single women have undergone a dramatic reversal. A precursor of this trend is Martha Vicinus, *Independent Women: Work and Community for Single Women, 1850–1920* (Chicago: University of Chicago Press, 1985); see also Rutgers Center for Historical Analysis (RCHA), "Single Women Bibliography" (2002), http://scc.rutgers.edu/rcha.

3. For a fuller discussion of the representation of these newly poor women, see Elaine S. Abelson, "Women Who Have No Men to Work for Them: Gender and Homelessness in the Great Depression, 1930–1934," *Feminist Studies* 29 (Spring 2003): 105–127.

4. Abramovitz, *Regulating the Lives of Women*, 22–22; for statistics on married women in the workforce, see Alice Kessler-Harris, *Out to Work: A History of Wage-Earning Women in the United States* (New York: Oxford University Press, 1982), 376n26; Women's Bureau, *Employment* 13, no. 4 (1 April 1933): 1.

5. Abramovitz writes that the situation changes with the New Deal; clerical work declined less rapidly and recovered more quickly. However, the data are often contradictory. See Abramovitz, *Regulating the Lives of Women*, 223.

6. U.S. Congress, Senate, Subcommittee of the Committee on Manufactures, *Federal Aid for Unemployment Relief, Hearings on S. 5125,* 72nd Cong., 2nd sess., 3–17 January 1933, statement of H. L. Lurie, 67; William Hodson, "Committee on Emergency Financing of Social Work," 8 July 1932, box 123, Community Service Society (CSS) Papers, Mss Division, Columbia University; see also David M. Kennedy, *Freedom from Fear: The American People in Depression and War, 1929–1945* (New York: Oxford University Press, 1999), 57.

7. The most recent book-length survey of homelessness in the United States follows this pattern in that it says little about the situation of women. Kenneth Kusmer, *Down and*

Out, on the Road: The Homeless in American History (Oxford: Oxford University Press, 2002).

8. *New York Times,* 2 January 1932, 9.

9. Laura Hapke, *Daughters of the Great Depression: Women, Work, and Fiction in the American 1930s* (Athens: University of Georgia Press, 1997), 24; Mrs. Harry Johnson, letter (Library of Congress), 17 August 1933, RG 9 NRA file 619, Wilmington, DE. See also Alice Kessler-Harris, "Gender Ideology in Historical Reconstruction: A Case Study from the 1930s," *Gender and History* 1 (Spring 1989): 31–49.

10. Edna Tibbets Hawley, "The Homeless Woman: A Study of Dependency among Unattached Women" (PhD diss., Washington University, St. Louis, MO, 1932).

11. Ibid., 15–16; *Channels: News Bulletin of the Social Work Publicity Council,* January 1933, 9; "Suggested Procedure for the Emergence Care of Unattached Men and Women in New York City," 24 September 1932, box 25, Lillian Wald Papers, Welfare Council, Mss Division, Columbia University.

12. "Correspondence August–December 1933," *Women's Bureau Bulletin,* 139, found in the National Archives, Washington, DC; quoted previously in Abelson, "Women Who Have No Men to Work for Them," 118.

13. "Correspondence January–July 1933," *Women's Bureau Bulletin,* 139; this letter exemplifies the confusion about the marital status of these women. The reference is to "unemployed unattached women." Presumably *Mrs.* Bishop is either widowed or divorced, but we cannot know.

14. "Correspondence August–December 1933," *Women's Bureau Bulletin,* 139.

15. Joanne J. Meyerowitz, *Women Adrift: Independent Wage Earners in Chicago, 1880–1930* (Chicago: University of Chicago Press, 1988), 117–139.

16. *Milwaukee Journal,* 26 July 1938.

17. Hawley, "Homeless Woman," 287.

18. Emily Hahn, "Women without Work," *New Republic,* 31 May 1933, 63–65.

19. Ibid., 63–65; also mentioned in Milton Meltzer, *Brother Can You Spare a Dime?* (New York: Signet, 1977), 38–40.

20. Meridel Le Sueur, "Women on the Breadlines," in *Women on the Bread Lines* (New York: West End Press, 1984).

21. Ibid.

22. Frederick Lewis Allen, *Since Yesterday: The 1930s in America* (New York: Harper and Row, 1939), 51–55; T. H. Watkins, *The Hungry Years: A Narrative History of the Great Depression in America* (New York: Henry Holt, 1999), 73ff.

23. Kennedy, *Freedom from Fear,* 57.

24. Josephine Chapin Brown, *Public Relief, 1929–1939* (New York: Henry Holt, 1940), 73.

25. Harry L. Hopkins, *Spending to Save: The Complete Story of Relief* (New York: W. W. Norton, 1936), 17.

26. Watkins, *Hungry Years,* 73; Frances Fox Piven and Richard Cloward, *Regulating the Poor: The Functions of Public Welfare* (New York: Vintage, 1971).

27. Allen, *Since Yesterday,* 53.

28. Alan Brinkley, *The End of Reform: New Deal Liberalism in Recession and War* (New York: Alfred A. Knopf, 1995), 68–72.

29. U.S. Congress, Senate, Appropriations Committee, *Hearing on Drought Relief and Unemployment,* 71st Cong., 3rd sess., 7 January 1931, statement of Col. Arthur Woods, 68.

30. Lizabeth Cohen discusses how, by the mid-1930s, industrial workers championed an expanded role for the state. See Cohen, *Making a New Deal: Industrial Workers in*

Chicago, 1919–1939 (New York: Cambridge University Press, 1990), 222–227, 252–257; *Outlook,* 13 January 1932, inside front cover.

31. Cohen, *Making a New Deal,* 225–235; *Chicago Daily Tribune,* 27 September 1931, D2, and 14 November 1931, 15; *Los Angeles Times,* 12 September 1932, A12, and 17 October 1932, A2.

32. Joanna C. Colcord, William C. Koplovitz, and Russell H. Kurtz, *Emergency Work Relief* (New York: Russell Sage Foundation, 1932), 17–18; William W. Bremer, *Depression Winters: New York Social Workers and the New Deal* (Philadelphia: Temple University Press, 1984), 31–32. In some states, limits of property taxation had been reached, and no additional funds were available; U.S. Congress, Senate, Subcommittee of the Committee on Manufactures, *Unemployment Relief, Hearings on S. 172 and S. 262,* 72nd Cong., 1st sess., December 1931–January 1932, statement of William Hodson, 14; *Emergency Relief in the State of New York: Statutes, Regulations, and Opinions and Interpretations of Counsel* (Albany, November 1934), 64ff.

33. *New York Times,* 26 October 1930, 20; *Los Angeles Times,* 24 March 1933, A3.

34. *Unemployment Relief, Hearings on S. 172 and S. 262,* statement of William Hodson, 19.

35. Colcord, Koplovitz, and Kurtz, *Emergency Work Relief,* 136–137.

36. Emergency Work Bureau Committee, Minutes of Meetings, 15 January 1931; W. H. Matthews, "The Story of the Emergency Work Bureau," New York City, 1 October 1930–1931, August 1933, box 67, CSS Papers, 44.

37. Colcord, Koplovitz, and Kurtz, *Emergency Work Relief,* 147; POUR, Women's Division, "Some Measures Used by Business Enterprises to Promote Regularization of Employment," 1930–1931; "Women Workers after a Plant Shutdown," Department of Labor and Industry, Commonwealth of Pennsylvania, 1933.

38. Matthews, "Story of the Emergency Work Bureau," 44; Edith Weller, "The Unattached Woman," *Jewish Social Service Quarterly* 10 (September 1933): 54.

39. Rockefeller Archive Center, Emergency Work Bureau, "Special Fund for Unemployed Girls," 14 January 1931; and memorandum of conversation, "Relief Needs of White Collar Girls," 13 January 1931.

40. Emergency Work Bureau Committee, Minutes of Meetings, 15 January 1931; Matthews, "Story of the Emergency Work Bureau," 44; POUR, "Diocese of New York," report, 1931, 34, Lillian Wald Papers; Colcord, Koplovitz, and Kurtz, *Emergency Work Relief,* 148–150; O. A. Randall, speech, 21 November 1932, Belmont Papers, Mss Division, Columbia University; an article in the *New York Herald Tribune,* 18 November 1930, said that "the greatest need of the unemployed girl in New York City was a fifty-cent hotel"; Abelson, "Women Who Have No Men to Work for Them," 121.

41. Colcord, Koplovitz, and Kurtz, *Emergency Work Relief,* 151; Meltzer, *Brother Can You Spare a Dime?* 99.

42. Alexander Leopold Radomski, *Work Relief in New York State, 1931–1935* (New York: King's Crown Press, 1947), 314. TERA provided reimbursement, from state funds, to the cities and counties of 40 percent of unemployment relief expenditures. See Brown, *Public Relief,* 92–93.

43. Brown, *Public Relief,* 90–91, 96; Radomski, *Work Relief,* 66–67; Kessler-Harris delineates the boundaries of what was possible in "In the Nation's Image."

44. Radomski, *Work Relief,* 135.

45. Box-Car Bertha, *Sister of the Road: The Autobiography of Box-Car Bertha,* as told to Dr. Ben Reitman (New York: Harper and Row, 1937), 134; see also Louis Adamic, *My America, 1928–1939* (New York: DaCapo Press, 1976), 292. These are just two of many such stories.

46. Bremer, *Depression Winters,* 68–69; *Channels,* November–December 1930, 2; an interview by Jeane Westin echoes this same sentiment. See Westin, *Making Do: How Women Survived the <apos>30s* (Chicago: Follett, 1976), 184.

47. *Buffalo Courier,* 8 December 1930; *New York Times,* 25 December 1932, 1. The Family Welfare Association of America published a monograph titled *Community Planning for Homeless Men and Boys* in 1931. Dealing with experiences in sixteen cities during the winter of 1930–1931, the authors gave no thought to the situation of homeless women; in a speech in November 1932 the assistant director of the Emergency Work Bureau in New York City conceded that this depression was the first to affect women in large numbers.

48. Gertrude Steel-Brooke, "The Single Woman on Relief: A Study of the Status of Two Hundred Sixty Single, Unattached, American-Born, White Women on Relief in the Heart of Downtown Los Angeles" (master's thesis, University of Southern California, 1936), 88.

49. Margaret Theresa McFadden, "Anything Goes: Gender and Knowledge in the Comic Popular Culture of the 1930s" (PhD diss., Yale University, 1996), 20.

50. Val Lewton, *No Bed of Her Own* (New York: Vanguard, 1932; repr., New York: Triangle Books, 1948), 31–32; Martin Field, *Jenny Jobless,* in New Theatre League Records, New York Public Library, n.d.

51. *New York Herald Tribune,* 23 October 1932, 1.

52. Nels Anderson, "Report on the Municipal Lodging House of New York City," Welfare Council Research Bureau, April 1932, xiii.

53. *New York World Telegram,* 27 October 1932, 9.

54. *Unemployment Relief, Hearings on S. 174 and S. 262,* statement of Herbert Benjamin, 195–196; *New York Times,* 20 September 1931, 2N; *War Cry,* 3 September 1932; Alexander Keyssar found that institutional relief was a last resort for virtually all the unemployed. See Keyssar, *Out of Work: The First Century of Unemployment in Massachusetts* (New York: Cambridge University Press, 1986), 153.

55. Esther Husman, "Care of Homeless Women in New York City" (master's thesis, Columbia University, July 1936), 3; W. H. Matthews writes that the single woman was "not recognized as the responsibility of any existing relief organization." See Matthews, "Story of the Emergency Work Bureau," 40. See also Allen, *Since Yesterday,* 54; Simkovitch is quoted by Lorena Hickok, in Richard Lewitt and Maurine Beasley, eds., *One Third of a Nation* (Chicago: University of Illinois Press, 1983), 49.

56. *Los Angeles Times,* 12 September 1932, A12.

57. Temporary Shelter for Homeless Persons in New York City, November, 1933, box 186, CSS Papers. See also letter to Welfare Commissioner Frank J. Taylor from the Welfare Council, April 16, 1932, box 123, CSS Papers. In discussing the administration of Home Relief on 26 October 1932, the Welfare Council selected five hundred cases for study from the five boroughs of New York and noted that only "4 households had 1 member." See reel 16, box 34, Lillian Wald Papers.

58. Steel-Brooke, "Single Woman on Relief," 49.

59. *New Leader,* 25 November 1933, 2A; *Unemployed Union,* 17 November 1934, 5.

60. Brown, *Public Relief,* 106–109.

61. *Unemployment Relief, Hearings on S. 174 and S. 262,* statement of Walter S. Gifford, 320.

62. Ibid., statement of Herbert Benjamin, 195–196; Lewton, *No Bed of Her Own,* 31ff.

63. *Federal Aid for Unemployment Relief, Hearings on S. 5125,* statement of Ralph E. Hurlin, 164–166.

64. Ibid., statement of William Hodson, 100–106; further testimony revealed the disarray in New York City where, in addition to single adults, at least 30,000 families entitled to relief were *not* receiving it, and some evicted families ended up separated and in shelters. Ibid., statements of William Hodson, Isaac M. Rubinow, and Edith Abbott, 250, 260; Box-Car Bertha, *Sister of the Road,* 134.

65. Brown, *Public Relief,* 147; for a discussion of these new attitudes, see Cohen, *Making a New Deal,* 251–261.

66. Brown, *Public Relief,* 153.

67. Hopkins, *Spending to Save,* 102; Husman, "Care of Homeless Women," 7.

68. Le Sueur, "Women on the Breadlines."

69. Mary Heaton Vorse, "Perkins, This Way!" *New Republic,* 21 February 1934, 44–45.

70. *New York Times,* 25 December 1932, 1.

71. Nancy Fraser and Linda Gordon, "A Genealogy of Dependency: Tracing a Keyword of the U.S. Welfare State," *Signs* 19 (Winter 1994): 310–311.

CHAPTER 11

Globalization, Inequality, and the Growth of Female-Headed Households in the Caribbean

HELEN I. SAFA

Globalization and neoliberal restructuring have produced growing inequality between advanced industrial and developing countries as well as between class segments within these economies. In developing countries, the internationalization and fragmentation of production result in fierce competition for foreign investment, largely by maintaining low levels of wages and other labor costs while sustaining high productivity. Cheap labor thus becomes a primary comparative advantage, and poor women provide much of it. This feminization of labor characterized by flexible, informal, and casual work has led to a decline in full-time, permanent wage employment among men as well as women, with lower rates of male labor force participation, lower real wages, and higher rates of unemployment.[1]

Women's participation in the labor force in the Latin American and Caribbean region increased 32.5 percent between 1980 and 2000, reaching 37.2 percent in 2000, while men's economic participation stagnated at around 72 percent in the same period.[2] A voluminous literature exists analyzing the factors responsible for this increase in female participation and its impact, but few have paid adequate attention to the gender implications of the concomitant stagnation in the rate of male participation. However, Amy Bellone Hite and Jocelyn S. Viterna demonstrate that this change in the gender composition of the labor force weakens the overall power of the working class, particularly the formal proletariat, in relation to the dominant classes. Hite and Viterna argue that gender discrimination, by facilitating deterioration in wages and working conditions among both sexes, may "be a vehicle by which global capitalism is becoming increasingly efficient in disempowering all of Latin America's workers."[3]

Women workers themselves are not to blame for this deterioration, but because they are relatively recent recruits to the Latin American labor market and are not as organized into unions as men, they are cheaper to employ and more exploitable. The recruitment of women, like immigration, expands the labor force, which in itself tends to depress wages. Recruitment of women also coincides with the massive turnover toward a new export economy in Latin America, which favors women workers, especially in labor-intensive industries, whereas investment declined in import substitution industries, in which male employment predominated. As wages and working conditions for men deteriorate, the men may be reincorporated into the export economy, but under less favorable conditions. Labor unions are now paying more attention to female workers, and women are becoming better organized, but much remains to be done.

While Hite and Viterna focus on class stratification, my own research documents the impact on the household of these changes in the gender composition of the labor force in the Latin American and Caribbean region. In *The Myth of the Male Breadwinner: Women and Industrialization in the Caribbean*, I show that as real wages and male employment deteriorate, women step in to bolster the household economy and have now become principal contributors to the household in Puerto Rico, the Dominican Republic, and Cuba.[4] Like most working women in the Latin American and Caribbean region, they have gained in economic autonomy, which is reflected in important changes such as lower fertility, higher levels of education, and smaller families.[5] Women's leverage in the household increases with job stability and occupational level, so middle-class professional women gain more than low-income women working in the informal sector. The massive increase in married women's labor force participation is also decisive, because it threatens the husband's or partner's role as provider—a role that traditionally forms the basis of his authority in the household. When married women have to substitute for men as principal breadwinners, family conflict and marital breakdown often ensue, contributing to the rising percentage of female heads of household in each of the Caribbean countries studied. This pattern is not confined to the Caribbean but may help explain the increase in female-headed households worldwide.[6]

Over 33 percent of households are now headed by women in Cuba, nearly 30 percent in the Dominican Republic, and 27 percent in Puerto Rico. Caribbean women are resisting marriage and remarriage because the "marriage market" of eligible men who could fulfill the role of male breadwinner has shrunk. The tendency toward the formation of female-headed households may be particularly marked in the Caribbean, where female-headed households have a long history, and where conjugal ties among the black working class have been weakened by slavery, migration, and a prevalence of consensual unions.[7] A dual marriage system that placed restrictions on legal marriage in the Caribbean was a way in which the elite maintained racial and class superiority over a population of color, who lived largely in consensual unions. The prevalence of consensual unions in colonial times helps explain the lack of stigma they still enjoy among the non-elite in the Caribbean today. Consensual unions, which are more unstable than civil marriages, are also the basis for many female-headed households.

Although this chapter focuses on the growth of the number of female-headed households in Cuba, Puerto Rico, and the Dominican Republic, I would argue that the results are applicable to a wider spectrum of households throughout the entire Latin American and Caribbean region. The deterioration in men's earning capacity has affected the entire region, changing the gender composition of the labor force as Hite and Viterna have shown. But the rate of female headship varies considerably, from a low of 19 percent in Mexico to a high of 35 percent in Nicaragua, based on a 1999 Economic Commission for Latin America and the Caribbean survey of urban households in which the woman reported herself as head.[8] In this same survey, the percentage of households in which the woman is listed as the primary contributor is always higher (except for Nicaragua), suggesting that these women do not automatically consider themselves the household head and continue to ascribe this role to men. Factors such as the strength of the Catholic Church, the importance of civil marriage versus consensual unions, and the difficulty or absence of divorce all contribute to the symbolic importance of the man as head of household, which in the Caribbean is particularly fragile. The aging of the Caribbean population, particularly in countries like Puerto Rico, where widows account for 30 percent of female-headed households, also affects the growth of female-headed households in the region. But the decline in the number of men who are able to fulfill the male role of economic provider has affected gender and particularly marital relations in the entire region, as we shall see in what follows.

The Economic Crisis in the Caribbean in the 1990s

Globalization and neoliberal reform have hit the small economies of the Caribbean even harder than they have the rest of the region. These countries had long been dependent on foreign investment and exports to sustain their economies, but as globalization opened up new markets for investment, particularly in Asia, they became less competitive and more dependent on cheap labor. Meanwhile, neoliberal reform was driving up the cost of living and reducing the value of real wages even more.

No country illustrates these effects of globalization better than the Dominican Republic. Once it abandoned sugar as a primary export commodity in the mid-1980s and sought foreign exchange through export manufacturing and tourism, it became even more dependent on the vagaries of the world market. Although the Dominican economy boomed through the late 1990s, by the end of the decade the Dominican peso had lost more than half its value as a result of an annual inflation rate of 42 percent.

Dominican free trade zones continued to prosper through the 1990s, spurred on by generous tax incentives and cheap labor, and employed 200,000 people by the end of 2001. The female share of the labor force increased to 38 percent in 2000, partly to meet the increasing cost of living. Since 1980, women's labor force participation has grown at a higher rate than men's, which continues to stagnate.[9] Women are still the predominant labor force in the free trade zones, but their numbers have been declining. The Dominican free trade zones are also under increasing pressure from international competition, because the North American Free Trade Agreement (NAFTA) lowered the tariff barriers to Mexico and Chinese exports dominate more of the U.S. market.

Puerto Rico has completely lost its comparative advantage over neighboring countries as a site for light manufacturing, and Operation Bootstrap, the government's ambitious industrialization program conceived in the 1950s as the engine of growth, became obsolete. The apparel industry, once the principal employer of women in Puerto Rico, has virtually ground to a halt. As educational levels rose, women shifted into white-collar and professional employment and into the service sector, and government employment became the most important source of job creation. Male labor force participation rates declined from 54 percent in 1980 to 49 percent in 2000, while the female rate rose to 35 percent, and from 1990 to 2000 also began to decline. Federal transfer payments, which since the late 1970s have approximated 20 percent of personal income, have become a major source of support for the Puerto Rican economy.[10]

Of the three countries discussed here, Cuba suffered the greatest economic crisis in the 1990s, due to the breakup of the socialist bloc and the elimination of trade and aid from the former Soviet Union. The 1990s in Cuba has become known as the Special Period, the worst peacetime economic crisis in its history. Between 1989 and 1993, Cuba's gross domestic product (GDP) declined 35 percent, as exports and imports collapsed and nutritional levels declined drastically. During the 1990s, as the Cuban state shifted priorities, a dual economy evolved, including a dynamic or emergent sector based largely on tourism and a traditional sector that included most agriculture and manufacturing.[11] As Cuba legalized the use of the U.S. dollar, a dual currency system emerged, benefiting those with access to dollars through tourism, remittances, and the informal sector. The result has been growing inequality and the erosion of the social contract that guaranteed everyone a minimum standard of living.[12] The Afro-Cuban population has been hit particularly hard by the Special Period, because they have less access to dollars through remittances (since the émigré population is largely white) and through the new tourist economy, which favors white employees. Shortcomings in public services, and particularly the low wage rate in the state sector, forced the Cuban population to develop survival techniques in which women played a critical role.

Cuba

Any analysis of Cuban family structure must take account of the dramatic changes ushered in by the Special Period in the 1990s but also examine the longer-term changes brought about by the revolutionary Cuban government's commitment to gender equality. The Cuban state tried to improve women's status through increasing their incorporation into the labor force, raising educational levels, increasing women's job opportunities, and providing generous maternity leave and free day care. Women's participation in the labor force increased rapidly, reaching 40.6 percent in 1993, and also changed qualitatively. As a result of rising education levels among women, two-thirds of technical and professional jobs in 1995 were held by females, a change that began in the 1970s.[13] But the Cuban state did not expect women's increased economic autonomy to contribute to marital instability. In an effort to stabilize the conjugal bond by reinforcing more egalitarian marital relations, the Cuban Family Code spelled out the sharing of rights and responsibilities of both spouses. The percentage of households headed by women has grown at an alarming rate, however, from 14 percent in 1953, to 28.1 percent in 1981, to 36 percent in 1995.[14] Various factors have produced this increase.

Historically, female-headed households were most characteristic of low-income, Afro-Cuban households and were often attributed, in Cuba and elsewhere, to the deleterious effects of slavery on the conjugal bond. However, the revolutionary commitment to the reduction in class and racial barriers contributed to a striking convergence of marital patterns among racial groups. Consensual unions have increased among the white population, whereas more blacks are getting married.[15] The rate of female heads of household traditionally was much higher among blacks, who had higher rates of conjugal dissolution, but by 1995 there was little difference by race. In addition, there is remarkable similarity among white, black, and mulatto female heads in educational level, labor force participation, and proportion of professionals, which is more than one-fourth in each case.[16] These high educational and occupational levels demonstrate the enormous progress black and mulatto women have made during the revolution. Also, the Cuban population is aging, leading to a higher number of widows, although the overall percentage of widows under sixty-five among female heads was only 10 percent in 1995.[17]

Certain features unique to Cuba may have contributed to the increase in female headship. Socialist Cuba was among one of the first Latin American countries to grant women in consensual unions, and their children, recognition and rights equal to those of women in legal marriage, further debilitating the legitimacy of legal marriage. The provision of free health care and education as well as the increase in educational and occupational opportunities for women made it easier for women to have children on their own and greatly weakened women's dependence on a male breadwinner. As one of our Cuban respondents in the mid-1980s, a woman textile worker who had raised three small children on her own, commented, "Ahora actualmente, cualquiera mujer, para mí, cualquiera mujer cría un hijo sola, porque hay mucho trabajo, hay más facilidades para la mujer." [Now, any woman, for me any woman raises a child alone, because there are a lot of jobs, there are more facilities for women.] In 1995, 47 percent of all women heading their households were employed.[18]

The extended family is essential to the survival of these Cuban female-headed households, especially for working adolescents who are mothers. The proportion of extended families in Cuba is generally high, due in part to a housing shortage, but it is higher still among female-headed households. In the study of Cuban women textile workers we conducted in the 1980s, over half of the female-headed households consisted of three generations. Adolescent mothers often live with their families of origin, which helps them to engage in paid employment but may contribute to marital dissolution because young couples lack privacy and financial and emotional autonomy. Young single mothers often live in a subordinate position in the household.[19] They generally pay a fixed sum to the head of household for rent and food, and maintain their own budget for clothing and other personal items for themselves and their children. Female-headed households receive no preference in housing or special payments from the state, unlike in the United States or Puerto Rico, although they have some priority in employment. Given the alarming increase in female-headed households, it could be argued that the Cuban state did not want to encourage their formation through additional support.

During the Special Period, the support services provided by the state have been sharply reduced, and the extended family has become even more essential. One of the extended families we interviewed in 1986 had twenty-six members, consisting of Rosa, the grandmother, and her five married children and their children. The family had been given a house by the government with a relatively large patio, on which each of the children had built an independent residence for him- or herself out of a communal fund. They continue to live together and now number about thirty-six, since Rosa has fifteen grandchildren and two great-grandchildren. Rosa is over sixty and no longer works but receives a small pension and earns some money sewing clothes at home for sale in a retail store. Previously, most of the family worked at the textile factory, but now only one of the daughters remains employed as a secretary. The textile factory, which previously operated for twenty-four hours on three and later four shifts, has now been reduced to a skeleton staff of one shift, due to a lack of fuel and spare parts. Initially, many of the factory workers were employed in agriculture, but now many are self-employed. Families like Rosa's continue to grow some of their own food as well as chickens and other livestock. They also make furniture out of makeshift materials like discarded plastic and wood, which they sell locally. The elderly grandfather, who worked as a cane cutter in Oriente in the pre-revolutionary period and then joined the rebel army, now earns money giving children rides in a goat cart. Here we see the variety of survival strategies that families have resorted to during the Special Period.

Ximena, Rosa's youngest daughter, in her early forties, illustrates how religion may contribute to changes in gender relations. She and her husband are active in a recent neighborhood Pentecostal church, which emphasizes the importance of the conjugal bond. Ximena says her twenty-year marriage only began to function after they joined the church and she learned to respect her husband as head of the household. She observes:

> Yo he aprendido a respetarlo a el, a ser sujeta, a obedecer, entiende? El ha reconocido su responsabilidad como varon, como cabeza del hogar, entiende? . . . Yo siempre era muy dominante, posesiva, me entiende? No queria que el me mandara y siempre teniamos problemas . . . Ellos estan hechos para ser el varon de la casa, para que se proven y cuando a ellos le quitamos ese lugar lo degradamos y entonces no funciona la cosa. Y hemos aprendido muchisimo de esto y realmente hemos llegado a ser uno, sinceramente, un solo corazon y una sola alma.

> [I have learned to respect him, to be subordinate, to obey, understand? He has recognized his responsibility as a man, as head of the household, understand? . . . I was always very dominant, possessive, understand? I didn't want him to give me orders, and we always had problems. . . . They

[men] are made to be the man of the house, to be the breadwinner, and when we take that place from them, we degrade them and then things don't work. And we have learned a lot from this, and we have really learned to be one, sincerely, one sole heart and one soul.]

Ximena and her husband were legally married after they joined the church, and she says she teaches her children that their father comes first, although he earns a minimal salary as a retail clerk. Her self-subordination is unusual for a young Cuban woman and may serve principally to support her stature in the church. Despite her rhetoric, Ximena appears to continue to be the dominant authority in the household, doing most of the talking and making most of the decisions.

Unemployment in Cuba was negligible before the Special Period, but in 1994 it was higher for women, 10.1 percent, compared with 4.4 percent for men. Some professional college-educated women are abandoning careers as teachers, doctors, and scientists in the state sector to work in higher-paid, less-skilled jobs in tourism. Studies by Nuñez Sarmiento and others suggest that even these professional women continue to "negotiate with patriarchy," as husbands reconcile themselves to wives who not only work but may earn more than they and are accustomed to making their own decisions.[20] I would argue that the kind of female headship found among these professional women may be quite different from that found among less-educated, nonprofessional women, although further research is needed.

Dominican Republic

No state support for female-headed households exists in the Dominican Republic, yet the percentage of these households increased from 21.7 percent in 1981 to 29.1 percent in 1991, and declined again to 26.8 percent in 1996. Female heads have a higher labor force participation rate than married or even single women, and this rate has increased rapidly for all women since 1960, standing at 37.6 percent in 2000. Here again the extended family plays a critical role, and women working in the free trade zones frequently leave their children with their parents in the rural area.[21] Women facing an emergency like illness, unemployment, or marital breakup seem to have no difficulty moving back with their parent(s) or other relatives, despite very crowded living conditions. Thus, Maria moved in with her parents and three brothers when the youngest of her three children became sick and she had to quit her job to take care of him. Her unemployed husband does not live with them. Maria previously had worked in the free trade zone and as a domestic in the capital. She says her brothers do not complain about supporting her because she does the cooking and the housework, noting, "When I worked, they didn't work, and I gave to them." Now apparently it is her turn.

Mothers and daughters are especially flexible at exchanging roles, which reflects the strength of the mother–daughter tie in most Dominican families. Dominica, at forty-seven, has been in three consensual unions and "raised her children [while] working in the factories." At her age, it would be difficult to find a factory job, so she stays home and watches her daughter's two pre-school children, while her daughter works in the free trade zone and also attends school every night until ten. Her daughter says she is lucky to have her mother's support, but Dominica claims, "I take care of her children and she studies at night. She is already in the second year of high school. If she really achieves something, then I also gain. I have to sit and take care of her children so that she can get ahead."

The household composition of female-headed households, whether living independently or in extended families, plays a fundamental role in determining the standard of living of these households. An analysis of the 1991 national-level Demographic and Health Survey (DHS) by the Instituto de Estudios de Población y Desarrollo in the Dominican Republic found that although female heads of household earn less than male heads and have a much higher rate of unemployment, the average household incomes of both groups are nearly equal.[22] Apparently female heads of household are able to raise their income through the contributions of other family members, particularly subheads, since over half (53 percent) of households headed by women are extended compared with only 35 percent of male-headed households. Extended households in the Dominican Republic represented 40 percent of all households surveyed in 1991 and are even more prevalent in urban than in rural areas.

Analysis of the DHS in the Dominican Republic shows that nearly three-fourths of these subheads living in extended families are daughters of the head of household, and over half have only one child. Many of these young, single mothers living as subheads go undetected in the census, because they are counted as part of the extended family in which they live. Households with subheads are found in even greater proportion among middle- and high-income groups than among the poor.[23] This outcome suggests that the incorporation of subheads or other additional wage earners is a strategy used not just by the poor but by the middle class to combat the economic crisis and the high cost of living.

My ethnographic research among Dominican free-trade-zone workers shows that female heads of household often resist marriage or remarriage and prefer to support themselves if they cannot find a good provider.[24] These women claim men have always been irresponsible but that unemployment has made them worse, because, as one women worker expressed, "if he doesn't get work, then he can't help. If you pressure him, he is resentful because he has no place to turn, to work." Even unemployed men, however, rarely look after children or do household chores, underlining the importance of female kin. Maintaining the gender division of labor in the home as well as in the workplace tends to bolster a man's sense of masculinity and self-esteem.

Initially men rejected employment in the free trade zones as "women's work," but since 1980, the percentage of men employed as workers nationally in the free trade zones has more than doubled, reaching 45.7 percent in 1999. Part of this increase can be explained through product diversification toward higher value added, a strategy used in the Dominican Republic to upgrade the apparel industry in a trend that has also been noted globally.[25] Men are employed in plants producing trousers and coats, which they have redefined as "men's work." But acceptance is also due to the drop in the kinds of employment considered suitable for men, which left men few alternatives. Here we have a concrete confirmation of Hite and Vitera's assertion that the increase in women's labor force participation, combined with stagnating employment among men, has resulted in a deterioration of wages and working conditions for all. At the same time, many attempts to improve working conditions for women, such as requiring women's consent to work overtime, have not been implemented. The generous maternity benefits women were granted under the 1992 Labor Code merely increased employers' preference for men.

Older men who have a particularly difficult time finding employment are resentful of the independence that paid employment has conferred on women working in the free trade zones. In Villa Altagracia, where a free trade zone replaced an older sugar mill, these older workers accuse the women workers of "having fun with men," spending their money in bars and beauty salons, and contributing little to the household economy.[26] This stereotype appears to reflect men's resentment at the erosion of their authority and the shattering of a gender hierarchy in which men were dominant as principal breadwinners and women were, at best, supplemental breadwinners.

Women clearly reject this stereotype, and most claim that they are working to support their children. One young woman worker argues that it was more difficult for women when the sugar mill was in operation, because men "worked and earned money for the home and did what they pleased, but now the woman works, she maintains herself, she dresses herself, it cannot be the same." As a result of their improved economic autonomy, women increasingly take the initiative in breaking off relationships that are unsatisfactory, whereas previously female heads of household were often the result of male abandonment.

While women are challenging patriarchal ideology at the household level, it is still prevalent at the public level in the Dominican Republic. Men are preferred in technical and managerial positions and receive higher salaries, even within the free trade zones in which women predominate. In spite of the labor code issued in 1992, few collective bargaining agreements have actually been signed and implemented in the free trade zones, and women workers in particular continue to be harassed and made to work overtime without due compensation.[27] The Dominican government has reasons for its reluctance to implement workers rights. Competition from cheaper wages elsewhere, like Mexico or Central America not to mention China, does not bode well for the future of the apparel industry in the Dominican Republic, which still constitutes the bulk of free-trade-zone manufacturing.

Puerto Rico

In Puerto Rico, the decline in export manufacturing is far more severe. Puerto Rico's industrialization program started in the 1950s and served as a model of export growth for much of the Caribbean (and other parts of the world). Decline began as other countries offered even cheaper wages and more lucrative tax incentives. U.S. government policies that favored export manufacturing in other countries in the region, such as the Caribbean Basin Initiative in the 1980s and NAFTA in the 1990s, accelerated this trend. The decline in garment production was already apparent in 1980, when I collected data on the original sample of women workers in Puerto Rico. Many of the women workers were older than forty and had been working in the same plant for twenty to thirty years. Life histories from some of the older female heads interviewed in the mid-1980s reveal that when they were younger and raising children on their own, most lived with or relied on the help of extended family members, usually female kin. Like Dominican women, two-thirds of the female heads of household in the Puerto Rican sample say they would prefer not to remarry. As Evarista, then a fifty-nine-year-old worker who had raised five children on her own, explains: "Porque que yo coja un hombre y que yo tenga que, que mantener ese hombre, pasar malos ratos y maltrato, pues me quedo sola veinte mil veces. Me encuentro mejor sola porque así sola yo tiro pa' donde quiera y no tengo que estarle pidiendo." [Why should I take a man and have to maintain him, have a hard time and suffer abuse, well I am twenty thousand times better off alone. I feel better alone because alone I take off for where I please and don't have to be asking.][28]

Clearly, Puerto Rican female heads of household differ in certain important respects from the profile of Cuban and Dominican female heads outlined earlier. Female household headship in Puerto Rico is lower, reaching only 27 percent in 2000. Consensual unions have largely disappeared, now numbering only 5 percent. This outcome is a deliberate result of state policy, which began as early as 1898, when Puerto Rico was occupied by the United States after the war with Spain. Subsequently the United States promoted a new civil code to broaden the definition of legal marriage in hopes of discouraging the population from living in consensual unions, which at the time were at 50 percent.[29] The promotion of legal marriage was defined as part of the United States' "civilizing mission" because consensual unions were considered immoral. The policy was later reinforced by Social Security and other federal transfer payments, which privileged women in legal unions. Widows or divorced women could claim benefits accruing to their former husband, but women in consensual unions had more difficulty. However, eliminating consensual unions has not brought about marital stability, because the divorce rate is so high. Nationally, 57 percent of female heads of household are divorced, a much higher rate than in Cuba or the Dominican Republic.

Puerto Rico's female heads of household are often poor, with 61 percent falling below the poverty line in 2000.[30] The absence of extended families and lack of support from additional wage earners appear to be part of the reason. Nationally 29 percent of female heads live alone, which again may reflect the high percentage of elderly widows. But in Cuba and the Dominican Republic, these elderly women are usually incorporated into extended families. Independent living is partly the result of public policy, which, through public housing and other social programs, stressed the American middle-class nuclear family as the ideal.[31]

Independent living has its advantages, and undoubtedly many women prefer living alone without having to accommodate to extended kin. But family fragmentation also helps account for the low labor force participation rate of

Puerto Rican female heads of household, which is much lower in Puerto Rico than in Cuba or the Dominican Republic. Only 35 percent of Puerto Rican female heads of household were employed in 2000, and 42 percent had no one employed in the household.[32] Again these data may be explained partially by the large percentage of elderly widows living on Social Security or other pension payments. Unemployment is high, but it is higher for men than for women in Puerto Rico. Female heads are also dependent on federal transfer payments, principally in the form of nutritional assistance, or what in Puerto Rico is known as *cupones,* food coupons, which were extended to Puerto Rico in the 1970s. In 2000, 35 percent of female heads were receiving public assistance, and 48 percent of these were living below the poverty line.[33] Many of these female heads might not have been eligible for public assistance if they had been formally employed or living in larger households with more total income. Welfare may have dampened female labor force participation, while also encouraging female heads to live alone, which makes it harder for mothers of young children to work outside the home. Nationally, only 16 percent of all Puerto Rican female heads have more than one person employed in the household compared with 39 percent among married couples.[34] Incomes in Puerto Rico are thus polarized between families in which no one is employed, which includes a large percentage of female heads, and those dual wage-earner families in which both husband and wife are employed.

Conclusion

Globalization has contributed to the increase in female-headed households in Cuba, Puerto Rico, and the Dominican Republic by weakening further the role of the male as breadwinner. Male unemployment has increased in all of these countries, while female employment and participation rates have increased. Women have become increasingly resistant to marriage because it offers them neither economic nor, apparently, emotional support. At the same time, the level of support that the state can provide to female-headed households has diminished considerably. As the Cuban state's resources have shrunk, women can no longer depend on free day-care centers or generous maternity leaves, and even the quality of free education and health services has eroded. The Dominican government never gave much support to women or the working class, and some recent attempts to aid them through support of unionization in the free trade zones or provision of maternity benefits have been weakened by international competition in export processing, which forces the state to keep wages low. Increasing numbers of men are employed in export processing, and they are still given preference in technical and managerial jobs and are paid more than women. In Puerto Rico, Operation Bootstrap is in total decline, and the island has become heavily dependent on federal transfer payments, with a large percentage of households in which no one is employed. The result in all three countries has been increased immigration to the United States, with women outnumbering men from both Puerto Rico and the Dominican Republic.[35]

A small class of professional women in the Caribbean has benefited from the changes globalization has helped produce. They have taken advantage of increased educational opportunities in Cuba, Puerto Rico, and the Dominican Republic and are surpassing men in university education and professional employment. The high rate of divorce among professional women in all three countries suggests that female educational and occupational advancement alone will not stem the increase in female-headed households. It may make them less poor.

Economic crisis is not the only factor responsible for the high level of female-headed households in the Caribbean. Historically, embedded cultural factors such as the dual marriage system, the prevalence of consensual unions, the fragility of the conjugal bond, and the strength of consanguine relationships facilitate the formation of female-headed households in the region.

The long history of female-headed households in the Caribbean suggests that they are not deviant and may be seen as an alternative form of family organization with its own legitimacy. I would argue that given the continuing economic crisis in the region, female-headed households are an adaptation to the weakening economic role of men and the growing economic importance of women in the region. The negative view of female-headed households in the United States is partly conceptual in that our Eurocentric emphasis on the nuclear family as the norm and the embodiment of modernity and progress leads us to view female-headed households as deviant, primarily because of the rupture of the conjugal bond. Against the assumption that the family is centered on marriage or the conjugal bond, I argue that in many urban low-income households, particularly in the Caribbean, conjugal bonds are weak and unstable in comparison to consanguine relationships between a mother, her children, and her female kin.[36]

The maintenance of consanguine ties that provide economic and emotional support either within extended households or through interhousehold forms of mutual aid appears to be essential for female-headed households to function adequately. My Caribbean data show that female heads of household are better off economically if, rather than being on their own, they share household tasks and expenses with relatives who provide additional sources of income or child care. This is particularly true of young mothers with small children, since in the Caribbean, older single mothers with larger numbers of children are more likely to live alone.

Social policy in advanced industrial countries like the United States, however, has worked to undermine the maintenance of extended family ties. Families are encouraged to be mobile, socially as well as physically, which impedes the maintenance of extended family ties. Public welfare makes it easier for single mothers to live independently and thus encourages their withdrawal from extended family households. This policy helps explain why female heads of household are more likely to live alone in Puerto Rico than in Cuba and the Dominican Republic, where they receive no special assistance. My study of African American single mothers suggests that their phenomenal increase in the 1960s may be due in part to their increased access to welfare, which enabled female heads to live independently of their parents or other extended kin.[37]

Encouraging female-headed households to live independently may lead to greater poverty, because it makes it more difficult for women with young children to work. This result may help explain the high incidence of poverty among female-headed households in Puerto Rico and among African Americans in the United States. Single mothers need the support of extended families, even when they have access to independent funds through public welfare. But I would argue that welfare policy could be modified to facilitate, rather than deter, household extension. Deterrence stems from a social policy based on the nuclear family model and on marriage as the primary mechanism for ensuring family stability. The opening statement of the Welfare Reform Act of 1997 enshrines marriage as essential to a successful society, while President George W. Bush sought and received special funds to promote marriage among low-income single mothers. Public policy needs to address male unemployment as the primary factor behind marital instability and the increase in female-headed households. Female heads of household will not marry the fathers of their children until these men are earning a decent salary and can help support their families.

Notes

1. Guy Standing, "Global Feminization through Flexible Labor: A Theme Revisited," *World Development* 27, no. 3 (1999): 583–602; Carlos Vilas, "The Decline of the Steady Job in Latin America," *Nacla* 32, no. 4 (1999): 15–17.
2. Amy Bellone Hite and Jocelyn S. Viterna, "Gendering Class in Latin America: How Women Effect and Experience Change in the Class Structure," *Latin American Research Review* 40, no. 2 (2005): 50.
3. Ibid., 50.
4. Helen I. Safa, *The Myth of the Male Breadwinner: Women and Industrialization in the Caribbean* (Boulder, CO: Westview Press, 1995).
5. Sylvia Chant with Nikki Craske, *Gender in Latin America* (New Brunswick, NJ: Rutgers University Press, 2003), 161–193.
6. Sylvia Chant, *Women-Headed Households: Diversity and Dynamics in the Developing World* (New York: St. Martin's Press, 1997).
7. Helen I. Safa, "Female-Headed Households in the Caribbean: Deviant or Alternative Form of Household Organization?" *Latino(a) Research Review* 4, no. 2 (1999): 16–26.
8. Carmen Diana Deere, "The Feminization of Agriculture? Economic Restructuring in Rural Latin America," occasional paper no. 1 (Geneva: United Nations Research Institute for Social Development UNRISD, 2005), 11, table 6.
9. Clara Báez, *Estadísticas para la planificación social con perspectiva de género,* Secretaría de la Mujer, Programa de las Naciones Unidas para el Desarrollo (Dominican Republic: Fondo de Población de las Naciones Unidas, 2000), 45, table 2.2.
10. Alice Colón, "Incremento en la mujeres jefas de familia y feminización de la pobreza en Puerto Rico" (paper presented at the International Congress of the Latin American Studies Association, Las Vegas, 2004), 8; James L. Dietz, *Puerto Rico: Negotiating Development and Change* (Boulder, CO: Lynne Rienner Publishers, 2003).
11. Pedro Monreal, "Cuba: The Challenge of Being Global and Socialist . . . at the Same Time," in "Cuba in the 1990s: Economy, Politics and Society," special issue, *Socialism and Democracy* 15, no. 1 (2001): 10.

12. Mayra Espina, "The Effects of the Reform on Cuba's Social Structure: An Overview," in "Cuba in the 1990's: Economy, Politics and Society," special issue, *Socialism and Democracy* 15, no. 1 (2001): 23–40.

13. Sonia Catasus, "Género, patrones reproductivos y jefatura de núcleo familiar por color de la piel en Cuba" (paper presented at the Red de Estudios de Poblacion ALFAPOP, Center of Demographic Studies, Bellaterra, Spain, 1999), 5, 3, table 1; http://www.ced.uab.es?PDFs/Papers PDF/Text.151.pdf.

14. Carollee Benglesdorf, "(Re) Considering Cuban Women in a Time of Troubles," in *Daughters of Caliban: Caribbean Women in the Twentieth Century,* ed. Consuelo L. Springfield, 229–258 (Bloomington: Indiana University Press, 1997); Catasus, "Género."

15. Alejandro de la Fuente, "Race and Inequality in Cuba, 1899–1981," *Journal of Contemporary History* 30 (1995): 147.

16. Catasus, "Género," 9, table 3.

17. Ibid.

18. Safa, *Myth of the Male Breadwinner,* 139; Marta Nuñez Sarmiento, "Cuban Strategies for Women's Employment in the 1990s: A Case Study of Professional Women," in "Cuba in the 1990s: Economy, Politics and Society," special issue, *Socialism and Democracy* 15, no. 1 (2001): 61.

19. Safa, *Myth of the Male Breadwinner;* Maura Toro-Morn, Anne Roschelle, and Elisa Facio, "Gender, Work and Family in Cuba: The Challenges of the Special Period," *Journal of Developing Societies* 18, no. 2/3 (2002): 51.

20. Miren Uriarte, *Cuba: Social Policy at the Crossroads* (Oxfam America report, 2002), 28; Toro-Morn, Roschelle, and Facio, "Gender, Work and Family in Cuba," 51; Nuñez Sarmiento, "Cuban Strategies for Women's Employment."

21. Isis Duarte and Ramón Tejeda, *Los hogares dominicanos: El mito de la familia nuclear y los tipos de jefaturas del hogar* (Santo Domingo: Instituto de Estudios de Población y Desarrollo, 1995), 47; Báez, *Estadísticas para la planificación social,* 33, table 1, 45, table 2.1; Safa, *Myth of the Male Breadwinner.*

22. Duarte and Tejeda, *Los hogares dominicanos,* 80–81; Helen I. Safa, "Questioning Globalization: Gender and Export Processing in the Dominican Republic," *Journal of Developing Societies* 18, no. 2/3 (2002): 11–31.

23. Duarte and Tejeda, *Los hogares dominicanos,* 90.

24. Safa, "Questioning Globalization."

25. Consejo Nacional de Zonas Francas de Exportación (CNZFE), *1999 Informe estadístico del sector de zonas francas* (Santo Domingo, Dominican Republic, 2000), 21, table 21; United Nations 1999 World Survey on the Role of Women in Development, *Globalizations, Gender and Work,* UN document A/54/227 (New York: Division for the Advancement of Women, Department of Economics and Social Affairs, 1999).

26. Safa, "Questioning Globalization."

27. Ibid.; U.S. Department of Labor, "Foreign Labor Trends: Dominican Republic," Washington, DC: Bureau of International Labor Affairs, Office of Foreign Relations, 2002.

28. Safa, *Myth of the Male Breadwinner,* 83.

29. Eileen Findlay, *Imposing Decency: The Politics of Sexuality and Race in Puerto Rico, 1870–1920* (Durham, NC: Duke University Press, 1999).

30. Colón, "Incremento en la mujeres jefas de familia," 24, table 1, 25, table 2.

31. Helen I. Safa, "Changing Forms of U.S. Hegemony in Puerto Rico: The Impact of the Family and Sexuality," *Itinerario: European Journal of Overseas History* 25, no. 3/4 (2001): 90–111.

32. Colón, "Incremento en la mujeres jefas de familia," 48.

33. Dietz, *Puerto Rico;* Colón, "Incremento en la mujeres jefas de familia," 16.
34. Colón, "Incremento en la mujeres jefas de familia."
35. Francisco Rivera-Batiz and Carlos Santiago, *Island Paradox: Puerto Rico in the 1990s* (New York: Russell Sage Foundation, 1996), 142; Peggy Levitt, *The Transnational Villagers* (Berkeley and Los Angeles: University of California Press, 2001), 220.
36. Safa, "Female-Headed Households in the Caribbean."
37. Helen I. Safa, "Welfare Reform, Racism, and Single Motherhood in the Americas," in *Resisting Racism and Xenophobia: Global Perspectives on Race, Gender, and Human Rights,* ed. Faye Harrison (Walnut Creek, CA: AltaMira Press, 2005), 105–122.

NOTES ON CONTRIBUTORS

ELAINE S. ABELSON is a senior lecturer in historical studies at the New School for Social Research (Graduate Faculty) of the New School in New York City. Her first book, *When Ladies Go a-Thieving: Middle-Class Shoplifters in the Victorian Department Store* (1990), explores the development of late nineteenth-century consumer culture and its relation to gender and class. She has published a number of articles on urban women and homelessness during the 1930s and is currently writing a book titled *The Dimensions of Inequality: Gender and Homelessness in the Great Depression.*

RUDOLPH M. BELL is a professor of history at Rutgers University, New Brunswick, where he has taught since 1968. He is the author of numerous scholarly articles and several books, among them *Fate and Honor, Family and Village: Demographic and Cultural Change in Rural Italy since 1800* (1979), *Holy Anorexia* (1985), *How to Do It: Guides to Good Living for Renaissance Italians* (1999), and, with Cristina Mazzoni, *The Voices of Gemma Galgani: The Life and Afterlife of a Modern Saint* (2003). He is currently working on a study of widows, property, and inheritance in early modern Sicily.

BETTINA BRADBURY is an associate professor of history and women's studies at York University. Her research focuses on feminist family history; Quebec and the British Empire; marriage and widowhood; marriage and inheritance laws; , and colonization as it pertains to Canada, Australia, New Zealand, and the Cape (South Africa). Her previous publications examine working-class families and how industrialization changed the lives of women and children in nineteenth-century Montreal. Her most recent publications are "Widows Negotiate the Law: The First Year of Widowhood in Early Nineteenth-Century Montreal," in *Intermediate Spaces: Sites of Identity Formation in Nineteenth- and Twentieth-Century Montreal,* ed. Tamara Myers and Bettina Bradbury (2005); and "Social, Economic, and Cultural Origins of Contemporary Families," in *Families: Changing Trends in Canada,* ed. Maureen Baker (2005).

ANNE BYRNE is a sociologist working in the Department of Political Science and Sociology, National University of Ireland, Galway, with research interests that span self and social identity, singleness studies, social exclusion, participative research methodologies, group work, and community relations. She has published in the area of identity, single women, and feminist research methodologies, and on aspects of the history of American social anthropology in Ireland. She is actively involved in both national and local research advisory groups. Recent publications include "Developing a Sociological Model for Researching Women's Self and Social Identities," *European Journal of Women's Studies* 10 (2003): 443–464; and, with Deborah Carr, "Caught in the Cultural Lag: The Stigma of Singlehood," *Psychological Inquiry* 16 (2005): 84–91. Byrne had the good fortune to participate as a senior research fellow in the Rutgers Center for Historical Analysis 2003–2004 project Gendered Passages in Historical Perspectives: Single Women.

DEBORAH CARR is an associate professor of sociology at Rutgers University. Her research focuses on the psychological consequences of work and family roles over the life course as well as issues facing older widows and widowers. Her publications have appeared in journals, including *Journal of Health and Social Behavior, Journal of Marriage and Family, Social Psychology Quarterly,* and *Sociological Methodology* as well as various edited volumes. She is also co-editor of *Spousal Bereavement in Late Life* (2006).

LEE V. CHAMBERS is a professor of history at the University of Colorado, where she has served as director of women studies and chair of the history department. Her pathbreaking study *Liberty, a Better Husband: Single Women in America: The Generations 1780–1840* (1984) still serves as the foundational text for singleness studies in a historical setting. More recently, she is completing a major study tentatively titled "Sister Works: Sibship, Gender Rebellion, and Moral Reform in Antebellum Massachusetts," a full-length study of Maria Weston Chapman, and an oral history anthology on Los Alamos, New Mexico, during the cold war.

RUTH CROCKER is a professor of history and director of the Women's Studies Program at Auburn University. She was educated in England and earned a degree in modern history at St. Anne's College, Oxford. She moved to the United States and completed a master's and PhD in U.S. history at Purdue. She is the author of *Social Work and Social Order: The Settlement Movement in Two Industrial Cities, 1889–1930* (1992) and of several essays on social work and welfare , as well as *Mrs. Russell Sage: Women's Activism and Philanthropy in Gilded Age and Progressive Era America* (2006), which is the first full-length, scholarly treatment of this significant early twentieth-century female philanthropist.

JENNIFER L. GROSS is an assistant professor of history at Jacksonville State University in Jacksonville, Alabama, where she teaches courses on the Civil War and Reconstruction, American women's history, and the antebellum South. Her most recent publication is "'And for the Widow and Orphan': Confederate Widows,

Poverty, and Public Assistance," in *Inside the Confederate Nation: Essays in Honor of Emory M. Thomas,* ed. Leslie J. Gordon and John C. Inscoe (2005). She is currently working on a book titled "'Good Angels': Confederate Widowhood and the Postbellum South."

CATHERINE KUDLICK teaches history at the University of California, Davis. A French historian by training, she has ventured into a comparative study of attitudes toward blind people and blindness in modern France and America. Her publications include "Disability History: Why We Need Another 'Other,'" *American Historical Review* (June 2003); "The Outlook of the Problem and the Problem with the Outlook: Two Advocacy Journals Reinvent Blind People in Turn-of-the-Century America," in *The New Disability History: American Perspectives,* ed. Paul Longmore and Lauri Umansky (2001); and, with Zina Weygand, *Reflections: The Life and Writings of a Young Blind Woman in Post-Revolutionary France* (2001, French translation 2004).

SUSAN INGALLS LEWIS is an assistant professor of history at the State University of New York at New Paltz. Her essay "Business or Labour? Blurred Boundaries in the Careers of Self-Employed Needlewomen" appears in *Famine and Fashion: Needlewomen in the Nineteenth Century* (2005), and her study *Unexceptional Women: Female Proprietors in Mid-Nineteenth-Century Albany, 1830–1885* will be published in 2008. Her current fields of interest include girls' culture during the Gilded Age and Progressive Era, and the fashion industry, particularly milliner Lilly Daché. Lewis acknowledges the valuable assistance of the Nuala McGann Drescher Affirmative Action Award from United University Professions in 2005, and she thanks the dean of liberal arts and the Department of History of the State University of New York at New Paltz for their support of this project.

HELEN I. SAFA, professor emerita in anthropology and Latin American studies at the University of Florida, has also taught at major universities in the United States, Spain, the Netherlands, and Mexico. As the author, editor, or co-editor of more than a dozen books and three times as many scholarly articles, she has been a moving force in shaping the field of singleness studies long before that term came into wide use. Her works explore the complexities of race, gender, and class in a wide variety of settings in North, Central, and South America, with particular emphasis on the Caribbean and on migration throughout these regions.

VIRGINIA YANS is Board of Governors Distinguished Service Professor of History at Rutgers University, New Brunswick, a chair recognizing her outstanding work as a public intellectual involved in projects such as the Ellis Island Museum and Women's Museum in Lower Manhattan, and the Women's Museum in San Francisco. After completing *Family and Community: Italian Immigrants in Buffalo, 1880–1930,* she turned to publishing studies of Margaret Mead, including several scholarly essays, and writing and producing the prize-winning film *Margaret Mead: An Observer Observed,* which was supported by major grants from the National Science Foundation, the Rockefeller Foundation, the Wenner-Gren Foundation, and the National Endowment for the Humanities and subsequently shown on PBS, the BBC, and in screenings throughout Europe and Asia.

EILEEN JANES YEO is a professor of social and cultural history and director of the Centre in Gender Studies at the University of Strathclyde, Glasgow, Scotland. She is editor of works on radical femininity and Mary Wollstonecraft, and the author of *The Contest for Social Science: Relations and Representations of Gender and Class* (1966), as well as numerous scholarly articles. Her current book, near completion, focuses on Britain, France, and the United States and is tentatively titled "Meanings of Motherhood in Europe and America, 1750 to the Present." Another of her works in progress explores the intersections of gender and class in Glasgow as women (and men) sat down for tea in public spaces.

INDEX